W9-BRW-262

SOUTH TO JAVA

A NOVEL

By

William P. Mack

and

William P. Mack, Jr.

The Nautical & Aviation Publishing
Company of America, Inc.
Baltimore, Maryland

Published in the United States of America by the
Nautical & Aviation Publishing Company of America, Inc.
101 West Read Street, Baltimore, Maryland, 21201.

ISBN:—0—933852—70—3
Library of Congress Catalog Number: 87-24768.

Printed in the United States of America.

Library of Congress Cataloging-in-Publication Data

Mack, William P., 1915–
South to Java.

1. World War, 1939–1945—Fiction. I. Mack, William, 1943–
II. Title.
PS3563.A3132S6 1987 813′.54 87-24768
ISBN—0—933852—69—X

PREFACE

The USS *O'Leary* never existed. No destroyer ever had that name nor the hull number DD 200. Over 200 nearly identical four-stackers were constructed during and after World War I. Outdated even when new, they were obsolete by the outbreak of World War II. That did not stop them from playing an important role in that conflict. Before Pearl Harbor, President Roosevelt leased 50 of the vessels to Britain to help combat Hitler's submarines. After our entry into the war, many of the old destroyers were converted to back-up roles as convoy escorts, mine sweepers, and troop transports.

Thirteen of the four-stackers had to face the Japanese onslaught in the Far East during the first months of World War II. The *O'Leary*'s story is based on the experiences of those ships.

The description of the battles and the ships that fought in them are as authentic as possible, based on battle reports, the sources listed below, eyewitness accounts, and the memories and notes of one of the authors, who served on the destroyer *John D. Ford.* The *O'Leary* has been added to the forces that actually took part in the various engagements in such a way as not to alter accurate description of the battles. In most cases, the Allied forces were so inferior that the presence of the extra destroyer would have been of little consequence.

The officers and men of the *O'Leary* are fictitious, with personalities and problems created by the authors. These characters are similar in many respects to the real men who manned the Asiatic Fleet destroyers. Those officers and men were a varied lot, mostly veterans, who made the most of their old ships. Their courage was above that required in the line of duty, their endurance under difficult weather and living conditions was outstanding, and their devotion to their country and to their Navy was deserving of the highest honor. Two destroyers, the *John D. Ford* and the *Pope,* were awarded the Presidential Unit citation for their accomplishments.

The authors are indebted to those authors who have produced the historical record of the first months of the war. We wish to acknowledge their works as well as to refer interested readers to them. The following were invaluable: Theodore Roscoe, *United States Destroyer Operations in World War II*; Samuel Eliot Morison, *History of United States Naval Operations in World War II*; John Toland, *But Not in Shame*; Walter Winslow, *The Fleet the Gods Forgot*; William Manchester, *American Caesar*; David Thomas, *Battle of Java Sea*; F. C. Van Oosten, *The Battle of the Java Sea*; Walter Karig and Welbourn Kelly, *Battle Report*; J. Daniel Mullin, who served on the *John D. Ford, Another Six-hundred.*

We are indebted to Professor Alan Lefcowitz, of the English and History Department of the U.S. Naval Academy and head of the Creative Writing Center, Bethesda, Maryland, for his advice and counsel.

CHAPTER ONE

The humid Philippine breeze veered to the north, gathered strength, and leaned against the USS *O'Leary*, trying to shove the elderly four-stack destroyer downwind of her anchor. The tide ebbing from Subic Bay resisted, and the anchor chain groaned and rattled in the hawsepipe. The wind overwhelmed the tide, and the destroyer began to swing downwind.

The dim illumination from the anchor light at the bow reflected off the high-necked white uniform of Lieutenant (Junior Grade) Ross Fraser as he emerged from the bridge structure. He picked his way around the mattresses of men sleeping on deck. Fraser snatched his hat off as a gust almost took it over the side, and the wind ruffled his dark hair. His gray eyes narrowed as the anchor chain jumped and shed a shower of rust, which the wind swept into the moonless night.

As the *O'Leary* settled in her new position, Fraser placed a foot on the heavy chain to check for the vibration of a dragging anchor. The wind picked up as he scanned the dark horizon. Lightning flickered to the east. Fraser looked down at the chain and shook his head because rust particles had speckled his white uniform.

"Whole damn ship's rusting away," he muttered, rubbing the crooked bridge of his nose.

Fraser turned and headed aft. He almost forgot his concern with the weather as he passed the number one gun and touched its long barrel. He remembered they would be firing a gunnery exercise the next evening, his first against a target in the three months since he had reported aboard as the gunnery officer. The number one gun was a chronic problem; it frequently failed to register the correct orders from the gun director during daily tests. Fraser wondered what would happen when they started shooting.

Another flash of lightning hurried him on his way. When he stepped on the quarterdeck, just aft of the bridge structure, he found the petty officer in charge of the watch, Jake Shifflet, leaning on the metal desk bolted to the bulkhead.

"Evenin' sir," said Shifflet, one of Fraser's gunner's mates. The enlisted man straightened quickly to his full height which enabled him to look down at Fraser. Almost six feet himself, Fraser felt slightly intimidated, but it wasn't just Shifflet's height advantage. The man's confident gap-toothed smile seemed to say that he had everything under control, a feeling Fraser had rarely experienced since reporting aboard.

Shifflet flexed a long leg and a tattooed snake seemed to wriggle up his leg and under his uniform shorts. "How's it feel to be left in charge of the ship for the first time, Mr. Fraser? Lot of responsibility."

Fraser nodded, wishing the captain were aboard. Although Fraser had found the captain remote, even a forbidding enigma, the captain always seemed to know what to do. The captain also expected his officers to do their jobs well. Fraser winced at the thought of explaining how he'd let the ship blow aground or suffer some other disaster.

"Shifflet, I'm concerned about that storm to the east. I don't want to drag our anchor if the wind picks up any more."

"Now that could ruin your whole night, Mr. Fraser. Don't worry none. That storm ain't gonna come close. Wind'll die down in a few minutes."

Fraser hoped Shifflet was right as thunder rumbled across the bay.

"Gonna be a lot more fireworks if the Japs start a war. Mr. Fraser, how about goin' to the old man and getting my restriction lifted so's I can go ashore when we hit Manila. I been stuck on board over a month now. Long time for a man of my powers."

"Sorry, Shifflet. I've already helped you twice. That didn't keep you out of trouble, so you'll just have to do your full sixty days."

"Seems like Saint Peter got three chances."

"You're not Saint Peter."

"Awww—Mr. Fraser. All the ladies say I'm downright heavenly. Have a heart. I might not get ashore no more if the war starts. I need to take care of my affairs and get things straight . . . so to speak."

"The exec says there'll never be a war in the Pacific."

Shifflet snorted. "That man's supposed to be the navigator, but he's lucky he can find his way to the head. You'd better hope he's right about the Japs. The Asiatic Fleet's behind the eight ball out here. Nossir, I take that back. The Japs come and it'll be like they dropped the whole damn pool table on us! Why, even that escape artist Houdini couldn't get out of the fix we might be in."

"Shifflet, stop trying to con me."

"Even a condemned man gets a last meal, Mr. Fraser. We ain't got nothin' but a couple of cruisers to help our old destroyers. We'll be like bugs hittin' the Jap windshields if the fleet don't get here from Pearl Harbor in time. Japs are a lot closer."

Fraser realized Shifflet was right and wondered how long it would take the fleet to arrive.

Shifflet licked his stubby pencil and looked over the quartermaster's notebook. "Look here, we've just about used up 1941. 'Zactly one month till Christmas, Mr. Fraser. If you could get me off, I'd have just enough time to take care of presents."

"You need a whole month to buy gifts?"

"I've got a lot of lady friends. Delivering 'em proper is what takes the time."

"Sorry, but I can't help you, Shifflet."

Shifflet shook his head mournfully. "Gonna be hard, in my condition, to keep the number one gun working. Whole ship needs an overhaul, but that gun's a menace—no telling where it might shoot."

Fraser shivered with apprehension. Shifflet was a skilled gunner's mate, but the wiring on number one was overdue for replacement. It was worn and corroded from the waves and salt spray the *O'Leary* had taken over her bow. If they hit the tug towing the target, Fraser knew the Navy would hold the captain and him responsible.

"Just do your best," Fraser said.

"Always do—and I know my job—not like you officers who're learning a new job every couple of years."

Fraser tried to think of a response but failed, so he decided to retreat to his stateroom. "Let me know if the wind picks up."

Shifflet directed a stream of tobacco juice over the nearby rail, clearing it cleanly. "Nothing to worry about, sir. Good bottom for the anchor. Been through many a storm here and never budged. Got two lights over in Olongapo lined up so I can tell if we start dragging."

"What if they turn the lights out?"

Shifflet smiled as he scratched his crotch. "They don't ever turn them red lights out. That first one, Mamacita's, knows how to take care of a man. Even a man who likes to save his money, such as yourself, they have some older ladies—."

"That's enough, Shifflet." Fraser realized that the wind had already diminished. "I'll be back in an hour when the liberty boat makes its last run. Any problems—call me."

"Yessir. Might have some real problems for you to worry about when the boat gets here."

As Fraser headed below, he heard a skitter in the passageway. He shivered; it was either a rat or a very large cockroach.

An hour later Fraser stood by the starboard rail and scanned the dark water between the *O'Leary* and the lights of Olongapo. He picked out the running lights of a boat. He closed his eyes and listened for the familiar engine, but the *O'Leary* vibrated with a life of her own. Ventilators and blowers whined and rattled. The engineering spaces added the hiss of steam and low-pitched vibrations from generators and pumps. Small waves slapped and slurped against the hull. Then Fraser heard the distant mutter of the boat engine, but that wasn't all; drunken laughter carried across the water.

Fraser sighed and realized his night might just be beginning.

Shifflet turned from the rail and bared his tobacco-stained teeth. "Yessir, that bunch sounds pretty well-oiled."

Fraser tried not to look worried. "Can't blame them. The last few weeks at sea were damned tough. Admiral Hart's been training the hell out of us."

Shifflet looked at Fraser reproachfully. "See! It's not just ol' Shifflet that's worried about the Japs."

Fraser frowned. Was Shifflet right? Were the Japanese going to start something?

Shifflet said, "Bet those boys have been making up for all that sea time tonight. Whole damn year's been screwed up by not goin' to China for the summer to cool off. Might be a real handful gettin' folks bedded down."

The whaleboat slid into the bright circle cast by a single floodlight. The engine backed down with a burbling roar, and the boat bumped against the bottom of the accommodation ladder rigged over the starboard side like a steep set of stairs. Fraser stepped onto the platform at the top of the ladder as the structure lurched and creaked. The tang of the boat's exhaust tickled Fraser's nose as he looked down.

"Shifflet! There's a body down there."

Shifflet's footsteps thudded as he ran to the rail.

The boat was crammed with white-suited sailors. Resting on the knees of the men sitting in the forward section of the boat, Water Tender First Class T. T. Simpson was spreadeagled and lashed to a door. His knees framed the sign "Senoritas."

"A dead warrior returning on his shield," muttered Fraser.

"Simpson alive?" yelled Shifflet.

"Aw, hell, yes!" shouted one of the men as his shipmates laughed raucously. "Had too much 'tubic' to drink."

The sailors scrambled to file up the ladder.

"Out of my way!"

"Hell, no! I ain't staying here to carry Simpson up."

Fraser summoned his most authoritative voice. "You men up forward. Stay where you are. Bring Simpson up last."

"Good thinking, sir!" piped up one of the men already on the ladder.

"Way to go, Mr. Fraser."

"These officers sure know how to solve a problem."

Fraser began to doubt his wisdom when he noted the condition of his stretcher-bearers; a few looked barely capable of walking. Fraser turned to select replacements from the men who had come aboard.

"Ready, alley-oop on three!" shouted one of the men in the boat.

"One."

"One!"

"Two."

"Twooooo!"

"Three!"

"Threeeeeeee!"

The door rose above the six bearers, who snorted and laughed as the boat rocked ominously. Somehow, looking like an albino caterpillar, they made it up the ladder.

Thank you, Lord, thought Fraser as Simpson was lowered to the deck. Simpson's balding head was bright red from coming up the ladder feet first. Thick glasses sat askew on a face dominated by a high forehead and fleshy cheeks.

"What's the matter, Mr. Fraser?" asked a grinning radioman whose right sleeve had been ripped off.

"I'm not complaining, but you guys almost dropped Simpson twice."

"No problem, sir. That door'd float."

Fraser shook his head. "There's no law of physics that says Simpson had to be on top."

Shifflet cleared his throat. "You worry too much, sir."

Fraser tried to ignore the criticism, but he could feel his face reddening. "What happened to Simpson?"

"He had a bad night, sir," said the sleeveless radioman, punctuating his report with a loud belch.

"Yeah," added one of the cooks, "he was pissed about the number two boiler acting up again. Then he got to dancing with this gal and spent all his money."

"That weren't the worst of it either," the radioman continued. "He's right proud of his dancing, but when he ran out of dough, that girl told him he don't dance no better'n a bear at the circus."

"That still doesn't explain his condition," Fraser said.

"Well, sir . . . we gave Simpson a bottle of 'tubic' to put him outta his misery. Turned into a wild man after he put that away. Chased that gal into the pisser—'scuse me, ladies' room—and ripped the door off after she locked it. Only way to stop him was to tie him to the door."

"You could have untied him after he passed out."

"Nossir! We had to pay for that door. We wanted our money's worth. Might add some class to the crew's head."

"You're sure he didn't get hurt?" Fraser asked.

Shifflet leaned over and gave Simpson a quick inspection. "He looks fine, sir. Just out cold."

"You sure?"

"Seen a lot like him, Mr. Fraser. You . . ."

". . . worry too much," Fraser said. He felt his jaw muscles bulge. "All right, get him below and into his bunk."

"Mr. Fraser."

"Yes . . . Shifflet."

"Might be a good idea to tie him to his bunk. Sometimes a man'll go wild again if he's had a lot of 'tubic'. 'Specially if he drinks some water."

Fraser picked up one of Simpson's limp arms and dropped it. Simpson's prominent Adam's apple bobbed but that was his only response.

"He's out of it," Fraser said. "I don't think he'll cause any trouble."

Shifflet scratched his jaw. "Don't be too sure, sir."

"Shifflet."

"Yessir?"

"You worry too much." Fraser turned on his heel and headed for the ladder down to his room feeling that, for once, he had gotten the better of Shifflet.

"Mr. Fraser! You'd better come quick!"

"Ummph." Fraser lifted his head from his pillow. The messenger of the watch stood in the doorway.

"Simpson looks like he's gonna cause trouble."

"Simpson?" Fraser felt his stomach drop. He could see Shifflet's knowing smile. He glanced at his watch—0500. At least another man would be in charge of the quarterdeck now.

Fraser jumped down from his bunk. He yanked on a khaki uniform, stuffed hand and leg irons under his belt, and shoved their keys in his pocket. He'd been surprised to find these restraints were standard equipment for Asiatic Fleet destroyer officers standing duty.

Fraser followed the messenger topside where he found the petty officer of the watch, Tim Egan, a torpedoman third class, warily watching Simpson, who was seated on a crate of bananas. Simpson was staring at the top of the second stack where a plume of steam drifted from the leaking safety valve.

"Damn! Something else wrong with number two," muttered Simpson in a gravelly voice. "That God damned bitch of a boiler is gonna kill me yet!"

The freckled Egan leaned toward Fraser. "He came up for a drink about ten minutes ago," the torpedoman whispered.

Fraser cleared his throat. "I know you had a tough night, Simpson. Maybe you could go on back to your bunk."

Simpson's eyes widened. He removed his glasses and slipped them in his pocket. "Tough night?" His bald head reddened. "Tough night! That floozy wouldn't know Jose Greco if he stomped her into the floor."

Simpson leaped up and began to flatten the crate of bananas in a passable flamenco style. When he finished, Simpson picked up one of the surviving bananas and hurled it at the number two stack. "Take that!"

"We'd better get those cuffs and irons on him," Egan said.

Simpson whirled around and fixed them with a wild look. "The hell you say! I'm going back ashore."

"No more boats tonight," Fraser said.

"Who needs a boat?" Simpson bolted for the rail, bowled over Egan, and catapulted over the side.

Egan picked himself up and put his white hat back over his wiry red hair. "That drinking water must have set him off. Looks like a 'tubic tear' all right."

Fraser watched Simpson flail toward the lights of Olongapo. "We'll have to get him with the boat."

"If he doesn't drown first." Egan ordered the messenger to wake the boat crew.

Fraser tried not think about Simpson drowning as he realized who would be blamed for that tragedy.

Out of the corner of his eye, he caught Egan's smile. "Are you going to sell tickets for this show?"

"No, sir. No customers at this hour, although Shifflet might pay good money to see this."

"Don't wake him up. I don't need any more of Shifflet tonight. I'm sure I'll hear from him soon enough."

"You can't take some of these Asiatic Fleet veterans too seriously, Mr. Fraser. This isn't like the battleship you were on."

"So I'm finding out. Damn, Shifflet warned me to tie Simpson to his bunk."

"Shifflet may be a hell-raiser, but he knows his stuff—if he's sober."

"It was different on the *Arizona*. We got rid of anybody who got in as much trouble ashore as Shifflet."

Egan's smile rearranged his face full of freckles. "And where do you think the Navy sends its Shifflets?"

Simpson seemed to miss a few strokes, and his head slid under for a few seconds. Fraser started breathing again as Simpson surfaced and struck out anew. "Egan how's your pitching arm? Are we going to win the fleet championship?"

"My arm feels great, but we're real underdogs."

Fraser laughed. "Maybe we'll get lucky."

"We'll take it any way we can get it. A couple of those *Holland* players are real brawlers. There may be trouble before that game's over."

Fraser began pacing the quarterdeck. He was thankful that Egan was in charge of the watch; the torpedoman was smart, dedicated, and responsible. Egan was not unusual. Since the onset of the depression, the Navy had been able to reject fifteen applicants for every man it enlisted. Egan was more intelligent than many of the officers Fraser knew. Fraser sighed as he thought of the men like Shifflet who anchored the opposite end of the enlisted spectrum. Many of the less-inhibited enlistees from the pre-depression era had gravitated to the Asiatic Fleet. Finding a way of life free of many of the constraints of Stateside society, many had stayed through several re-enlistments.

"Sir, the boat crew is ready," Egan prompted.

Fraser tried not to look down as he followed the sleepy men out the narrow wooden boat boom projecting from the destroyer's side. Fraser climbed down the swaying rope ladder and dropped into the whaleboat. The cough of the starting engine shook the boat. The coxswain guided the boat toward the distant splashes as the engine increased its beat.

Fraser steadied himself with one hand and moved to the bow where fine sheets of spray drifted over the gunwale and cooled his face. Next to Fraser stood Seaman Hank Landry, who wiped his black eyes with the back of a deeply tanned hand. Landry shook his wiry body and seemed to snap awake. He tapped his boat hook slowly against the gunwale as he stared out at Simpson.

"Be careful with the boat hook if we have to use it," Fraser said. "The engineers can't afford to lose Simpson."

Landry spat over the side. "Damn snipes piss me off."

As if one of the engineers in the forward fireroom had heard Landry, a blast of steam erupted from the number two stack. Tiny particles of soot hung in the gray-tinged sky and floated down.

Landry seemed to vibrate. His forearms corded and his knuckles whitened as his lean hands squeezed the wooden pole of the boat hook. "See what I mean. Every time those snipes blow tubes, they dump soot all over the topsides. I have to clean that crap up. Goddamn steam! Goddamn boilers!"

Fraser wondered about Landry's bitterness. Deck hands and engineers were traditional antagonists, but Landry's anger seemed to go deeper.

As the boat maneuvered behind Simpson, Fraser watched the pale blue-green glow that streamed behind the swimmer. His ragged kick had stimulated millions of tiny micro-organisms into temporary phosphorescence. When the boat pulled alongside Simpson, the engineer slowed the engine to a burbling idle to match the sailor's pace.

Fraser leaned over the side and tried to sound authoritative. "Okay, Simpson, give up and get in the boat."

The swimmer's uneven strokes continued.

"Come on now. This is Mr. Fraser. Make it easy on all of us and get in the boat."

The culprit plowed on.

Fraser sighed. "Landry, get ready to slow him down with your boat hook."

Landry unstrapped his watch. "You'd better take yours off, Mr. Fraser, unless it's waterproof."

"Thanks, I almost forgot. Okay, I'm ready now."

Landry's mouth twitched. "You better leave the cuffs and leg irons in the boat, sir. Unless you want to sink."

"Right, thanks." Fraser pulled the equipment free and ripped two of his belt loops in his haste.

There were snickers from the back of the boat.

Landry hefted his long pole.

"Don't hurt him," Fraser said, knowing the engineering officer would not be pleased if Simpson were injured.

Landry's head snapped up and his black eyes flashed. "You're talking to an artist with this boat hook." He leaned out and rapped the back of Simpson's balding head three times. The swimmer's arms began to flop aimlessly. Landry poised himself for another shot.

"That's enough," Fraser said. "Let's go. Keep him under just long enough so he won't give us any more trouble."

Landry hesitated and jerked his boat hook back with obvious reluctance. "If you say so, sir."

Fraser followed Landry over the side. Subic Bay was tepid, but when Fraser opened his eyes underwater, he saw nothing but blue-green fire. He panicked for a second before he remembered the phosphorescent organisms. Fraser kicked to the surface beside Simpson. A flailing arm caught Fraser behind the ear, dazed him, and wrapped around his neck. Another hand seized his shirt and ripped a pocket. Buttons popped. Fraser gasped and inhaled a mouthful of water. He coughed and retched as he tried to free himself from Simpson's tenacious grip. Fraser was forced down into a glowing emerald maelstrom where there was no air. He fought. His chest convulsed with spasms. He struggled. The underwater glow reddened and swiftly turned black.

The next Fraser knew, Landry was towing him to the boat. The boat engineer pulled the now slack Simpson into the whaleboat while the coxswain pushed from the water. After the engineer pulled the coxswain aboard, the two men dragged Landry and Fraser up. A motionless Simpson sprawled in the bilges. Fraser slumped on a seat, dazed and coughing salt water.

Landry rubbed his knuckles. "I hit Simpson a good shot in the chops, Mr. Fraser. Should keep him quiet for a few minutes."

"Thanks," Fraser said between coughs.

The coxswain laughed. "Simpson won't be dancing soon."

"The hell you say!" Simpson sat slowly upright like a vampire rising from his casket. "Where's Olongapo?" he slurred.

"Hold him down!" shouted Fraser, searching frantically for the wrist and leg irons. Fraser finally found his equipment. He circled the pile of men, lunged, snapped on the irons and handcuffs. He stepped back to survey the results.

"Ah, hell!" One end of the leg irons was shackled to Landry's ankle. The sailor shook his leg, and Simpson's left leg bobbed up and down.

Landry's tanned face grew even darker. "Turn me loose, Mr. Fraser."

Simpson smiled vacantly as he examined his handcuffed wrists. He looked at Landry. "Wanna dance?"

Landry answered the invitation with a left to the jaw.

Fraser winced. "Another poor choice of partners." He wasn't sure which of them was having the worse night. "Just a minute Landry, I'll find the keys." Fraser searched his pockets. "They're gone."

Landry held his head. "Jesus! Over the side."

"Coxswain, take us back to the ship," Fraser ordered. "There should be some spare keys there."

"I hope so," muttered Landry. "But if you want to saw this snipe's foot off, that's fine with me. Chief Mortland's gonna be pissed if I can't do my work this morning."

Wonderful, thought Fraser. The chief bosun'll be mad at me too. Damn, I know the engineering officer won't be happy about Simpson. And what's the captain going to say when he gets back?

CHAPTER TWO

The bottom of the whaleboat vibrated under Hank Landry as it headed toward the *O'Leary*. Landry sat in the bilges next to Simpson and clenched his fists. Some of his anger evaporated when he looked up at Lieutenant Fraser sitting alone in the bow of the boat. The officer's sturdy shoulders slumped and his matted black hair framed a bruise on his forehead. The gray eyes above Fraser's prominent cheekbones stared at his shoes. Landry felt a partial sense of comradeship as he noted the bridge of Fraser's nose. Landry had suffered three broken noses himself, and he knew a carelessly reset nose when he saw one. The last of Landry's anger cooled when he remembered that Fraser had always treated him with concern and respect, unlike some of the officers he had run across.

Fraser had taken time to help coach the ship's baseball team, which had impressed Landry, who was the team's catcher. Fraser was one of the few people who seemed to appreciate what a hot and dirty job it was behind the plate. Hell, Landry thought, guess I did the right thing to save Mr. Fraser from drowning.

Landry turned his gaze to the *O'Leary*, outlined by the predawn light. He had to admit her lines were almost graceful. The destroyer's main deck swept in a flowing line from bow to stern. Forward, she was dominated by the low bridge and a single, long-barreled 4-inch gun on the forecastle. The rakish set of the four slender smokestacks was spoiled by the blocky deckhouse between the second and third stacks, which gave the vessel a humpbacked appearance. Two 4-inch guns crouched atop the deckhouse, one on each side. Aft of the stacks, a pair of triple-tube torpedo mounts squatted on the main deck along each rail. Near the stern, another 4-inch gun sat on a small deckhouse. The fantail tapered to a sharp point, leaving little room for a stubby 3-inch antiaircraft gun and two depth charge racks.

Landry rattled the shackle on his ankle. "Damn! No way I'll have time to get back to my bunk now." He looked around the whaleboat at the litter the liberty parties had left and realized he had work to do. But he didn't mind. He considered the whaleboat his personal possession and never resented the hours required to clean it. He'd grown up poor—no toys, no family car. He loved the whaleboat; not even the rich kids had boats in Wyoming. He ran his hand along the newly painted gunwale. It was almost as smooth as Teresa's silky thighs. Three more days and they'd be back in Manila. Landry felt a stirring between his legs. He'd be back in their bed soon.

Shortly after dawn, Ross Fraser sat on a mooring bitt on the *O'Leary*'s forecastle. The unconscious Simpson lay in a puddle on deck next to Landry, who looked as if he wouldn't mind another excuse to punch Simpson.

"How much longer before I get loose, Mr. Fraser?"

"We'll just have to be patient."

The morning sun slanted under the awning and added sweat to the bay water that still soaked Fraser's uniform. The awnings would intercept some of the sun's energy during the middle of the day, but by late afternoon the sun would slant under the awnings again and turn the destroyer into an oven.

Fraser shifted his position on the bitt to ease a case of heat rash and tried to forget his problems. Off the port side, a flotilla of small fishing "bancas" headed toward the morning fish market in Olongapo. The fishermen wore conical hats and glistened with sweat as their paddles flashed in the sunlight.

Fraser realized that the fragile craft would probably outlast the *O'Leary* by many years. If the Japanese didn't sink the destroyer, the scrapyard would soon claim her. She was already three years past her designed life span of twenty years. The long career since her launching, much of it spent in tropical heat and humidity, had exacted a toll. Corrosion had cost the hull plating a third of its original thickness. Internally, much of the electrical wiring, auxiliary equipment, and piping was rusted, corroded, and worn. Fraser was certain his ship was no match for a modern Japanese destroyer.

A twinge in Fraser's knee reminded him of the injury responsible for his present duty. He had first hurt the knee his third year at Annapolis during one of his few chances as a varsity running back. The doctors hadn't operated, but they decreed no more football. Eight months ago, during flight training, he reinjured his knee in a softball game. Despite surgical repairs, the Navy doctors had ruled out any more flying.

Fraser grunted with disgust as he squished his toes in his sodden shoes. I asked for duty on a new destroyer and look what they gave me. Just don't fit in here. Should have asked for a cruiser . . . in the Atlantic. Anywhere but out here.

Landry rattled his leg iron as he shifted his position.

"Landry, I don't remember much, but I think I almost drowned last night. Thanks."

"Just promise you won't lock me up with a snipe again, or I'll let you go next time."

"I hope there won't be a next time," Fraser said.

Christ, Fraser thought. I almost died last night. Died . . . dead . . . the end. If Shifflet is right about the Japs coming . . . might not have gained much time. I'm sure as hell not ready to die. All I've ever done is keep my nose to the grindstone. Studied like hell to get into the Naval Academy. Worked harder there. Busted my butt aboard the *Arizona* to get flight school. Never had time for fun. Almost got enough saved up for the red Ford convertible I've always wanted. Imagine a beautiful girl, a mountain road. . . .

Fraser's fantasy evaporated as he remembered that most of the American women had been evacuated from the Philippines.

He looked around the forecastle and realized he'd be riding a gray rust-bucket instead of a red convertible.

Simpson moaned softly but didn't wake up. Fraser started to worry that Simpson might be injured. "Landry, keep an eye on Simpson for a few minutes while I wake up Doc Laster."

Landry nodded at the leg irons. "Ain't going nowhere."

Fraser stepped into the bridge structure and knocked at the door of the single cabin there. "Have a case for you Doc."

A single sheet was draped over Doctor Herman Laster like a shroud over a dead hippopotamus. "Ummmph. Tell him to take two . . . two . . .

"Aspirin?"

"Right," Laster said. "And call me in the morning."

"It is the morning."

"Try this afternoon."

"I think you should see Simpson now."

"Simpson! Christ! Don't want anything to happen to him!"

Laster threw his pillow aside and groped for his black rimmed glasses with a thick fingered hand and jammed them on his round face.

Fraser looked around the room which was stuffed with boxes of books and papers. The bulkheads were covered with maps of Europe and the Far East. "You sure you're really a doctor and not a spy?"

When Laster stood, fatty folds around his middle hid the top of his baggy boxer shorts. "Somebody's got to keep track of the big picture. You line officers are nothing but ignorant ship drivers."

"Oh, come now."

"Okay, that's an overstatement. The captain is fairly well informed. But the rest of you . . . What's happening outside Moscow and Leningrad right now?"

"Haven't the foggiest."

"Just as I thought. The future of the world is being determined there. Millions are dying to see whether Hitler or Stalin is going to come out on top." Laster began stuffing himself into his uniform.

Fraser thought again of what Shifflet had said. "Doc, what about out here. Think the Japs will start something soon?"

"No."

Fraser let out a relieved breath.

"I don't think they will," Laster continued. "I know they will. Roosevelt's cut off the oil we were selling them. The Japs can't keep fighting the Chinese unless they get oil . . . soon."

"Where'll they buy it?" Fraser asked.

"They won't buy it. They'll invade the Dutch East Indies. One problem—we're right between Japan and the oil."

"How soon you think we could get help from Pearl Harbor?"

"The old plan projected three to six months," Laster said.

"And the new plan?"

Laster began rummaging through his desk. "Europe gets priority first. Roosevelt's already sent some of the ships from Pearl to the Atlantic."

"Maybe we'll retreat if the war starts," Fraser said hopefully.

"Yeah, I've heard some rumors," Laster said as he pawed through some drawers. "We may fall back to Java."

Fraser looked at the map again. The large island of Java sat in the center of the Dutch East Indies. "Right in the middle of all that oil? You're kidding me?"

"No."

Fraser felt his stomach sink. "You looking for your black bag, Doc? It's right here.

"I'm looking for some cigarettes. Got one?"

"No, always heard they're bad for the lungs."

"Only if you get old," Laster said.

"You're not going to get old?"

Laster looked up at the map of the Far East. "Who knows?" he said softly. "You're sure the exec didn't tell you to get me up?"

"No, he's still ashore."

"Just as well. Useless bastard."

Fraser said, "Seems like the Navy should have gotten rid of the exec by now."

"Unh-hunh!" grunted Laster as he strained to tie his shoes. "His uncle is a big wheel in Congress. And his committee doles out the money for the Navy. Beringer is just one of the ways the Navy has to cozy up to Congress. He's had mostly staff jobs until now. I think he's here just so he'll sound dashing and daring when he runs for his uncle's seat some day."

"Good thing the captain knows his job," Fraser said.

"Yeah, Haven't seen him make many mistakes. In fact, he's stepped in several times just in time to keep the exec from screwing up."

Fraser remembered what he'd heard about the captain's family dying in an auto accident two years before. "You ever see the captain looking happy?"

Laster frowned. "He's not a cheerful sort and keeps to his cabin. But after losing his family—that's normal, I guess. Only thing I can't figure out is why he asked for this job. He was all set to command a new destroyer."

"And he asked for one of these old buckets? You must be kidding."

"No. It's true," Laster said.

"I wonder why."

"Don't ask me. I slept through all my psychiatry lectures."

"What kind of a doctor are you?"

"I wanted to be an obstetrician . . ."

"Just what we need. What do you mean by 'wanted'?"

"A long story."

Laster was interrupted by a thud against his door. Fraser pulled it open and Bull Durham, the ship's first lieutenant, fell into the room. The compact but broad-shouldered body of the former Naval Academy gymnast lay motionless on the green linoleum.

"Bull, you're not much shorter lying down than you are standing up," Laster said.

"I do my best work lying down," Durham slurred, his dark brown hair rumpled. Lipstick marks circled his collar and headed down his shirt.

Fraser wrinkled his nose at the aroma of alcohol and cheap perfume.

"I hope you used proper precautions before consorting with the bar girls ashore," Laster said.

"A man of my experience, no problem," Durham said.

"What are you doing here?" Laster asked.

"My aspirin supply is getting low . . ."

Laster's eyes glinted behind his glasses. "A man in need indeed. Maybe I can help you . . . in exchange for a few of your trade secrets with the ladies."

"I keep telling you, no. They wouldn't be secrets if I told everyone," Durham said.

Fraser grabbed a bottle of aspirin and flipped it to Durham. "Come on Doc, you've got another patient to treat."

They pushed Durham out the door and Fraser followed Laster toward the forecastle. Fraser was glad the destroyer division doctor was riding the *O'Leary*. If the war was coming, they might soon need Laster's skills.

The messenger of the watch caught up with them just as Fraser was about to step out onto the forecastle. "Mr. Fraser, the *Pope*'s boat is coming alongside with the captain."

"Our captain?" Fraser's stomach dropped. The captain wasn't due back until ten.

"How close is the boat?" Fraser asked the messenger, hoping he'd have time to change his uniform.

"Just about alongside, sir. You'd better hurry."

Fraser bolted for the quarterdeck. The boat was 20 feet away. Perched in the bow was the *O'Leary*'s commanding officer, Lieutenant Commander Gerald Arkwright. A rumpled linen suit bagged around the captain's stocky frame; he had obviously lost some weight since its purchase. His closely cropped thatch of light brown hair receded at the temples, and the sun glinted off a bald spot at the crown. A jagged pink scar ran diagonally down the middle of his forehead and into one of his bushy eyebrows. The captain scanned the bay and appeared to be sniffing the breeze.

The old man doesn't miss much, Fraser thought. What the hell is he going to say when he sees me?

Arkwright jumped onto the lower platform and trotted up the ladder. Fraser tried to tuck in his shirt, but the buttonless front still gaped open.

The captain paused at the upper platform and faced the colors but, hatless, did not salute. Arkwright turned to the petty officer in charge of the quarterdeck. "I report my return aboard, sir," he said in a quiet, low-pitched, but authoritative voice.

Fraser tried to look inconspicuous, but the captain's piercing pale blue eyes found him immediately. Arkwright's strong Roman nose rose perceptibly.

"I didn't expect you back for hours, Captain," Fraser said lamely.

"Obviously." The one word said paragraphs in the short silence that followed. "Sorry to surprise you. The poker game ended early, and I wanted to get some work done. Have an interesting night, Ross?"

Even though Fraser was several inches taller than the captain, he felt completely intimidated by Arkwright's look of appraisal. "Ah . . . yes, sir. Very."

"The ship appears to be riding normally. I assume we're not taking on water, although your uniform would indicate otherwise."

"The ship is fine, sir. No damage."

"Anyone hurt?"

"Simpson is still passed out. I think he's all right. Doc Laster is examining him now. No other problems, Captain."

"Only Simpson? It looks like you had to subdue half the crew. Maybe you'd better come down to my cabin and tell me about it."

Fraser followed Arkwright down below, feeling like a boy on his way to the woodshed.

"Sit down, " Arkwright said in his cabin. "Let me write down some of the unofficial intelligence I picked up at the poker game last night while it's still fresh in my mind." Arkwright opened his safe and pulled out a notebook and scrawled several entries while Fraser squirmed in his chair.

The room, larger than Fraser's, was still cramped and monastic. Almost all the contents were gray-painted Navy issue. A framed picture on the desk showed an attractive dark-haired woman with a boy and a girl on her lap. A partially completed wooden model of the *O'Leary* sat next to the picture; Fraser was fascinated by the intricate, hand-carved detail on the few sections that were finished. The shelf over the desk was packed with a line of books, starting with the Bible. Fraser scanned the rest of the row: Plato, Shakespeare, Marx, Freud, Darwin, Faulkner, among others. Tucked between a Hemingway novel and the end of the shelf was a leather holster, which covered all but the gleaming black butt of a .45-caliber automatic pistol.

The captain closed the notebook with what sounded like a satisfied grunt.

Fraser wondered what that implied about the start of the war.

"You like my model of the *O'Leary*?" Arkwright asked. "I've put several months into it already. Aside from reading, there's not much to do at night."

"You have an impressive bookshelf," Fraser said.

"I'm about halfway through it. Enlightening as those books are, they don't explain everything."

Fraser looked up again at the gun at the end of the row of books.

"Tell me about your night," Arkwright said.

Fraser took several minutes to tell his story. "Captain, I'm having trouble adjusting out here."

"That should change with time. Also, you should realize you have more responsibility on a small ship. It's not as easy to turn to someone above you for all your problems. But that's what command is all about."

Fraser wondered how anyone could want to sit in a captain's chair.

"Maybe the gunnery exercise tonight will give you some confidence," Arkwright said.

Fraser realized that a successful exercise would help, but that would depend on how the number one gun behaved.

The deep lines in Arkwright's weathered, sun-reddened face softened slightly. "Learn anything last night?"

Fraser thought for a moment. "I guess so, sir."

"Well? I'm curious."

"Ahh . . . two things. Alcohol can be bad stuff, even in a good man like Simpson. And . . . not to ignore good advice because of my pride."

Arkwright closed his eyes and rubbed the scar on his forehead with one finger. The scar reddened and seemed to pulse. Ten seconds later, the captain's eyes opened, unfocused and misty under his bushy brows. "Your night wasn't wasted. Those lessons can be expensive." The captain's voice was almost inaudible.

There was a long silence while the captain stared at the picture of his family. Arkwright shifted his eyes up to the bookshelf, and the lines around his mouth deepened.

Fraser swallowed when he realized the captain's eyes were focused on the pistol.

"Is that all, Captain?"

"That's all."

Fraser eased the door shut behind him as he left.

CHAPTER THREE

Hank Landry knelt in the bobbing whaleboat, cleaning up the trash and San Miguel beer bottles left by the returning liberty parties. He'd finally been hacksawed free of Simpson just before noon. He knew he had a lot of work to do on the boat before they got underway later that afternoon. Landry lifted a seat cushion and frowned when he found a half-empty pint of Ginebra gin. Landry flipped it over the side where the tide carried the bottle slowly away. "Good thing I found that," he muttered. "If that prick Mortland found it, he'd put me on report. Sure don't want that now."

Hours later, Landry finished his cleaning and polishing and began to ready the boat for hoisting aboard. As he worked, he thought of their scheduled return to Manila in a few days. Erotic thoughts of Teresa, the half-Filipino, half-American girl he had lived with for several months, drifted through his mind.

A rumbling, derisive grunt broke his reverie. "Can't see what that little gal back in Manila sees in you."

Landry squinted up at the rail of the *O'Leary* where the chief boatswain's mate, George Mortland, stood, almost blotting out the sun. Well over six feet, his heavily muscled frame was padded with a layer of fat. A roll of flesh hung over his tightly cinched belt. Hairy, thick hands grasped a stanchion, and a tuft of hair sprouted out the neck of Mortland's shirt.

"I just got a check in the mail from my bank. That girl'll pay some attention to me now. Money talks with women."

"Don't be too sure, Chief. Teresa's got taste."

Mortland's knuckles whitened. "I'd better come down there and see if you've done your job right for a change." The chief clambered down the ladder, and the boat jolted as he dropped the last two feet.

"Best looking whaleboat in the squadron, Chief."

"Only because I taught you how to keep it up."

Mortland went over the boat, poking into corners, missing nothing.

"All ship-shape, Chief?"

"Don't smartass me, Landry. I know you young sailors. Always trying to get away with something. I've caught a few trying to hide booze in boats. Can't fool me, though. A stupid mistake like that'll cost you a few weeks of liberty."

Mortland's meaty lips retracted triumphantly as he lifted the cushion where Landry had discovered the gin bottle earlier. "What have we here?"

"A cushion?" Landry said.

Mortland looked down at the empty space; his mouth opened and snapped shut. His face reddened. "This cover needs work."

Landry inspected the spotless canvas. "Good eye, Chief. Looks like a mosquito crapped here on the corner." Landry gave the cushion a flick with his finger. "Satisfied?"

Mortland's jaw muscles bulged. "For now. I wouldn't make any social plans if I was you."

As the chief hauled himself up the ladder like a gorilla clambering up a tree, Landry felt a spasm of anger. If I'm not careful, he thought, that jerk is gonna keep me aboard while he goes after Teresa with his money. Landry wished his nearby boat hook were a harpoon. "Then I'd stick it to that big bastard," he muttered.

Landry climbed the ladder and joined the deck hands who were dismantling the awnings rigged over the forecastle. Like ants returning with booty to their anthole, men carried burdens of canvas and pipes down the forward hatch.

"Hey, Chief," said one of the deck hands, "you hear anything about the Japs?"

"Japs—why should we worry about them?" Mortland said in his loud, rumbling voice. "We'll kick their asses all the way back to Tokyo if they try anything."

Landry remembered the modern Japanese warships he had seen in the ports the *O'Leary* had visited. I wouldn't be so damned confident, Landry said to himself.

"Landry!" shouted Mortland. "Get to work."

A high-pitched boatswain's pipe twittered.

Landry straightened up. "Special sea detail, Chief. I have to get up to the bridge. See you later."

Mortland's small, close-set eyes narrowed. "Count on it."

Fraser stood in front of his men, who were lined up on the after deckhouse. If the destroyer were alongside a pier they would handle lines, but today they would be spectators as the ship left her anchorage. At 1500 the *Ford*, the destroyer division flagship, hauled down a flag signal to order the destroyers to get underway. The flagship hoisted signal flags indicating her course and speed and the *O'Leary* fell in behind her with the *Pope* and *Jones* astern at three-hundred-yard intervals. Within minutes the formation increased speed to 15 knots.

The breeze created by their movement cooled Fraser's sweaty body. The national ensigns and the signal flags snapped from their halyards, and Fraser had to admit it was a stirring sight as they steamed out to sea. When Fraser dismissed his men from their stations, he heard a familiar chuckle.

"Mr. Fraser, heard you been doing some swimming," Shifflet said.

Fraser felt his face redden as he heard a snicker behind him.

"Shifflet." The voice was quiet, almost soft, but there was iron in it.

"Yes, Chief."

"You'd better check number one gun again."

"Right away, Chief."

Chief Gunner's Mate Byron Hanlon's patient brown eyes regarded Fraser with the same steady look he seemed to give officers and seamen alike. Stocky, rugged, of medium height, he might have been hewn from a block of teak. Hanlon's face, neck, and arms were deeply tanned from eleven years of service in the Far East.

"Thanks, Chief. Are we still in good shape for the gunnery exercises?"

"Never can tell about number one," Hanlon said quietly. Fraser had never heard the chief raise his voice. Hanlon paused and looked at the horizon for a few seconds as if carefully selecting the few words he would utter. "Everything checks out."

Fraser knew all that could have been done was done. The chief did not permit sloppy work on his guns. "But you think number one will act up?"

"Not even the Lord could predict that," Hanlon said. "But Shifflet's a good gun captain. He won't let them put a round into the tug."

"Shifflet!" Fraser felt goose bumps on his neck as the breeze evaporated his sweat.

"Good man when we shoot the guns. Wild man ashore, though. The Japs come, we'll need more like him."

Fraser contemplated a shipload of Shifflets laying waste to foes, friends, and civilians alike. He shuddered.

"Mr. Fraser, you hear any information about the war starting? I need to make plans with Maria. Her church won't let us marry, but I'll always treat her like we are."

Fraser watched the foaming bow wave curl away to starboard as he considered his answer. A gull swooped down and plucked a squirming fish from the water. A hundred feet in the air, the fish fell free and splashed back into the water.

"Lucky fish," Fraser said.

"Until something else eats him," Hanlon said.

"Chief, nobody knows anything for sure about the war. Doc

Laster thinks it's going to start soon. Let me see if the captain has any good advice for you."

"Thanks, Mr. Fraser. That'll ease my mind. I didn't like what the Japs were doing to Chinese civilians when we stopped in Chefoo last year."

"Was it bad?"

"Bad."

"You should have a chance to get things settled when we get back to Manila."

Hanlon nodded. "We'll have to take care of our exercises the next few days first."

"Tonight's the one I'm worried about," Fraser said.

In the forward fireroom, T. T. Simpson had managed to stay on his feet on the grating between the two boilers while the ship got underway.

"You still don't look so hot," said Simpson's assistant, Ralph Burley. "That 'tubic' must have really done you in."

"Ask Mr. Fraser."

"You look about as bad off as the boilers," Burley said.

"Don't give me a hard time," said Simpson as he shifted position under the blower duct to get the coolest air. His head throbbed, and waves of nausea swept up from his stomach. He vowed never to use rubbing alcohol again, much less drink anything as potent as "tubic."

Simpson tried to take his mind off his misery. He looked over the familiar maze of piping and valves that was no mystery to him because he had been aboard for eight years. There were often times when he felt like a part of the *O'Leary*'s machinery. Simpson faced aft and gazed at the front of number two boiler, which almost filled the width of the hull. Number two was making steam, as was number four in the after fireroom. Number one boiler sat cold and silent at Simpson's back. Both boilers ran from the bilges up to the main deck ten feet over Simpson's head. The boiler room, like its twin just aft, and the two engine rooms were not subdivided into smaller compartments. Aside from the transverse bulkheads, their boundaries were the hull and main deck of the destroyer.

The bell on the repeater from the engine order telegraph jangled, calling for more speed. Without waiting for the steam pressure to drop as the turbines in the engine rooms demanded more steam, Simpson cut in another burner on the face of the roaring boiler. The grate underfoot vibrated as the steam sang through the lines at a higher pitch.

"Need to put bigger atomizer plates in the burners?" Burley asked.

"Not unless we speed up more." Simpson twisted the fuel flow valve, making a minor adjustment.

The forced draft blowers whined louder as they adjusted to the boiler's demand for more air.

Burley increased the feedwater supply and checked the long glass tube that ran up in front of the boiler. "Water glass is still okay."

"Good," Simpson said. The supply of feedwater was critical and had to be increased during periods of high demand. Too much feedwater would permit water to enter the steam line and damage the turbine blades. Too little water in the boiler would allow it to overheat and damage the boiler itself.

Simpson relaxed and felt a quiet sense of pride, secure in the knowledge that his boilers served as the heart of the *O'Leary*, generating the steam necessary to turn the propellers and run all the auxiliary equipment. But unease began to nag at Simpson. He checked the gauges on the front of the boiler, looked at the water glass, and cocked his ear for the individual sounds of the feed and fuel pumps against the background roar of the air blowers. All seemed normal, the steam pressure was holding steady at 200 pounds-per-square-inch; the water level was normal and all systems appeared to be functioning properly. But there had been a subtle change during the last few weeks of steaming.

"What the hell is different," he muttered.

He prowled the grating looking for an answer but found none.

Simpson heard the door of the airlock open and realized his watch was over. He shook his head. "Just have to find what's bothering me later."

After turning the watch over to their reliefs, Simpson led Burley into the airlock, turned the wheel to dog the lower door, and climbed the ladder to the upper hatch, which could not be opened unless the lower door were closed. The hatches were interlocked to keep the fireroom pressurized to force air into the boilers. If the fireroom were suddenly depressurized, the fires in the boilers might flash back into the fireroom.

Simpson knew the interlock system was safe, but an enemy shell could quickly depressurize the boiler room. The threat of a flashback paled when compared to that of a rupture in the steam system itself. Men trapped in the engineering spaces could be cooked in a matter of minutes.

Simpson put those unpleasant thoughts from his mind and savored the breeze as he crawled out the upper hatch and stood on the main deck.

Burley wiped a greasy forearm across his brow. "Damn, all we got off is the two dog watches. Four hours off ain't enough."

Simpson grunted. "Be a little cooler this evening."

"Big deal," Burley said. "What's 5 degrees when it's 130?"

"Not much. The chief down in main control?"

"Yeah, he's got this watch. Why?" asked Burley.

"Want to talk to him about number two."

"Quit worrying, Simpson. You're worse'n my mother."

Aft of the amidships deckhouse, Simpson twirled the shiny wheel that opened the hatch to the forward engine room. He climbed down the vertical ladder and crossed the grating to the main throttle station, which was dominated by large gleaming control wheels and backed by a mass of gauges and valves. Bulky turbines, auxiliary equipment, and a maze of steam lines filled the large compartment. The air smelled of lubricating oil and steam. Simpson not only heard but felt the whine of the high and low pressure turbines as steam sang against the whirling blades. Vibrations from pumps and heavy machinery throbbed through the metal grating under his feet. A nearby valve hissed and dripped into the bilges.

The chief machinist's mate turned from the throttle station and smiled. "We thought you'd be out of commission for a while."

Simpson shouted over the roar of the ventilation blowers. "You know I'm always on the job when we get under way."

"Maybe that forward boiler room sweated some of that 'tubic' out of you," the chief said. "You still worried about number two?"

"That's why I'm here. That damn boiler . . . I just don't know. Something ain't been right for weeks now. Just can't figure out what it is."

"Be plenty of time when we go in the yard next week. You'll have over two months to find it then."

"I hope so," Simpson said. "Got a lot of other things to fix, too. Most of the gasketing in main steam line joints is in bad shape. Whole damn ship's falling apart. Hope they have some miracle workers there at Cavite."

The chief frowned. "Just hope the Japs don't start anything before we're done in the yard."

Simpson felt a chill despite the 125-degree heat. "Don't know what'd be worse: getting caught all taken apart in the yard, or trying to fight without an overhaul."

"Lotta folks say something might happen soon," the chief said.

"Christ, I haven't got time to worry about that. I got troubles keeping the boilers going," Simpson said.

In the lingering twilight, Ross Fraser climbed the ladder at the rear of the bridge structure with a feeling of apprehension. He nodded at the signalman on duty on the signal bridge as he stepped off the ladder. Bull Durham was forward on the port bridge wing watching the flagship 300 yards ahead. Durham turned and looked aft where the other two destroyers followed close astern. Durham gave Fraser a quick wave and went back to checking the horizon. Fraser smiled to himself. Despite his wild life ashore, Durham seemed just as respectful of the captain's high standards as everyone else aboard.

Fraser climbed another ladder to the small range finder platform on top of the bridge. Just aft was the elevated gun director platform. Two fire controlmen wearing headsets were swinging the director to various positions and listening to the men verifying the readouts on the guns to see if they were following properly.

After a few minutes the stream of technical chatter ceased. "I don't believe it," said one fire controlman.

Fraser glanced over his shoulder where the round, spectacled face of Doctor Laster rose slowly over the top of the ladder.

"What are you doing here, Doc?" Fraser asked.

"It's so calm tonight, I thought I'd try some fresh air. The bastards on the bridge didn't trust me not to throw up and chased me off. Wait'll they get sick and need me."

Fraser laughed. "Grab that bucket, and we'll give you a chance."

Laster plunked his heavy body on the platform beside Fraser. "Explain what you're doing. I need to keep my mind on something besides my stomach."

"We're testing for the gun shoot tonight."

"I know that. First, tell me why your main battery can't shoot at airplanes," Laster said.

"It was designed before air threats existed. The guns won't elevate high enough to shoot at most aircraft and the computer won't work with the speeds at which an aircraft moves."

Laster frowned. "We're almost defenseless then."

"Except for two .50-caliber machine guns and a puny 3-incher," Fraser said. "Our best defense is to move like hell."

"Damn, cheer me up by telling me what you can do against surface targets."

Fraser thought for a minute how to put it all in simple terms. "It's a hard enough problem to hit a target with a rifle at a few hundred yards. With a big gun at long range it gets harder. Our 4-inch guns might be shooting at a target six or seven miles away. The target's moving. We're moving. We might be pitching and rolling. The earth's rotating, and the wind's blowing. Even the air temperature affects the powder charge."

"A wonder you can hit anything," Laster said.

"Can't be done reliably by the men at the gun except at close ranges. The equipment up here solves most of our problems. The men on the director and the range finder track the target, and the computer uses a bunch of gears and wheels to figure out target course and speed. When we enter in all the other variables, the computer comes up with orders to point the guns so the projectile will hit the target. The men on the guns just match up with order dials rather than watching the target."

"What about the pitching and rolling?"

"There's a stable element—a gyro—that closes the firing circuit when the ship rolls through level."

"Sounds like all your problems are solved," Laster said. "How can you miss?"

"Lots of reasons. The target can change course while the shell is in the air. An optical range finder isn't perfect under the best of circumstances. The one we have is useless at high speeds because the ship vibrates so much."

"Wonderful. We slow down, we'll be easy to hit."

"We won't do that," Fraser said. "We have to rely on me to estimate the initial range, and then we shoot a spotting ladder to make sure."

"Spotting ladder?"

"Sure, the first salvo goes out 500 yards under my range estimate, the second right on, and the third 500 yards over. Then the spotter in the crow's nest gives me a correction."

Laster looked up at the cylinder near the top of the mast. The mast oscillated through a few cycles as the ship rolled gently.

"You want to go up there, Doc?"

Laster had already turned pale. "No, thanks. It's time for me to go back to my bunk."

Fraser realized that he hadn't warned Laster about the possibility of the number one gun's read-out dials running amok. "See you later, Doc."

"Much later. Don't let anyone get hurt."

Wonderful, Fraser thought. Imagine lying down there in the wardroom with a seasick doctor operating on you.

"Everything checks out, Mr. Fraser," said one of his fire controlmen. "Won't be long now."

The *Ford* led the four destroyers away from the tug and the slender barge. The target, a large canvas screen suspended between tall masts at the ends of the long barge, was visible until the last light faded from the western sky.

Fraser hoped the number one gun wouldn't pump a round into the tug. That'll end my career in a hurry, he thought.

The rhythmic gong-gong of the general quarters alarm jolted Fraser from his thoughts. Feet pounded on steel decks and clattered up ladders as the crew raced to their battle stations. He took a deep breath, buckled his life jacket, and put on his sound-powered headset and steel battle helmet.

Fraser adjusted his headset so one earpiece was over his right ear. The earpiece and his microphone connected him to the main battle circuit, which included the captain's talker and the spotter in the crow's nest, Bull Durham.

Fraser pushed the left earpiece off his ear so that he could hear the men on the director platform. One of the new arrivals was a storekeeper third class named Eckersly, a solemn, beagle-like sailor, who put on a phoneset that communicated with the guns. Wherever Fraser went, Eckersly followed like a faithful hound, ready to relay Fraser's orders. With his uncovered left ear, Fraser could also keep track of activity on the bridge wings just below and anticipate the captain's orders. Fraser often felt like a fly on the wall as he watched the captain, who preferred to run his ship from the open wings instead of the covered pilot-house.

"Gun control on the line," Fraser reported when the bridge talker came on the line.

"All guns manned and ready," Eckersly said at Fraser's elbow.

"Crows nest manned and ready," came Durham's tinny voice over the headset.

Fraser took a deep breath to calm the butterflies in his stomach. His mouth felt dry, and he tried to keep his voice from cracking. "Bridge, gun control. The gun battery is manned and ready."

The *O'Leary* heeled over as the flagship led the column of four destroyers back toward the now invisible tug and target. The steel deck trembled as they accelerated to their attack speed of

27 knots. The blowers whined and picked up volume and pitch as they crammed air into the firerooms for combustion in the boilers. Equipment shook and rattled in harmony with the beat of the propellers. The wake boiled into a rooster-tail which hung several feet above the fantail.

Fraser lifted his binoculars and scanned the horizon ahead. The overcast sky blotted out light from the moon and stars. The division commander on the *Ford* would lead them by the target. Only he knew whether the target would be to port or starboard. When the destroyers were on a safe firing bearing, the tug would play a spotlight on the target for a few seconds. Then it would be up to the destroyers.

"Keep a sharp lookout," Fraser ordered. "It shouldn't be long now."

Fraser glanced down at the open bridge wings below. The compact figure of the captain was wedged into the forward corner of the port wing and several other helmeted figures stood nearby. The minutes crawled by, and Fraser strained to catch sight of the target. Suddenly, a stabbing flash of white light transfixed the barge off the port beam.

Fraser reacted quickly. "Surface target! Port beam! Fire a star shell spread! Get the director on him!"

A sharp crack shook the ship. A flash from the fantail lit up the night as the 3-inch antiaircraft gun pumped out the first of several star shells, set to explode above and beyond the target. The other ships followed the *O'Leary*'s lead. Seconds later bright points of light flashed and grew in intensity as the illuminant in the shells began to burn. The flaring lights descended slowly, swaying gently from their supporting parachutes. The illumination of the target wasn't as effective as a searchlight, but it wouldn't offer a target for enemy fire.

Durham's report sounded in Fraser's right earpiece. "Range six oh double oh. Target angle zero eight zero. Speed five knots."

Fraser knew their range finder was useless. After many gunnery exercises aboard the battleship, he felt confident about estimating ranges. It looked longer than 6,000 yards. He hesitated but finally passed Durham's estimates to the computer operator who entered them into the box mounted on the side of the gun director.

"Fire up ladder. Range six oh, double oh," Fraser said.

"On target!" the director trainer said.

"On target!" echoed the director pointer.

"I have a solution," the computer operator said.

"Surface action port. Match pointers," Fraser ordered.

Seconds later Eckersly reported the guns were ready.

"The captain says open fire when ready," reported the bridge talker in Fraser's headset.

"Load all guns," Fraser ordered. He looked down at the number one gun; it seemed to be pointed in the right direction. Fraser took a deep breath. "Three rounds salvo fire, commence firing."

The salvo buzzer rattled in his ears. Fraser shut his eyes to protect his night vision from the gunflash. A giant hand shook his body, and the ship jolted sideways as the first salvo crashed from the guns. Fraser opened his eyes and searched the sky for the glowing tracer elements, which looked like angry fireflies in a hurry to get somewhere.

Thank God! Fraser thought. Tracers are tightly bunched. Means number one's okay and not shooting somewhere else. Salvo buzzer. Close your eyes. Second salvo on the way. Look for first salvo landing. Red splashes—our dye color. Damn! Way short. Should have added five hundred yards to Bull's estimate. Buzzer! Close eyes!

As the acrid smell of burnt gunpowder stung Fraser's nose, the second salvo landed at least 500 yards short. "Last one should be close," he muttered as more star shells continued to blossom in the sky behind the target.

"Damn, still short," he said when the third salvo of the spotting ladder hit. Fraser agreed with Durham's report that the third salvo was 100 yards shy of the target, but correct in deflection. "Up two, no change," he ordered the computer operator. The next salvo threw up red columns of water just beyond the target. "Beautiful! Right through the target screen. No change! No change! Rapid salvo fire!"

The guns began to hammer out salvos. "Looks good," Fraser muttered. After the fifth salvo, Fraser looked down at the number one gun. The crew danced about their old-fashioned open weapon with practiced ease. The pointer and trainer crouched in metal seats on either side of the gun, cranking handwheels to keep the gun matched up with orders from the computer. The gun captain, Shifflet, yanked the breech block open. A smoking brass cartridge case flew to the deck where an asbestos-gloved sailor snatched it aside. The first loader shoved home a new round and turned back to the second loader, who was waiting with the next round.

Fraser closed his eyes when the salvo buzzer rattled again and turned to pick up the next salvo in flight. The distant sled was surrounded by multicolored spashes as salvos from the four destroyers lifted water all around it. The *O'Leary*'s crimson columns were still falling just behind the target.

"Perfect, perfect!" Fraser said as the eighth salvo left.

His mouth opened after the ninth crashed out. One glowing tracer diverged from its fellows, heading up and to the left. Fraser whirled to check the number one gun. The pointer and trainer were cranking their hand wheels furiously. Fraser froze. The trainer looked up as the gun slammed into its stops with the barrel pointed within inches of the port bridge wing. Fraser watched in horror as the captain leaned forward and seemingly peered straight down the barrel of the loaded gun.

The salvo buzzer rattled as Fraser shouted, "Cease firing!"

Too late. The deck jolted and Fraser was temporarily blinded by yellow flashes. Fraser stared down at the bridge wing. Several figures had retreated aft toward the signal bridge, but Arkwright still leaned from the forward corner.

"Thank God!" Fraser said when he realized the forward gun hadn't fired.

Eckersly came to life at Fraser's elbow. "Casualty on number one. Ceased firing one round early. Request permission to fire at the target under local control."

"Permission granted," Fraser said.

Fraser watched Shifflet crouch behind the pointer and coach

his gun back on the target. The last round slammed out toward the sled. Fraser watched in amazement as it threw up a splash just behind the target, having passed through the target screen—a hit.

The gun crew cheered as Fraser watched Gerald Arkwright disengage himself from his spot at the forward corner of the bridge wing. The last star shells floated low behind the sled and cast an eerie yellow-green light on the captain's features.

My God, thought Fraser. He looks disappointed. Did he want that last round to take his head off?

The clank of shell casings being gathered by the gun crews stirred a perplexed Fraser back into action. He ordered Eckersly to ask all stations for their final reports.

CHAPTER FOUR

The morning after the gunnery exercise, Fraser sat in his stateroom, trying to concentrate on an ammunition inventory. He remembered how the starshells had illuminated the captain's face. Fraser wondered why the captain hadn't retreated from the threat of the loaded gun. He shook his head and forced himself back to work.

His eyes felt like sandpaper. He'd had the midwatch on the bridge and hadn't turned in until 0400. Like the other junior officers, he stood one watch in four while under way, averaging six hours a day on the bridge. Watchstanding didn't solve his administrative responsibilities, so Fraser was trying to reduce the pile of paperwork that kept rising in his "IN" basket.

Fraser yawned and looked up at his bunk, perched above a four-foot high set of metal drawers, but the bed was off-limits during working hours. The tiny patch of open floor was half-filled by his single chair which was pulled up to a flip-down desk top attached to another metal cabinet. A small closet and a wash basin completed the contents of Fraser's so-called stateroom.

"Damn shoebox," Fraser said, remembering that the bathrooms back home had been larger. Still, it was a palace compared to what the crew had, so he couldn't complain. Fraser leaned his head back to catch the current of humid air from a humming electric fan mounted on the bulkhead. A flake of mildewed paint spiraled to the green linoleum-covered deck. A cockroach, alerted by Fraser's movement, scurried under the green curtain that covered the doorway.

Fraser looked at his watch and realized it was time for lunch. He walked a few steps aft to the wardroom, which was below the main deck just forward of the bridge. The narrow wardroom ran the width of the ship's hull. The eight-place table took up most of the space, and two rattan lounge chairs sat in the open area. A large operating room light loomed over the table like a chrome vulture waiting for a meal. The light bothered Fraser because it always reminded him that the table would be used for surgery on battle casualties. Fraser pulled a chair away from the table and joined the officers sitting at the open end of the wardroom.

Bull Durham, the diminutive first lieutenant, and Jack Meredith, the engineering officer, were playing cribbage. Meredith's wispy mustache accentuated the dark circles under his brown eyes. Even his curly brown hair seemed limp with fatigue. His thin hands shook slightly as he dealt the cards.

"Any new problems, Jack?" Fraser asked.

"Same old ones. I'll be glad when we get in the yard. It's going to take all of our overhaul to fix the engineering plant."

"Any news about your getting relieved?"

Meredith's narrow shoulders slumped. "Only bad news. One of my friends in Olongapo said nobody would get relieved until the threat of war dies down."

"But you're months overdue already," Fraser said.

Durham's pug face wrinkled with disgust. "That's the Navy for you."

"I've been a father for six months now and never seen my son," Meredith said with a slight trace of a Tennessee twang. "I haven't even seen my wife for a year now."

"Cheer up," Durham said. "At least your wife doesn't have a brand new baby. Then it wouldn't be yours."

The wardroom door opened and the executive officer, Robert Beringer, strode in. His legs were short compared with his elongated trunk and neck, and his long nose and upper lip gave his face an equine look. The executive officer's uniform was well cut and tailored. It had to be, Fraser thought; no off-the-rack uniform would fit that body.

Beringer wrinkled his nose. "I hope the menu isn't as plebian as usual."

Fraser usually liked southern drawls, but Beringer's nasal intonation grated on his ears.

"Sir, I have a suggestion to spice up the meal," said Durham.

Beringer's swamp-colored eyes looked suspicious. "You did such a deplorable job during your term as mess caterer, I'm not sure I want to listen."

"Doc Laster is trying out a new seasick medication. He said he's coming to lunch today," Durham's innocent blue eyes took on a glint of mischief.

Meredith's thin fingers folded the cribbage board. "Not much of a test. It's dead calm."

Durham smiled and showed even white teeth. "We could make it a test."

Beringer looked down his long nose. "I don't normally approve of such shenanigans. Since it's Laster, all right. Sort of thing we used to do at Choate."

"I'll go along," Fraser said. "Here he comes now."

"Time to eat, gentlemen," Beringer said.

The officers took their regular places. The captain's chair remained empty because the *O'Leary* was still steaming in a tight formation. The captain would take his meal from a tray while sitting in his bridge chair. He would catnap in the chair or sleep in a pipe rail bunk in the chart house, never straying far from the bridge.

As the rest of the officers took their places, Durham said, "Doc, I think I know your problem with seasickness. Your seat at the end of the table makes things worse."

Fraser nodded. "Take my seat, Doc, it's right in the middle. I'll just move down one."

"Why not?" Laster eased his belly under the table. "Might as well give this medicine every chance. This is wonderful. I feel great! The wonders of chemistry and medical pharmacology."

"Can't seasickness be partly psychological?" Fraser asked.

"Nonsense!" said Laster. "Psychiatry is nothing but mumbo-jumbo. Don't believe in it myself."

Durham's eyes seemed innocent again. "Real smooth now, but I heard it's not going to last long."

"Long enough for lunch, I hope," Laster said.

"You never know about the weather," said Meredith. "Ah, here's the soup."

As Laster lowered his head to take his first spoonful, Durham winked, and the officers swayed slightly to starboard, stopped, and swayed slowly back. They settled into a comfortable rhythm and began eating and talking normally. Laster looked up from his soup dish as Fraser leaned against him and then away. Out of the corner of his eye, Fraser saw Laster blink several times as he watched the officers opposite him. It was still dead calm.

"Sea's picking up," said Durham as he increased his sway and the others followed. The next time Fraser leaned against Laster, the doctor began to sway with them.

The conversation turned to the prospect of war.

"Shouldn't be long now," the swaying Laster said. "Just as well."

Beringer rattled his soup spoon. "Oh come now, Doc. Just how is your hero Roosevelt going to inveigle us into it? He won the election by promising to keep us out."

Laster's thick hand held his spoon in mid-air. "You and your uncle's isolationist friends in Congress just want us to stand aside and let Hitler take over?"

Beringer was silent for a few seconds. "The Europeans will always be fighting each other. Why should we partake in their imbroglios?"

Imbroglio? What a windbag, Fraser thought.

"Hitler's not just another European," Laster said.

Beringer's nasal voice rose a notch. "Your paragon Joe Stalin's no prize."

"He isn't my paragon."

"I thought all you liberals loved communists."

Laster took off his glasses and wiped them as he swayed. "Stalin's as bad as Hitler. He's knocked off millions of his people, ruined their agricultural system, and almost destroyed their army."

"And you want us to help him?" Beringer asked.

"Not especially. I want us to stop Hitler."

"Why bother?" Beringer said. "We've got two good oceans to protect us. Congress will never declare war."

"Political discussions are boring!" said Durham as he increased the sway, and the officers followed.

"Sure is warm in here," Meredith said.

"Stuffy, too," Fraser said.

Laster was paler, but he dug into his plate of spareribs as he swayed to the increased tempo.

"Doc, you really think the war will start soon for us?" Meredith asked.

"Certainly. The Japs are desperate for oil. Back in 1905 they defeated the Russians with a surprise attack."

"Come now," Beringer said. "They wouldn't dare attack us. After all, they're only Orientals."

"Those mere Orientals may be smarter than we are," Laster said sharply.

The officers swayed farther now. "Damn, it's going bad in a hurry!" Durham said.

Meredith said, "At least we're not pitching too much. I hate that up and down, up and down."

The officers added a subtle vertical component to their motion. A few beads of sweat appeared on Laster's brow.

"Anything the matter, Doc?" Durham asked.

"Just thinking. I know the Japs are going to spring a surprise attack. But the Asiatic Fleet isn't worth one."

"What is," Fraser asked.

"Pearl Harbor."

The wardroom echoed with guffaws and laughter. Meredith's tired face came to life. "You may know some military history, Doc, but the Japs would never try to hit Pearl. Hell, it's 3,500 miles from Japan. The Army has the place covered with hundreds of aircraft and all kinds of antiaircraft guns. Someone told me they have radar there now."

"He's got you, Laster." Beringer's smile was contemptuous.

"I've never heard anyone idiotic enough to suggest the Japs would attack Pearl Harbor. I don't think the Japs will start hostilities, but if they do, everyone knows it would be out here."

"Okay, okay. I just wanted to see if you guys were awake," Laster said.

"Nice to hear you admit defeat for once," Fraser said.

That appeared to be too much for Laster's pride. He frowned for a few seconds. "If their carriers could catch our fleet in Pearl Harbor . . ." His assertive look faded as sweat rolled down his face, and he jumped from his chair. Still swaying in time with his shipmates, he weaved and bobbed across the rock-steady deck and out the door leading forward.

Beringer frowned. "That's funny, he usually heads aft to go up to his room."

"Probably wants to throw up in the head," Meredith said.

The sounds of retching confirmed his observation.

The steward shook his head, "I don't think he likes my cooking."

Fraser said, "He likes it all right. He eats enough of it in port."

A pale Laster walked back into the wardroom and stopped beside Beringer. "I should apologize—"

"No, no. When nature urgently calls, you don't have to ask to be excused."

"But—"

"You still look pale. So much for medical miracles," Beringer said in a condescending tone. "You'd better go up and lie down before you get sick again. I insist. The case is closed. No more apologies."

"If you say so." Laster hurried out the door aft.

When the officers finished, Beringer pushed back his chair. "End of November coming up. You gentlemen make sure all your monthly reports are ready to submit on time."

Wonderful, Fraser thought. The Japs are probably coming, and he's worried about reports.

The rest of the officers were still talking over their coffee when there was a roar from the passageway forward. Fraser and the other officers ran for the door. Beringer emerged from his room holding his long nose. "Laster threw up all over my desk. A month's work of paper work is ruined!"

Durham snickered behind Fraser. "Now that's what I call a successful surprise attack."

Fraser wondered if Laster had really stumbled in the wrong door by accident. Maybe the doctor had realized what the officers were doing. Or had Laster and Durham set up the whole thing to get Beringer?

Later that afternoon, Fraser stood on the fire control platform and buckled on his headset as the last rhythmic "gong-gong" of the general quarters alarm died away. The familiar fleet tug steamed on the horizon to starboard. The column of destroyers sliced through a 3-foot swell as a 10-knot breeze ruffled the surface.

"The maneuvering we do for one of these torpedo attacks always gives me the sweats," said his talker, Eckersly. "We almost got run over last year."

"Don't even mention that," Fraser said as he thought of another destroyer's bow slicing into them at 27 knots.

Fraser looked down at the starboard bridge wing where Ensign Chuck Steiner, the heavyset torpedo officer, wedged himself behind his torpedo director. Steiner adjusted the headset connecting him with his mount captains stationed on top of mounts behind the amidships deckhouse. The torpedo officer was a placid, thick-limbed native of Wisconsin who was a class behind Fraser at Annapolis. Steiner always seemed to take adversity with a smile, and Fraser envied his easy affability.

Steiner's broad brow was furrowed with concentration as he listened to the captain's final instructions. Steiner would be responsible for aiming and firing the exercise torpedo. His director, like its twin on the port bridge wing, tracked the target and generated firing orders that might allow the torpedoes to hit their targets at ranges up to 8 miles.

The four destroyers accelerated to their attack speed of 27 knots, and headed for the tug, now a dot on the horizon. The

O'Leary was second in the tight column of four ships with only 300 yards between each destroyer. As they made the long run toward the target, Fraser's mind replaced the fleet tug with an enemy battle line, the target the old destroyers had been designed to strike with their main armament of twelve torpedoes. Two or three torpedo hits could sink or cripple a battleship. But the enemy would know that and respond to an impending torpedo attack with a blizzard of gunfire. The *O'Leary* had only her speed to protect her. Her thin skin left her vulnerable even to small shells.

Fraser groaned as he thought about the possibility of heading for the Japanese Fleet in an attack like they were rehearsing. Down on the bridge wing, the captain gazed straight ahead at the tug with almost an exultant look. Fraser remembered Laster telling him the captain had asked for this command. How could anyone ask for the possiblity of charging the Japanese Fleet like this, Fraser wondered.

Fraser's thoughts were interrupted when the *Ford*'s fluttering signal hoist snapped down. An intricate sea ballet began, mesmerizing Fraser with the foaming wakes which curved and intersected as the ships moved into a line abreast formation for the final stage of the attack. The destroyers pounded toward the target, spray flying from their bows. Drops of warm Pacific salt water carried up to Fraser, cooled his face, and fogged his binoculars.

When the target range dropped to three miles, the next flag hoist at the *Ford*'s yard arm whipped down. "Fire your torpedo," Arkwright ordered Steiner.

Fraser craned his head aft, waiting for the single exercise torpedo that would be fired 30 degrees off the starboard bow. Suddenly a long metal cylinder leaped through a blast of smoke toward the water. The weapon's steel body and yellow exercise head glinted in the afternoon sun. The propellers whirled, and a plume of steam trailed behind. After the weapon splashed into the water, a trail of exhaust bubbles rose. The torpedo obediently made its programmed 30-degree turn, paralleled the ship's heading, and left them behind.

When all torpedoes were clear ahead, the destroyers wheeled away in a simultaneous turn and made black smoke from all stacks to cover their withdrawal. Fraser realized that they had been completely naked during their approach. Even at this stage, an unfavorable wind might scatter the frail cocoon of their protective smoke screen. Fraser shuddered. If this had been war, he might be lucky to be swimming away from the *O'Leary*'s shattered hull. He took a deep breath and his shivering stopped. He wondered how he would stand up to the test of real combat. Death might be only weeks away if the war started.

The flagship signaled the end of the exercise and released the destroyers to recover their torpedoes. The *O'Leary* wheeled back through the remnants of the oily smoke to hunt for the torpedo by following the faint trail of bubbles.

Durham made the first report from the crow's nest. "Our fish passed right under the target!"

"No more excitement today," Eckersly, Fraser's talker, said dolefully.

"Cheer up, Eckersly. It's a beautiful day."

"I am cheerful, Mr. Fraser. I grew up this way. My family runs a funeral parlor."

"A profitable business. Why'd you leave for the Navy?"

"I'm from Florida. It's always hot down there, and I have a sensitive nose and—"

"I understand," Fraser said quickly.

Eckersly looked him over as if measuring him for a coffin. "If the Japs get you, I'd be happy to see your remains are treated right."

"Thanks, but I'm not sure it'll make much difference."

The voice of the bridge talker crackled in Fraser's right earpiece. "Mr. Fraser, the captain wants you to come down to conn the ship for the torpedo recovery."

The boatswain's pipe twittered to secure from general quarters as Fraser hurriedly stowed his equipment. He climbed down to the bridge and went in the pilothouse.

Arkwright nodded his short-cropped head. "This is a good chance for you to handle the ship. I want you to stop about 100 feet upwind of the torpedo and keep it in our lee. There's just enough of a swell to make the recovery tough for the whaleboat."

"Aye, aye, Captain. I'll do my best."

"Mr. Fraser has the conn," the captain announced, beginning the required ritual to turn over control of the ship.

"This is Mr. Fraser, I have the conn."

"Rudder's amidships, steering one four zero," announced the helmsman behind the spoked wheel.

"Very well," Fraser said trying to keep his voice from cracking.

"All engines ahead standard, indicating 235 turns for 20 knots," said the lee helmsman at the shining brass engine-order telegraph with its twin handles.

"Very well," Fraser said.

The required ritual complete, Fraser stepped out to the pelorus on the starboard wing and took a bearing on the smoke plume the torpedo was releasing. "Come right to one five eight." He continued to adjust their ship's course to keep the torpedo dead ahead as the *O'Leary* closed. As they drew near, he noted the wind direction and maneuvered upwind with the torpedo off the starboard side, where the whaleboat waited to be lowered.

Fraser knew it would be easy to over- or under-shoot the torpedo's position. He could only stop exactly if he picked the right time. Feeling the pressure, Fraser bit his lip and made his decision. "All engines stop. All engines back two-thirds."

The ship shuddered as the propellers bit the water. Thirty seconds later the destroyer halted.

"All engines stop," Fraser ordered to prevent the *O'Leary* from gathering sternway.

From his bridge chair, the captain peered over his sunglasses at the torpedo as it bobbed 100 feet off the starboard beam. "Good work. Make sure you maintain your position."

The whaleboat danced across the medium-sized swells toward the torpedo. Fraser saw Torpedoman Tim Egan poised in the bow of the boat, ready to secure a line to the torpedo. Even in the protective lee of the ship, the torpedo bobbed erratically. Fraser was so engrossed with the recovery that it wasn't until

Arkwright coughed several times that he realized the destroyer, with an almost imperceptible amount of sternway, had drifted enough to move the ship's protective lee away from the torpedo.

Fraser reacted. "All ahead one-third." He waited agonizing seconds for the *O'Leary* to pick up headway. By the time he stopped the ship again, it had moved too far.

Damn! he thought. "All back one-third." He prayed he would be able to stop the 1200 tons of steel in the right spot.

"Boat's goin' after it anyway," came a voice from the signal bridge.

"Come on, Egan, be careful. We need you to pitch against the *Holland*," said another voice.

Fraser gave his last order with a dry mouth as the ship stopped again.

"I think you're all right now," Arkwright's low-pitched voice said.

But the boat moved alongside the torpedo before the new lee formed. Egan deftly secured the huge metal beast with his line, but the whaleboat slammed against the torpedo several times. The crunch of splintering wood came across the water. Triumphant but battered, the boat towed the captive torpedo to the side of the ship where both were hoisted aboard.

"Oooee! Landry looks pissed about his boat," said the voice on the signal bridge.

The captain eyed Fraser with a flat expression. "Nice approach." The following seconds of silence said more than any chewing out could have. "But you let yourself get lulled by your success. You always have to be alert. Trouble can come when you least expect it." The next words were almost inaudible. "And not just aboard ship."

That night Hank Landry had just fallen asleep in his bunk in the forward berthing compartment when the messenger shook him for the mid-watch; there were groans from the rows of triple-tiered bunks as the messenger poked his red flashlight in other faces. Landry stared for a few seconds at the bundle of wire cables that ran just above his face. Above them was the steel overhead that separated the large berthing space from the wardroom and officer's country one deck above. Landry often found himself thinking there was a hell of a lot more than a quarter of an inch of steel between his way of life and an officer's. The familiar rattle of the ventilator almost lulled him back to sleep, but he forced himself to roll out of his bunk and jump down to the deck. He pulled on his uniform and followed the other members of the on-going watch to the galley. A cup of black coffee burned all the way down his throat but helped clear his head.

Despite the coffee, Landry found it difficult to stay awake when he took over as the lookout on the starboard bridge wing. The four destroyers steamed in column at 10 knots with no other shipping in sight. Landry circled his post several times to revive his tired brain. The pair of binoculars felt as if they weighed 20 pounds. His aching feet nagged his brain for the luxury of sitting down.

As the humid night wore on, Landry began thinking of their last port call in Manila a few weeks ago. The night before his departure Teresa had seemed almost sad. In bed, she had raised herself to one elbow and stroked his face tenderly, watching him with brown eyes flecked with green and gold.

"I love you, Hank."

"Hmmm. You're very beautiful." He stroked her firm thigh. He wasn't just flattering her. Her long black hair framed a high-cheekboned, oval face. Her dusky skin was soft and smooth and covered a body that he never ceased to admire.

"I love you, Hank."

Landry fondled her breasts, which seemed fuller.

She moved his hand away. "I love you, Hank." Her eyes were misty.

"What is this? Some kind of a game?"

"No. I need some security." Her soft voice was accented with her native Tagalog.

"Will twenty pesos do you?"

She turned away and refused to talk to him the rest of the night. He had left their bed before dawn to return to the *O'Leary*.

Never have understood women, he thought as he paced the bridge wing, scanning the horizon. He had been too poor to afford dates while growing up in Cheyenne, Wyoming. His father, a fireman on the Union Pacific Railroad, had been killed in a locomotive derailment. He remembered how his father had loved the locomotives. Only seven when his father died, Landry had grown up hating the chuffing black steam engines that had killed his father. Landry still hadn't forgiven his father for dying and leaving his family behind.

Poverty wasn't the only legacy from his father. His father's mother was an Arapaho Indian. Landry had been the butt of classmates' taunts of, "Hey, Injun! Damn halfbreed!"

Landry doubled his fists as he remembered some of the fights he had been lured into, always by bigger kids. The last had been the mayor's son, a notorious bully. Landry had beaten him in a clean fight, breaking the boy's jaw. The mayor had pressed charges. "Son," the judge had said, "I'll give you the choice of enlisting or sixty days on the county work farm."

Landry had taken the Navy and left his past behind. In a setting where many of his shipmates accepted nicknames such as "Frenchy," "Swede," or "Dutch," Landry answered any inquiry about his ancestors with a curt, "American."

As Landry leaned against the wing of the bridge, he was surprised by the strength of his feelings for Teresa. Early in life he had developed a fierce sense of independence and had rarely developed close friendships. Aboard the *O'Leary*, his few friends were other members of the ship's baseball team. But since he and Teresa had taken an apartment together two months ago, she had penetrated his shell. It wasn't just the sex, which was very good, but something deeper. She had broken through the layers of scar tissue that had built up over the years. She was closer to him than anyone had ever been.

He wondered what kind of security she wanted. He wasn't sure he was ready to settle down for good. The taunts of his childhood tormentors echoed in his head. If he and Teresa ever had kids, they'd be part oriental. He didn't want his kids to face the problems he had endured.

If it was money she wanted, he was in trouble. He had never

saved any of his pay. Landry knew there was no way he could match Chief Mortland's savings. The thought of losing her to Mortland and his wad of money was unbearable.

Landry's thoughts were interrupted when it was time to take his turn behind the wheel. He forced himself to concentrate on his job because a mistake by the helmsman could create a disaster at close quarters. But he enjoyed the feeling of control. Every time the destroyer started to nudge off course, he brought her back by turning the spoked wheel.

After Landry took his turn behind the engine-order telegraph, he rotated out to the other bridge wing as a lookout. His feet ached and he was ready for his bunk. "Two more days and we'll be back in Manila," Landry muttered softly as he shifted his weight wearily from one aching foot to the other. Finally, he greeted his sleepy relief and headed below for two hours in his bunk before reveille.

In the forward fireroom, T. T. Simpson watched the airlock door close behind the men who'd just been relieved. As a rule Simpson didn't mind the 0400-0800 watch, but the effects of his "tubic tear" hadn't completely worn off.

"You're not very frisky this morning," said Simpson's assistant, Ralph Burley.

"Enough," said Simpson. "Show some respect for your elders. Be quiet so I can enjoy a peaceful watch." Simpson turned his back on the heavyset Burley and checked the forest of pipes for any signs of leaks. The activity soothed him. Although his world was hot, crowded, and noisy, its familiarity was a comfort to him whenever he felt depressed or angry.

Simpson leaned back against the smooth metal railing and regarded the number two boiler. Its huge bulk reminded him of one of the massive squatting stone Buddhas he had visited in a Japanese port. The boiler seemed to exude power; Simpson could feel the heat radiating from its metal surface. Simpson gazed at the fire in the boiler through a smoked glass viewing port and shivered as the flames flickered and swirled in the heart of the inferno.

As he realized the gases in the boiler were slightly opaque, Simpson frowned. Dirty brown smoke would be rising from the stack, indicating inefficient use of fuel and sloppy watchstanding. He gestured to Burley, and the fireman closed the fuel valve slightly, clearing the gases. "Just right," said Simpson, knowing too great a reduction would have sent white smoke up the stack, also sure to invite criticism from the bridge.

Simpson smiled to himself. Big bitch of a boiler'll pump out more power than a hundred cars, he thought. And I'm in charge. She works just as hard as I want her to.

Above all, Simpson respected the power trapped within the boilers. The steam would be his servant only as long as it remained confined within the boiler, piping, and machinery. A small steam leak could burn a man's skin severely. A large one could turn an engineering compartment into a searing cauldron, scalding and cooking anyone who did not escape quickly.

Wiping his damp forehead, Simpson wished they were steaming on number one instead of number two. He felt all his boilers had personalities; they were as different as women. Number one was a proper lady, always dependable and efficient, but she was near the limit of her steaming hours before a required overhaul. They had to use number two—a fallen lady if there ever was one. She was a battered whore and nothing but trouble. She always used too much feedwater and was difficult to control. A real bitch, Simpson thought.

As Simpson patrolled his station, the unease that had troubled him for weeks began to gnaw at him again. He checked all the gauges on the boiler front and listened for the sounds of the feedwater and fuel pumps. There was no problem he could detect, but the nagging feeling increased, and he knew that something wasn't right. He leaned against the railing and checked again. The gauges were steady; the steam pressure was an even 200 pounds-per-square-inch. All still seemed normal. He cocked his head and listened to the rush of air and the roar of the boiler. Nothing wrong there.

Still, Simpson was uneasy. A certain noise—that was it! Something didn't sound right. What was it? Shut your eyes. Listen. There. No, not that. There it was again. Damn! Now it's gone.

The elusive vibration tantalized Simpson. He shut his eyes again and listened. He sorted through the general roar for discrete sounds, each with its own message: the familiar noisy bearings in the huge blower in the galley passageway above; the steady swish from the fuel atomizers in the boiler front; the whine of rotary pumps; the clanks and wheezes from the reciprocating pumps. But he could hear nothing abnormal aside from the sound of a few loose valve linkages that needed work.

"Hey, Burley! Tend the boiler while I look around."

Prowling the upper platform, Simpson followed each pipe, inspected each valve. All seemed normal. He walked by the boiler front again and inspected all the pipes leading in and out. He frowned as he gazed up at the pipe from the steam drum near the top of the boiler. The pipe mated with the main steam line at a large flanged joint. All the bolts around the joint appeared tight, and he hoped the gasketing would hold up until their overhaul.

"Dammit!" Simpson shouted as he kicked the boiler front, but a sense of guilt overcame him. "Sorry, old bitch, I guess you're doing your best." Simpson remembered the hard life the boiler had led. Once, during a dull watch, he had calculated she had logged seven years' worth of continuous steaming.

"Burley, I'm going down to the lower level," Simpson shouted over the roar of the blowers. He slid down the polished metal rails without even touching the treads of the ladder. He dropped to the shiny metal grating two feet above the oily bilge water, which sloshed back and forth below him with each roll of the ship. The surface jittered and roiled and seemed more active than usual. Simpson made a systematic check of every pipe, pump, and valve. Nothing. He bit his lip with frustration.

There! No. Something else! Louder now. From above! His mind raced. Get your ass back to the upper level!

"Simpson!" Burley's shout had a note of panic.

Damn night watches, Fraser thought as he scratched his heat rash. Nothing ever happens. He leaned against the edge of the starboard bridge wing, yawned, scanned the dark horizon carefully, and checked the positions of the ships in the column. His legs ached, and he eyed the vacant captain's chair. But the privilege of that seat belonged to the man saddled with the responsibility of command. No one else ever dared to sit there. The empty chair seemed to rebuke him for his problems with the torpedo recovery, but Fraser felt some sense of accomplishment because he had performed adequately during the shiphandling drills the captain had held for the junior officers later that afternoon. At one point, Arkwright had even praised one of Fraser's efforts.

Fraser sighed and entered the covered pilothouse where the quartermaster and the boatswain's mate of the watch were drinking coffee at the chart table. The men behind the helm and lee helm swayed slowly with the motion of the ship. Fraser continued across the pilothouse and stepped out on the port wing, where the lookout straightened as Fraser's feet rocked a loose wooden grating on the metal deck.

"Horizon's clear, sir."

"Very well."

Fraser heard a low hiss and turned to look aft where wisps of white steam rose from the second stack. Fraser frowned; the only time steam came up the stack was when the engineers blew tubes. Narrow tendrils widened and coalesced into a solid stream. Fraser's knees weakened, and his stomach dropped as he realized there must be a serious casualty. "Lee helm, tell main control to check with the forward fireroom," Fraser ordered. "Steam's coming out the number two stack."

Thirty seconds passed. The flow of steam increased.

"Main control reports no answer from the forward fireroom," Mr. Fraser.

"Bosun, wake the captain! Send the messenger to tell Mr. Meredith there's a breakdown in the forward fireroom!"

Simpson pounded up the ladder from the lower level. When his head rose over the level of the grating, he turned and looked at the number two boiler. He could see nothing, but he heard a keening wail from above. Still he could see nothing, but now he knew what it was, escaping high-pressure steam. There! The large flange where the pipe from the boiler was mated to the main steamline.

In seconds, the pin-sized jet of steam expanded to a pencil-thick plume. As Simpson watched, more of the gasket material blew out. The leak became a frantic rush of steam, which filled Simpson's ears with a menacing roar.

"Burley! Get out!" Simpson shouted. "We'll shut her down from topside!" Without waiting for a reply, Simpson headed for the airlock and twisted the wheel to open the door. "Let's go. Goddamn!"

Burley wasn't behind him; the fireman was climbing toward the small platform by the main steam stop valve near the top of the boiler.

"Burley! Get the hell out!"

Burley kept going, pulled himself onto the platform, straightened, and grabbed the huge wheel of the valve that would isolate the leak. Before he could turn the wheel, the swirling white mist engulfed his head and shoulders. He convulsed backwards and fell screaming to the grating where one leg bent under him at an unnatural angle. The searing blanket of steam descended from the overhead foot by foot. Simpson slammed the door shut and headed for Burley, crouching as the cloud of steam swirled ever closer.

Simpson slid to a stop on the slick grating, seized Burley's shirt collar, and dragged him toward the airlock. Ten feet from their destination, the scorching heat of the approaching steam forced Simpson to his knees. Burley's shirt ripped, and the collar came away in Simpson's hand.

"Damn!" Simpson scrambled back and grabbed Burley's arm; he covered the last few feet by sliding along the grating and dragging Burley. "Take a deep breath!" Simpson shouted.

Simpson lowered his face to the grate and inhaled deeply. It wasn't steam. The air was hot and moist, but it didn't burn. He pulled himself to a crouch and was enveloped in steam. The hot gas went up his nose and into his ears. He yanked open the door, but the steam was already burning his exposed skin and seeping into the gaps in his clothing. Oh, Jesus! Simpson's mind screamed. It's hot! Hot! He dragged Burley inside the airlock trunk, and slammed the door shut, turning the wheel with burned hands. Cooler air settled to the bottom of the trunk and Simpson took another breath and headed up the ladder to the hatch ten feet above. The steam that had entered with them had risen, so the further he went, the hotter it got.

His face contorted in pain when his burned hands seized the wheel to open the hatch. Turn you bastard, turn! Air! I need air! Christ! I can't do it!

His hands slipped off the wheel, and he grabbed the ladder with the last of his strength. The small bulb lighting the narrow trunk seemed to dim. Just as he was about to fall backwards down the trunk, the wheel above him squealed. The hatch crashed back on screeching hinges. Hands grabbed his forearms and yanked him into the night air. The humid 90-degree air felt like a cooling breath from the Arctic.

Simpson groaned. "Burley . . . he's at the bottom of the trunk. Burned bad . . . leg's broke. Get Doc Laster."

More men ran up and secured the boiler by shutting the control valves that protruded from the main deck. The column of steam from the stack slowly subsided. Simpson thought it sounded like the breathing of a hungry beast prowling for a meal.

Simpson pulled himself to his feet and staggered across the quarterdeck to the large refrigerator sitting next to the amidships deckhouse. He yanked open the door and thrust his hands into a large bucket of ice. "Rub some ice on my neck," he told a nearby sailor.

Simpson looked over to where Doc Laster was bent over Burley. He had cut the rest of Burley's shirt off and smeared salve over Burley's face, neck, and back. Much of the skin had already blistered and some of it wrinkled and pulled away despite Laster's efforts.

Simpson winced as he watched Laster work. It had been a

close call. The blown gasket didn't explain his apprehensions of the last few weeks. The gasket material had been old, but it shouldn't have blown. It hadn't caused the vibration he had finally detected in number two. What had?

"Get over here so we can treat your burns," Laster said.

"My grandmother taught me to use ice first, Doc."

"That's not what my professors taught me in medical school."

"What the hell do they know," Simpson said. "Grandmothers know best."

Fraser conned the *O'Leary* back to their station in the column while the captain paced the bridge. Fifteen minutes after number two was secured, Jack Meredith shuffled across the bridge, shirt tail flapping and shoelaces trailing. "Casualty's under control, Captain. It'll take a while to see if there's any serious damage."

"What about your men?"

The black circles under Meredith's eyes deepened. "Not so good there. Simpson has some moderate burns where his clothes didn't cover his skin. Burley has a compound fracture of the leg and some nasty burns on his face and neck. Laster said they both should be hospitalized immediately. He'll be up soon with a report."

"Better light off number four for the run to Manila. Any other problems?"

"None that we don't already know about," Meredith said. "Thank God we're going in for our overhaul next week. I don't think we could keep her going much longer."

Fraser thought the engineering officer was right.

Arkwright rubbed the scar on his forehead. "The Japs may not permit us the luxury of an overhaul."

Meredith's thin body seemed to wilt. "Don't even mention that possibility. An overhaul is a necessity, not a luxury." Meredith shook his head, pulled out a red bandana and wiped his face. "Hot! Never know it's almost December, would you?"

CHAPTER FIVE

The next afternoon, Fraser sat at the green-covered wardroom table with the rest of the officers, waiting for the captain to come out of his cabin and give them a briefing. After a highspeed run, the *O'Leary* had anchored off the Manila waterfront that morning and sent her injured men to a hospital. The captain had just returned from a meeting at the fleet commander's headquarters ashore.

When Arkwright took his seat at the head of the table, his bushy eyebrows were set in a horizontal line. "Gentlemen, Admiral Hart has received a war warning from Washington." Arkwright paused, and his pale blue eyes looked around the table.

Lord, Fraser thought. An official war warning, not just some rumor. Laster was right.

The lines around the captain's mouth deepened. "The message said negotiations with Japan have ceased. Aggressive action by the Japs is probable. We can expect an amphibious expedition against targets in this region—maybe Borneo, maybe the Philippines, or possibly the Thai or Kra Peninsulas. The Asiatic Fleet has been directed to prepare to execute its war plans."

Beringer smiled. "The Asiatic Fleet can't do anything unless

Congress declares war. That's unlikely, no matter what Roosevelt wants."

"That's for the politicians to figure out," the captain said.

Laster let out a stream of cigarette smoke and coughed. "Any mention of Pearl Harbor?"

"No," Arkwright said. "The only specific targets mentioned were in the Far East. Why?"

Beringer's nasal laugh was derisive. "Our supreme strategist, Doctor Laster, was semi-delirious at lunch one day. He prognosticated a Japanese attack on Pearl Harbor."

"I haven't heard anyone else suggest that," Arkwright said.

Beringer sniffed. "Not likely to, either. Idiotic idea!"

Arkwright frowned, wrinkling the scar across his forehead. "Maybe not. British carrier aircraft surprised the Italian fleet anchored at Taranto last year."

Beringer waved a hand. "The Japanese aren't the British. They may have the aircraft carriers, but they're only Orientals. They're not capable of doing what the British did."

"I wonder . . ." The captain looked up for several seconds at the large slowly twirling fan. "Back to our immediate problem. I told Admiral Hart I didn't want us helpless in the Navy Yard if the war came. But he insisted we start our overhaul next week. He said the Army Air Force should be able to protect us from air attack."

"MacArthur propaganda!" Durham's eyes were scornful.

"I agree, Bull," the captain said. "I told Admiral Hart that, but he overruled me."

Meredith, the engineering officer, ran a hand through his curly hair. "Then he must know the condition of this ship, Captain. We're desperate for that overhaul. I don't know how long we could keep steaming without it. There'll just be more problems like the fireroom casualty."

"We'll be in worse shape if the Japs bomb us," Durham said.

"Correct," Arkwright said. "That's why I intend to do everything I can to prevent this ship from being destroyed in the yard."

Fraser wondered why the captain's low-pitched voice had taken on such a hard edge.

Arkwright continued, "Therefore, we'll carry out our orders, but within limits. When we go into the yard, I want us to be able to move on one engine and one boiler on twenty-four hours' notice. Hopefully, we can fix many of our problems within my limitations. If the diplomats make progress, we can conduct our overhaul normally."

Meredith straightened his narrow shoulders. "Captain, we can't even begin a regular overhaul under those conditions. We'll wind up doing jobs over again later. For one thing, we need to tear down the main steam line and replace all the gaskets."

Arkwright's stubby hands grasped a brass ash tray that had been made out of the end of a 4-inch powder casing. "Jack, efficiency will have to be sacrificed. I want you to work on the main steam line right away, but in sections so that one engine and one boiler can be hooked up quickly."

"Captain," replied Meredith, "trying to steam on some kind of a jury rig could cause another accident. I've already had two men hurt."

Arkwright slid the brass ash tray across the green table cover from one hand to the other. He fixed his pale blue eyes on Meredith. "We'd only take that kind of risk if the war starts. I think your men would prefer not to be sitting ducks for Jap bombs and bullets."

Meredith squirmed but said nothing.

Arkwright looked around the table. "We'll be anchored here five days before entering the yard on the fourth of December. If you can fix anything without affecting our combat efficiency for more than a few hours—do it. Every morning I want the duty section to man our antiaircraft battery—such as it is. Your other job is to make sure your people get ashore for some recreation. It may be their last chance."

Fraser cleared his throat. "Captain, do you have any advice for the men who have Filipino girl friends or common-law Filipino wives?"

Arkwright tapped the ashtray for a few seconds. "We may be sent south to the Dutch East Indies or Singapore. I'd advise the so-called 'shackmasters' to give as much money to their women as they can. If the Japanese invade, they may abuse Filipinos who were friendly with Americans. Civilians have been raped or killed in China. I'd suggest moving to a new neighborhood or living in the country with relatives."

Arkwright looked around the table. "Any other questions? That's it, then."

As the officers began to file out the captain beckoned Fraser aside. "Ross, two things for you. When we move to the yard, I want you to conn the ship."

Fraser felt his stomach flutter. He'd never taken a ship alongside a pier before.

"Also, I was asked to furnish a presentable junior officer to serve as an escort. The Dutch have sent a senior officer here to confer with Admiral Hart. His daughter has accompanied him. Can you be at the Army Navy Club at 1600 tomorrow for a reception?"

"I just happen to be free, sir."

"No guarantees. She may be fat and wear wooden shoes."

"Has to be better than nothing."

Arkwright's slight smile disappeared. "I expect you to take this job seriously. The Dutch may soon be our allies. American lives may depend on them. Neither I nor Admiral Hart will be pleased if you cause any problems."

"Would he send me home, sir?"

"No. He'd find you a worse job and see that you stayed here for twenty years."

"Sir," Fraser said quickly, "there'll be no problems." He remembered the other difficulties he'd had aboard recently and vowed to stay out of trouble. Fraser wasn't sure who he feared more, Admiral Hart or the captain.

That afternoon Landry waited on the quarterdeck to board the first liberty boat to Manila. He remembered the injured men who had been sent ashore strapped in stretchers. Jesus, thought Landry, my old man probably got burned like that when his locomotive derailed.

Landry shook his head and lifted his eyes to the familiar Manila skyline. The white bulk of the Manila Hotel rose north of the green stretch of Quezon Park. A maze of low office buildings and apartments surrounded the hotel and receded in the distance. He felt comforted by the sight. It was as much a home as he'd ever known, but that was mainly due to Teresa.

When the boat bumped alongside the Fleet Landing, Landry leaped ashore and strode toward a line of waiting cabs. The breeze flapped his bell-bottom trousers around his ankles. He pushed his hat off-center enough to assert his independence, but not enough to catch the eye of the Shore Patrol. Two young Filipino women giggled admiringly, but Landry only smiled and hurried on.

When he walked in the door of their small apartment, Teresa's brown eyes widened. She ran to him and Landry wrapped her in his arms and stroked her long black hair.

"So many rumors about war," she murmured. "I worry you never come back."

"The whole Jap fleet couldn't keep me away."

"You a day early."

"Yeah, some snipes got burned bad down in a fireroom."

"I glad you not work down there."

"Might be better'n working for that pig, Mortland."

"He always nice to me when I work at the restaurant."

"Yeah. Old man's trying to sweet-talk you."

"He not that old."

"Enough of him. I have other things on my mind."

"Yes?"

He nodded toward the bedroom.

"Oh, yes," she said.

He picked her up, skirted the rattan couch, carried her to the small bedroom, pushed aside the mosquito netting, and lowered her gently to the bed. Landry slid off her thin cotton shift and underwear. He gazed at her brown-nippled breasts and silky thighs. "It's been too long."

Teresa's eyes were moist. "Hold me first. When you go, you may never come back."

Landry sighed, trying to conceal his own worry. "The war ain't nothin' but talk. Put it out of your mind."

The flood tide of their passion floated his worries away and left them soaking, but soon ready for more.

"Hungry? she asked.

"Just for you." Landry ran his hand over her bottom.

She laughed. "If rest of Navy ready like you, Japanese in trouble."

Later, Landry woke from a doze. Teresa was already up and dressed. She had hung up the clothes they had so hastily discarded. The bedroom, like the rest of the apartment, was immaculate.

Landry propped himself with an elbow. "You only wear that dress to work at Sagun's. I thought you were going to quit."

"I change my mind."

"Why? I give you enough money to live on. I don't make much, but things are cheap."

She stared at the crucifix she had mounted over the bed and lowered her gaze to the floor. "I need some . . . security. If war come you be gone, and I be left with . . ."

"I thought you'd be happy not working. None of the girls who live with our men work. It'll make me look bad if you work at the restaurant. Besides, I can't stand Mortland looking at you like he always does."

"Chief Hanlon's Maria works there."

"That's different. She's a part owner."

"She save her money and work her way up. I do that, too. Almost late. See you later."

She walked quickly into the living room before Landry could respond. He rose to follow her but she was already out the door. He realized a naked man wouldn't get far on the street. He kicked the arm of a bamboo chair. "Damn! Why won't she do what I want!"

Fraser rose the next morning, refreshed by an uninterrupted night's sleep even though he'd had the duty. For once there had been no problems with the returning liberty parties. He headed topside to inspect the readiness of the antiaircraft batteries. He found Shifflet manning one of the two .50-caliber machine guns atop the amidships deckhouse.

"You look cheerful this morning, Shifflet."

"Yessir. Today'll be my first day ashore in a month and a half. Thanks for gettin' me off."

"You deserve it for not blowing the captain's head off the other night. You saved his head and my career. Tomorrow's the first of December. That should give you enough time for your Christmas shopping."

"Thanks, sir. The ladies are always tickled when Santa Shifflet comes."

"I hope you won't have any more trouble ashore."

Shifflet coughed. "Well, I'll make sure nobody catches me."

"I was hoping you'd learned a lesson."

"Jeez, Mr. Fraser, a man's got to have some fun, 'specially if he's been restricted aboard."

Fraser shook his head. "Be careful. I hope to have you promoted back to first class before long."

"Don't worry, Mr. Fraser. It's no big thing. Been there three, no, four times before."

Fraser resolved to talk sense into Shifflet. "Stay out of trouble, and you'd be a chief in a few years."

"Can't say as that's important to me, sir. Third class, first class, chief, it don't make no difference. I'll be doin' the same work on the guns no matter how many stripes I wear. Hell, I'd rather enjoy just being what I am."

Fraser searched for a reply, but Shifflet interrupted him. "Mr. Fraser, I'll bet you look at them admirals and think how great it would be to be one. But I'll guarantee you when they take off that uniform at night, they'd trade places in a minute, just so's to be young again."

"You're quite a philosopher, Shifflet."

"Yessir, my pappy died in a coal mine when I was still a little sprout. He must of felt it coming 'cause he sat me down one day and told me not to waste my life doin' what other folks expected.

He told me to work to be rich and famous if that's what I enjoyed doin', but mainly I should do what's right for me."

Fraser felt like he was sailing into troubled waters. "I don't think he would have recommended bar fights."

"Don't knock a good bar brawl. Hell, it's as much fun as football, and you don't have to practice or wear one of them hot uniforms. Same thing, really. Gives a man a chance to test himself."

Fraser thought of another tack; he felt trapped on a lee shore. "You might get hurt, or hurt someone else."

"Not if it's a good fair fight. 'Bout the same chances as football. They carried you off, didn't they?"

"Yes."

"A man pays his money and takes his chances. Mind you, I never pick on a man who's not interested. Don't mind going up against a man spoiling for trouble. Sort of like I'm doin' him a favor lettin' him get rid of the poison in his system."

Fraser realized he had run aground and shook his head. "Guess I'm not going to change you, Shifflet."

"Nossir, I'm pretty set in my ways. Seems like what I am's right for me. I'm comfortable with myself. Hell, we could all be dead anytime now. Most folks think death will never happen to them, but it will."

"Can't argue with that." Fraser realized how rarely he had considered the inevitability of his own death. He walked away with a sudden sense of envy. If the Japs got them, Shifflet could die knowing he'd had a full life. Fraser knew he couldn't say the same thing. He felt a desperate urge to do some living before it was too late.

After Fraser finished his inspection of the guns, ate breakfast, and turned over the duty to Jack Meredith, he decided to take a boat to the Army Navy Club to exercise his knee in the swimming pool.

As Fraser floated on his back in the pool, he heard a plonk-plonk from two nearby tennis courts. The Army Navy Club rose three stories above the pool and was encircled by wide awning-shaded verandas.

He forced himself to swim five more quick laps and was panting by the time he finished. He began to think about his assignment to the reception. The military had ordered all wives and dependents home a year ago, so there were few women available to date. He hoped the Dutch girl could speak English; Fraser wasn't much at social conversation under the best of circumstances.

Fraser's half-closed eyes snapped open. Two figures stood on the porch near the pool. One was an army general; despite his ribbons, his chest was nothing inspirational. His companion's chest could have inspired anyone, Fraser thought. Even from a distance Fraser could tell she was blonde, tall, and well-endowed. The girl laughed, and they turned and disappeared into the club.

"I thought all the dependents had been sent home," he muttered. "Must be some general's daughter passing through on her way to the States."

Fraser hauled himself out of the pool and headed for the locker room to change so he could find the girl before the other woman-starved military officers in Manila caught scent of her.

"Never saw her before, sir," a club waiter said.

"The general?"

"Must be somebody just arrived, sir. Maybe someone else can help . . ."

"I've asked everyone else."

"Have you tried the cab drivers?"

The fourth driver in the cab line was the only one who could help Fraser, telling him that the general and the girl had left with Felipe, one of the drivers who regularly waited in the cab line at the club. Fraser knew Felipe, so he decided to wait for the driver's return. Almost an hour passed before the balding driver stopped his cab at the back of the line.

Fraser leaned in the cab window. "Just need some information. The general and the blonde girl who left about two hours ago, where'd you take them?"

"The Manila Hotel."

Fraser checked his watch; he'd never make it to the hotel and back in time for the reception. Muttering with frustration, Fraser walked into the bar on the main floor of the club, ready for a drink. The bar was a sea of khaki Army Air Force uniforms interspersed with an occasional white uniform or civilian suit of a naval officer. The *O'Leary*'s first lieutenant, Bull Durham, was perched on a stool at the end of the mahogany bar. Fraser made his way to a seat next to him.

"What are all these Army people doing here, Bull?"

"Latest bunch of P-40 fighter jockeys to hit Clark Field. They're down here drinking booze instead of getting ready to fight." Durham banged his fist on the bar and his eyes flashed. "I'm burned up. We've been training our butts off for months. Half the crew is still aboard ready to fight."

One of the Army pilots slid a chair to the middle of the room and put on a set of rimless glasses. He stuck his front teeth out over his lower lip and held an imaginary stick in his hands. His friends extended their arms like wings and flew around him making machine gun noises. The "Japanese" pilot looked terrified, tipped over his chair, and crashed while his friends howled with laughter.

"Looks like they're taking the Japs real seriously," Fraser said.

Durham looked contemptuously at one shouting Army officer. "Nothing wrong with a little fun, but we're going to be in trouble if we have to depend on these idiots. They're laughing at the base commander because he wants them to dig trenches and protect their aircraft with revetments."

"Bull, let me buy you a drink before I take off for this reception."

"I need another drink. Jesus, I'll bet I could outfly any ten of these guys."

"If you were such a hot flyer, why'd they throw you out of flight school?"

"Caught me in bed with an instructor's wife."

"That'll do it." Fraser suddenly remembered how Laster had thrown up on Beringer's desk. "Bull, I've been wondering. Did you and Doc work together to set Beringer up at lunch the other day?"

Durham's eyes narrowed. "Let me get this straight. You think Doc and I were in cahoots from the start?"

"It did occur to me."

Durham's pug face broke into a smile. "What a suspicious mind you have."

"You haven't answered the question."

"I'd never take credit for it. Suppose it got back to Beringer. Besides, I'd be betraying my associate in crime."

"You could deny it."

Durham's eyes were mischievious. "I think I'll let you wonder."

Fraser shook his head and sipped his drink. As the Jack Daniels and water slid down his throat Fraser felt his frustration mount. He desperately wanted to leave for the Manila Hotel. With all the Army pilots in town, he knew he had to find the blonde quickly. Visions of her riding alongside him in a convertible flashed though his head. Maybe Bull would stand in at the reception, he thought. Jesus, isn't that asking for trouble? Hell, how much longer do I have to live anyway? Take a chance for once in your life!

"Bull, can I ask you a favor? I'll make it worth your while."

Durham looked skeptical. "Depends."

"I need you to stand in as an escort for me at the reception this afternoon. I'll take your duty for three nights."

"Are you kidding? For one of these formal affairs? Boy, I'll bet she's ugly, too! Five nights."

"Four."

"Five."

Fraser spotted Admiral Hart's aide entering the bar and knew he had no choice but to concede. "Okay, five it is."

The bulky aide made his way to the bar. "Ah, Fraser, just the man I've been looking for."

"Commander, I'm sorry, but I've just got word that there's an emergency I've got to take care of. Lieutenant Durham, here, has agreed to take my place."

"Hmmm." The aide frowned.

"Don't worry, sir. Durham is a product of the Naval Academy's best training in the social and diplomatic arts."

"Six," Durham mouthed silently over the aide's shoulder.

Fraser gave him a slight nod. "If you two will excuse me, I'll be on my way."

"Very well, Fraser," the aide said. "Durham, follow me."

Fraser trotted out of the bar, ran down the stairs, and jumped into a cab for the Manila Hotel. During the ride, all he could think about was the blonde and her magnificent body.

At the hotel, he strode across the luxurious lobby to the registration desk. He beckoned the clerk aside and described the young lady he was looking for.

The clerk's face was frosty. "Sir, we respect the privacy of our clientele. I can't tell you anything."

Fraser opened his wallet. "Here's a picture of my uncle. You may know him." He slid a ten dollar bill toward the clerk.

The clerk's hooded eyes darted down and then right and left. The money was gone. Fraser blinked. Christ, Fraser thought, this guy was faster than a gecko taking a fly. He took a firmer grip on his wallet.

"Your uncle is an excellent reference. The young lady you're describing went into the bar about ten minutes ago."

Fraser crossed the lobby and entered the bar, searching the nearly deserted gloom. There was a flash of blonde hair in the corner. Fraser took a deep breath and walked to the table, wondering what to say.

"Ah . . ."

"Yes." Her bright red lipstick was slightly smudged.

"May I join you?"

Her blue eyes looked him over, as if she were inspecting a piece of furniture. "Why not?"

"Ahh . . ."

"Hey, that's different. Usually it's, 'Haven't we met before?' Or some sophisticated line. Except for that nose, you're kind of cute—in a rugged sort of way."

"Thanks."

"You do have a name?"

"Ross Fraser."

"Shirley McGee. Sorry I'm not very friendly, but I just had a terrible fight with my . . . boyfriend."

"That's too bad."

"Oh, well, I'm not sure it was meant to last. Tell me, Ross, is it?"

"Yes."

Her eyes took on an appraising glint, like a jeweler inspecting a large gem. "You're obviously a naval officer. Do you have any money?"

"Well, I've got some put away for a convertible when I get back to the States."

"No, I mean *money* money. Do you come from a rich family?"

"No."

"Too bad. My boyfriend is filthy rich. But you're definitely cuter."

"Thanks. That's something."

"Not nearly enough, though."

Fraser saw the army general enter the bar and look around. "Here comes your father. I'd like to meet him."

"Wrong, sailor. That's my boyfriend. Bye."

A half hour later, Fraser neared the steps to the Army Navy Club, his face dripping sweat. There had been no cabs at the Manila Hotel so he had been forced to walk back. Lust for the grapefruit-like charms of Shirley McGee had long since wilted, and now he was worrying about the chance he had taken by entrusting the Dutch girl to Bull Durham. Durham had no scruples about women. Even now, Fraser thought, Durham might be administering his coup de grace or the more erotic coup d'Alice. Fraser shuddered as he thought of the wrath of Admiral Hart and Gerald Arkwright. He might be condemned to ride the *O'Leary* forever.

Fraser ran up the front stairs of the club to the hall outside the reception room. The sound of clinking glasses and the drone of voices came from the reception room, so Fraser's hopes rose. He moved to a bulletin board by the doorway and pretended to study it while taking in the large reception room out of the corner of his eye. He scanned each group in turn but failed to spot Durham. There was a rift in a group just in front of him, and he caught a glimpse of Durham in profile, laughing.

"That horny little leprechaun!" Fraser muttered, turning on his heel. He found a waiter and slipped him some money to page Lieutenant Durham for a phone call in the hallway around the corner. He pulled one of the phones off its hook, left it dangling, and slipped into the men's room across the hall.

Two minutes later, footsteps sounded in the hallway. "Durham here," said the cocky voice, which grated on Fraser's taut nerves.

Fraser opened the door of the men's room, collared Durham, and yanked him out of the hallway. "Sorry, Bull. Your evening is over."

"I thought you had other plans."

"Didn't work out. You have an emergency on the ship."

"There's nothing that Chief Mortland can't handle."

"The question is, can you handle me here?"

Durham's eyes narrowed. "That does put another light on the situation. Okay, okay. I think you should take a few more nights of duty if I relinquish this prize."

"Okay, one more."

Durham rubbed his hands. "Seven it is, then. Just as well. This girl isn't responding to my overtures."

Fraser wasn't sure whether that was good news or not. At least there was less danger of getting in trouble with the captain now. While Durham went out to make excuses, Fraser washed his sweaty face in the men's room. He checked himself in the mirror, took a deep breath, and headed for the reception.

The sandy-haired girl talking with Durham was a few inches shorter than Fraser. A sleeveless silk cocktail dress displayed firm arms and shoulders.

"Ah, here he is now," Durham said. "Ilsa Van Dorn, allow me to introduce Ross Fraser."

"Nice to meet you, Lieutenant." Her voice was as calm and

reserved as her large green eyes. "This is the second emergency aboard your ship today. I hope she isn't sinking. We may need your services before long."

"She's still floating," Fraser said, "but that's about all I can guarantee. I'm afraid the *O'Leary* isn't much of a threat to the Japanese."

"Neither is the Dutch Navy," Ilsa said. She shook her head and her glossy hair swirled around her oval face, which was neither stunningly beautiful nor striking, but honestly attractive.

"If you two will excuse me," Durham said.

"It was interesting talking with you." Ilsa smiled and sipped her drink as Durham headed for the exit. The bridge of her nose was a shade too prominent, Fraser thought. She wasn't built like the general's girlfriend, but she held herself proudly, her tanned, arms suggesting a body that was sleek and efficient.

"Ahh, I hope Bull wasn't . . ."

"Offensive? No. Most interesting, but rather too smooth and aggressive for my taste."

"Please don't judge me because of Bull. We don't see eye-to-eye on a lot of things."

"Ilsa, is everything going well?" asked another voice.

"Yes, Father. I'd like you to meet Lieutenant Ross Fraser, my original escort, who was delayed."

"Nice to meet you, Lieutenant."

Fraser took the tall captain's large hand. The grip was firm. The lean Dutchman's blue eyes were deep set, and his nose was a larger version of his daughter's. His face was sun-reddened, and a fine network of purplish vessels crisscrossed his nose.

"Sorry I was held up, sir," Fraser said.

"Maybe you wouldn't mind taking care of my daughter this evening. Some of my friends from Washington want to get together for a poker game."

"Lieutenant Fraser may have other plans," Ilsa said.

"Oh, no. There isn't any one here to date," Fraser said.

"So I'll do."

Fraser felt himself in trouble. "Certainly not."

"I won't do then." Her green eyes seemed amused.

"Yes. No. I mean you will. I mean you would. Anytime. Anywhere. Please. Let me take you to dinner."

"You left out anyplace."

"Anyplace. Ahhhh . . . please."

"Since you put it that way, I'd be delighted. If you'll excuse me for a minute, I need to powder my nose."

Fraser watched Ilsa head for the door and admired her shapely nylon-clad legs. Van Dorn coughed. "Thank you for being patient. Her fiance' was killed when the Germans invaded Holland last year. Died trying to stop a tank. He was very gallant . . . but now he's just very dead. Since then, she's refused to date military men. Unfortunate—since most of our eligible young men are now in uniform."

"I'm surprised she agreed to go to dinner, then."

"Yes. Maybe she's taken a fancy to you . . ."

"Or she thinks I'm too harmless to give her any trouble."

"Well, hmmmm."

Van Dorn and Fraser traded stories of their experiences in the Philippines for a few minutes.

"Here Ilsa comes now," said her father. "Good luck to you."

Fraser escorted Ilsa to the dining room where only a few tables were occupied.

"Before the dependents were evacuated, this place used to be jammed," Fraser said. "The food's very good. Would you like another drink?"

"A glass of Chablis will be fine."

After he gave the waiter their drink orders, he turned back to Ilsa. "How did you learn to speak English so well?"

"My father had two separate tours in Washington as a naval attache. I was in grade school during the first one so it was easy to pick up your language.I continued to study English when we returned to Holland."

"You sound like an American college girl."

"I should. I spent four years at Smith while my father was our senior naval attache."

"You enjoyed that?"

"Yes."

"And Washington. Did you like our capital?"

Ilsa's large green eyes clouded and her shoulders sagged slightly. "I'm afraid I have some bad memories. My mother died of cancer during those years in Washington."

"I'm sorry. I didn't mean to . . ."

"Not your fault." She lifted her glass of wine with a slender hand.

"I know your father must appreciate your helping with his social obligations."

"It's the least I can do. My sister did it for several years, but she got married three years ago. Now it's my turn. I'm also acting as his secretary on this trip."

"It seems foolish for you to be in a prospective war zone," Fraser said after he had given the dinner orders.

"Where would I go? Holland has been occupied by the Nazis. Almost all Europe is under Hitler's control. The Dutch East Indies are more than just a colony. Generations of my people have lived there and consider it a permanent home. I'd never leave my father, even if I had somewhere else to go."

Fraser was surprised by her intensity. "The threat of war doesn't seem to scare you."

Her eyes seemed angry. "Only because I won't have to fight in it. But there are times when I wish I could shoot a few people. I'd start at the top . . . Hitler . . . Stalin . . . Mussolini. They've all caused so much misery."

"Ummmm. Let's just be thankful the war's still half a world away," Fraser said. "Here comes our dinner. Maybe it will take our minds off the world's problems."

An hour later Ilsa took the first taste of her dessert. "You were right about the food. This mango ice cream is superb."

"It's the specialty of the house." As Fraser spooned the last of his ice cream from his dish, he reflected that Ilsa had remained about as cool as the dessert. No wonder Durham hadn't minded turning her over to him. Fraser wondered if he should ask her to visit some of the night spots in Manila.

"Excuse me, Ross. What time is it?"

"Almost nine."

"I'm sorry, but I have to get back to the hotel to transcribe some notes for my father. He has a meeting first thing in the morning."

"Oh." Fraser was sure she was dumping him.

"After tomorrow morning, the meetings will be classified. I won't have anything to do. If you have any free time, could you show me Manila?"

"Ah . . ." Fraser was surprised. "Well . . . of course. My ship doesn't go into the yard until the fifth."

"How convenient. That's the morning we fly home. If you take care of me I won't have to fend off any more eager beavers like Lieutenant Durham."

Fraser knew the evening had been pleasant. But the prospect of romance seemed remote. The lusty pleasures awaiting the rich man who found Shirley McGee were out of the question.

CHAPTER SIX

Byron Hanlon, the chief gunner's mate of the *O'Leary*, shifted carefully in his chair, his head pounding with a ferocious hangover. His seven shipmates sitting at the table in the cramped chiefs' quarters appeared to be in the same condition. Hanlon smiled as he watched Mortland, the chief boatswain, shove his scrambled eggs back and forth across his plate without eating any.

"Next re-enlistment party has to be on a Saturday night so we don't have to work the next day," Hanlon said.

"Don't let them start the war today," said John Jablonski, the chief quartermaster. His deepset eyes squinted painfully behind his wire-rimmed glasses. "If I see someone load a gun, I'm jumping over the side."

Mortland stood up and flipped the switch of the electric fan with a thick finger. "Thing's too loud."

"Thank God we don't have to go to sea today," said "Beerbarrel" Robustelli, the rotund chief torpedoman.

Hanlon agreed with that thought. Like any four-stacker the *O'Leary* rolled heavily in bad weather. But that wasn't the worst part about living in the chiefs' quarters, located forward of officers' country, close to the bow. When the *O'Leary* headed into weather heavier than a moderate sea, the bow was like an express elevator, climbing each wave rapidly and dropping with a sickening swoop into the trough.

Mortland lifted his large head and glared at the chief machinist's mate. "Hope your head don't hurt too bad, snipe. I'm gonna have my men chip some paint right over your engine rooms."

The other chief's neck reddened. "Just try it, you big deck ape. You'll be sorry you dropped out of your tree this morning. Start banging away, and I'll guarantee an oil spill on your deck."

"Mortland, why don't you knock off chipping today," Hanlon said. "Everyone's hung over."

Mortland pursed his thick lips and finally nodded. "Not a bad idea, but we'll never get away with it. It'll be too damn quiet. The old man will think nobody's working and start walking around."

"You're right," Hanlon said. "Anyone want to volunteer his part of the ship for some chipping?"

There was a long silence, and Hanlon knew why. Being anywhere near a sailor pounding a heavy chipping hammer against a steel deck or bulkhead was annoying. Being caught inside a compartment where chipping was being done outside was torture—even without a hangover.

Chief Quartermaster Jablonski massaged his prominent forehead. "Seems like we're at an impasse."

"Thought we was anchored off Manila," Mortland said.

"He means we can't decide, you dumb deck ape," the chief machinist said.

Mortland's close-set eyes narrowed. "Don't you tell me about the King's English, you ignorant snipe!"

"Gentlemen, gentlemen, we won't solve our problem this way." Jablonski stroked his long jaw. The quartermaster's large brown eyes glinted distantly behind his wire-rimmed glasses. "Let's lay the problem out. We need to do some chipping to keep the officers happy, right?"

There were nods of assent.

"We just have to make sure it's far enough away so it won't bother anybody," Jablonski said.

"How the hell we gonna do that?" Mortland asked. "No matter where we chip somebody's gonna bitch."

"Ahhh." Jablonski smiled. "The answer! The crow's nest!"

"Perfect!" Hanlon said as the rest of the chiefs nodded.

"Mortland," Jablonski said, "to be safe, have someone do some work above the old man's cabin every now and then."

Mortland's chair creaked under his heavy weight as the boatswain rocked back. "You're okay, Jablonski. Even though you do waste your time reading all those damn books. That one you're reading now got some good skin? *Madame Bovary*—must be about a whorehouse, right?"

"Sorry," said Jablonski. "It's a great work of literature. I don't think it's really up your alley."

"Don't get snooty with me," said Mortland. "I don't care if you are smarter than most of the officers. Just because you do all the exec's navigation don't mean you can put on airs."

Jablonski laughed. "Don't count on me outsmarting the old man, though. He's a sharp cookie."

Hanlon had to agree. He was also thankful for Jablonski's quiet intelligence and his ability to resolve the conflicts that sometimes disturbed the chiefs' quarters. Aside from Mortland, Hanlon felt lucky to have this group of chief petty officers, all of them veterans of fifteen years or more. He knew the survival of the ship might depend on their keeping the *O'Leary* going. The officers could give the orders, but it was the enlisted men who operated and maintained the ship and her equipment.

Hanlon's thoughts were interrupted by a nasty chuckle from Mortland. "I know just the man to send up to the crow's nest."

Hanlon caught Mortland's eye. "Landry?"

"What's it to you, Hanlon?"

"He's a good sailor, Mortland. The way I see it, you're close to getting out of line with him."

"Keep your damn opinions to yourself. Ain't none of your business," Mortland said.

"Go too far, and I'll make it my business," Hanlon said.

"I'll second that," Jablonski said.

There were other murmurs of agreement.

"One other thing," Hanlon said. "I don't want to hear about you making any trouble at Maria's restaurant. They want to make that into something special. No fights or arguments over Teresa or you'll have to settle with me."

"Okay, I'll behave at the restaurant." Mortland's eyes narrowed. "As for Landry, I won't do nothin' you can take me to the captain for." He stalked out and slammed the door behind him.

"Good for you," Jablonski said. "I'll back you up."

"Got to stand up against the jerks or they'll make folks miserable," Hanlon said.

"He'll still make it tough for Landry," Robustelli, the chief torpedoman, said.

"Kid's got a decent chance now," Hanlon said.

At two o'clock that afternoon, Fraser waited in the lobby of the Manila Hotel for Ilsa to meet him. He brushed some lint off his new five dollar suit and checked the shine on the one dollar shoes he had picked up from the Filipino shoemaker that morning. The captain had given Fraser the next three afternoons off to continue his escort duties. Arkwright had again made it clear that Fraser's primary responsibility was to avoid any incidents.

A few minutes later, Ilsa crossed the lobby and greeted Fraser. Her Batik sun dress revealed tanned shoulders and arms. Her smile was pleasant, but her green eyes seemed cool. Fraser saw the Filipino desk clerk raise an appreciative eyebrow.

They took a taxi to "Intramuros," the historic fortified section of the city which had been turned into a combination of apartments and little stores called "tiendas." Wandering inside the walls, they spent several hours looking through the shops and talking to the friendly proprietors.

Ilsa opened a mahogany cabinet in one shop.

The diminutive Chinese proprietor smiled and stroked his wispy mustache. "All yours, one hundred pesos."

"It's very nice—forty pesos?"

"Aieee! Aleady special plice for pletty lady. Ninety."

Ilsa smiled. "Sixty."

"Only one like it! My glandchi'llen will spit on my grave. But for you—eighty."

Ilsa's cool green eyes warmed. "Seventy. That's my final offer."

"Aieee. Toothless wife would not let me rest at night."

"Seventy is my top offer."

"Cash?"

"How are you going to get that on the plane?" Fraser asked.

"Oh, I forgot about that," Ilsa said. "I'm sorry, I guess I can't buy it after all."

The merchant chuckled. "That's all right. Some dumb American will probably pay a hundred pesos for it."

You lost your accent," said Fraser.

"I save it for the live customers."

As they walked away, Ilsa couldn't stop laughing. For a minute, Fraser thought he saw another person behind her reserved exterior.

"Too bad you couldn't buy that," Fraser said.

"It doesn't make any difference with the war coming." Some of the life left her face.

Fraser found himself enjoying just wandering with Ilsa. The afternoon passed quickly, and Fraser realized he was hungry. "Ready to try something unusual for dinner?"

"Yes, that might be fun," she said.

At the Manila Jai Alai Fronton, Ilsa told Fraser she'd never watched the game before. The large playing court filled one side of the huge building. The vocal spectators watched on three levels behind a glass wall that lined one end of the court. Shouts of joy and despair punctuated the end of each game. After a half-hour of mingling with the volatile spectators on the lower level, Fraser escorted Ilsa up to the night club on the third floor. From their table, they watched the agile jai alai players as they skillfully caught and hurled the ball in one flowing motion.

"It looks dangerous," Ilsa said.

"It is. Players have been killed."

Ilsa shuddered. "I don't know why men need that."

"I've been told some men find the threat of death stimulating. That's why they enjoy war, I guess."

"What about you?" she asked.

"I can live without that type of thrill."

"Why are you in the Navy then?"

"Same reason as most folks—to make a living. Times have been hard since the depression started. My Dad runs an insurance agency in Columbus, Ohio. Business went way down because most people were struggling just to eat. My older brother had just started law school. The family was hurting for money, so a service academy sounded like a good way to get a free education.

"The Navy's not a lifelong ambition?"

"Not exactly." He recounted his problems with his knee and the events that had resulted in orders to the *O'Leary*.

"Is everyone in your Asiatic Fleet as unenthusiastic as you are?"

"Actually, most of the enlisted men love it out here. Many expect to retire and stay. Until this year most of the officers enjoyed their tours because they could have their families here with them."

Ilsa took a sip from her glass of wine. "Maybe it will work out. You said you enjoyed your tour on the battleship, so you don't hate the whole Navy. You may find the Far East grows on you. It's very different from America. Once you get to know the people and their ways, you may like it."

A Filipino combo unlimbered its instruments and swung into their version of "Two O'Clock Jump," trombone slides pumping and trumpets blaring.

"Not quite like the record," Ilsa said.

Fraser laughed. "Harry James would probably sue the lead trumpet for libel."

"You like music?" she asked.

"Yes. Benny Goodman, Glenn Miller, Harry James. I wish I had some time to try some more serious music, but some of the modern classical music sounds like noise."

"Not all modern classical music is bad. Try some Sibelius or Rachmaninoff or your American composer, Aaron Copeland. Do you play a musical instrument?"

"No," Fraser said, "but I must confess to a secret ambition. My family's of Scottish descent on both sides. I've only heard bagpipes a few times, but they stir my blood. If I had the time, I might try to learn how to play them."

"I hope it's easier than the violin. I was a complete failure."

The band broke into a passable rendition of "Smoke Gets in Your Eyes."

"I think my knee could handle a slow one like this if you'd like to dance."

"Yes, I'd like that."

Fraser discovered that Ilsa danced well, but she maintained a polite six inches of distance between them as they circled the floor.

As he returned her to their table, he took a deep breath. "There's a polo match tomorrow afternoon. Would you like to go?"

"That would be nice," she said politely.

That evening, Hank Landry led the *O'Leary*'s sweaty baseball team into the Mabuhay Bar and Grille. The owner, a retired Navy man, waved them to a group of corner tables. The bar was one of Landry's favorite watering holes, a spot many of the fleet's athletic teams frequented. The owner had adapted to his patrons by bolting solid mahogany tables and benches to the floor. Landry had helped splinter several earlier generations of less sturdy furniture.

"Best peanuts in Manila," said the red-haired Tim Egan, tossing shells to the floor among several thousand of their dead comrades.

"Careful, Egan," said Eckersly, the storekeeper. "Watch your arm. We need you to pitch a helluva game tomorrow if we're gonna have any chance at all."

"Eckersly, Don't be so damn gloomy," Landry said.

"Just keeping in practice in case I decide to go back to the family funeral home."

"Hey, we would have beat the *Holland* early in the season if we didn't make so many errors," Landry said.

"Don't get too cocky," Egan said. "Those tender guys are in port all the time so they've been practicing a lot. They have three times as many men to draw from."

"My money's on your curve ball," said Landry. "They had a tough time hitting you last time."

The freckled Egan took a long pull from his bottle of San Miguel beer. "You look a little tired, Landry."

"I should be. I was chipping paint in the damn crow's nest all day. Try working inside a big tin can in this sun."

"I know how you love chipping paint," Egan said.

"Jesus, I do hate it." Landry shook his head at the thought of the unending task. The rust always came back, so the old paint would have to be chipped off and replaced.

"Mortland still after Teresa?" Egan asked.

"Yeah. He just won't accept she's my girl now. He ain't gonna quit trying to get her."

"I don't know what you're worried about," Egan said. "It's obvious Teresa loves you. You're set for life, man."

Landry picked his beer bottle up and rolled it between his hands, avoiding the red-haired torpedoman's eyes.

"You mean you don't want to marry that girl someday?" Egan said. "You're crazy. She's beautiful . . . bright. Maybe a little stubborn, but who's perfect?"

"Don't know if I'm ready to settle down for good." Christ, Landry thought, what would happen to their kids if they had any? They'd be real half-breeds. Hell, what's bothering Teresa anyway. Hell of an argument we had last night. Why won't she quit her job?

"A piece of advice about Mortland," Egan said. "Never get in a pissing contest with a skunk. That goes double if you have to work for him."

"I'd love to punch Mortland right in his ugly face."

Egan's freckles shifted as he frowned. "Don't be a fool. He'd love that. You'll get yourself court-martialed. You won't get to see much of Teresa if you're locked up in the brig."

The team was just starting its second round of beer when Egan froze. "Here comes the whole damned *Holland* team."

They watched quietly as the tender's players found chairs at nearby tables. A heavy-set sailor who was the *Holland*'s catcher noticed the smaller group from the *O'Leary* and smiled derisively. "Are you guys really going to show up tomorrow?"

Landry snapped, "Why not, fatso?"

"Your pitcher was lucky last time," a *Holland* sailor said.

"Five to one says we win," the fat catcher said. "Any of you destroyer pukes man enough to put up a hundred?"

The *O'Leary* table was silent. Landry remembered he had borrowed against his next two paychecks in order to have some cash to show Teresa. The catcher's smile was unbearable. "Okay, fatso, here's a hundred that says we'll beat you." Landry handed his money to the bar owner. "Put up or shut up!"

The *Holland* man frowned, pulled a sheaf of bills from his wallet, and borrowed some from his friends. He swaggered to the bar and laid his money next to Landry's.

Landry eyed the pile of bills hungrily. Love to see Mortland's face if I won that, he thought.

"Six hundred," said the bar owner. "I'll put it in my safe right now."

The fat sailor laughed as he walked back to his table. "Easiest hundred bucks I'll ever earn."

The tension grew but then subsided as the bar owner rushed frosty bottles of San Miguel to the other team. The *Holland* team ignored the destroyer men and talked among themselves. Landry noticed the fat catcher looking their way from time to time and whispering to his buddies.

A half-hour later, Egan rose and headed for the men's room. As he walked by the *Holland*'s team, the fat sailor rose and bumped Egan. "Watch where you're going."

"Didn't see anything in front of me," Egan said.

"Chickenshit destroyer puke!"

"Who are you calling chicken, Fatso?"

The heavy sailor threw his beer in Egan's face and wrestled him to the floor. Several *Holland* sailors jumped on the pile.

Landry leaped over his table and led his shipmates to the rescue. The sailors from the *Holland* backed away when threatened by the angry men from the *O'Leary* and the bar's three burly bouncers. The last of the sailors who had piled on Egan was finally pulled away.

The *O'Leary*'s only good pitcher lay among the peanut shells clutching his hand. "That bastard broke one of my pitching fingers."

Eckersly's long face looked even more somber. "Landry, my deepest sympathy about your departed money."

An hour before game time, the bleachers were only partly filled. "We're gonna get those *Holland* bastards!" one of the *O'Leary*'s men shouted from the third base side where sailors from the destroyer force sat. One of his buddies gave him an elbow and he turned around. "Sorry, Ma'am, I clean forgot you were there."

Ilsa nodded politely. "I learned a lot worse in college."

"Maybe we'd better leave," Fraser said. "It will get a lot worse."

Ilsa shook her head and her sandy hair swirled in the breeze. "I'd rather stay. It's a good thing I read about this game in the morning paper. Otherwise we'd be watching a stuffy polo match. I'm glad we came early. I like to watch batting practice."

God, thought Fraser, I just hope there's not a riot here today.

Fifteen minutes later Hank Landry and Bull Durham, the team's coach, climbed into the stands and approached Fraser. "Ross, we got problems," Durham said.

"I heard about Egan's finger. You might do okay with Nystrom. He's got the strongest arm I've ever seen."

"His arm's fine," Durham said. "It's his head. He's an outfielder—never pitched in a big game before. He's so nervous he'll walk everyone."

"Don't look at me," Fraser said. "All I ever did was pitch a few J. V. games at Annapolis. I'm just your batting practice pitcher."

Landry tapped his spikes on the wooden bleachers. "You're all we got, Mr. Fraser." The deckhand gave Fraser a long look. "Sir, you owe me for pulling you out of Subic Bay."

Fraser remembered how he could have drowned. And there was the banged up whaleboat. Landry had been polite enough not to mention the bungled torpedo recovery. "Yeah, I do owe you. But I just can't leave Miss Van Dorn alone up here. I'm responsible for her."

"Don't be silly," Ilsa said. "I can take care of myself. You're not afraid to play are you?" Her green eyes teased him.

"Of course not," Fraser lied, knowing how much the crew wanted to win. Jesus, he thought, if I go out there and do something stupid to lose the game . . .

"It's all settled, then," Durham said. "There's a uniform for you in the clubhouse."

As Durham and Landry returned to the field, Fraser scanned the stands for somebody to sit with Ilsa. None of the other officers had arrived yet. Shifflet was several rows away and Fraser shuddered. Then he saw Chief Hanlon walking up into the bleachers and Fraser knew part of his problem was solved.

The stocky Hanlon smiled after Fraser described his problem. "Happy to take care of a beautiful young lady."

Landry squatted in the dust of the bullpen and warmed up Fraser. His sense of despair mounted as Fraser began to throw in earnest. The fastball wasn't fast and had no movement. After the warmup, Landry trudged toward the field with Fraser, knowing his money was lost. "Mr. Fraser, I'm going to call for mostly slow junk. I'll just call for your fastball as a change of pace. Keep your fastball off the plate where they can't get a good swing at it."

Landry buckled on the heavy catcher's equipment, trotted out to to home plate, and took his crouch in the thick dust. Fraser served the first batter a tantalizing curve that broke just outside the plate. The batter swung, topped the ball, and hit a futile roller to the second baseman. As the batter, a hulking bruiser, trotted back to the bench, Landry looked over to the *Holland*'s bench and thumbed his nose. "You'd better send up someone bigger."

One batter later the *Holland*'s fat catcher crowded the plate, pawed the dirt, and dug his spikes in. "Watch your ear, Fatso," Landry whispered.

"An officer wouldn't throw at me."

Landry held his mitt behind the hitter's head. Fraser shook his head.

Landry trotted out to the mound. "You gotta move this guy off the plate, Mr. Fraser."

"I'm not throwing at anyone's head," Fraser said.

"You're too goddamned nice, Mr. Fraser. The rest of them will dig in if you don't dust this guy off."

Bull Durham ran out from the dugout.

"What's that midget doing on the field?" shouted a voice from the *Holland*'s dugout.

"Send that jockey to the race track."

Durham glared into the enemy dugout when he arrived at the mound. "What's the problem?"

"We gotta move that fat bastard off the plate," Landry said. "Besides he's the one who broke Egan's finger. We can't let him get away with that."

Fraser's gray eyes hardened. "I'll move him off my way."

Durham scowled at another insult from the *Holland*'s dugout. "Just get him off the plate." Durham spat contemptuously at his hecklers in the enemy dugout. The breeze blew some of the saliva back on Durham's shoe.

Landry shook his head and walked back to the plate, wondering why the Naval Academy couldn't even teach an officer to spit right.

Fraser's next pitch headed for the batter's ankles. "Shit!" yelped the fat batter as he toppled into the dust.

"Fatty, tell your buddies to stay loose if they wanna walk back to the ship," Landry said with new respect for Fraser.

As the game went on, Fraser surprised Landry. He kept his junk just far enough off the plate to coax many pop-ups and slow grounders out of the other team. Ben Nystrom, a rangy deck hand, roamed centerfield and ran down several line drives. But their luck ran out in the fifth inning. Two errors and three solid hits produced three runs for the *Holland*.

The *O'Leary*'s scoring prospects looked dim. The *Holland*'s pitcher overwhelmed them with a hopping fastball and a sharp curve. But the *O'Leary* scratched out a run in the sixth. Landry took a pitch in the ribs that had been called by his opposite number. "I'm stealing second on that rag arm of yours," Landry told the catcher before he left the plate. The pitcher walked the next batter after the catcher called three straight pitchouts. Eckersly sliced a single allowing Landry to score while the destroyer rooters roared and rocked their bleachers.

The next inning, Fraser threw a fast ball too close to the plate, and the obnoxious catcher crunched a home run.

Landry ran out to the mound. "One more fast ball over the plate, and I'll chase you back to the ship with a bat."

Fraser's mouth opened.

"I don't care if you are an officer. I'm the catcher. You'd better give me the pitches I call for."

"You're the catcher," Fraser said.

Through the eighth inning, Fraser's pitches continued to frustrate the opponents, so the score remained four to one. Between innings, the banter from the stands intensified and took on a more urgent tone.

As they walked out for the top of the ninth, Fraser asked Landry, "What's all the noise for? We'll never get enough runs off that pitcher to win."

Eckersly heard the question and his long face smiled. "Didn't you hear? The *Holland*'s sailors were offering three and a half runs just before the game to get bets from our people. If we hold on, we'll cost those pricks a lot of money."

"Why'd I put my money down so early?" Landry muttered, knowing his hundred dollars was down the drain. He watched Fraser trudge off to the mound and noticed the officer's grim face. Landry followed him out to the mound. "Mr. Fraser, don't change what you've been doing. Stay loose."

"Easy for you to say. If I give up another run the crew may dump me over the side."

The first batter struck out in his eagerness to belt a lazy curve. The noise from the bleachers rose another notch. The fat catcher who had broken Egan's finger stepped up to the plate and muttered obscenities.

"That's not polite," Landry said. He eased his aching legs as he gave the target for the next pitch.

The batter laughed as two of Fraser's best curves broke in the dirt. Landry groaned as the next pitch wandered into the strike zone. The ball rocketed toward the outfield. By the time the left fielder threw it back, the beefy catcher was puffing on third base.

Landry trudged to the mound. "Damn, we're in it now. The next hitter is their clean-up batter, and he's been tattooing you all day."

"What the hell can we do?" Fraser asked. "One more run and they'll win all the money, too."

Landry kicked the dirt as he considered the problem. "Nystrom's in centerfield with his catapult arm. Keep the ball up and outside. The hitter'll probably fly to center."

"That's just what they want. That batter will hit it a mile, and the runner will tag up and score."

"Yeah, but they haven't seen that arm of Nystrom's yet. That fat slob on third is slow. He's still puffing."

Fraser took off his cap and ran a hand through his black hair. "You're the boss. High and outside it is."

"Waste one way outside first. We want him hungry."

As ordered, the first pitch was a foot outside, and the big hitter watched it go by. He banged the plate with his bat and kicked the dirt.

Fraser peered in from the mound with a worried look on his face.

Come on, Mister Fraser, Landry thought. Don't let us down. Gimme a good pitch.

The next pitch was right to Landry's specifications, a lazy slow curve, high and six inches outside. The batter leaned out and swung, sending a soaring fly to deep center field. Nystrom backed up behind the ball, set himself, and took a few steps in to make the catch. There was a roar from the *Holland*'s rooters as the runner chugged toward home; the run looked like a sure thing.

Landry tossed his mask aside, planted himself in front of the plate, and watched Nystrom's throw come. The ball bounced in front of the pitcher's mound, raised a small puff of dust, and homed into Landry's glove. The lumbering runner lowered his shoulder and barrelled over Landry, trying to knock the ball loose. The impact drove the air from Landry's lungs and sent him rolling in the dust, but he still had his bare hand clamped over the ball in his glove. Landry scrambled to his feet and held the ball aloft. The runner lay in the dirt holding his bleeding nose where Landry had tagged him.

The umpire threw his arm skyward, and bellowed, "You're out!"

The *Holland*'s catcher jumped up and faced Landry, clutching his nose. "I'll get you for this!"

Landry flipped the ball to the umpire and faced his adversary. "Why not now, Fatso?"

The fat sailor cocked his right fist and charged. Landry stepped inside the threat and drilled a short left to the jaw. The impact shot up Landry's arm. The other man dropped like a steer shot between the eyes.

Landry turned to the other team's dugout. "Anyone else?"

There were a few murmurs but no takers.

The umpire banished both combatants to their benches and hurriedly shepherded the teams through the last half-inning. The *Holland*'s pitcher mowed down the *O'Leary*'s last hitters, but none of the destroyermen seemed to care; they danced and cheered with each out, waving their wallets at the glowering tender sailors across the field. As the last *O'Leary* batter watched a third strike whiz by, the shore patrol rushed on the field, hefting their wooden billy clubs, and kept the two sides away from each other.

Landry left the dugout with Fraser and started for the clubhouse. "Don't much care for losing," Landry said. "But we made 'em pay for that trophy, didn't we?"

"Damned if we didn't," Fraser said.

Landry tossed a ball to Fraser. "A souvenir. You earned it."

Fraser caught the ball and turned it over. He showed Landry a patch of dried blood. "Thanks. This is the only game I ever won by a minus score. Hell of a job on that bastard's nose!"

"Thanks, . . . sir," Landry was suddenly aware that he was no longer the boss, nor even an equal under the Navy system. Then he remembered he was not only broke, but two paychecks in debt. "Awwww shit!" he muttered.

"That game was fun," Ilsa said as Fraser escorted her to their table at a night club on Dewey Boulevard.

"I'm glad you enjoyed it," he said, thinking they were lucky to have escaped without being caught in a riot. Lord, he thought, Admiral Hart would feed me to the sharks at dawn if something had happened to Ilsa.

"Your men certainly are uninhibited."

"So were the Mongol hordes," Fraser said.

"You judge them too harshly. Your Chief Hanlon is a fine man. When a few of the men were a little too friendly, all he had to do was look at them."

"I don't know anybody our men respect more—except the captain."

After dinner, they moved toward the dance floor. Ilsa still maintained a polite distance. "You dance very well despite your knee injury."

"Yes, I guess I should thank the surgeons for that. But I can't say as much for the guy who fixed my nose."

"Don't worry. That nose just gives your face character."

"In that case, I'll change my story. This nose has been handed down through generations of Frasers. If a male child doesn't have one like mine, he's put up for adoption."

"You'd better stick with the first story."

As they moved around the dance floor, Fraser saw a familiar blonde head nearby—Shirley McGee, the general's girlfriend. She appeared to be dancing alone. Then she turned with the music, and Fraser's jaw dropped as he saw Bull Durham's chin nestled in Shirley's formidable cleavage.

As the music stopped, Fraser looked for the nearest exit.

"Oh look, there's your friend, Lieutenant Durham. Let's say hello."

Ilsa towed Fraser across the floor where Durham and his date had both turned the other way. "Lieutenant Durham! Your team played so well today."

Durham turned, almost guiltily, Fraser thought. "Oh, hello again. Shirley, I'd like you to meet Ilsa Van Dorn and a shipmate of mine, Ross Fraser."

Fraser was surprised when the girl only raised one eyebrow slightly. "Ross, is it? Pleased to meet you," was all she said.

"Nice to meet you, Shirley," Fraser said. "Having a good time, Bull?"

Shirley giggled. "Rocky, do they call you 'Bull' on your ship?"

"Rocky?" Fraser said.

"Sure," Shirley said. "After his mother's maiden name—Rockefeller."

Fraser thought he could see the dollar signs in her eyes.

"Shirley, now you've done it," said Durham quickly. "I try not to let my Navy friends know about that. The Navy doesn't pay very well, and I don't want to flaunt my money."

"Ohhh, I'm sorry Rocky. You're just so considerate," Shirley said. "You're not like so many rich people."

"No, he isn't, is he?" Fraser said.

"I hope you two will excuse us," Durham said. "I have to call my broker in New York."

"Selling short, Rocky?" Fraser asked.

Durham just glared.

Shirley squeezed Durham's arm. "And then the two of us can have a little party of our own at the hotel."

"I think I can work it in," Durham said.

After they said goodnight to Durham and Shirley, Fraser escorted Ilsa back to their table.

"Hmmmm. An interesting couple," she said.

"You mentioned Corregidor yesterday," Fraser said quickly. "Would you like to see it tomorrow?"

"That would be interesting. I'll be able to tell my father I'm seeing something of military interest."

"I've heard the Army has a nice beach there. We can go swimming if you'd like."

"I could use the exercise," she said. "And you . . ."

". . . may need the practice, if my ship sinks."

Ilsa's sandy hair fluttered in the breeze the next morning as they neared Corregidor. They sat by the rail of the high-speed boat that had taken them thirty miles west to the entrance of Manila Bay where the fortress stood guard. The dominant part of the island was a circular, 600-foot-high section, which tapered to a narrow, low-lying peninsula pointing east toward Manila. A smaller rocky hill thrust its way skyward from the narrow part of the island.

Fraser pointed. "That's Malinta Hill in the middle. The Army's tunneled into it for protection."

"My father's not impressed by Corregidor. He said most of its guns are exposed to bombs and howitzers."

An hour later Fraser realized the wisdom of Captain Van Dorn's opinion. The huge guns and mortars were mounted behind concrete parapets with no overhead protection. The fortress had been designed for an era when the only threat was from high-velocity, low-angle naval bombardment. The island's antiaircraft defenses were meager. Fraser felt like he was looking at a dinosaur, ready for extinction.

An electric tramway carried them from the heavily fortified main section known as "Topside" down to the narrower part of the island. Suddenly, the grim mood was broken. They were surrounded by orchids and a myriad of flowering trees and shrubs: frangipani, bougainviliea, hibiscus.

"Lunch and a swim?" Fraser asked.

"Good idea."

At the nearly deserted beach, they visited the snack bar and took a table under an awning. Fraser sat back when they finished eating. "Maybe we should lie in the sun for a while before we go swimming."

"Let me change. I'll meet you in a few minutes."

Fraser was almost asleep on his blanket when he saw Ilsa walking toward him. A light blue one-piece suit hugged her body. Her lightly tanned legs were well-shaped and firm.

"Look's like you get a lot of exercise."

"Tennis and some swimming," she said.

After an hour of sunning and talking, they went in the water and floated in the gentle swells. As Fraser swam by Ilsa, who was standing in the shoulder-deep water, she jumped on his back and dragged him under the surface. He broke her grip and thrashed to the surface.

She laughed. "Just testing to see if you're ready for a surprise attack."

"Always ready."

He jumped and pulled her under. She fought him for a few seconds, and then her body was against his. She was smooth and firm and slippery; the contact was electrifying. Fraser felt his body respond and released her.

Ilsa looked at him appraisingly as he surfaced. "I think I'll get some more sun."

"I'll be in after I swim some more."

Fraser watched her walk toward the beach. The suit clung to her narrow waist and flaring hips like a shiny second skin. The muscles of her well-shaped bottom bunched and worked as she pushed through the water. Wet legs gleamed as she emerged from the shallows.

When he returned to the blanket, she rolled on her side and propped herself on her elbow. Her wet hair was slicked back and exposed the pleasant symmetry of her face. Her cool green eyes looked into his. "I have to leave tomorrow on the flying boat with my father."

"Yes, I know."

"I don't suppose I'll ever see you again."

"Java is 2,000 miles away," he said.

"A long way."

"Dinner tonight?" Fraser asked.

"That would be nice."

Ilsa lay back down on the blanket, beads of water still clinging to her sleek body.

As they sat down at the table at the Manila Hotel, Ilsa smiled. "You've been so nice showing me around, I have a present for you. Don't let me forget to give it to you tonight."

"Any hints?"

"No, you'll be surprised. It wasn't easy to find."

"A glass of Chablis for the lady," Fraser told the waiter.

"Excuse me, but I think I'll try a martini," Ilsa said.

"Jack Daniels and water for me please," Fraser ordered.

"You've been taking me all over town. I really haven't had a chance to try the food here at the hotel," Ilsa said.

"Some say this is the best hotel in the Far East. I think you'll be impressed with dinner. It's still the center of local society. General MacArthur lives in the penthouse. That's his table over there."

"What about the empty table next to MacArthur's?" asked Ilsa.

"That's reserved for MacArthur's Chief of Staff, General Sutherland. Nobody seems to like him. But I've heard people speak well of his predecessor. Eisenhower, I think his name was."

The food was as good as Fraser had promised, but he was

surprised when Ilsa had two more martinis. He was even more surprised when they arrived at the Army Navy Club and took the dance floor. The polite six inches that had previously separated them was reduced to zero. Fraser realized that there was only a sixteenth of an inch of warm and damp cotton between him and Ilsa. When she lifted her arms to join him in a slow number, Fraser could feel her firm breasts pressing into his jacket.

"I think I'm ready for another martini," she said as the band finished an off-key version of "Temptation."

"Maybe you'd better slow down," Fraser said.

"How much longer do we have for this kind of fun?"

"Don't let me spoil it for you, then."

"Eat, drink, and be merry, Lieutenant, for tomorrow . . . Who knows if there will be a tomorrow. The Japanese will show the other Asiatics that they can get along fine without the white man. This whole way of life will be gone soon."

"Maybe you're being too pessimistic."

Her look seemed both sad and sympathetic. "I've already seen what war can do."

An hour later, as the band mauled "In the Mood," Fraser realized that Ilsa was getting wobbly. "I think it's about time to get you back to the hotel."

Her head nodded against his shoulder. "Yes, by all means, the hotel."

As Fraser helped Ilsa out of the taxi at the hotel, she looked up at the sky. "Look at that full moon. It's gorgeous."

Alone in the elevator at the hotel, Ilsa wrapped her arms around his neck. She hiccupped, kissed him, and then leaned against him. "Having trouble schtanding up. Must be that moon."

Fraser supported her as they stumbled to her suite. He took her key and opened the door after knocking politely.

"My father . . . my father is . . ."

Ilsa slumped against him, and Fraser grabbed her as her knees buckled. He carried her across the sitting room of the suite and lowered her gently to the brocade couch.

"Captain Van Dorn? Sir, are you here?"

Silence from the two bedrooms.

What had she been trying to tell him? Her father wouldn't be back tonight? He'd be back shortly? He patted her cheek gently, but there was no response. His mind raced. What to do? Her father might be here any minute. What will Van Dorn say if he finds me here with his unconscious daughter. If the story gets to Admiral Hart . . .

Despite his concern, Fraser felt a surge of lust. He'd let himself enjoy life so little. Ilsa seemed incredibly attractive, more so in her own way than Shirley McGee.

He looked down at the oval face. Her helpless vulnerability cooled his desire. Death had claimed both her mother and her fiance' and now threatened her father. He was suddenly ashamed at the thought of taking advantage of her condition.

Ilsa looked comfortable on the couch so he decided to leave her there. Regretfully, Fraser rearranged the hem of her skirt to cover an exposed knee. He saw some hotel stationery on a nearby desk, and thought for a minute before writing:

Ilsa,

I'm sorry you're leaving tomorrow. My ship is going in the yard. If the threat of war dies down, I should be able to take a few weeks of leave. I would like to see Java if you would care to show it to me.

Ross

Not very poetic, he thought, but she should have no illusions about his finesse with words. He retreated to the door where he paused for a minute to look back at her. He felt incredibly attracted to Ilsa. He saw a gift-wrapped box on a nearby table. The card had his name on it, so he tucked the box under his arm. He closed the door softly behind him.

Will I ever see her again, he wondered. Yesterday, it didn't much matter. Tonight . . . tonight, it matters a lot. Tomorrow . . . oh Lord. Tomorrow, I have to conn the ship over to the yard.

CHAPTER SEVEN

Fraser rubbed his throbbing temples as he left the wardroom after breakfast for officers' call. He had only nibbled at a piece of dry toast. I wish the hell it were yesterday, he thought. Then I'd have another day with Ilsa. Lord, hope I don't bang up the ship this morning.

The slanting sunlight seemed to pierce Fraser's eyeballs and lance through his brain as he took his place in the line of officers facing Beringer.

The executive officer paced back and forth as he gave them routine information. "Now I have a more serious matter to discuss. I thought you gentlemen realized that officers' country is not a proper place for sexual liaisons." Beringer stopped pacing and faced Durham. "Last night, I was roused out of a sound slumber by the damndest squeals. It must have been one of your women, Durham. Your proclivities are well known."

"My what, sir?"

"Your . . . er . . . umm . . . habits."

"I didn't have a woman in my room, sir."

Beringer's eyes narrowed. "Good God! I never would have believed you'd turn into a . . ."

". . . fairy? Never, sir."

"What was it? An animal! Have you no morals at all? What if the men find out?"

"I'm innocent, sir," Durham said. "I didn't even get back to the ship until just before dawn."

Beringer walked up and down the line of officers. "It seems someone else is the guilty party."

Fraser raised his hand. "Was it about 0100, sir?"

Beringer stopped in front of Fraser and looked contemptuously down his long nose. "Yes. Explain yourself, Mr. Fraser. Just what kind of a pervert are you?"

"I was just testing a present from a young lady. I obviously need some practice."

Beringer's muddy eyes narrowed. "What in God's name was it?"

"A bagpipe chanter, sir. It's the part the bagpiper uses to play the tune. You don't need the bag and other pipes to practice. You just blow in the chanter."

Beringer stared at Fraser. "I hate bagpipes, even when they're played properly. You will hereafter conduct any practice sessions ashore or some place where I can't hear you. That's an order!"

After Beringer dismissed them and stalked away, Durham snickered. "I wonder if you can buy bagpipe records. I might start a collection just to drive that prick up the wall."

After morning quarters with his men on the after deckhouse, Fraser walked reluctantly to the bridge, stepped into the pilothouse, and leaned over the chart table to inspect the approach to the Cavite Navy Yard.

"Not very complicated," the captain said. "All you have to do is follow the buoys around Sangley Point, put the bow alongside the pier, and twist the stern in."

It was the final approach that worried Fraser. Despite their small size and high-powered engines, the four-stack destroyers had small single rudders, which limited their maneuverability, particularly at slow speeds. In the confined area between the piers at Cavite, there would be little margin for error.

Fraser felt his stomach churning, and his palms were sweaty. He was surprised when Arkwright smiled.

"I'll be here if you need me," the captain said. "This may be your last chance to take her alongside for a while."

Minutes later men bustled around Fraser as the special sea and anchor detail took their stations. Fraser accepted a pair of binoculars from a quartermaster and hung the thin strap around his neck.

The bridge phone talker buckled on his headset. He soon turned to Fraser. "Sir, all stations manned and ready."

"Very well."

The captain climbed into the chair mounted to the starboard side of the forward bridge bulkhead. "She's all yours, Ross."

"Aye, aye, sir." Fraser turned toward the helm. "This is Mr. Fraser, I have the deck and the conn."

"Aye, aye, sir," chorused the helmsman and lee-helmsman.

Beringer, officially the navigator, slid over behind the chart table where he yawned. He stared vacantly toward the square windows running across the front of the bridge while Chief Jablonski coordinated the efforts of the quartermasters.

Arkwright nodded to Fraser, who turned to the phone talker. "Tell the foc'sle to heave around to short stay."

The capstan clanked as it pulled the heavy anchor chain aboard. Muddy links began to appear, and the chain groaned and jumped under the strain. Chief Mortland leaned over the bow and bellowed a steady stream of reports at his phone talker. The bridge talker labored trying to keep up but was always about two reports behind.

Fraser laughed. "Talker, belay repeating those reports from the foc'sle. I can hear the chief fine."

"Avast heaving. Anchor's at short stay-y-y," boomed Mortland.

"Very well. Tell them to stand by," said Fraser, who stepped out on the starboard wing to take a last look around.

Another nod from Arkwright, and Fraser took a deep breath. As soon as the anchor left the bottom, he would have to control the ship.

"Hoist the anchor," Fraser ordered.

The capstan resumed its clank.

"Anchor's aweigh!" Mortland shouted. "Get the hose going on that muddy chain."

An answering blast of water erupted, and spray cascaded into the air, creating several small rainbows.

"Get that spray away from me, you idiot!" Mortland shouted at the deck hand directing the hose.

"I owe Nystrom a beer," Fraser heard Landry mutter at his lookout post.

"All ahead one-third," Fraser ordered.

The deck shuddered, and Fraser heard a froth of water aft. Fraser conned the ship from her anchorage and headed her toward the anchored submarine tenders, *Holland* and *Canopus*, each with a nest of black submarines alongside for repairs. As they passed the *Holland*, the boatswain of the watch blew a whistle calling the crew to attention to render passing honors. As the whistle shrilled, signalling the men to salute, a series of soft curses rippled across the bridge. Aboard the *Holland*, her fat catcher stood next to his captain holding the fleet trophy aloft.

"Ross, take us around again," the captain said. He instructed the messenger to have Egan report to the bridge.

As the *O'Leary* made her next pass, Egan stood at attention next to Arkwright on the bridge wing, displaying his wallet in his left hand. At the signal for hand salute, Egan thrust his splinted middle finger skyward.

"Now they know what I think of them for breaking Egan's finger," Arkwright said.

As the *O'Leary* steamed south, the haze dispersed to reveal the Cavite Navy Yard. Masts, giant cranes, and smokestacks appeared to sprout from a maze of shops and offices, which were topped with galvanized iron roofs. Near their destination, several ungainly PBY seaplanes floated at their moorings like giant sea gulls. With a growing feeling of apprehension, Fraser threaded the *O'Leary* by several smaller vessels anchored off the yard.

Fraser groaned when he saw the final task ahead. There had been plenty of room for all his previous maneuvers, but now he would have to conn the ship into a tight berth. The *Pillsbury*, another destroyer, lay further to seaward along the pier and would have to be passed close aboard. There was just enough room for the *O'Leary* between the bow of the *Pillsbury* and the sea wall at the base of the pier. The breeze had freshened and was blowing directly across the pier, making his task even more difficult. Fortunately, the tide was slack, so there was no current to compound the problem.

"Captain, the wind . . ." Fraser hoped the captain would take the conn.

"Glad you caught that, Ross. It'll push you off the pier. Just means you'll have to make your final approach a little sharper, right?"

For an instant, anxiety seized Fraser. Then he was buoyed by the fact that the captain appeared to have confidence in him. He turned to his task.

"All engines ahead one-third," he ordered, slowing the ship to 5 knots. He conned the *O'Leary* close by her sister ship, which temporarily shielded them from the breeze. "All engines stop," Fraser ordered, letting ship's momentum carry her forward.

He knew the breeze would require him to turn the bow toward the pier sooner and more sharply than normal. He bit his tongue and waited for the right moment. "Left ten degrees rudder." After letting the bow swing, he ordered, "Rudder amidships. All engines back one-third."

Fraser clenched his fists as the propellers bit into the water. The ship shuddered to a halt in nearly perfect position with the bow only fifteen feet from the pier, safely short of the bulkhead just ahead.

"All engines stop." Fraser let out a long breath.

Durham's men on the forecastle threw the weighted ends of their light heaving lines over to the line-handling party on the pier. The men ashore pulled the stout mooring lines over to the pier and dropped the looped ends over the mooring bollards. The deckhands wrapped their end of the number one line around the capstan so that the bow could be pulled closer to the pier.

With the bow under control, Fraser ordered, "Port ahead one-third. Starboard back one-third. Right full rudder." The *O'Leary* vibrated and rattled as the stern slowly twisted through the dirty water toward the pier. Soon, the after mooring lines followed the heaving lines over to the pier.

As the ship settled into her final position, Fraser gave his last orders with a combined feeling of exhilaration and relief.

From his bridge chair, Arkwright nodded. "Good job, Ross. Nothing to it, eh?"

You'll never know, Fraser thought. "I guess not. I hope I didn't worry you, Captain."

"Oh, no."

Fraser felt a surge of pride because of the captain's confidence in him, but then he noticed the large circles of sweat under Arkwright's arms.

A raucous "toot! toot!" reverberated off the walls of the yard buildings.

Fraser looked over at the Guadaloupe Pier where a yard tug was preparing to move a barge. A stout chief petty officer leaned out the wheel house door and saluted the bridge of the *O'Leary* with a wave.

"Looks like that chief liked your work, too," the captain said.

Fraser was flattered by the compliment from the old professional. He also felt comforted by the cranes and shops of the yard. Whatever the *O'Leary* needed for repairs would be available at Cavite. Fraser hoped the war warning Admiral Hart had received from Washington would prove to be groundless.

When all six mooring lines were doubled up, Hank Landry and the other deck hands began installing circular metal rat guards on each mooring line.

"I wish the hell we were some place farther from the Japs," said Ben Nystrom, the rangy deckhand who had thrown out the fat catcher.

"Like where?" asked Landry.

Nystrom took his hat off and ran a hand through his fair hair. "Pearl Harbor'd be nice."

"You men quit farting around and get those rat guards on," shouted Mortland from the forecastle.

"Right away, Chief," said Nystrom.

Mortland walked over and tested one of the metal stanchions. "Heard you lost all your money, Landry. How 'bout if I take over your apartment. I'll give you a couple of hundred for it—and the girl, of course."

Landry clenched his fists and fought to keep them at his sides. "Rent's paid through the end of the month."

"Have it your way. Keep the damn apartment. It's gonna seem mighty empty before long." Mortland was humming as he walked away.

"Damn! What am I gonna do?" Landry said.

The sun-reddened Nystrom smiled. "Hey, don't worry."

"Don't worry? I was already in hock for my next two paychecks before I lost all my cash."

"From what I hear, a lot of folks are chipping in some money for you."

"Won't take no charity."

"Ain't charity. Most of it's money guys won when you tagged that bastard out at home. Or it's money from folks like the snipes who hate Mortland."

"Maybe that's different, then," said Landry.

Later that day, when the word had been passed to knock off ship's work, Landry cleaned up and found a taxi for the 10-mile trip back to Manila. The wallet tucked in his pants was heavy with the money his shipmates had kicked in. As the cab approached Landry's neighborhood, he thought about the argument he had gotten into with Teresa the night of the baseball game. She had again refused to quit her job, and Landry had stormed out and returned to the ship that night instead of waiting until the next morning. He wondered how wise that had been.

When Landry walked into the apartment, he was covered with sweat and road dust. "Teresa, I'm home."

Silence.

"Dammit, where is she?"

Landry washed some of the dust off and waited for Teresa to return. As light began to fade from the sky outside the windows, he realized she must be working at the restaurant.

After a quick walk through the darkening streets, Landry

pushed his way through the door of Sagun's Restaurant and scanned the dining room. Teresa was laying a plate of food on the small table where Chief Mortland sat, smiling up at her.

Landry strode across the room. "Teresa!"

Her brown eyes seemed calm, even remote.

Mortland showed his teeth. "Well, if it ain't poor Landry, and by poor, I mean stone broke." Mortland smiled up at Teresa. "Maybe you better think about moving in with a man of means, little lady." Mortland reached into his pocket and pulled out a sheaf of bills and ruffled through them. "Seems like I have enough here to keep a lady in proper fashion."

"You ain't the only one with some money," Landry said.

Mortland guffawed. "Couldn't be you. You lost it all on a damn-fool bet is what I heard."

Landry pulled his wallet out and showed the bills. "Seems I have some friends. Come on, Teresa, you don't have to work here anymore."

"No, Hank. I do."

"You mean you're letting him buy you?"

"No. I not for sale. Not to Chief Mortland and not to you. Not to anyone. Both of you . . . leave me alone!" Tears began to slip down her cheeks and she ran into the kitchen.

Landry turned on his heel and headed back to the ship.

After quarters the next morning, Doctor Laster held sick call. Aside from a few cases of tuberculosis, malaria, dengue, and other tropical fevers, he hadn't encountered many interesting cases during his year aboard. He sighed as he thought of his most frequent problems: venereal disease and malingerers trying to avoid a day's work.

Laster's two patients that day had the "Asiatic foot crud," a common fungus infection that thrived in the heat and humidity. Laster painted the affected areas with a purple solution of gentian violet. "Come back each morning for repeat applications and wear 'go-aheads' for a week."

After he had dismissed his customers, Laster decided it was time to buy a pair of "go-aheads" for his own use. He found the

Filipino shoemaker on the *O'Leary*'s fantail. The little man whipped out two wooden soles, and cut tops from a piece of canvas. He stretched the canvas over Laster's left foot and hammered a fierce-looking steel tack home to hold one side in place.

"Jesus! Watch that hammer!"

"My name's pronounced Hey-zoos," the shoemaker said.

"Just don't stick one of those nails in my foot."

"I never hurt no one. Why worry? Doctor fix if I miss."

"He is the doctor," said a nearby electrician's mate.

"Don't make him nervous," Laster said.

"Why I be nervous?" the shoemaker said. "Not my foot."

His new purchase under his arm, Laster headed forward toward his stateroom. Laster was stopped by the executive officer, whose long upper lip quivered with anger. "Laster, what are you doing? I took a count at quarters this morning and half the crew has purple feet and 'go-aheads.'"

"Half? I know I'm not treating that many." Laster thought for a few seconds. "Of course! Counterfeet!"

"What?" Beringer's horse-like face looked puzzled.

"Counterfeit feet. The men are using grape juice or paint."

Beringer glowered. "Hereafter, issue chits to all the men with genuine infections. I won't tolerate so many men looking unmilitary."

As the executive officer walked away, Laster hoped Beringer would contract a terminal case of the foot crud.

In his room, Laster decided to try out his new footwear. He was clunking around the deck when Bull Durham walked in.

"Hi, Doc. New 'go-aheads'? Try backing up."

Laster tried, but his foot slid back and the wooden sole gouged the sensitive bottom of his foot. Laster yelped and took a skidding fall to the deck. "You bastard! Now I know why they're called 'go-aheads!'"

Durham hoisted a pile of books off a chair and sat down. "What the hell are you doing reading Mahan's books on seapower?"

Laster adjusted his thick glasses. "I was a history major in college and studied the Napoleonic Wars. Besides, I need something to keep my mind off being seasick."

"I guess we all have our frustrations," Durham said. "I was

going to be a pilot. I was booted out of flight school when they caught me in the sack with an instructor's wife. Now there was a lady who could do some stunts."

"Not flying still bothers you?"

"Yeah, I keep thinking I should be flying instead of sitting on this rusty old bucket."

"Why are you here today? What about that bruise on your jaw?"

"I got belted by a lady, when my millions ran out."

"Millions?"

"Just a line I was conning her with. Boy, she had the biggest pair I've ever seen. I could put one in each ear."

"How big?"

Durham held up both his hands to demonstrate. "And that was only one."

"Amazing! But remember they're mostly fat. The bigger they are, the farther they fall. Why are you here? Looking for sympathy?"

"For one thing, I'd like some sleeping pills."

"Sleeping pills?"

"Yeah, I 've been worrying about the war coming. This old bucket leaks enough without the Japs putting holes in her rusty hull. Even with the overhaul, we'll still have problems."

"Bull, I never thought you'd be one to worry."

"Why do you think I'm trying to get in all the living I can? Hell, I've been having nightmares. I dreamed I was a Japanese pilot in a ready room being briefed to attack our destroyers. As they went over our air defenses, the pilots began to laugh. At the end of the briefing, we were rolling in the aisles with a mixture of laughter and anticipation. Thank God I woke up before I had to sink you."

Laster remembered how defenseless they were. "I'd laugh too, if I were a Jap pilot."

Durham squirmed in his chair and looked sheepish. "Doc . . . I'm afraid I have another problem . . . something personal . . . kind of a steady drip."

"Let's take a look," Laster said.

Durham dropped his pants.

"Looks like the clap," said Laster.

"Can't be," said Durham. "I always use protection . . . except a couple of nights ago with Shirley."

"Bingo," said Laster. "Normal incubation is two to eight days. A parting gift for you."

"Boy, she really screwed me."

"Literally or figuratively?" Laster looked at Durham again and was puzzled. "Bull, your equipment is nothing exceptional. I thought you had something special to please the ladies with."

"Size is unimportant, Doc."

"What is?"

"There you go again. Why are you interested?"

"Professional reasons, I assure you. I hope to do some scientific research and publish a book."

"On sex?"

"Yes. It's a field which has never been investigated properly. I hope to do that someday."

"You mean like in a laboratory?"

"That's what I had proposed to do . . ."

"Had proposed?"

"I asked to be allowed to do some research as part of the obstetrical training programs I applied for. They must have thought I was strange, because nobody accepted me . . . and here I am."

"Sorry, but I won't tell you any of my secrets," Durham said. "Can't let the competition catch up."

"I knew you'd say that," Laster said. "I should refuse to treat you, but that would be unethical. The treatment will cure your problem, but you'll have to take the standard sanitary precautions. Any questions?"

"Is there any way we can keep it unofficial?"

"No. Someone finds out and we'll both be in big trouble. Medical officers have ruined their careers making that mistake. I've got to enter it in your record and tell the exec."

"Okay, do what you have to do. If the war starts, that kind of a black mark won't matter anymore. I'll either be dead or a hero."

"Or both."

Late Saturday afternoon, after a long day working on the number one gun, Chief Hanlon paced the packed dirt outside the yard entrance. After a frustrating wait for a taxi, a horse-drawn carriage known as a "calesa" appeared. Hanlon flagged the driver and promised to make it worth his while for the 10-mile trip to Manila. The ride was bumpy, dusty, and backbreaking.

As the horse churned up clouds of swirling dust, memories danced through Hanlon's mind—images of eleven years in the Far East. Arrival on the "China Station" in 1930. Three years on a gunboat patrolling the Yangtze River. Finding a permanent home aboard the *O'Leary*. Seeing a slender, dark-haired Maria for the first time as she worked in a small Filipino cafe. The honesty and simplicity in her face. Her graceful swaying walk in her dresses of delicate woven fiber. The months before he summoned the courage to ask her for a date. A long shy courtship filled with the joy of a growing love. Anger and despair that her religion would never let her marry a divorced man. Deciding to live together as if married. The joy of their love-making. The happiness of a life together despite the absence of a hoped-for child.

The years have gone so fast, he thought, as the "calesa" ended its two-hour trip. Stiff and weary, Hanlon opened the door to his apartment, but the sight of Maria's dancing eyes helped to erase the worst of his aches. The woman in his arms was no longer the slender girl he had met seven years ago but a full-figured woman of twenty-seven. The memories of six years of love-making swirled through his mind.

"I'm surprised you'd take a Saturday night off from the restaurant," he said.

She waved a graceful hand. "Some things are more important than business. Go change while I finish dinner."

"Can I help?"

"Not tonight. This is special."

Hanlon smiled. If Maria said it was special, it would be. Hanlon had long since discovered she was a determined lady. After he met her, she had announced she would learn to speak English properly. And she had. When no children had arrived, she had gone back to work at Sagun's Restaurant and worked her way into a partnership. Hanlon shook his head. Maria was different from most of the Filipino girls who lived with American military men.

In the bedroom, Hanlon took off his uniform and donned his usual attire: shorts, a pair of "go-aheads," and a light shirt known as a "barong." Before he returned to Maria, he gazed at the familiar room with the gossamer mosquito net hanging over the bed and the crucifix on the wall. He remembered the long battle with Maria over the crucifix. She had won when she convinced him that it represented their Lord himself rather than the church that denied them the sanctity of marriage. Hanlon sighed as he wondered how many more times he would share their bed before the war came.

When he walked out of the bedroom, Maria led him to his favorite chair, handed him a bottle of San Miguel beer, and moved behind him. Gently, she reached forward, loosened his shirt, and began a slow massage of his neck and shoulders. "You're so tense," she said. Maria must have sensed his mood because she said no more. Hanlon missed her usual pleasant gossip of the neighborhood. As she reached forward to massage his temples, her full breasts brushed against the back of his head. With a searing pang of realization, Hanlon tried to come to grips with the fact that this night might be their last. He reached back and patted her thigh gently.

"Dinner should be ready," she said.

The Tagalog-style baked chicken, vegetables, and fruit were perfectly prepared. After they finished clearing the table, they walked the tree-lined streets of the middle-class neighborhood. Hanlon knew most of the Filipino families sitting in front of their doors, and he exchanged greetings in Tagalog and English. As they strolled, Hanlon realized that he felt a permanent part of this community. When he retired from the Navy, he would be content to spend the rest of his life with Maria.

"Dominoes tonight, Chief?" yelled a Filipino friend from his porch.

"Not tonight. Another time, I'll be ready to beat you."

As darkness fell, they returned to their apartment and prepared for bed. Still, Hanlon's mind dwelt on the oncoming war. The passion of their love-making was restrained.

"Byron, what's bothering you? Is it the war?"

"Maria, I don't want to worry you, but it could start soon. The captain said we should prepare for the worst. We have to talk about your safety because any night could be my last."

"I'll be safe. My friends will take care of me."

"Someone's bound to tell the Japanese about me. I think you should go back to Pampanga to live with your parents."

She sighed. "The 'barrio' will seem boring after Manila."

"I know, but you'll be safe. After the war I'll come get you."

"I guess you're right, Byron. But I hate to give up the restaurant."

"You can start over again after the war."

She snuggled closer to him. "I've become good friends with Teresa. She doesn't get along with her mother so maybe she would like to go to the country with me."

"Did Landry and Teresa break up the other night?"

"It looks that way, but she really loves him. I think they'll get back together."

"What's their problem?" Hanlon asked.

"You men can be so stupid."

"There must be something else."

"There is. She's going to have his baby."

"Does he know that?"

"No."

"Why doesn't she tell him?" Hanlon asked.

"He's so independent. She doesn't want him to feel trapped. She wants to be sure he loves her."

"Sometimes you women ask too much."

"That's not too much."

"You're right. Should I say something to Landry?"

"Not now. They should have a chance to work it out themselves. It will be better that way."

"You'd better tell her to hurry up since the Japs could start something any day now." Hanlon felt a stab of regret as he thought of Teresa's pregnancy. "It would be nice if you two went to the country together since we've never been able to have a child."

She clung to him even more tightly, and he felt her warm tears against his chest. Hanlon stared up at the crucifix and wondered why God sent children to those who didn't want them while denying them to someone like Maria.

An hour later Hanlon left their bed and looked through a small desk. He pulled out his checkbook from a local bank. "What's the date today?" he asked.

"December sixth."

"This check is for all my savings," he said. "Monday, cash it, and hide the pesos until you're ready to leave."

The finality of his words seemed to burst an emotional dam inside Maria, and she cried for over an hour before lapsing into a troubled sleep in Hanlon's arms. Before dawn she woke him, and they made love gently and slowly.

When the first gray light of dawn filtered through the mosquito netting, Hanlon rose and dressed. Maria watched him from the bed, her eyes misty. When he was ready, Hanlon bent over and kissed her softly one last time before he walked out of the room and through the front door.

Fraser stood in the shade of the quarterdeck awning and watched Hanlon walk down the pier. When the chief boarded the destroyer, Fraser asked, "Everything all right, Chief?"

"Not if the Japs are coming."

"Let's just hope they aren't," Fraser said. "I've been ordered up to Clark Field for a briefing. The captain wants me to find out how we can work with the Army fliers."

Hanlon's square face was grim. "We'll sure as hell need them if we want to stay around here."

"And you're hoping to stay?"

"Yes, sir. I'll never leave here if I have a choice."

"You're never going back to the States? Why not?"

"Maria for one thing. This is her home, and now I feel like it's my home. But I guess there's more to it than that. I got a bellyful of the way civilians treated enlisted folks back home—like we're some kind of dirt. Hell of a thing. Comes a war, we're gonna be shot at and even killed, so the fat cats back home can stay safe. But strangers weren't the worst of it. My brother-in-law kept rubbing his success in my wife's face. She finally divorced me for someone who was making some money."

"And things are different for you out here?"

"Yes, sir. Folks are so poor here, I'm the rich man. I don't care for that either, but it's easier to take."

Fraser paused and thought what a competent man Hanlon was. He couldn't fathom how anyone could ever look down at Hanlon.

"Anything we need to talk over before I leave?" Fraser asked.

"I guess everything's under control. We're finding a lot of bad wiring on number one. Be a lot easier if we could rip the whole thing apart."

"But that's not what the captain wants."

Hanlon shrugged his heavy shoulders. "He's the captain."

"Chief, we got bad news in the latest mail. Those idiots back in Bu Ord won't give us two more machine guns like we asked. Too much topside weight, they say."

Hanlon shook his head. "No problem to strike 'em below in heavy weather."

"Logic won't get us the guns."

"Figured there might be a problem, Mr. Fraser. I went over to the ordnance shop and talked to a chief I know. He's going to give us the pieces we need to add to the spare parts we have so we can make up another gun. He might even be able to come up with another gun on the sly." Hanlon smiled. "Course, I had to promise him a couple of Maria's chicken dinners."

Fraser laughed for several seconds. "I wonder what those bureaucrats in Washington would say if they knew Maria's cooking overcame their veto."

"They wouldn't complain if they tried one of her dinners."

"Anything else we need to talk about?" asked Fraser.

"I'd like to move Shifflet to the amidships 4-inch guns. I'd like to have him where he can get behind one of the machine guns in a hurry."

"As long as there's still a good man in charge of number one."

"I'll make sure of that," Hanlon said.

When Fraser left the chief and headed for his room, he found himself envying Hanlon's relationship with Maria. Suddenly his mind was filled with images of Ilsa, walking through the water at the beach, dancing in his arms, and kissing him in the elevator. Fraser packed his bag, wishing he were heading south to Java rather than north to Clark Field.

The dusty ride on the Army bus gave Fraser a look at the interior of Luzon, one of the largest of the thousands of islands that made up the Philippines. Clark Field was 65 miles north of Manila on a large central plain, with the Zambales Mountains to the east. The solitary volcanic cone of Mount Arayat thrust over 3,000 feet skyward only 15 miles west of the airfield. Fraser realized that the peak would make it easy for any Japanese planes to find Clark Field.

After unpacking in his BOQ room at the base, Fraser headed for the officers' club. The dark but well-appointed bar was almost deserted. He took a stool at the polished teak bar, placed his order, and surveyed the room. A pilot sitting alone at a nearby table looked familiar. Then he realized it was Joe Costanzo, the all-American West Point linebacker.

"Excuse me, I'm Ross Fraser, Navy '38. I believe you knocked the hell out of me once in the '35 game."

"Hey, that was a good one for us, twenty-eight to six."

"Don't remind me," said Fraser.

The thickset pilot smiled apologetically. "Sorry, but I don't seem to remember you."

"Not surprising. I was only a sub that year. Banged up my knee early the next year and that was that."

"We all have to give up football sooner or later," Costanzo said wistfully. "Gonna be a different game now. One 120-pound Jap in a Zero could wipe out the whole Notre Dame team."

"Or my ship," Fraser said. "I'm up here to find out how to get some air support. You guys are our only air cover."

"Hell, I just got here, but I hope you'll be more impressed than I am," the pilot said.

"How so?"

"No protective revetments have been built to protect our planes from air attack," Costanzo said. "The planes are all bunched together to prevent sabotage."

"Sabotage? There aren't any Japs around here."

"Yeah, but the Army is paranoid about sabotage. Before I left Hawaii last week, we got a war warning. Protection against sabotage was the only real precaution they took."

"You're kidding?"

"No." Costanzo's voice took on an angry note. "The aircraft were all parked in neat rows to minimize the number of guards. Makes a beautiful target for an air attack. Not only that, all the ammunition was locked up. Hawaii is ripe for the picking."

Fraser hoped the Japanese wouldn't take advantage of Hawaii's vulnerability.

"The situation isn't much better here," said the pilot. "We're a damned long way from being ready to fight."

"But you've got those new B-17s and P-40s."

"The pilots and crews aren't comfortable with them, yet. And we don't have enough tools, spare parts, or replacement engines."

Fraser felt compelled to bring up something positive. "I hear the P-40 is a hot airplane."

"That's what the Army wants you and the pilots to think. Good for morale, I suppose. Truth is, the P-40 can't match the Jap Zero."

"How do you know?"

"Chennault's Flying Tigers have been using the P-40 in China. They found the Zero is a much better dog-fighter. Climbs and turns better. Only way to stay alive in a P-40 is to attack out of a dive or fight in pairs and larger groups, so we can protect each other."

"You must be working like hell to adjust your tactics."

"Nope, the information has been ignored and filed away in Washington. Military politics. They don't care for Chennault back there. I only found out about all this on the sly from a classmate. A lot of pilots are going to find out the truth the hard way."

Fraser looked around the nearly empty bar. "A lot of your buddies must be working."

Costanzo snorted. "Guess again. There's a big party down in Manila for our commanding general. Almost everyone is down there. The B-17s stationed here were ordered to move south to Mindanao two weeks ago so they'd be out of range of the Jap planes on Formosa. Supposedly, their departure was stalled so everyone could stay around for this party."

"Amazing," Fraser said.

Costanzo took a long pull from his drink. "I hope you're not expecting the B-17s to stop the Jap Navy."

"They'd better. The Asiatic Fleet doesn't have enough ships to do the job."

Costanzo laughed derisively. "The bomber boys expect to cruise over at 20,000 feet and sink the Jap Navy in one pass. Hell, they'd have trouble hitting a football field from that altitude."

"Christ!" Fraser said. "It must take over a minute for a bomb to fall from that height. A ship can evade easily."

"Yup. Bet the bomber boys are going to rip up a lot of ocean." Costanzo drained the last of his drink. "Maybe I'll see you tomorrow. My P-40 has big number '62' on its sides. It reminds me of my academy days when I was naive enough to think the Army knew what it was doing."

Fraser laughed and fingered the rib that had been cracked by Costanzo's helmet. "I remember that number all too well. Just don't run over me like you did in '35."

Fraser enjoyed a quiet dinner by himself, but he kept thinking back to the disturbing information that Costanzo had revealed. The Asiatic Fleet needed the Army Air Force for air defense. How long would their air support last if the situation was as bad as Costanzo painted it?

Fraser returned to his room and tried to sleep but found it difficult. He finally drifted into a troubled sleep. Loud voices and slamming doors dragged him back to consciousness. He poked his head out of his room and stopped an officer who was running down the corridor, hoisting his trousers as he ran.

"It's four in the morning! What the hell is going on?"

The pilot's eyes were wide. "The Japs have bombed Pearl Harbor!"

CHAPTER EIGHT

"Doc! Wake up!"

Laster rolled over and lifted his head. Bull Durham's head poked in the doorway. Laster buried his face in the soft pillow. "Mmmfff. No such thing as an emergency case of V. D."

"Doc, the war! It's started!"

"Here?"

"Not yet."

"Then I'll worry about it in the morning."

"The captain's holding a meeting in the wardroom."

"I only take care of dying people at this hour."

"If they're dying, why bother?" Durham asked.

"Good point. Now I won't get up anymore. Where'd the Japs hit?"

"Pearl Harbor," Durham said.

"I'll be right there."

"I thought you weren't getting up."

"I want to see Beringer's face."

After he took his seat at the foot of the green-covered wardroom table, Laster buttoned his shirt. The other officers straggled in, some trailing shoelaces across the deck. Both of Chuck Steiner's shoes were brown, but from different pairs. Dazed, unfocused eyes looked out of unshaven faces. Laster glanced at his watch; it was 0330.

At the head of the table, the captain seemed totally alert. His mouth was a narrow line. "The yard copied an uncoded signal a half-hour ago. He looked down at the piece of paper. "'Air Raid on Pearl Harbor. This is no drill.'"

"Pearl!" Beringer fumbled with a pack of cigarettes. "It must be a prank."

Laster couldn't resist a backhanded dig at Beringer. "I never would have predicted a night attack."

Meredith ran a shaking hand through his curly hair. "It's Sunday morning there."

"Sunday?" said Laster.

Meredith nodded. "By the sun, we're five hours behind Hawaii, but the International Date Line puts us a calendar day ahead."

"Sunday morning," mused Laster. "A perfect time."

A radioman knocked, ran in, and handed a message to the captain. Laster stopped breathing while the captain read the message.

Arkwright looked up, his pale eyes hard. "No doubt, now. This is from Admiral Hart to the Asiatic Fleet. 'Japan started hostilities. Govern yourselves accordingly. Execute War Plan 46.'"

Beringer emitted a strangled cough as he blew out cigarette smoke. "Impossible. I don't believe it. The Japanese would never dare . . ."

"Believe it," Arkwright said. "Gentlemen, you can be sure that the yard and the ships here will be high on the list of Jap targets. Jack, how soon can we move?"

The engineering officer frowned. "Captain, the steam lines are the problem. We should be able to hook up the number one boiler and the starboard engine within twenty-four hours."

"Let me know what you need. Along with the antiaircraft weapons, the engineering plant is our top priority. Bull, what about the gunnery department?"

"We're ready, Captain. Ross briefed me before he left. The .50-caliber machine guns and the old 3-inch are in good shape."

Arkwright said, "Be ready to shoot by first light."

"G. Q. for the whole ship?" Meredith asked.

The captain shook his head. "Not until we know they're coming. We can't waste time standing around. I want hoses and damage control equipment rigged, and as much watertight integrity as possible. But the important thing is to get the ship ready to move. Any questions? Let's go."

Two hours later, as Laster finished counting scalpel blades, he was satisfied that there were no shortages of medical supplies. But he wasn't reassured. There was only one corpsman aboard to assist him, and their facilities and equipment were limited.

Laster wasn't sleepy, so he climbed the ladders to the bridge and joined the captain on the starboard wing. At 0600 the first flush of dawn began to appear over Manila. Lookouts and antiaircraft crews manned their stations and scanned the sky.

"I feel like we're trapped here in the yard," Laster said.

"You and everyone else," the captain said. "Our best defense is open water and a healthy engineering plant."

Dawn changed to full daylight and nothing happened. An hour later Laster said, "Where are the Japs?"

"Hard to believe they're not here," the captain said.

Durham leaned over the rail of the fire control platform. "Captain, the extra .50-caliber machine gun is now mounted and ready to go. That gives us a 50 percent boost in firepower."

Laster knew the .50 caliber machine guns were almost useless. One hundred and fifty percent of nothing is still nothing, Laster said to himself.

Sixty-five miles north of the *O'Leary*, at Clark Field, Ross Fraser wondered if he were doing the right thing by staying there. He had packed his bag and hustled over to the motor pool before dawn, only to find the facility totally disorganized. The first bus for Manila wasn't due to depart for hours, if then. When he stopped to think the situation through, he realized he hadn't obtained any information about how to work with the Army Air Force. He knew the *O'Leary* couldn't move for at least twenty-four hours. After some thought, he had decided to remain at Clark to see if he could complete his assignment.

Fraser finally tracked down the officer who had been scheduled to run the briefing.

The harried major tossed his clipboard to his desk. "Hell, Lieutenant, we've got a war on our hands this morning. Maybe I can find someone to give you a quick run-through this afternoon. Take a look through some of these publications."

Fraser eyed the stack of thick manuals. "Thanks."

"Don't give up," the major said. "Once we send our B-17s to kick the hell out of the Japs, maybe I can help."

Fraser settled down in a corner of the large office to find out as much as he could about the Army Air Force's equipment and procedures. As he leafed through a manual, a heated voice rose above the hubbub.

"You mean we don't have permission to attack?" a colonel shouted. "Let us know as soon as you can." He slammed the phone down. "General Brereton has gone to MacArthur's headquarters to try to get permission to bomb Formosa."

There were murmurs of disgust and frustration as the angry aviators tried to figure out what was going on in Manila and why they weren't allowed to attack the Japanese.

The pre-dawn gray yielded to the sun. Fraser continued his reading as the anger of the pilots around him mounted. Suddenly, the silence was broken by the wail of an air raid siren and shouts from men manning phones in the office.

"The radar station on the coast says Jap planes are on the way! Let's get everything airborne!"

The pilots and aircrews ran for their aircraft. High-powered aircraft engines whined, coughed, sputtered, and roared to life. Lumbering B-17s turned for the end of the runway like a herd of large geese waddling across the grass. One by one, the huge four-engined aircraft rolled down the grass runway, engines bellowing, and climbed slowly into the morning light. Some of the bombers were so new they were unpainted; their gleaming aluminum surfaces reflected shafts of sunlight as they receded into the distance. A covey of aggressive-looking P-40 fighters scrambled into the air and followed the bombers as an escort.

Fraser was impressed as he watched plane after plane climb into the morning sky. "Those P-40s are mean-looking."

"Yeah," said the Army officer standing next to him. "Not like the Navy's stubby Wildcat fighters. Wait'll we tear the hell out of those Jap Zeros."

The men on the ground at Clark waited for the expected air raid, but nothing happened. Word came that outposts to the north had been hit. The bombers were left aloft, but most of the P-40s returned to Clark. Joe Costanzo's "62" slid in for a smooth landing and Fraser envied the pilot's obvious skill.

Fraser returned to his work and made notes on the ranges and capabilities of the Army's aircraft, as well as their communications frequencies and procedures.

Several hours after the false alarm, Fraser heard the multi-engined drone of the B-17s as they straggled back to base. The big bombers landed, taxied, and parked in neat rows in front of their hangars, where their service crews swarmed over them and began pumping them full of high-octane aviation fuel.

Fraser went back to work; soon there was a bustle of activity.

"We finally got permission to hit the Japs," one of the pilots said. "Now we'll have those bastards on the run!"

"Not quite yet," another said. "They've ordered us to send a recon flight to Formosa first."

"Why?"

"Nobody has any idea what to bomb up there."

"You're kidding," a lieutenant said. "Jap scout planes have been flying over the Philippines for almost a year."

"No big deal," a heavyset flyer said. "This'll give us time for lunch. No sense fighting on an empty stomach."

Apparently, the rest of those at Clark Field felt the same way because almost everyone adjourned for the noon meal. The remaining P-40s landed, and the pilots joined their colleagues for lunch. Fraser was hungry, too. The energy from two pre-dawn doughnuts had long since been consumed.

A pilot turned to Fraser at the lunch table. "How long does the Navy think the war will last?"

"Hard to tell. The Navy's short on ships out here."

"No matter. We'll sink the Jap Navy for you."

"Gonna be a piece of cake," another pilot said. "Hell, those Japs can't fly worth a damn."

Finished with his beef stew, Fraser glanced at his watch. It was past noon. No one seemed in any hurry, so he continued discussing the situation with a group of pilots. B-17 engines coughed to life, interrupting their conversation.

"Sounds like the recon flight is leaving. Took a while to get the cameras installed," said one of the Army pilots.

"Had to fly 'em up here," said another. "If things go right, we should have the results in time for an attack at dusk. Hey, listen to the radio!"

Station KMZH in Manila announced a special bulletin: Clark Field was reported under attack. The announcer's voice rose with excitement through the static.

Hoots of laughter and scorn erupted from the tables. "What the hell does he know?" a major said.

One of the officers standing in the doorway called to Fraser, "Hey, Lieutenant, is the Navy sending us some reinforcements?"

"You must be dreaming," Fraser said.

"That's the Japs up there!" shouted a voice outside.

The air raid sirens began their gut-chilling whine, and the few obsolete antiaircraft guns dug in around the field banged away. Fraser joined the stampede for the door. The three B-17 reconnaissance planes were trundling toward the runway. P-40 pilots sprinted for their planes where the frantic ground crews started the engines. But the first flight of twenty-seven Japanese bombers high overhead had already released their deadly cargo. Bombs caught the three bombers while they were still on the runway; their full gas tanks blossomed into huge balls of fire. Of the seven P-40s that got rolling, only three made it into the air. The others disintegrated from direct hits or caught their wheels in bomb craters in the runway.

One of the last P-40's to roll was Joe Costanzo's, its gold "62" glinting in the sun. The P-40, engine snarling, hurtled down the runway. As it neared flying speed a bomb exploded in its path and flipped the speeding aircraft over like a child's toy. It cartwheeled, shedding chunks of metal as it turned. After a final bounce it skidded to a halt and erupted in flames. Fraser groaned, his gut pulling into a tight knot. Jesus, he thought. Costanzo was so tough, so smart, our whole football team couldn't hold him. The damn Japs just exterminated him like he was a bug.

More bombs rained down and shook Fraser, nearly knocking him off his feet. He bolted for one of the few slit trenches and slid into an empty space. The ground heaved from the concussion of the exploding bombs. Pieces of earth from the side of the trench showered down. Red dust and smoke swirled over the edges of the trench, choking Fraser's lungs.

"Goddamn," muttered the man next to Fraser, "I'm a supply sergeant. I ain't used to this."

Fraser coughed. "You're not the only one."

It didn't take long for Fraser to decide that war ashore was not what he wanted. The protective trench was a fixed target. At least the *O'Leary* could maneuver at 30 knots to avoid being hit—if her engineering plant worked. Fraser missed the reassuring solidity of the destroyer's steel decks.

The relentless rain of bombs continued as several formations of bombers hammered Clark Field. When the pounding finally ended, Fraser dragged himself out of the trench. Other figures emerged from the scanty cover available. Smoke from burning aircraft swirled across the field. Despite the bombing, the planes, including the B-17s on the flight line, were still intact.

"Look out! Here come Jap fighters!" shouted a soldier.

Fraser swung around and spotted a stream of diving Japanese Zeros. Their top surfaces were greenish-blue; their bellies, buff. Rising sun insignia glinted blood red in the midday sun. The first strafer winked orange flashes and sent Fraser sprinting for his trench. Machine gun bullets whined and ricocheted by. Men who had just emerged from cover were caught in the open and the machine guns of the strafing fighters scythed them down.

Back in his trench, Fraser tried to burrow into the dirt. Zeros rocketed overhead, fourteen-cylinder radial engines snarling, machine guns stuttering, 20-millimeter cannons wham-whaming.

Crumpling explosions from the fuel tanks of parked aircraft shook the trench. Fraser coughed dust and smoke from his lungs and prayed for the ordeal to end. Enemy strafers kept coming in a murderous stream, like a swarm of angry bees defending their hive. Finally, the attack slowed, and the scores of enemy strafers droned away. Fraser crawled out of the trench and blinked the smoke out of his watering eyes.

"Damn!"

The B-17s were funeral pyres. Rows of parked P-40s and medium bombers were twisted, fire-blackened skeletons. Dead and wounded men were everywhere. Injured men screamed and groaned. Some bodies lay in contorted positions impossible in life. Assorted body parts littered the ground. A perfect hand and arm lay nearby; one finger twitched.

A pall of smoke and dust hung over the field, drifting slowly downwind. The oil and fuel dumps burned furiously, adding ugly black smoke. The air stank of explosives and burning oil. Most of the buildings and hangars were demolished.

"We won't get any air cover from these guys," muttered Fraser, as he turned to help the wounded. Ambulances departed with their sirens screaming. More help arrived as ambulances and trucks from nearby Fort Stotsenburg rolled onto the scene. One young driver lost his lunch on the fender of his vehicle.

"Don't worry, son, I don't feel so hot either," a grizzled sergeant said.

Fraser was relieved to see others were sickened by the scene. He came very close to losing his beef stew several times as he helped during that long afternoon. Only his fierce desire to protect the Navy's reputation made him swallow the bile rising in his throat.

Late that afternoon, Fraser heard an officer shouting instructions to a truck driver to take his load of wounded to Manila because the local hospital was full.

Fraser flagged the truck down. "Can I hitch a ride?"

"Hop in," the pale corporal said. "I may need help."

Fraser jumped in the front seat and slammed the door. The

driver eased the clutch out slowly, but the truck bucked as it moved off. There were moans and muffled screams from the cargo area.

"Got some shot-up guys back there," the driver said. "Hope the roads are in good shape."

The trip seemed endless as they lumbered along roads clogged with military traffic. Fraser winced with every bump and pothole. After one bone-shaking jolt, there was a desperate pounding on the back of the cab of the truck, but it died away. Fraser and the driver exchanged guilty looks, but Fraser knew there was nothing they could do.

As they passed rice paddies and villages in the twilight, Fraser thought about what he had witnessed. Clark Field should never have been caught by surprise. What had happened? But that hadn't been the only problem. He had heard men from the antiaircraft crews cursing the many shells that had failed to explode. Fraser wondered who was responsible for sending men to die with obsolete weapons and ammunition that didn't work.

Outside Manila, they hit another traffic jam, so it was well after dark when they arrived at Sternberg General Hospital. Fraser's trip from Manila to Cavite was not much easier. It was almost midnight when Marine guards halted Fraser's cab at the gate of the Navy Yard.

"Sorry, sir. No civilian vehicles." One guard looked disdainfully at Fraser as he regarded the officer's white uniform, which was caked with dirt, grime, and blood.

"Anything happen here today?" Fraser asked.

"No, sir. But we saw the smoke from attacks on the Army airfields near here."

As Fraser walked toward the piers, he felt he had returned to another world. Which was the real one: the calm, clean, orderly streets of the yard; or the blasted, smoking, bloodstained field at Clark? The yard looked so normal that he wondered if his day had been some kind of nightmare. He rounded the corner of a yard building and saw the *O'Leary* and the other ships floating untouched at their berths. As Fraser walked down the pier, he saw a furry shape clinging to the number two line below the rat guard. Fraser shuddered, trotted up the brow, and made his way to the captain's cabin.

"Come in," Arkwright called in response to Fraser's knock. "Ross! I was beginning to wonder if we'd ever see you again. We've heard rumors of disaster at Clark. From the way you look, they must be true."

"They're true all right."

"That bad?"

"Worse." Fraser described the events at Clark Field.

Arkwright frowned. "You've confirmed what I heard at Admiral Hart's headquarters this evening. I went there to find out what happened at Pearl."

"I hope they made out better than Clark Field."

"Afraid not. Most of our Pacific Fleet battleships were sunk or crippled today."

"We've been dispersed for months," Fraser said. "What were they all doing in port at the same time?"

"I don't know," the captain said.

Fraser thought of the inevitable air attack that would be coming their way. "Sir, will we be able to move tomorrow?"

"That's my goal. Jack said we're on schedule."

"Only good thing I've heard all day," Fraser said.

Arkwright's face was grim. "Things aren't so simple. Fleet headquarters has ordered us to go ahead with our overhaul at full speed."

Fraser snapped back in his chair. "That's crazy! The Japs will fly down here and pound us."

"They're going to catch the *Ford*, too. She's been ordered into drydock the day after tomorrow."

"I can't believe this," Fraser said. "They must be getting advice from Army headquarters."

Arkwright nodded. "I agree with your sentiments. So we're going to keep putting machinery and equipment back together as fast as possible."

"But the yard people will realize what we're doing," Fraser said.

The captain picked up his partially completed wooden model of the *O'Leary* and held it in his stubby hands for a few seconds. "Hopefully, the yard won't catch on for a while. The yard is supposed to work at top speed on the *Peary* and *Pillsbury* because they're well along with their overhauls. We won't see many yard workers for over a week. This place should be rubble by then."

Fraser hoped Arkwright's decision would save them from destruction in the yard. But he realized escape would be no guarantee of safety. Without air support, how long could they survive? The horror of the day surged back into his mind. Suddenly he began to tremble and grabbed the arms of his chair.

"You all right?"

A day's worth of emotions welled up in Fraser. "No, sir. I feel like hell. I know . . . because that's where I've been today. I . . . I never want to see anything like that again. Lord . . . maybe I'm in the wrong business."

The lines on Arkwright's face softened. "I'd say this is a normal reaction. What you saw today would shake any man. These feelings should ease."

A surge of anger rose in Fraser. "You weren't there. Men were blown to pieces. The blood! My God! The blood was the least of it."

Arkwright shifted in his chair. "Give yourself a chance. Get through today, and tomorrow may be easier."

"You don't know. You've never seen anything like that!"

"No, I haven't." There was a long pause as the captain stared at the picture on his desk. He locked his pale eyes with Fraser's. "But I've seen worse. Just be thankful that it wasn't your family you saw dying today." Arkwright paused for a half-minute. "I've seen blood all right—the blood of my wife and children. My wife went through the windshield of our car. My son was dead of a broken neck. My little girl bled to death in my arms."

Fraser recoiled against the back of his chair. The captain's words had been flat, even dull. But the lines in his face had deepened. Arkwright's icy blue eyes had been a momentary window into a private hell even worse than what Fraser had witnessed. The scar on the captain's forehead reddened and pulsed with a life of its own.

Fraser groped for words but none would come.

The captain shifted his gaze to the picture and then to the holstered .45 automatic at the end of his bookshelf. "And thank your God that what you saw today wasn't your fault."

"But how . . ."

"It was after a party. I had too much to drink. My wife wanted to drive, but I was too damn proud. Didn't want my friends to think I couldn't hold my liquor. Just too goddamn proud."

"I didn't know," Fraser said.

Arkwright's eyes bored into his. "Nobody else does. I'd rather you didn't discuss my history with anyone. Maybe Doc can give you something to sleep tonight. You'll survive."

"Yes, sir. I'll try."

Just after dawn on the second day of the war, T. T. Simpson rubbed a bandaged hand across his itching nose as the engineering officer emerged from the airlock in the forward fireroom.

"How'd the captain take the bad news?" Simpson asked Meredith.

The officer's lined face smiled briefly. "First, I tried to cheer him up by telling him you'd snuck out of the hospital. He wanted to know if they'll come looking for you."

"Don't think they'll miss me," Simpson said. "Lot of casualties were just coming in. Tell me, was the captain pissed about us needing another day before we can move?"

"He wasn't happy," Meredith said. "When I told him we could steam about thirty minutes before blowing the main steam line, he agreed to let us do the job right."

"Question is—will the Japs give us another day?" Simpson tried to mop his forehead with the back of a forearm. "Goddam bandages! We'll have to keep busting ass if we want to move by tomorrow."

Meredith looked around the fireroom. "Some of the men are starting to drag."

Simpson nodded. "Sir, with the hatches shut, the heat's pretty bad. We worked right through last night, and you got 'em up at four in the morning the night before."

Meredith massaged his temples with thin fingers. "If I can get some extra men down here, will it help?"

Simpson was silent for many seconds before he could forget his pride. "Dammit, Mr. Meredith, we're used to handling our own problems down here. But maybe this is a special situation. Even some guy who knows how to use a wrench could help. I need somebody to serve as my pair of hands."

Meredith said, "Getting help should take some of the strain off our men. Don't forget that this is only the beginning."

"Yeah, we got a lot more work to do before the whole plant's back together."

"Let's get at it then." The engineering officer paused. "Do you mind if I ask you something personal?"

"Shoot," Simpson said.

"Just how the hell do you go to the bathroom with those bandages on your hands?"

The morning sun slanted across the pier alongside the *O'Leary*. Sweating members of the deck force carried the ship's awnings and other flammable or non-essential items ashore and stacked them.

"We're gonna miss these awnings," Seaman Ben Nystrom said.

Hank Landry heaved a heavy roll of canvas on top of the growing pile. "Yeah, I could use some shade right now." He paused and wondered if he'd ever see Teresa again. He hadn't been back to Manila since she'd told him to leave the restaurant. He knew his pride had made him stay away. Damn, he thought, if I'd patched things up, I could have had another two nights with her.

Nystrom stretched his rangy frame and yawned. "Second day of the war already. Where the hell are the Japs?"

"They'll find us soon enough," Landry said. "Don't go asking for trouble."

"Speaking of trouble, here comes Chief Mortland," Nystrom said.

"Got some special work for you two," Mortland said. "Report to the forward fireroom."

"Snipe work?" Landry said.

"You're kidding us," Nystrom said.

"Nope. I would've told 'em to go to hell, but these orders came from the old man. Besides, we're stuck here until you help 'em put things back together."

"Gonna be hot down there, even without a boiler lit off," Nystrom said.

"Yeah, that's why I put you two right at the top of my list. Have a nice day. You'll probably be down there all night, too. Maybe you'll be done by dawn—just in time to do some of the work I got planned."

"I ain't looking forward to this," Nystrom said.

Landry wasn't either. He hated the thought of going down in the fireroom. The boilers reminded him of the steam locomotives his father had worked and died on.

Five minutes later, Landry led Nystrom and three other deck hands out of the airlock and into the forward fireroom. The heat hit Landry and sweat began to flow. It wasn't noon yet, and he knew it was over a hundred.

Simpson was crouched over a valve laid out on the grating between the boilers. He looked up and tapped his assistant on the shoulder. "Looks like the cavalry has arrived, or maybe it's the Indians."

Landry clenched his fists. Did Simpson know about his Arapaho grandmother?

Another water tender laughed. "Indians, hell. All I see is deck apes. Ain't no bananas down here."

"We're here to help so the Japs won't drop bombs down your goddamn stacks," Landry said.

Simpson shoved his glasses up his nose with a bandaged hand. "Landry, I don't mind taking some crap from you as long as you keep pissing Mortland off. Come on over and get to work."

An hour later, Landry sat on the top of an overturned bucket.

Simpson nodded approvingly. "Now you know how to take apart a feedwater stop and check valve."

"Probably would have ruined the damn thing if you hadn't shown me a few tricks," Landry said.

Simpson pointed to a corroded spring lying on a greasy piece of canvas. "We'll need to replace that and install a new set of gaskets. Then she'll be good as new. You handle a wrench good, Landry. But I could still show you a thing or two if my hands were okay."

Landry looked at Simpson's bandages and turned his eyes to the maze of pipes around them. He remembered how his father had been burned to death. "Could something blow up today?"

"Naw. We ain't even got a boiler lit off."

"But when you start things up?"

Simpson delivered a kick to the stout casing of the number two boiler. "Dunno. I still think there's something wrong with this old bitch. Won't know until I have time to go inside. Don't know when that'll be. We're just busting ass to put number one back together so we can get the hell out of here."

In just an hour, Landry had been impressed by Simpson's competence. "My money's on you to find the problem."

"I hope you're right." Simpson held up his hands. "If not, I may not get off this easy next time."

"Any idea what the problem is?" Landry asked.

"Nope. All I know is that something was bothering me for weeks. Whatever it was got a little worse just before the gaskets blew."

"What was it?"

"A vibration. I don't think it was the joint itself. I think the vibration helped cause the joint to blow."

Landry frowned. "Looks like an awful lot of things to go wrong down here."

Simpson nodded. "But we got other fish to fry first, like putting this valve back together."

"First, I got one question. How the hell do you blow tubes?"

Simpson laughed and pointed to a chain hanging over Landry's shoulder. "Pull that and steam blasts the soot inside the boiler right up the stack."

"Don't I know."

"Don't take it personally, kid. By the way, where'd you learn to handle a wrench like that?"

"Worked weekends and evenings at a service station back home. We were too damn poor to have a car of our own."

Simpson's prominent Adam's apple bobbed. "My family didn't have much money either. I grew up near Cleveland on Lake Erie. My family had to scrape to pay the food bills. Not much money for heat. Damn near froze to death. Promised myself I'd never be cold again."

Landry chuckled, but he wasn't smiling several hours later when the temperature passed 115. Several of the weary engineers and some of their new helpers were overcome by heat and exhaustion. They had to be carried up to the main deck and treated by Doctor Laster. Only a steady intake of water and salt tablets enabled Landry to avoid the humiliation of being carried off. "I'm gonna climb outta here on my own when we're done," he muttered.

But that wasn't until almost dawn the next day.

Simpson looked up as Landry torqued the last bolt on the metal flange of a main steam line joint. "This is the last section we need to run the starboard engine."

"Never thought we'd be done." Landry's back ached and his hands were blistered raw from the heavy wrench work of the last eighteen hours.

"Now we're ready to test the system," Simpson said.

Landry eyed the softly roaring number one boiler, lit off two hours before. He thought he could feel the power of the steam trapped in the boiler. He remembered his father's death and felt an urge to run topside.

"Looks like that pump we rebuilt is doing fine," Simpson said.

Landry inspected it and found no signs of leakage. He was surprised to feel a sense of pride.

"You can knock off and get some sleep," Simpson said.

Landry wanted to leave, but he fought the urge to go. "I'd like to stick around and see if everything works."

"Nice to find a man who takes some pride in his work," Simpson said.

An hour later, Simpson and Landry watched as an engineer opened the main steam stop valve. Steam hissed into the main steam line, and Simpson followed the line to check for leaks. "No problems, yet," he said.

"Yet?" Landry said.

"We only replaced some of the steam line gaskets. I don't like the looks of some of the other joints."

In a few minutes they were ready for a test of the starboard engine. Simpson cocked his head toward the main steam line. "Should be anytime now."

Suddenly steam sang through the pipes and the grating trembled underfoot as the turbines in the after engine room turned the starboard propeller.

Simpson turned to Landry. "Looks like we did it."

"I guess you snipes have a lot more work to do."

"Yup, and that'll just make things pretty much like they were before we came here."

"Cheer up, Simpson," Landry said. "Maybe you'll even figure out what's wrong with number two."

Simpson pushed his glasses back up his nose with a grimy bandage, turned, and stared at the number two boiler. "I hope so. This bitch is a problem. But nothing like the old man's problem when the yard finds out what we're doing. There'll be hell to pay then."

CHAPTER NINE

Fraser climbed to the fire control platform as the dark horizon began to lighten on the third morning of the war. He wondered if the day would be a repeat of the one before when there had been no sign of the Japanese. Smoke trailed aft from the number one stack, and dirty froth boiled behind the starboard propeller. The mooring lines creaked under the strain of holding the ship stationary in her berth.

"Looks like we can move again," Fraser muttered, but he wondered how long and how far.

As the sky brightened, the gun crews emerged from below, yawning and scratching in the humidity. Most stopped at the galley and walked out of the amidships deckhouse with steaming cups of coffee to take to their stations.

As Fraser pulled his headphones from their stowage, the captain looked up from the bridge wing. "Mind if I come up?"

"Plenty of room, sir. We're not manning the main battery director."

Arkwright was soon beside him. "It's a shame we don't have a dual-purpose main battery like the new destroyers."

"Yes, sir." Fraser remembered the captain could have had one of those destroyers with its modern 5-inch guns, which were effective antiaircraft weapons.

A sweat-soaked but smiling Meredith climbed up to join them. "Captain, the starboard engine and number one boiler are ready."

"Good work, Jack."

As Meredith left, Arkwright said, "Good thing it's the starboard engine."

"Why?" Fraser asked.

"Think about the shiphandling problem. How do we get out of here?"

"We twist the stern away from the pier so we clear the *Pillsbury* as we back out," Fraser answered.

"Right, but you need two engines to twist the ship."

"Oh." Fraser thought for a moment. "Now I understand. With just the starboard engine, we keep the number two spring line over to the pier. Then go ahead on the starboard engine. The stern will swing out."

"You've got it," Arkwright said.

Fraser bit his lip. "It'll be tough backing out with one engine. That'll swing the stern to port, right into the *Pillsbury*."

"I'd use the rudder to compensate. About twenty degrees right rudder should do it. See, now you know as much as I do."

"Not quite."

As they continued their vigil, Fraser heard a soft hiss from the main deck where a charged fire hose sprayed a small stream. Filipino workmen chattered in Tagalog as they scurried aboard the *Peary*, across the pier. Her collision-damaged bow had been partially amputated so it could be replaced with a structure being fabricated in the yard. The *Peary*'s boilers and engines were still disassembled.

"*Peary* looks like hell, doesn't she?" Fraser said.

"Looks don't matter now." Arkwright's voice was grim. "I don't want to be caught with our engineering plant ripped apart like the *Peary*'s. I won't have my ship destroyed alongside a goddamned pier!"

Fraser thought there might be certain advantages to that; he wouldn't have far to swim here at Cavite. Fraser glanced at the *Pillsbury*, which was berthed just astern of the *O'Leary*. Smoke drifted skyward from her number one stack, indicating the boiler was steaming.

Arkwright raised his head. "Look at all the yard workmen going aboard the *Pillsbury*. She should be ready in a few weeks. Hopefully, the yard won't pay any attention to us for a while."

Fraser wondered about the wisdom of Arkwright's course of action. "Captain, for your sake, I hope you're right about the Japs attacking. If they don't, and Admiral Hart gets wind of what we're doing . . ."

"It'll be my career," the captain finished.

"Definitely not a way to make admiral," Fraser said.

"Hell, I gave up thinking about making admiral two years ago."

Fraser thought of what the captain had been through. It reminded him of the horror at Clark Field two days before; Fraser shuddered.

"You're recovering from the other day?" the captain asked.

"So far. Time seems to be helping."

"Good. I thought it would."

Fraser remembered how the captain had looked, and he wondered if there were some things time couldn't cure.

An hour after dawn, Arkwright lowered his binoculars and turned to Fraser. "Secure the antiaircraft batteries. The men have other work to do. Just make sure the guns and ammunition are ready to go. I'll be in my chair."

As Fraser climbed down to the bridge a few minutes later, he heard a loud voice in the pilothouse. An irate-looking yard supervisor in a hard hat was shouting at the captain.

"What the hell is going on here? Your men aren't following the overhaul schedule. Hell, they aren't tearing machinery down. They're putting it back together again."

Arkwright looked coldly at the man. "A command decision, I'm afraid."

"Whose?"

"You should look into it. The *Peary* and *Pillsbury* need all the yard's resources. Don't worry about us."

"Don't give me a lot of crap! I'm going to get to the bottom of this!"

The supervisor left the *O'Leary* and headed down the pier toward the yard office.

Arkwright turned to Fraser. "It's going to hit the fan."

"I figured we'd have a few more days," Fraser said.

Arkwright's bushy eyebrows drooped. "So did I."

Two hours later the captain summoned Fraser to the bridge and waved a message. "The game's up. I'm to report to Admiral Hart's office at 1300 with the exec and the engineering officer. That means you'll be in charge. Carry out my orders until I . . . or my relief notifies you otherwise."

"How do you want to go?" Fraser asked. "The gig's engine is down for repairs. Should I get a car from the motor pool?"

"The whaleboat will do fine," said Arkwright bleakly. "Maybe it will give Beringer some humility for his new job."

Dear God! Fraser thought. Don't let them put Beringer in command.

Hank Landry stood on the pier and held the bow of the whaleboat against the piles. Landry ached from his labors in the fireroom, and his eyes burned from lack of sleep. As he looked at the familiar whaleboat he felt like a husband who'd been running around with another woman. He remembered the smooth feel of the heavy chrome-plated wrenches, the discovery of the internal secrets of the pump, and the satisfaction of making it whole again. Somehow, he felt he'd been unfaithful to his boat.

As soon as the three officers boarded the whaleboat, Landry jumped in and shoved the bow away from the pier with his boat hook. When they headed toward Manila, Landry was surprised that the captain failed to assume his usual position next to the coxswain. All three officers were seated in the after cockpit. Lieutenant Meredith slumped against the cushions, almost asleep. Remnants of grime stained the back of one hand, matching the dark circles under his eyes. Landry remembered how the engineering officer had worked with them all night.

Beringer looked fresh and alert, his uniform and shoes were immaculate, but his movements were quick and nervous. He pulled a cigarette out and started to light it.

"Sorry, sir. No smoking in the boats," Landry said.

Beringer frowned, nodded, and flicked the cigarette over the side.

The coxswain glanced at Beringer and faced forward and winked at Landry. "Dumb shithead," his mouth said silently.

I hope the rumors aren't true, thought Landry. If they put the exec in command, we're all up the creek. Landry looked back at the captain, whose head was slumped forward, his chin almost on his chest. Unlike Meredith, Arkwright's eyes were wide open, staring at his outstretched feet.

Halfway there, Landry scanned the Manila waterfront five miles ahead. The Marsman Building, a white five-story structure, stood out against the skyline. The Navy had taken over a suite of offices on the third floor for the fleet headquarters. Signal flags flapped from a mast on the roof of the building. Landry figured that on a clear day, Admiral Hart could see Cavite.

When the whaleboat nosed against the stone steps of the landing, Arkwright stood, almost reluctantly. Even the grating of the boat against the stone steps failed to wake Meredith. Landry signalled to the boat engineer who leaned back and gently poked the engineering officer. Meredith awakened with a start just as the white-clad legs of Arkwright and Beringer stepped over the side of the boat.

Landry whispered, "Shake a leg, Mr. Meredith."

A pretty Filipino girl stood on the landing, and Landry noticed Beringer and Meredith gave her appreciative looks, but the captain didn't even turn his head. The breeze wafted a suggestion of her perfume to Landry, and he ached for Teresa. He wondered if he would be able to see her again. As Landry watched the white-uniformed officers enter the Marsman Building, he realized he wasn't the only one with problems. He wondered who would be in command of the *O'Leary* when they returned.

On the bridge of the *O'Leary*, a radioman rushed across the wooden gratings. Fraser's knees buckled slightly as he read the message from fleet headquarters.

"What is it, Mr. Fraser?" asked Jablonski, the chief quartermaster, who was bent over his chart table.

"A large formation of Japanese aircraft has been sighted to the north. This may be it for us. Pass the word to prepare to get under way."

"What the hell are you doing now?" asked an angry voice. It was the yard supervisor who had been aboard that morning.

"We're getting out if the Japs show up," Fraser said.

The supervisor shook his head. "You'd better not try that. My men just drained the lube oil out of your starboard reduction gear. You'll burn it up if you move."

Fraser's jaw tightened. He felt compelled to do what Arkwright would have done, but then he began to think about the consequences of taking responsibility for the *O'Leary*. Doubt gnawed at him, and his stomach churned. Fraser made his decision. He turned to the voice tube to the engine room and rang the call bell.

"Main control," echoed the voice of the chief machinist.

"Chief, check the lube oil level in the starboard reduction gear. The yard says they drained it. If so, replace it as soon as you can. The Japs may be on the way. Let me know when you're ready."

"Christ! If you're right, it'll be a half-hour before we can move."

"Make it fast!" Fraser said.

The yard supervisor's neck reddened. "You're a damned fool!"

Fraser straightened up from the voice tube and stared at the portly man. "You'd better leave before we put the brow over. Unless you want to swim ashore."

"You're going to be the exec of your skipper's next command—a garbage scow!" The supervisor turned on his heel and headed for the pier.

Fraser called the remaining officers and the chiefs to the bridge and instructed them to prepare to get under way. "We'll go to general quarters when we're ready," he finished.

Chief Hanlon asked, "Sir, how soon are we leaving?"

"We'll be delayed for half an hour. Why?"

"I'd like to go over to the yard to pick up our fire control computer. Don't want it bombed in the shop."

"Go ahead. We won't be using the 4-inch guns today, but we may need them soon."

"Sir," Chief Mortland said, "request permission to rig the lines so we can slip them off without line handlers on the pier."

"Good idea," Fraser said. "Let's get at it."

From the wing of the bridge, Fraser watched Hanlon trot toward the yard shops. Fifty-caliber ammunition belts clattered on the amidships deckhouse. Fraser scanned the skies for the Japanese. He didn't have long to wait. Three nine-plane vees of bombers appeared to the north and leisurely attacked a few targets out in the bay and on the Manila waterfront. Minutes later, another formation of twenty-seven aircraft turned toward Cavite from the west.

"General quarters," Fraser ordered. "Tell the 4-inch gun crews to stand by the lines." Fraser anxiously watched the incoming flight. He ran over to the voice tube and rang the bell. "How much longer?"

"Fifteen more minutes. Then we'll have enough oil in the gear to prevent damage if you keep the speed down."

"Let me know! All hell is about to break loose up here."

His fingers tense, Fraser looked through his binoculars helplessly as the Japanese formation approached high overhead. Memories of the horror at Clark surged through his mind. When the bombers neared the approximate bomb release point to hit the *O'Leary*, Fraser's sphincter tightened and his throat went dry. Seconds passed, and no bombs appeared. Fraser let out his breath.

Cavite's nine 3-inch antiaircraft guns barked, but their black bursts were far short of the formation sailing serenely over them.

"Might as well throw my library at them," said Chief Jablonski next to Fraser.

"Why didn't they drop any bombs?" a relieved-sounding quartermaster asked.

"Getting a measure of the wind," Jablonski said. "They'll be back."

The Japanese turned in a wide arc and began another run. Dozens of tiny specks separated from their bellies and began an agonizingly slow descent. The sun glinted off silver fins. When the bombs were half-way down, Fraser noticed that the 4-inch gun crew on the forecastle was scattering for cover. "Hit the deck!" he ordered. "All hands take cover!"

Fraser felt an urge to run, but there was nothing for him to do but drop to the wooden grating on the bridge wing and pray. Although he had less protection than the trench had afforded at Clark, he felt reassured by the familiar surroundings and the presence of friends. The approaching horror seemed more bearable than it had two days before.

When the explosions stopped, Fraser jumped up and saw that Cavite's main power plant had been devastated along with several other buildings. Dirty swirls of foam marked the water just off the ends of the piers where several bombs had narrowly missed the moored ships.

A late bomb whistled down and hit the tug which had saluted Fraser's shiphandling efforts only a few days before. The small vessel disintegrated in the blast. One moment it was there; in the blink of an eye, it ceased to exist. Fraser trembled for a few seconds as he thought of the salty chief who had given him the encouraging wave.

"P-40s!" a lookout shouted.

As the formation of Japanese bombers turned for another run, a few distant dots approached the enemy. An overwhelming number of Zeros jumped the Army fighters and hounded them from the sky, except for one P-40 that was chased into the antiaircraft barrage from Cavite's gunners. A black burst caught the Army fighter; within seconds an orange flicker blossomed and consumed the P-40.

The bell from the forward engine room rang urgently. Fraser beat three other men to the voice tube. "Yes?" he shouted.

"Ready to get under way!" came the echoing voice.

Fraser turned to the telephone talker. "Stand by to get under way!" His voice shook slightly, then steadied. "Take in all lines except number two!"

The talker repeated the order, and Fraser walked over to the port wing of the bridge with the talker following, his long length of black telephone wire dragging behind. Fraser looked aft where men aboard the *Pillsbury* worked frantically to ready their ship to get under way. "Can't wait for them to get out of our way," he muttered. Fraser looked over the side, noted that all the *O'Leary*'s lines except number two were in and took a deep breath. "Left full rudder. Starboard ahead one-third."

Foam boiled under the starboard quarter. The bow began to swing to port, toward the pier, as the ship was restrained from moving forward by the number two mooring line. The heavy manila line, which angled from the bow aft to the pier, creaked and groaned as it took the strain. The stern began to swing out, and it soon pointed at the open water outboard of the *Pillsbury*.

"Starboard engine stop! Rudder amidships!" Suddenly, Fraser remembered Chief Hanlon. Where was he? Fraser scanned the pier and the streets nearby but there was no sign of Hanlon. A quick glance at the sky revealed the Japanese were beginning another bombing run. Fraser bit his lip. "Take in number two line! Right twenty degrees rudder! Starboard engine back two-thirds!"

The *O'Leary* shuddered and began to move astern, ever so slowly at first, and then faster. Some of the dirty harbor water stirred up by the starboard propeller came up along the port side as the *O'Leary* accelerated. Pieces of garbage and trash swirled about in a mindless dance. The bridge gratings vibrated with the off-balance effort of the single screw. For a moment, Fraser feared that the *O'Leary*'s fan-shaped propeller guard would scrape against the *Pillsbury*, but it cleared with two feet to spare.

As they slid by their sister and toward open water, Fraser looked up. More bombs were on the way down.

Doctor Laster ambled down the third-floor corridor of the Marsman Building. As he passed Admiral Hart's office, he saw familiar faces in the reception area. He poked his head in the doorway and caught Meredith's eye.

The engineering officer stepped out into the corridor. "What are you doing here, Doc?"

"Officially—trying to get more medical supplies. Unofficially—pumping friends on the staff for intelligence."

"Find out much?"

"Enough to curl your hair—or in your case straighten it. What are all of you doing here?"

Meredith explained what had happened.

"Ah, hell! The captain's in for it now."

"Yeah." Meredith nodded toward Beringer. "The rest of us are in for a lot worse if they give him the ship."

"Oh, Lord! They wouldn't!"

"Say a prayer," Meredith said.

"Think the captain will mind if I ride back with you?"

"I doubt it."

Meredith and Laster went in and took seats.

Arkwright was standing by the window, staring out, his shoulders slumped. He turned and saw Laster. "Do they need a doctor present for a public hanging?"

Laster explained what he'd been doing at headquarters. "If you need a character reference, I'll be happy to step forward, Captain. I think you were doing the right thing."

"In this case, the opinion of a medical officer won't count for much," Arkwright said.

"Even if he is a supreme military strategist," Beringer said sarcastically.

Laster decided to ignore Beringer and picked up the morning edition of the *Manila Bulletin*. Ten minutes later, the chief of staff and the fleet material officer walked through the doorway and greeted them with icy expressions.

"Sit down," the chief of staff said. "We'll send for you in a few minutes." He and the fleet material officer went into the admiral's office.

Arkwright began pacing the room. The wait ended when the door jolted open. The chief of staff and the fleet material officer ran through the waiting room. Laster watched in amazement.

"The Japs are bombing Cavite!" the chief of staff yelled over his shoulder.

The *O'Leary*'s officers jumped up and followed the sound of pounding feet up the stairway to the roof of the building. Beringer and Meredith were close behind Arkwright, but Laster lagged as he puffed up the steps. He finally stumbled out on the roof and staggered across to the fleet signal station, where the other officers clustered. A signalman was bent over a high-powered telescope, giving a running commentary on what he was seeing ten miles away. All Laster could see was a billow of ugly black smoke.

The signalman's voice rose. "Jesus, Cavite's taking a beating. The yard's going up in flames. I can't even make out the ships at the piers. I can see the masts of the destroyers, but the submarines are too low."

"Are any of the destroyers leaving?" Arkwright asked.

"I don't think so," the signalman said. "They're all supposed to be in overhaul. I don't think they can move."

Arkwright grimaced and looked at the fleet material officer. "Maybe one can."

The fleet material officer looked uncomfortable, but he said nothing.

The signalman shouted again. "Christ, I think the destroyers just caught it. A bomb seemed to hit the mast of one. Sparks and pieces showered all over. One destroyer is on fire."

"Damn!" Laster said.

There was a moment of silence before the signalman spoke again. "Wait a minute, there's a destroyer coming around Sangley Point and turning. I'll be able to see her bow numbers in a few seconds."

They waited.

Laster knew it had to be either the *Pillsbury* or the *O'Leary*. Even he knew there was no way the *Peary* could move. Laster turned from the distant scene and looked at Arkwright, who stood silently. The captain seemed to have retained his aplomb except for the white knuckles of his clenched hands.

The signalman turned his telescope slightly. "Here comes the destroyer. Her first number is two."

"So is the first number of all of our destroyers," Meredith said.

"The last two numbers are zero zero. It's the deuce double hole!"

"The *O'Leary*!" the chief of staff said.

The signalman continued to recount the action. "Christ, she's zigzagging in the channel so the Japs can't hit her."

The chief of staff nodded his head admiringly. "That takes guts in those restricted waters."

Arkwright grunted.

"What was that?" the chief of staff asked.

"Nothing," Arkwright said. He wiped the perspiration off his forehead. "I assume Admiral Hart no longer needs to see me. With your permission, I'll go back to my ship and get her ready to fight."

The chief of staff nodded grimly as he looked toward the flames consuming Cavite. "I'll be the first to apologize. You were right."

"Not necessarily, I know you have a lot more to think about than one destroyer."

"You did what was best for your ship," the chief of staff said. "We'll have one more ship to fight with."

"If she doesn't fall apart," Arkwright said.

"When can you be ready?" asked the chief of staff.

"A couple of days," said Arkwright.

"You'll have your chance to fight," the chief of staff said.

"Good, I'm ready to take on the Japs," Arkwright said.

Laster didn't much care for that idea, but it seemed better than having Beringer in command.

An hour after the last enemy bomber droned away to the north, Fraser conned the *O'Leary* back off Sangley Point and anchored the ship. He kept the antiaircraft battery manned but instructed the remainder of the crew to go back to work. Fraser kept a vigilant watch for Japanese planes while Cavite continued to burn.

Fraser's vigil was broken by a shout from the signal bridge. "Here comes Admiral Hart's barge!"

Fraser raised his binoculars and caught a glimpse of four gleaming stars on the bow of the sleek power boat. There was no doubt it was Admiral Hart's barge.

Durham ran over from the other wing, "I can't make out any flags or pennants flying anywhere, so I don't think the admiral's aboard."

Fraser was puzzled. "Let's go down to the quarterdeck."

Deck hands rigged a sea ladder as the barge pulled alongside smartly. The powerful exhaust died to a slow burble as it bobbed against the fenders dropped over the *O'Leary*'s side. Gerald Arkwright climbed out the after cockpit and deftly caught the flying tail of the sea ladder. As his head poked above the deck level, Fraser thought he could see a trace of a smile.

When the captain reached the deck, he straightened his shoulders and looked past Fraser at the blazing yard. "Hell of a way to have your career saved," Arkwright said.

Fraser nodded at the barge. "You must be in favor with someone."

"The chief of staff offered it to us. It's a lot faster than our whaleboat. Did you conn the ship out?"

"Yes, sir. Just as we discussed."

"Nice job," the captain said.

"He also told the yard to stuff it," Durham said. "Didn't know Ross had it in him."

After the other officers went below, Arkwright turned back to Fraser and raised a bushy eyebrow. "About that zig-zagging as you came out the channel?"

"Ahhh . . . Captain, that wasn't really intentional. I lost my bearings twice, but Chief Jablonski set me straight."

"You made it. That's what counts. Any damage?"

"Nothing serious. We may find some shrapnel damage."

"Casualties?"

Fraser turned to look at the mass of flames consuming Cavite. "Chief Hanlon's missing, sir. My fault. I let him go ashore to pick up the computer. I thought he had plenty of time."

"Maybe he'll be all right. Let's go up to the bridge," Arkwright said.

Fraser spent the afternoon on the bridge wing watching Cavite burn and wondering what had happened to Hanlon.

"Looks like most of the fires are out," the captain said as evening neared.

"I think most of them just burned themselves out," Fraser said.

"At least the ammo dump is all right."

"How do you know?"

Arkwright's laugh was short, even grim. "Believe me, we'd all know if the ammo dump went up."

Fraser paused for several seconds. "I can't believe I sent Chief Hanlon over there."

"You made a reasonable decision. Without the computer our main battery is crippled."

"I still feel bad."

"Better get used to this kind of situation," Arkwright said. "It may be a long war."

A radioman ran up with the message board. "Just in from Admiral Hart, sir."

"Probably wants to know why I stood him up," the captain muttered. He scanned the message and let out a deep breath. "He wants to know how soon we'll be ready to fight."

"That's all?"

"That's it. If he's not going to worry, why should I?"

Fraser saw the captain's eyes narrow, so he turned to look at Cavite. Flames shot up from one section of the yard. "Not much left except the ammo dump," Arkwright said.

If that goes up, Fraser thought, there won't be many survivors over there.

Before the bombs began to fall on the yard that afternoon, Hanlon had run for the shops as fast as his stocky legs allowed.

The air raid sirens had just begun to wail as he reached the door of the fire control shop.

"Where is everyone?" Hanlon asked a half-asleep Filipino behind a desk.

The Filipino rubbed his eyes. "Out to lunch, Chief. They be back soon."

"What the hell is this siesta and lunch stuff? The Japs are about to start bombing."

"Jesu Cristo!" The Filipino leaped up and bolted out the door.

"Damn! I'll find the computer myself."

In the clutter of the shop it took Hanlon fifteen nerve-wracking minutes to find the computer on a rear shelf. The tag indicated it was completed. Hanlon twisted the dials and tested it as best he could. "It looks okay."

He hefted the 50-pound gray metal box and headed for the door. The eerie whistle of falling bombs sent him scuttling for a sheltered space under a sturdy metal workbench. Hanlon cradled the computer under his stomach. A blinding yellow burst of light flashed through the windows. The cement floor bucked and heaved like a cheap mattress. A concussive blast deafened Hanlon and shook his body, driving the air from his lungs. Dust rose from the floor and choked his mouth and nostrils. Stone blocks from the walls joined falling beams and roofing material. Debris fell all around him, but the heavy steel bench held.

When the avalanche stopped, Hanlon raised his head. Dust, smoke, and debris swirled through the air. He could see little and coughed to clear the dust from his lungs. The chief rose and lugged the computer through the debris to the smoke-filled street. Many of the yard buildings were either flattened or burning. Flames sprouted from heaps of debris, and smoke billowed around him. Hanlon staggered toward the waterfront, choking and coughing.

A voice shouted, "Here they come again!"

Hanlon ran for a nearby ditch and pushed the computer into a culvert. Bombs shook the ground and showered him with dirt. "Not as bad this time," he muttered.

As soon as the explosions stopped, he left the computer in the culvert and ran down to a low wall just short of the pier. Hanlon looked around the corner and saw the *O'Leary* backing from her berth, barely easing by the *Pillsbury*.

He looked toward the other piers. Most of the ships had departed, but two submarines and the two other destroyers remained. The *Peary* amd *Pillsbury* appeared undamaged, but as he looked at them another load of bombs arrived. Tall spouts of water rose near the *Peary*'s stern, and one bomb hit her mast and exploded just above the director platform. Shrapnel and incendiary materials sprayed the *Peary*'s bridge, setting it aflame and mowing down nearby men. Across the pier, shrapnel from the same bomb raked the *Pillsbury*.

"Damn!" Hanlon muttered as he realized the death-dealing cone of the explosion would have swept across the *O'Leary*'s decks if she were still in her berth. Hanlon ran from the sheltering wall and sprinted along the pier. The upper decks of the destroyers were strewn with dead, wounded, and scarlet splashes of blood. Dazed survivors moved among the wounded as flames flickered. Sailors played the few undamaged fire hoses on the blazes.

Hanlon trotted up the brow of the *Peary* and helped throw burning supplies off the forecastle. By then the fires were out on the *Pillsbury*, and sailors carried some of her hoses across the pier to the burning *Peary*, where they brought her fires under control.

"We're getting under way!" came a shout from the *Pillsbury*.

Hanlon ran to the pier and helped throw her lines off the mooring bollards. As she backed away, another load of bombs whistled from the sky. The men who could still move scurried for what little cover there was on the naked expanse of pier. The first bombs exploded in the water alongside, lifting towering columns of dirty water that cascaded down and drenched the cowering men. Shattering explosions rocked the pier and demolished nearby buildings.

When the bomb blasts ended, Hanlon ran aboard the *Peary*. "Need a hand with the wounded?" he asked.

"Do we ever," said a pale corpsman.

Hanlon helped carry stretchers down to the pier, where other men carried them off toward the yard dispensary. As Hanlon bent down to pick up one of the last stretchers, a weak but familiar voice stopped him.

"Always knew I could count on an old China hand."

Hanlon looked down at the man on the stretcher, a shipmate from his first tour in the Far East. One of the man's arms was a bloody stump. Blood seeped from a dozen shrapnel wounds.

"Easy, Swede, we're gonna get you some help."

His friend coughed up a bloody froth. "Too damn late," he whispered. "Had us a hell of a time up the Yangtze, didn't we?"

"Yeah, we did," said Hanlon as he helped lift the stretcher. Hell, he thought, that's all gone now, just like life here in the Philippines.

As Hanlon helped carry the stretcher along the pier, secondary explosions from the torpedo workshop on the adjacent Machina Wharf rocked them with concussive blasts and showered the piers with shards of metal and burning debris. At the head of the pier Hanlon relinquished his friend's stretcher to other men.

As he watched him being carried off, he suddenly felt his knees weaken and he shivered. Christ, he thought, the world is falling apart around me. More explosions from the torpedo workshop reinforced that thought. Hanlon shook himself to stop his shivering and peered through the smoke and spotted a small gray shape nosing toward the *Peary*'s stern. Hanlon watched with admiration as the minesweeper *Whippoorwill* braved the heat of the flames, made its approach, and passed a line to the destroyer's fantail. Foam boiled under the minesweeper's stern, but the *Peary* refused to budge. The line parted with a crack.

"Damn! That's the end of that!" Hanlon said.

The minesweeper tried again with the same results. Hanlon saw the problem: some of the *Peary*'s mooring lines were still over to the pier. Hanlon gathered three lightly wounded men, and they ran down the pier where they threw the mooring lines off the bollards. With the *Peary*'s lines free, the little minesweeper pulled the destroyer away from the pier like a feisty terrier tugging at the tail of a greyhound.

Back under cover at the foot of the pier, Hanlon looked over at the Machina Wharf. The submarine rescue ship *Pigeon* was pulling a submarine clear of a sunken sister. The valiant rescue was completed just before a flood of burning oil rolled over the pier from ruptured tanks nearby.

After the last of the wounded men had been carried away, Hanlon realized that there was nothing left to accomplish at the piers. He led a group of men through the burning yard and joined the makeshift fire fighting parties. Although they had manpower and hoses, the fire mains had ruptured, so there was no water until two fire engines arrived and began to pump a few futile streams from the bay. But the fire engines had little effect as secondary explosions and ruptured fuel tanks added to the inferno the bombs had begun. By late afternoon, many of the wind-whipped fires began to die out because there was little left to burn.

Hanlon and the men around him realized they had no more to do and retreated to a clear spot. Hanlon dropped to the ground and coughed up gobs of gray-streaked phlegm while he tried to ignore the burns inflicted by flying embers.

"At least we saved the ammo depot," a soot-streaked sailor said.

"That's about all," Hanlon said.

An hour later, Hanlon was chewing on a Spam sandwich when a man ran up. "The lumber yard's on fire!"

"Oh, shit," the man next to Hanlon said. "That's right next to the ammo dump."

One of the fire engines roared by them, its bell clanging.

"Let's go. There's work to do," Hanlon said.

CHAPTER TEN

Shortly after sunrise the next day, the *O'Leary* steamed around Sangley Point and anchored off the piers, where debris-filled water lapped at her hull. Fraser boarded the whaleboat with Meredith and several enlisted men to go ashore to see if they could salvage anything from the yard. Doctor Laster went along to offer medical assistance.

When Fraser jumped to the pier from the whaleboat, he was stunned by the devastation ashore. The shop areas were no more than twisted girders and galvanized roof sheeting. Only an occasional utility pole stood unscathed. In a few spots, there were piles of equipment intact, protected by parts of the thick stone walls that were still standing despite the explosions. A few fire fighters were hosing down smoking rubble. The smell of smoke, burning rubber, and explosives was intense.

A blackened figure shuffled toward them, and Fraser noted the man's smoke-stained uniform, dotted with blackened holes.

"Aren't you guys going to say 'Good morning'?" a quiet voice said.

"Jesus, that's Chief Hanlon!" Laster said.

"I hope so," Hanlon said.

Fraser stared at the sooty man for several seconds. His eyebrows and half his hair were gone, but it was Hanlon. "Thank God!" Fraser said. "We thought you were dead."

"So did I, until we stopped the fire short of the ammo dump. What're you here for? You're not going to find much."

"The captain wanted us to do some salvaging," Fraser said. "Doc's going to help with the wounded. What happened to the computer?"

"Should be okay," Hanlon said. "Would have been blasted if I hadn't saved it. We can pick it up later. Let's go see what else we can find."

Under the protection of a section of a stone wall in the ordnance shop, they found a .50-caliber machine gun. Nearby, they recovered some spare parts for the 4-inch guns. While Meredith led his men off to another shop, Fraser and Hanlon packed the parts they had found in wooden boxes. When they finished, Hanlon sat on a piece of rubble. As he wiped his hand on his grimy pants, it trembled slightly.

"Damn, Mr. Fraser, look around us. Took just one afternoon to level the yard. Nothing but cinders now. What's a whole war going to do? This is insane. I saw good men die yesterday."

"Chief, I know how you feel. The dying men I saw up at Clark Field will haunt me forever."

A silent understanding seemed to pass between the two men. Hanlon let out a long breath. "Most folks got no idea what war's all about. I know I didn't."

"No argument," Fraser said. "What's the alternative? Stand back and let Hitler and the Japs do what they want?"

Hanlon poked a shoe at a pile of ashes. "S'pose you're right. If the good folks don't stand up, the bastards will take over." He rose from his seat. "Let's get at it."

They joined the engineers in their hunt for salvagable material. Amidst the wreckage of another shop Meredith unearthed some gaskets. In the pump shop, Fraser found the destroyer's number one fire and bilge pump still bearing a scorched tag with the *O'Leary*'s name on it.

"Damn shop didn't overhaul it," Meredith said. "But Simpson'll make it work."

When they headed back toward the piers, Hanlon stopped by a culvert and slid the undamaged computer out of the drainage pipe. A solemn group of men boarded the whaleboat.

As he settled back in the boat, Fraser shifted his gaze from the yard to Hanlon's determined jaw and blackened face. He felt a sudden surge of respect and affection for the older man, who seemed ready to take on the whole Japanese Navy despite his condition.

"This is the last we'll see of Cavite," Fraser said.

"I'll be back here someday," Hanlon said in his quiet, firm voice.

Fraser was surprised at Hanlon's acceptance that they would soon have to leave. He wondered where the Navy would send them.

Chief Hanlon winced as he took his chair in chiefs' quarters. Three days after the destruction of Cavite, his burns still hurt. He was thankful the *O'Leary* had done nothing more than steam on one engine around Manila Bay to avoid Japanese air attacks. The bay was almost empty now; two days ago, Admiral Hart had ordered the operational ships to escort a large convoy of merchant vessels south to the Dutch East Indies. The *O'Leary* was virtually alone. The only other major naval units left in the Philippines were the submarines, their tenders, and destroyers *Peary* and *Pillsbury*, now undergoing emergency repairs in a civilian yard.

Chief Mortland rattled his coffee cup at the end of the table. "You hear the order on uniforms? Everybody's supposed to bring two sets of whites to the galley this afternoon."

"The galley?" Hanlon said. "Cooks have a new soup recipe?"

"Naw," Mortland said. "A message came in to get everyone out of whites because they make good targets."

"Too hot for blues," said Jablonski, the chief quartermaster.

"We're dyeing whites khaki," Mortland said.

"How?" Hanlon asked. "I'll bet we don't have any khaki dye."

"Using coffee," Mortland said.

"Just so long as I don't have to drink it afterwards," said "Beerbarrel" Robustelli.

When Hanlon took his uniforms to the galley two hours later, he saw that the cooks had been hard at work. Drying uniforms flapped from every available topside surface. They were khaki-colored but hardly uniform, varying from a medium brown to a sickly mustard tan.

Hanlon had to laugh. "We look like a floating Chinese laundry. No Jap pilot could hit us because he'd be laughing too hard."

Mortland was standing nearby. "It ain't funny. That damn coffee is dripping all over my decks. Sheeeit! If we hit a squall, the whole damn ship will turn coffee-colored. Then they might as well give us to the Army!"

"You'd make a great sergeant," Hanlon said. "Maybe you missed your calling."

"Might beat the hell out of this crap," muttered Mortland.

Hanlon chuckled and headed forward to return to chiefs' quarters. On the forecastle, Hanlon saw Hank Landry chipping a rusted stanchion. "Landry, better tell the deck hands to look out. Chief Mortland's pissed."

Landry stood and stretched his wiry frame. "When isn't Mortland pissed? Chief, you hear anything about getting some liberty in Manila?"

"No," Hanlon said. "I wouldn't count on it any time soon. I hope you patched things up with Teresa."

"No such luck. Haven't seen her since she told me to get my butt out of Sagun's."

"You'd better send her a letter with some money the next time they send mail ashore."

Landry's deeply tanned face was bleak. "Dunno, Chief. Maybe it's better to let things be. Something just wasn't right the last few weeks. I guess she didn't want me around anymore."

Hanlon didn't know what to tell Landry. "I know that's not true," he finally said.

"How do you explain the way she was acting. She didn't have to keep working. Hell, once the girls out here take up with a man, they don't work anymore."

"You two ever talk about making things permanent?"

"No. Seemed like things were okay the way they were."

"She's a fine girl. You must've thought about it."

"Marriage didn't seem like such a hot idea."

"Why not?" Hanlon asked.

"Kids, for one thing."

"What's the matter with kids? Maria's been praying for one for years."

Landry looked down. "Just not right to bring half-breeds into the world."

"Better a half-breed than not living at all."

Landry raised his black eyes and his face twisted. "How can you know? It's hell."

"How do you know?" Hanlon asked softly.

There was a long silence as Landry stared at the deck. "This is between you and me, right?"

"Sure."

"My grandmother was a full-blooded Arapaho Indian. I took all kinds of crap from the other kids. I wouldn't want to wish that on a kid of my own."

Hanlon scuffed at the deck with his shoe. "Son, Teresa's of mixed stock—American father, Filipino mother. Her kids aren't going to be pure-blooded anything. Seems like they could use a father who'd understand their problems."

Landry's jaw took a firm set. "She'd be better off with someone else to father those kids. I just don't think I'm up to it."

"Son, I'm not sure I should tell you this . . ."

"Tell me what."

"Even if you never see Teresa again . . . her first kid's going to be yours."

Landry's mouth opened. He finally shut it, took off his hat, and ran a hand through his black hair. "Why didn't she tell me?"

"That girl's got a lot of pride. Didn't want you to feel trapped. She wanted you to want her. That explain the last few weeks for you?"

"Yeah, I guess it does."

"If it's any consolation, if the Japs invade, Maria will probably take Teresa to the country to stay with Maria's folks. Think about that letter, will you?"

"Letter, hell. I gotta see her, Chief."

"No one's getting ashore son. A letter's about the best you can do."

Two days later the engineers had both engines and all boilers but number two ready. That evening Fraser sat in the wardroom waiting for the captain to return from fleet headquarters. Fraser stirred his coffee and wondered when they'd get orders. His thoughts turned to Ilsa and how she'd looked lying beside him on the beach at Corregidor.

Woody Korchak took a seat across from Fraser. The chunky reserve ensign had just returned to the *O'Leary* after a six-week stay in a Manila hospital. A routine hernia operation had become infected and required prolonged treatment. Fraser was happy to see Korchak return, partly because it meant there was someone aboard who knew less than Fraser did. But Korchak, a graduate of the University of Michigan, was a hard worker and catching on fast as the ship's communications officer.

Korchak's broad Slavic brow furrowed. "I wonder where Admiral Hart's going to send us."

"To the States for an overhaul would be nice," Meredith said.

Bull Durham's eyes took on a distant look. "I'll vote for Tahiti."

The captain strode into the wardroom, and Doctor Laster trailed in behind him like a fat waterskier in the wake of a speedboat.

Arkwright's mouth was set in an angry line. He waved a large envelope. "Gentlemen, we've been ordered to leave the Philippines. I have to read these sealed orders to find out where we're going and then digest some other information. I'll brief you in fifteen minutes."

The doctor, dark circles under his eyes, settled in his chair at the foot of the wardroom table.

Beringer lifted a corner of his prominent upper lip. "Doctor, that uniform is a disgrace. It looks like you've been sleeping in it for days."

"Too many wounded patients for much sleep," Laster said. "I was sent over to the Army Hospital in Manila because facilities at Cavite were limited."

Meredith broke in before Beringer could reply. "Doc, you hear any good news ashore?"

"None. They're still talking about how MacArthur's headquarters delayed so long in granting permission for Clark Field's B-17s to attack."

Durham crushed his cigarette in his ash tray. "Who was responsible?"

"Nobody seemed sure who made that decision," Laster said. "Rumor has it that MacArthur thought he'd get more support from the government here if the Japs made the first hostile move against the Philippines."

"Why didn't the radar on the coast warn Clark?" Fraser asked.

Laster coughed heavily as he lit a cigarette. "The radar worked perfectly, and the station notified headquarters here. Somehow, headquarters couldn't get through to Clark. There are rumors about communication problems, someone failing to pass the word. I'm not sure anyone knows for sure."

"Maybe everyone at Clark was having lunch," Fraser said bitterly.

Durham looked up at the overhead. "Christ! Our air cover shot to hell because of sheer incompetence."

"There may be worse yet to come for the Philippines," Laster said. "I had a very interesting ulcer patient while I was ashore."

Beringer snorted. "Ulcers? What could be interesting about that. A mundane problem."

Laster raised a pudgy finger. "Ah—what was interesting was why he had ulcers. This colonel is a member of MacArthur's staff—one of those who've been begging the general to revert to the old Orange Plan. That plan would withdraw the troops to Bataan and Corregidor."

"That plan's been around for years," Beringer said.

"But little was ever done to get Bataan ready," Laster said. "There's not much food stored over there. MacArthur's holding fast to his scheme to stop the Japs on the beaches. His plans are totally unrealistic because most of his troops are raw recruits who aren't equipped properly or ready to maneuver."

Laster seemed ready to say more but was cut short when the captain opened the door to his cabin and walked to the head of the table. "Let's get down to business. I don't have any good news about the war from fleet headquarters. The problems here won't concern us much longer. We have orders to leave."

The captain's words seemed to hang in the air. Orders to the States would mean a safe overhaul. Orders to the Dutch East Indies might enable Fraser to see Ilsa again, but that destination would put them in the path of the Japanese steamroller.

"We're to escort a convoy leaving tomorrow," said Arkwright. Wherever the convoy was bound, the captain looked satisfied now that he had opened their orders. "The convoy's headed south to Java. When we get there, we'll join other elements of the Asiatic Fleet for operations against the Japanese."

"Better than staying here," Durham said. "It's been lonely the last few days. Maybe we'll get some help from the Dutch and British."

"Not much," the captain said. "The *Prince of Wales* and the *Repulse*—you're thinking the rumors about their coming to Singapore were true?"

"Yes, sir," Durham said. "We could use a brand-new battleship and a battle cruiser."

"Jap aircraft sank them at sea a week ago," Arkwright said.

Christ, thought Fraser, if Jap planes could sink a modern battleship that easily, what are our chances?

"We'll have to make do with what we have," Arkwright said. "We'll load water, fresh food, and supplies from barges tomorrow morning. We get under way at 1500. Any questions? Get some sleep if you don't have any problems to solve."

That evening Landry climbed to the signal bridge to search the Manila skyline through a telescope. The pain of his separation from Teresa seemed worse now that they were only a few miles apart, and he was hearing so many rumors about the *O'Leary*'s departure the next day. Landry had watched the captain in the boat when he returned from fleet headquarters for a clues of where they were headed, but the captain's face had been impassive.

Landry turned the heavy telescope and scanned the water

between the anchored *O'Leary* and the commercial piers. Something caught his eye on one pier—a ladder down to the water.

"By God! I'm going to see Teresa," he said softly.

He left the signal bridge, checked the watch list, and discovered Ben Nystrom would be the stern sentry the next morning.

Landry found Nystrom in his bunk and explained the situation to him. "Just look the other way," he asked.

"I won't shoot. I'll do my best."

"Thanks," Landry said.

Landry borrowed as much money as he could find and added it to the money his shipmates had previously chipped in. He put on his darkest set of coffee-dyed whites and headed up to the quarterdeck with a bucket.

"Going down to clean up the whaleboat," he told Shifflet, who had the watch.

"Jesus, Landry. It's time for lights out. Take a break."

"You know Chief Mortland," Landry said.

"Yeah, too well. Don't fall in. I ain't jumpin' in to fish you out."

"Don't worry," Landry said. "I might try to get some shut-eye on the cushions if it's nice down there."

The boat bobbed gently as it accepted Landry's weight. He dampened a rag and started wiping down the boat, pausing to watch the *O'Leary* and the routine of the two sentries. When the word for lights out was passed, some of the men dragged mattresses up to the main deck and curled up to sleep, avoiding the heat below decks. Landry stretched out on the boat cushions and waited until both sentries were headed away from him. He sat up and slipped over the gunwale. He waited for a shout. Silence. He glided away with a gentle breast stroke through the lukewarm water and headed for the piers. There was no moon yet, and the blackout had eliminated the harbor lights. The stars cast an uncomfortable amount of light, but the water was dotted with debris. There were no challenges from the sentries.

The swim took longer than Landry planned, but he finally pulled himself up the ladder he had picked out earlier. He looked down at his uniform, which had lost most of the coffee coloring. "Shit!" he muttered as he ran for a protective shadow.

Trailing dribbles of water, shoes squishing, he trotted toward town looking for a cab. The blackout suited him perfectly; he kept to the shadows, not wanting to be seen by the police or a military patrol. He spotted a cab waiting by a movie theater.

When Landry jumped into the back of his cab, the little Filipino turned. "Hey, man, you get my cab wet!"

"You won't get any complaints from other passengers," Landry promised. "I'll pay for the whole night."

The driver hesitated. "Twenty pesos?"

Landry knew it was too much, but he didn't have time to argue. "Fine. I'll give you ten now and the other ten when you drop me back here."

At their destination, Landry jumped out. "You'll stay here, right?"

"Where else I make money middle of night with wet cab?"

Just before midnight, Landry slipped into the apartment. "Teresa, it's me," he said softly so as not to alarm her.

"Oh, Hank! Thank God," her sleepy voice said from the tiny bedroom.

When he rushed to join her, her look of joy was replaced by laughter. "Where you been? It not raining."

"I had to swim ashore." He began stripping his wet uniform off.

"My turn now." Teresa voice was husky and she sat up and pulled her night dress over her head. Behind the mosquito net, her dusky, brown-nippled breasts seemed to beckon him. "Tell me about it later."

He slid into bed beside Teresa. Her body was warm and smooth. She wrapped her arms around him and he felt her firm breasts press against his chest. Joy, passion, and regret surged through Landry. She groaned as he entered her. Their lovemaking was quick and frenzied. He held her tightly when they finished. He wanted time to stop so he could stay locked in that moment forever. As they lay in each other's arms, he stroked her breasts which were larger and even firmer than they had been before.

"It looks like your body's getting ready for our little one," he said softly.

"Hank, you guessed." Her voice was anxious.

"No. Chief Hanlon told me. I was too damn stupid to figure it out. Yeah, I still love you. If it wasn't for the war, I'd marry you."

"What going to happen?" Teresa asked.

"Everyone says the ship is leaving tomorrow, but I don't know where."

"When you come back?"

He hesitated, dreading facing the truth himself, much less having to tell Teresa. "I don't know. Months. Maybe years."

She buried her head on his shoulder. "You leave me before dawn?"

"Yes."

Teresa cried softly in his arms, and Landry stroked her silky body softly to console her. Soon, she kissed him with a demanding intensity, and her soft hands aroused him. Their lovemaking this time was slow and patient as if each wanted to prolong an ecstasy which might never be theirs again. The intensity of his shuddering climax drained Landry.

He lay back on the pillow as he realized how much he hated leaving Teresa. There seemed little reason to go back to the *O'Leary*. He had few friends aboard, and there was Mortland.

"Maybe I'll let the ship leave without me," he said.

"That not be trouble?"

"The brig if they catch me. Maybe worse. Maybe a firing squad."

Her intake of breath was sharp.

"The Japs may get me if I go back."

Teresa was silent for a long time. "If you not go back, we live in fear forever. If . . . if I lose you, I'd rather you be on ship. I live with that. I not bear it if you dead because of me. What should I tell our child?"

Landry stared at a crack in the plaster ceiling. It ran to meet another crack—which spread to another. Just like life, he thought, it wasn't simple.

"Okay, I'll go back."

Landry could feel her tears on his chest. He refused to fall asleep, trying to make the most of each minute, knowing he would have to leave soon. They made love gently for one final time, as if to seal their commitment to one another.

Landry put on a dry uniform. "This won't stay dry, but it won't do me any good here in the closet." He realized that they would share no more hours of happiness in this place.

She said goodbye to him at the door.

"You'll stay with Maria?"

"Yes, I think she enjoy the baby. It sad they not have any of their own. It be all right to tell her they be godparents?"

"Perfect. I can't think of anyone I respect more'n Chief Hanlon."

They said their final goodbye. As she clung to him, he stroked her hair. After a final lingering kiss, he left and closed the door. Out front, he roused the cabdriver. "Here's the rest of your money. Take me back."

"We be there half-hour. Before dawn."

The driver dropped Landry a block away from the piers. Landry dug into his pockets for the few pesos he hadn't left with Teresa. "Here, take these. I won't be needing them."

The little man smiled and stuffed the bills in his pocket. "Bet she worth the trip! Good luck! As we say—Mabuhay!"

Landry slipped through the shadows cast by the large warehouses and headed toward the pier where he had climbed ashore. He paused before crossing the last few yards in the open. He took a deep breath and trotted out of the shadows.

"Halt, swabbie! Or I'll blow your ass off!" Two Army M.P.s stepped out of the shadow of a building. "Look what we got, Corporal." A beefy, red-faced sergeant chortled.

"Yep, we caught one going over the hill, all right," agreed his companion, who levelled a rifle at Landry's mid-section.

Landry's gut tightened. He was too far from the edge of the pier to run. He raised his hands. "You guys got me. I've already been to visit my girl. I'm headed back to my ship." He pointed at the dark shape of the *O'Leary*.

The sergeant laughed contemptuously. "You gonna walk out there? Maybe you have your own private speedboat?"

"Same way I got here—swim. If you take me to the brig, I'll miss my ship. She's leaving today. All you'll be doing is helping the Japs."

"Seems he's got a point, Sarge. Save us filling out a lot of paperwork."

The sergeant was silent. He moved some pebbles about with his polished boots. "Ah, hell! I must be getting soft. Who am I to stop someone who would swim that far for a crack at the Nips. My brother's on a battleship at Pearl. I still don't know if he's okay."

"Thanks, Sarge." Landry suddenly thought that the Army wasn't hopeless after all.

As he climbed down the ladder, the two M.P.s stood over him at the pier's edge. "Good luck, swabbie. We'll be watching. If you head somewhere besides that ship, we'll nail you with this rifle. That's a promise."

"Thanks again." Landry waved and pushed off. The swim seemed to take longer than before because he felt drained of physical and emotional energy. By the time he reached the *O'Leary*, his arms and legs were shaking with fatigue.

He grabbed the first of a series of rungs welded to the ship's side and hung on. When he heard the tread of the stern sentry above, he whispered hoarsely, "Pssst! Don't look down, just stop." Nystrom's tall form halted alongside the lifelines. "When you see the coast is clear, just turn around and head back the other way."

When Nystrom pivoted and resumed his slow patrol, Landry clambered up the ladder. He peeped over the deck edge, saw nothing but shadows, and scrambled through the lifelines. He turned for the after head where he had stashed a dry uniform.

"Stop right there!" Chief Mortland walked up to Landry. "You're on report—AWOL. You're in deep shit now!"

CHAPTER ELEVEN

The next afternoon, shortly before their departure, Chief Hanlon peered through the big signal bridge telescope, hoping to see the suburb where Maria lived.

"It's no use, Chief," Landry said. "I just looked. It's too hazy to see anything."

Hanlon shook his head. "Thought I'd give it a try. We may not have a chance to see our neighborhood for a while. You know, someone told me our Navy's been out here on the China Station since 1835."

"Getting our butts booted out now," Landry said.

Hanlon considered the rumors he'd heard about Pearl Harbor. If they were true, he knew it might be years before the Navy would be strong enough to fight the Japanese so near their home waters. As he looked down at the main deck, he realized that he and Landry weren't the only ones with the same problem. Two Filipino stewards stood at the starboard rail, gazing at Manila. "Poor stewards," Hanlon said. "Gonna be even harder for them to leave."

"Surprised they haven't jumped ship," Landry said.

"My hat's off to 'em for staying."

The bosun's pipe shrilled, calling the special sea detail.

"Guess we'd better get to work," said Hanlon, as he headed back to the after deckhouse. There he stood in front of the rest of the men in his division. At anchor, there were no lines to handle; Hanlon had nothing to do but stare at the Manila waterfront as they slid away, the deck vibrating with the beat of the propellers. Familiar landmarks, part of his life for almost a decade, grew smaller and smaller and faded into the haze as if they never had existed.

Memories of Hanlon's years with the Asiatic Fleet surged through his mind. Yangtze River patrol—the muddy water full of garbage. Shanghai—beggars dying in the streets. Manila—meeting Maria. Summers in Chefoo—rickshaws for a dime. Subic Bay and Olongapo. Maria. Hong Kong—trips across the harbor to Kowloon. Tsingtao—liberty in north China. Singapore—huge guns pointing to sea. Manila and Maria at night. Maria—Maria—Maria.

Fraser had the watch as officer of the deck after the *O'Leary* rendezvoused with three merchant ships late that afternoon. They would make a night departure through the minefields at the entrance to the bay.

"Merchant ships are starting to bunch up again, Captain," Fraser reported.

Muttering, Arkwright hopped down from his bridge chair and walked the few steps back to the signal bridge. Seconds later one of the hooded signal lamps began to chatter.

The captain returned to his chair. "Maybe that blast will keep them in position."

"Maybe not," Fraser said as signal lamps astern winked acknowledgments. "Those merchant captains seem to have minds of their own. Captain, do you expect a Jap submarine outside the entrance?"

"The fleet staff must be worried. Otherwise, we wouldn't be going out at night."

Fraser was suddenly glad his general quarters station wasn't below decks. If they hit a mine, at least he had a chance to swim away.

After Chuck Steiner relieved him, Fraser just had time for a quick dinner before the general quarters alarm sounded for the trip out through the minefield. By the time they reached the mined channel, darkness had descended. The moon would not rise until after midnight, but brilliant stars cast a pale light. From his station on the fire control platform, Fraser watched a quartermaster on each bridge wing take bearings on nearby landmarks. Chief Jablonski was plotting cross bearings on the chart table in the pilot house to obtain their position. The navigational task was difficult: the normal navigational lights ashore or on buoys had been turned off to hinder enemy submarines and aircraft. Fortunately, the light from the stars outlined the buoys, as well as nearby points of land on Corregidor and the end of Bataan Peninsula.

"Twenty yards right of the center of the channel," Jablonski sang out from the pilot house. "Recommend two seven eight, Captain."

Down on the port wing, Arkwright answered, "Very well. Come left to two seven eight. Woody, take a look astern and make sure all our friends are still with us."

Woody Korchak, their reserve ensign, clumped back to the signal bridge. The chunky Korchak ran back seconds later. "The ship astern has closed to about 200 yards and is about 30 yards out to port. The others are closing up, too."

"Dammit!" Arkwright said. "There's enough light for them to keep station better than that. Signal watch! Tell those civilians to get back on station!"

"Aye, aye, Captain." The hooded light chattered.

Jablonski called out, "I have us near the center of the channel now, Captain. Recommend two eight zero."

The captain ordered the course change. He elevated his Roman nose and began to sniff the breeze as if seeking to confirm the navigational information with his own senses. Fraser thought the captain looked like a hunting dog straining for a scent.

"I make us near the right edge of the channel now. Recommend two seven eight," Jablonski said.

Before Arkwright could order the change, the port lookout shouted, "Mine! Just off the port bow! One hundred yards!"

Fraser was stunned. Port bow! We must be in the minefield! Have to come left to get out! No! We'll turn into the mine ahead. Christ, what should we do?

Arkwright's calm voice cut through the confusion below. "Is your last fix a good one, Chief?"

"Yessir! All four bearings intersect at the same point. That mine must be a floater."

Fraser realized the chief was right: they wouldn't have seen the mine if it were still attached to its moorings.

"Helmsman, nothing to the left of our present course," the captain ordered.

"Aye, aye, sir. Nothing to the left of two eight zero," repeated the helmsman, his voice cracking with tension.

"We're getting pretty close to the right edge of the channel, Captain," Jablonski reported.

"No choice, Chief," Arkwright said.

Fraser realized they faced a tight squeeze between the floating mine and its tethered brethren. There was more room to clear the drifting mine on the left side of the channel, but it was too late for that option.

The captain looked up from the bridge wing. "Ross, get your machine gun battery ready to destroy the mine after we pass it! I'll have the signalmen illuminate it."

Fraser passed the word through his talker, Eckersly. A machine gun breech clattered on the amidships deckhouse as the gun was loaded. Fraser leaned against the rail of the fire control platform and watched the bobbing sphere approach. Protruding horns—detonators—glinted in the starlight. The mine was bigger than Fraser expected, and he wondered how much explosive it contained. "Christ!" he muttered. "This'll be close!"

The captain turned and looked aft. "God damn!"

Fraser wheeled around. The first merchant ship was only 200 yards off the port quarter. The mine was almost sure to hit the merchant ship if it missed the *O'Leary*. Fraser had expected to leave the mine well astern before the order to commence firing. Now he realized they wouldn't have much margin for error. It would have to be destroyed when it passed far enough astern not to damage the *O'Leary*, but not so far that the mine might endanger the merchant ship. The civilian vessel also was going to be near the line of fire from the *O'Leary*'s machine gun.

"Tell your gunner to be ready to shoot when the mine's about 75 yards off our quarter," the captain shouted. "He'd better not miss."

"Shifflet's on the gun," Fraser said. "He can do it."

The *O'Leary* glided through the dark water toward the deadly sphere. It slid by the port side, barely 10 feet away. The ugly shape glistened as small waves lapped around it. Fraser shuddered. The mine could have blown their bow off if they'd run into it. Fraser prayed that the buffeting of the bow wave wouldn't set it off. He knew it shouldn't. The mine wasn't designed to be that sensitive; one of the horns had to be bent or broken. But it wasn't designed to break away from its mooring, either. The sinister black shape heaved up and down as the bow wave caught it, but nothing happened.

Fraser felt sweat trickle down his sides as the mine cleared the fantail. As the *O'Leary* pulled away, the first merchant ship plowed inexorably toward the mine.

"Illuminate with the light!" Arkwright ordered.

The white beam shot toward the bobbing black mine and settled on it.

Fraser took a deep breath and waited for the order.

"Commence firing!" Fraser's shout echoed the captain's.

The tense silence was ripped by the roar of Shifflet's machine gun spitting tracers at the mine. A line of splashes walked up to the mine and past it, but nothing happened.

"Come on you bastard! Explode!" pleaded Fraser.

The angle between the *O'Leary*'s line of fire and the first merchant ship narrowed second by second. The vessel appeared to be headed directly for the bobbing menace. The stream of projectiles walked back over the mine. Some of the bullets bounced off and ricocheted toward the merchant ship, but minor damage seemed the least of the large ship's problems; she was barely 50 yards from the mine.

Suddenly, there was a blinding flash. A shattering roar shook the *O'Leary*, and Fraser had to grab the rail to stay upright. A huge spout of water rose into the air and hung suspended before tumbling back. Seconds later, small pieces of metal rattled down around Fraser.

"Ask all stations for damage reports," the captain ordered from the bridge wing.

The destroyer had been severely shaken, but all the reports from the talkers were negative.

"Captain, we're 30 yards right of the center of the channel," Jablonski reported. "Recommend steer two seven six."

"Very well," said Arkwright, who gave the order to the helmsman. "Keep up the good work, Chief."

Five minutes later, Korchak came back from the signal bridge where he had just checked the ships astern. "They're all exactly where they're supposed to be, Captain."

Arkwright grunted. "I guess that mine was worth a hundred nasty messages."

Fraser looked down at the bridge wing at Arkwright's dim figure and envied the way the captain had handled the situation. He thought back to the crucial moment and realized that he would probably have maneuvered the ship out of the channel and right into the minefield. Fraser was thankful the captain had been in control.

As they passed Corregidor, the dark mass of the island fortress looked as indestructible as ever to Fraser. He now knew that was just an illusion. If the Japanese could take the nearby Bataan Peninsula, Corregidor was doomed. In the starlight, the massive rocks and walls of the immense fortress seemed to project an aura of gloom. The fall of Bataan and Corregidor seemed as inevitable as death. Fraser knew a lot of good men were going to die there. He felt guilty about leaving the Army defenders behind, but then he remembered how the Army air resources had been squandered. The situation was now so bad, the Army was sending its remaining B-17s south to Australia. That eased Fraser's sense of guilt, but not much.

As they neared the end of the channel, the antisubmarine battle stations were manned. From the fire control platform, Fraser could hear the high-pitched pings of the sonar in the charthouse near the back of the bridge. Although their sonar was a big improvement over the primitive passive listening equipment of World War I, its detection range was about 2,000 yards in good conditions. The sonar could be almost useless if water temperatures and gradients were not favorable. The steady pinging continued but there were no tell-tale echoes to indicate a submarine as the little convoy left the mouth of the bay.

"Captain," the lee helmsman called from the pilot house, "main control requests permission to shut down the number four boiler. That mine explosion did some damage inside."

"How soon can they fix it?"

"They think it's gonna take a yard or a tender to help us, sir."

Oh-oh, Fraser thought after he heard the last report. Now we're down to two boilers.

After clearing the minefields, Arkwright ordered the course changed to the south. The convoy pointed its bows toward Java, almost 2,000 miles away. The *O'Leary* took station several thousand yards in front of the plodding merchant vessels to guard against enemy submarines. They secured from general quarters and assumed a Condition III watch—one-third of the crew on watch with some of the weapons manned.

Fraser was depressed by the prospect of his upcoming midwatch; it would allow only a few hours' sleep before pre-dawn general quarters. But then his fatigue eased as he thought of their destination: Java and Ilsa Van Dorn. He wondered would she even see him again? How much would she remember of the last evening? He sighed as he realized those questions wouldn't be answered before seven or eight days of steaming through hazardous waters. Fraser consoled himself with the thought that, despite the disasters which the Navy and Army had suffered so far, the *O'Leary* had been fortunate. He hoped their luck would continue.

It did not. Three days later, after a numbing succession of Condition III watches, a weary Fraser had taken over the first dog watch. Ten minutes into the watch, the lee helmsman yelled, "Mr. Fraser, main control reports casualty in the number three boiler! They're shutting it down."

"Very well. Messenger, go tell the captain."

While Fraser was waiting for Arkwright, he realized they were down to the number one boiler.

Arkwright arrived on the bridge, buttoning his shirt and carrying his shoes. One arm gleamed with soap suds. "Can't even get a shower," he muttered.

As soon as the boiler was secured, Jack Meredith reported to the captain, now in his bridge chair. Meredith's eyes were red, and the dark circles under his eyes matched the grime on his hands.

"Looks bad, Captain. It'll be a few hours before we can get inside the boiler. We'll probably need yard or tender help and maybe a week."

"Just like number four," Arkwright said.

"Yes, sir. I'm afraid that mine explosion did some real damage. Another day or two and we may have number two ready to steam again, but I don't know how long she'll hold up."

The captain nodded grimly. "Now I know why you wanted that overhaul so badly. Tell your men to keep up their hard work. This would be a hell of a place to break down completely."

Fraser heard the clatter of leather shoes on the ladder at the back of the bridge. The oil-streaked messenger of the engineering watch ran up to Meredith. "Sir, Simpson says he needs you in the forward fireroom as soon as possible!"

Meredith closed his eyes and leaned against the bridge bulwark. "Did he say what the trouble was?"

"Main steam line's starting to leak."

"Damn!" Meredith shook his head and groaned. "Excuse me, Captain, I'd better go right down."

"Keep me informed, Jack." Arkwright got down from his chair and began pacing the deck restlessly, his bushy eyebrows furrowed.

Fraser glanced at the chart. They were about 600 miles south of Manila, still undiscovered by the enemy. Fraser wondered what they would do if they lost their last boiler. He didn't envy the captain. Not only was Arkwright responsible for his ship, but he was also responsible for the three merchant ships.

Twenty minutes later, Meredith returned. "Two of the old gaskets in the steam lines in the forward fire room are about to go. If we reduce pressure and slow down to 6 or 7 knots, they might last until morning."

"How long to replace them?" Arkwright asked grimly.

"Probably twenty-four hours to do the job right. We can probably have number two ready by then, too."

Meredith and Jablonski, the chief quartermaster, joined the captain at the chart table. "Jolo Harbor is only about 60 miles away," Jablonski said.

"They've been reporting air attacks recently," Arkwright said.

Jablonski tapped the chart with his pencil. "I've been there before. The islands are of volcanic origin. There's deep water right next to some of them. I think we could get in close to shore and camouflage ourselves."

"That means letting the convoy go ahead on its own," Arkwright said.

"Yes, sir. No way to hide all of them," Jablonski said.

Arkwright frowned. "I'm not sure we're doing these civilians much good anyway. There haven't been any reports of Japanese submarine activity to the south. God knows, we can barely protect ourselves against air attack, much less them."

Minutes later, the signal lamp chattered Arkwright's instructions for the merchant ships to continue south independently. The *O'Leary*'s bow swung to port as she changed course for Jolo in the Sulu Archipelago. Fraser watched the merchant ships disappear over the horizon and wondered who felt more alone.

Hank Landry had the 04-08 watch the next morning. His Condition III station was on the amidships deckhouse where he strapped himself behind one of the .50-caliber machine guns. If they ran into a Japanese surface ship, he and the other three men around him would run for one of the nearby 4-inch guns. Landry had compared some of their drills to a game of reverse musical chairs; the problem was knowing which weapon to man. Even at general quarters, the amidships deckhouse only had enough men to man one of the 4-inch guns near each rail. The gun crew was supposed to man whichever gun was toward the enemy.

Landry spent most of the watch with an ear cocked toward the number one stack, listening for sounds of trouble. He was well aware that the boiler below was their only source of power. There was only the gentle whoosh of hot gases rising from the round metal rim of the gray stack.

Just before dawn steam jetted out of the stack and Landry jumped.

"Just blowing tubes," Shifflet said.

"Ready for a fight?" said Landry.

"Bet your ass! I ain't been ashore for over a week. Didn't finish lettin' off steam from my restriction."

"You look a lot healthier than when you were raising hell all the time," Landry said.

"Healthy, hell! Gonna die of boredom afore long." Shifflet turned to his loader. "Take over the gun." The gunner's mate strolled over to Landry's gun. "Rumors about you bein' AWOL true?"

"Mortland wrote me up."

"I remember you goin' down to the boat that night. Did you go over the hill?"

"Could be."

"Bad business, boy."

"You're a fine one to talk."

"Got us a war on now. Probably means a court martial."

"Damn."

"Come see me, sometime. Maybe I can give you some advice. If'n anybody knows how to beat the system, I do."

"Thanks," Landry said.

Reveille sounded when the first gray light began to appear in the moonless sky.

"Be at G. Q. in a few minutes," Shifflet said.

"Why the hell do we do this every morning," Landry asked.

"Might be somebody out there in the dark," Shifflet said. "First one to start shooting would probably win. Just like a bar fight—never let someone sneak up and get the first punch."

Dawn revealed the islands of the Sulu Archipelago just ahead. The *O'Leary* slipped into Jolo Harbor and anchored off a small island with a steep shoreline. Landry took his station in the bow of the whaleboat, and it headed for the nearby shoreline. Beringer sat back and watched Chief Mortland sound the bottom with a hand-held lead line. Landry had to admit Mortland handled the line with skill.

"Plenty deep right along this shore," Mortland said after he finished his survey.

"All set then," Beringer said.

"Not quite, sir. We have some work to do ashore first." Fifteen minutes later, Landry and the rest of the boat crew were sweating in the humidity as they took turns chopping at a tree near the water's edge.

Mortland sat on a nearby rock and puffed a cigarette. "We ain't got all day! Japs may be coming. Hurry up!"

Ten minutes later there was a splitting crack. The tree toppled into the water, jutting out from the shore.

"Now we got something to keep the stern from swinging aground," Mortland said.

Landry admired the captain's skill as the *O'Leary* glided in, dropped anchor, and twisted around to butt her stern against the fallen tree. Lines were sent ashore, and the destroyer's bow was secured between the anchor on one side and lines ashore on the other. The stern was moored to the tree.

"Glad that's over with," Landry said.

"Your work's just beginning," Mortland said.

The ship's boats ferried men ashore to cut vegetation for camouflaging the *O'Leary*. Some of the more adventurous foragers clambered across the tree butted against the stern.

"Hard work," Ben Nystrom said as he slashed vines alongside Landry.

"Worth it," said Tim Egan, the torpedoman, swinging a machete with his good left hand. "Until we get some camouflage, we're sitting ducks."

"Let's get with it," Landry said. "I don't want to spend the rest of the war stuck here."

Nystrom slapped at mosquitoes. "Yeah, this place is bad. But not as bad as when Mortland shipped us off to the snipes."

Landry remembered the terrible heat in the fireroom. "Yeah, even the bugs are smart enough not to go down there."

The boats ferried heaps of vegetation back to the ship. Soon the main deck and upper works were covered with palm branches, small trees, and trailing vines.

"Looks just like a little island," Nystrom said.

"Let's hope the Japs think so," said Egan.

When Landry and Nystrom crawled aboard over the large tree, Simpson was taking a break, sitting on a mooring bitt. "I always knew there was a reason for calling you guys 'deck apes.' You look right at home in that tree. I hope you brought a bunch of bananas for Mortland."

Landry expected Mortland to be pleased with their work, but when they found him on the forecastle, the chief boatswain was steaming. "Hell's fire! Wouldn't you know it! Took a week to get the coffee drippings from those damned uniforms cleaned up! Now it's dirt! Mud! Berries! All over the decks . . . on my frigging ship!"

Mortland paced up and down the forecastle, red-faced and muttering obscenities. "It's those frigging snipes' fault. If they hadn't broken down, this never would have happened. I hope the Japs drop a bomb right down a frigging stack. Damn those soot-belching boilers!"

"Aircraft!" shouted a lookout from the crows nest, which now resembled the top of a palm tree.

The four-engined seaplane orbited slowly in the distance. Landry peered through the foliage and tried to guess whether it had seen them.

"What do you think, Chief?" Nystrom asked Mortland.

"This ship is such a God-awful mess! How could a Jap think this pile of crap is the property of the U.S. Navy?"

The plane banked and flew off to the southeast.

"We'll know whether he saw us in a few hours," Landry said. "He may be radioing his friends."

They manned the antiaircraft guns and waited for the Japanese. Landry kept adjusting his position behind the machine gun to take advantage of the shade cast by the foliage overhead. "Not as good as the awnings, but at least it's shade," he muttered. From time to time, a grimy, soot-stained man emerged from the forward fireroom and shuffled aft to the crews' head for relief. "Poor bastards," Landry said, surprised at his sympathy.

Dusk finally came and ended the possibility of a Japanese attack that day. Landry spent a restless night trying to sleep. He kept wondering if the Japanese would find them before the engineers finished their repairs. Lying in his bunk, he felt almost guilty because he knew the engineers were working and sweating in the forward fireroom.

Morning brought reveille and general quarters. On the amidships deckhouse, Landry, ready for action, elevated his machine gun and swung it fore and aft. The sky remained empty. Two hours after dawn, they secured from general quarters and Landry turned his gun over to a relief. He reported to the forecastle where Mortland gave his men instructions to start cleaning up. The chief wrinkled his nose in disgust. Piles of bird droppings littered the decks. The *O'Leary*'s disguise had been so effective that several flocks of tropical birds had spent the night in the foliage.

Mortland mumbled obscenities through his clenched jaw. "I don't know why we bother to throw the garbage over the fantail anymore. Might as well toss it on my decks."

Landry struggled to keep a straight face. "War is hell, ain't it, Chief?" He pointed at a pile of brown bark lying near Mortland. "Watch your step. That monkey shit smells awful."

"Monkey shit?" Mortland sputtered, turned even redder, and stomped toward the fantail.

The boatswain trotted back ten minutes later. "Snipes are ready to go! Get rid of the rest of this damn camouflage!"

Before the cleanup was half done, the special sea and anchor detail was called. Landry ran up to his lookout post on the bridge wing and watched as the lines were taken in and the anchor was hoisted. Mortland stamped around the forecastle glaring at the festoons of vines fluttering in the breeze.

"Seems the bosun is not pleased with our appearance," the captain said.

Landry didn't stop smiling until he thought of the Japanese aircraft that would be waiting for any ships headed south.

CHAPTER TWELVE

Fraser stepped out on the bridge wing ready to take over the afternoon watch. It felt good to be on the move again after lying helpless in Jolo. The chart showed the ship near the mouth of Sibutu Strait which would allow her to leave the Sulu Sea and enter the Celebes Sea.

"Any sign of the Japs?" Fraser asked after Durham briefed him on the routine information of the watch.

"Not yet," Durham said. "But the Japs know everything heading south has to go through Sibutu Strait. Bound to be somebody waiting for us."

"Probably some shore-based bombers," Fraser said.

"Still have two boilers, so we've got 25 knots on tap to dodge 'em," Durham said.

In his head Fraser said a word of thanks for the laws of physics which meant that half-power could give them about three-fourths of their top speed. The third and fourth boilers would have only added a few knots each. But the extra boilers would have given them a valuable backup; both steaming boilers were in the forward fireroom. One bomb or one blown steam line could leave them powerless.

"Any problems with the boilers?" Fraser said.

"Nothing during my watch," Durham said.

"No news is good news. I relieve you, sir."

Thirty minutes later, Arkwright eased down from his bridge chair, glanced at the chart, and joined Fraser on the bridge wing where he scanned the horizon and sniffed the breeze. "Ross, everyone's had time to eat. We're close enough to Sibutu Strait to get some air activity any time now. Let's go to general quarters."

Minutes later, Fraser turned the deck over to Woody Korchak and climbed to the fire control platform, where he buckled on his headset. Durham joined him as an additional spotter since the threat was from the air; a surface contact would have sent Durham up to the crow's nest.

Fraser took a mental inventory of his assets. The 3-inch gun was ready to fire a fixed barrage with fuzes set at 2,000 yards. The four .50-caliber machine guns were loaded and ready. It wasn't much.

A half-hour of waiting began to dull the edge of Fraser's tension. But a lookout's shouted report jerked him back to full alert. Fraser swung his binoculars around and scanned the sky off the starboard bow. There! Just over ten miles away. A high-flying four-engined seaplane banked and began to circle the ship.

"Kawanishi flying boat," Durham said. "Bet he's sending our position back to base right now."

Fraser looked down to the bridge wing where Arkwright dropped his binoculars and looked up. "I hope those extra machine guns are ready," the captain said.

They could only stand and wait as the distant shores of the Sibutu Strait approached and narrowed down. The flying boat dogging the *O'Leary* finally turned away and disappeared.

"Feel like a damn steer being driven into the slaughter pen," said Durham as they entered the confined strait.

The sun burned high in a clear sky. Far to the south, the tops of cumulus clouds poked over the horizon. A shouted report from another lookout marked the end of their wait. Three twin-engined Japanese Army bombers turned and circled the destroyer, far outside the ship's limited antiaircraft range. The enemy slowly descended to 8,000 feet and made a wide turn, heading toward the *O'Leary*.

Arkwright snapped his order from the bridge wing. "All ahead flank. Make turns for 25 knots."

The men at the throttles below were apparently well aware of the danger above; the destroyer's stern squatted quickly and her bow raised a ribbon of water. The blowers whined at a higher pitch, and the ship vibrated as the screws bit into the blue-green water. The wake boiled up as high as the fantail.

Durham lowered his binoculars. "I just hope these Jap Army pilots aren't any better than ours."

That thought encouraged Fraser, but only for a few seconds. Even though he had been under enemy attack twice, the gravity of their position suddenly dawned on him as he scanned the horizon. There were no friendly forces nearby. The nearest land other than small islands was hundreds of miles away. Fraser yearned for the solid ground of Ohio and the comfort of his family, almost half a world away.

The enemy formation arrowed for the *O'Leary* but remained at 8,000 feet. Fraser tensed, waiting for the captain's next order. He bit his lip and locked his binoculars on the oncoming enemy aircraft.

When the bombs fell free, the captain snapped his order, "Right full rudder!"

"Right full rudder, sir," the helmsman shouted from the pilothouse, and the big wheel whined.

The *O'Leary* heeled heavily to port in her high-speed turn. Fraser heard loose pencils slide across the chart table and rattle on the pilothouse gratings. There was no sound from the men around him as the bombs descended. The unemployed gun crew on the forecastle scurried for cover or hit the deck. The bombs neared with a whistling shriek and exploded in a neat pattern a safe distance to port, lifting plumes of white water mixed with ugly black smoke.

"Left standard rudder!" Arkwright ordered, conning the ship back into the center of the deep water, where they would have maneuvering room on either side for the next attack.

Durham slapped Fraser on the back of his life jacket. "Maybe these guys aren't so tough after all."

Fraser felt some of his apprehension lift.

Three times, the deadly dance was repeated; the bombers came lower on each run as they discovered the limitations of the destroyer's antiaircraft defenses. Each time, Arkwright outguessed the bombers and maneuvered clear of the bombs, which did no more than shake the ship.

"You'd think these guys would get tired and go home," Durham said as the attacks continued.

"You'd better get used to this." Fraser clutched the rail for reassurance.

After a last run, the bombers withdrew.

"Maybe we can get to that cloud cover before their friends show up." Durham pointed toward the growing gray masses to the south.

They were still miles from cover when another three twin-engined bombers, neatly arranged in a vee-shaped formation, appeared over the horizon. Again the Japanese repeated their tactics, but Arkwright avoided the plummeting bombs. Three near misses shook the ship, but only a few pieces of shrapnel hit with metallic clanks, doing no real damage to the destroyer or its crew.

By the end of the second series of attacks, the *O'Leary* had sprinted through the confines of Sibutu Strait and into open water. As a third wave of bombers appeared, the destroyer dodged into a squall line. Tropical rain splatted off metal surfaces and drowned out the drone of the circling bombers. Arkwright maneuvered from squall to squall until the approach of darkness offered more permanent protection.

Just as the sun dipped below the horizon, another shower swept the ship. Fraser had just put away his headset and stood in the downpour letting the water wash away the afternoon's sweat. He watched Chief Mortland gather some of his hands on the forecastle and put them to work sweeping away the bird droppings. When they finished, Mortland seemed to straighten, as if he were no longer ashamed of the *O'Leary*'s appearance. Fraser shook his head at Mortland's perseverance and climbed down to the bridge.

Fraser stepped into the pilothouse where the captain was bent over the chart table. "How does the situation look?" Fraser asked.

"We'll be entering Makassar Strait in the morning."

"Another strait," Fraser said.

"Not as confined. There's plenty of maneuvering room."

"But Japanese patrol planes will find us."

Arkwright nodded. "That's not our only problem. We've already used a lot of fuel by maneuvering at high speed. We'll have to stop at Balikpapan tomorrow night for refueling."

"I'd forgotten about fuel," Fraser said.

"A destroyer captain always worries about fuel. So does any higher officer with destroyers under his command."

Fraser knew that the captain was right. The *O'Leary*'s engineering plant produced as much power as an old battleship, but it also took up a lot of hull space, leaving little room for fuel tanks. High speeds like they had employed that afternoon rapidly drained their 110,000-gallon fuel supply.

"More time in destroyers and you won't forget about fuel," the captain said.

Fraser wished he were aboard a new cruiser in safer waters.

The next morning, T. T. Simpson roamed his general quarters station on the grating in the forward fireroom. Simpson stopped pacing and leaned against a railing and watched his men tending the demands of the boilers for fuel oil and feedwater.

"Where are the Japs?" one of the younger men asked. "Damn waiting is getting to me."

"Be here soon enough," Simpson said. Got enough problems already, he thought. Number two still ain't right.

Suddenly, the order for maximum speed came down from the bridge. Simpson's men inserted additional burners in the fire box fronts to increase the flow of fuel oil inside the boilers. Simpson gazed at the number two boiler and its maze of piping, knowing it might be dangerous to strain the boiler. Then he thought of the havoc a Japanese bomb would cause in the fireroom. He decided it was safer to take a chance on number two.

"Hope the bitch holds together," Simpson muttered.

As their speed picked up, Simpson listened to the rising howl of the blowers and the roar from the boilers. Vibrations from the turbines and propellers filtered through the grating under his feet. But there was something else. There. He prowled the grating and looked at the face of the number two boiler. He placed his foot against the boiler casing; a low-frequency vibration pulsed through the sole of his shoe. It was the sort of vibration that could resonate through the piping and eventually cause the kind of casualty they had experienced a month ago. He turned and put his foot against number one. Much steadier—no vibration.

The man on the feed check valve wiped his neck and looked over his shoulder at Simpson. "Shouldn't we slow down?"

Before Simpson could answer, he had to grab the rail as the ship heeled in a hard turn. Explosions rocked the hull and drove any thought of securing number two from Simpson's mind.

"Too close," one man said as dust filtered down from the overhead.

"Both boilers at maximum power?" Simpson asked.

His men answered affirmatively.

Simpson stared at number two. Just get us to Java, he thought. Know damn well something's wrong. Just don't shake a steam line apart.

More explosions shook the grating.

Two hours of intermittent attacks continued before the bridge slowed to 16 knots. The men in the forward fireroom sweated the rest of the afternoon away.

"Don't hear anyone asking where the Japs are now," Simpson said.

"Long as it ain't here, I don't care," said a sweat-soaked water tender.

At dusk the *O'Leary* steamed into the Borneo port of Balikpapan, used by the Dutch to export oil. As the destroyer glided across the still water, a launch approached with a Dutch naval officer who boarded and guided them alongside a pier for refueling. After the black oil started pulsing aboard, the officers gathered at the wardroom table to attack a backlog of paperwork.

Fraser sipped a cup of coffee as he shuffled through a report. He glanced around the green-covered table and noted that the stress of combat seemed to be aging the younger officers although the war was only two weeks old. Faces were drawn and lined. Several officers leaned on the arms of their chairs, too tired to sit erect.

"Balikpapan is a veritable magnet for the Japs," Laster said. "The oil here is what they want."

Beringer rattled his coffee cup. "That wouldn't be so if that idiot Roosevelt hadn't cut off our oil shipments to the Japs. They would never have started this war if he hadn't done so many stupid things."

"If your uncle's buddies had given the military some more money, the Japs wouldn't have done anything," Laster said.

Durham yawned. "Maybe you two gentlemen could settle this another time."

But Fraser thought Laster was right. Why hadn't the country done more for the armed services? If the men out here were ready to sacrifice their lives, why couldn't the civilians have made some financial sacrifices to equip them properly?

The captain walked into the wardroom. "Jack, how are we doing with the refueling?"

"It's almost finished, Captain. We should be ready to leave within the hour. We'll have enough fuel aboard to maneuver at high speed and still reach Surabaya."

"Are we leaving tonight?" Durham asked.

Arkwright shook his head. "I think we'll wait until first light. Coming in, the reefs and minefields were difficult enough to avoid in the daylight. I think we'd be foolish to try it in the dark."

"I agree," Beringer said quickly.

Arkwright said, "Reveille at 0430 so we can feed everyone before getting under way. Any other questions? Ross, put on a clean uniform. I want you to go over to the Dutch governor's mansion with me."

Fraser pushed back his chair as the captain walked into his cabin. "I hope the captain doesn't think I learned much Dutch from Ilsa."

"You must have learned something," Laster said.

"Only a few words."

Durham smirked. "If they're words she whispered in your ear, the governor might chuck you in the local jail."

"I'm afraid I don't work as fast as you, Bull."

"Don't feel bad. Few do."

A half-hour later Arkwright and Fraser walked up the gravel path to the governor's mansion, a wood-framed house with a thatched roof surrounded by tropical plants and trees. Inside, they settled in rattan chairs. A servant handed them warm pink gins. Arkwright held his as if he'd been given a hand grenade. The governor welcomed them in passable English; Fraser was thankful his few words of Dutch wouldn't be needed.

The governor sat back in his chair and unbuttoned his bulging jacket with a chuckle. "I've put on a few pounds lately. I'll be damned if the Japs will capture my best food."

Arkwright leaned forward. "What are your chances of holding out or escaping?"

The governor shifted his heavy body and wiped his face. "Our chances? Nonexistent. We'll disable the machinery, burn the oil, and fight as long as we can. Then we'll head for the jungle."

"Can you escape to the south?" Fraser asked.

The governor shrugged. "Very difficult. Almost impassable jungle, even for the natives. If we get through, we'll probably find more Japanese."

"What's the air situation here?" Arkwright asked.

"We're still out of range of land-based bombers. I'll call my intelligence officer for the latest information."

While the governor talked on the phone, Fraser finished his pink gin and placed the glass on the table next to Arkwright. The captain nodded, put his full glass down, and picked up Fraser's glass. Fraser drained half of the captain's drink while the governor rattled off rapid-fire Dutch.

When the governor returned he was frowning. "Latest reports indicate a Japanese carrier may be in range tomorrow."

"We'll be under way at first light," Arkwright said.

"Good luck to you," the governor said.

"The same to you, sir," Arkwright said. "I admire your courage, Governor."

The governor smiled ruefully. "I assure you I have little choice in the matter."

Fraser looked at the sweating but composed Dutchman with compassion and thought about the thousands of men like him, trapped by the advancing Japanese war machine. They had no chance of being reinforced or rescued; they were sacrificial pawns of their governments, just as the Americans trapped on the islands of Wake and Guam had been.

Arkwright interrupted his thoughts. "Come on, Ross. Drink up. Governor, thank you for your hospitality. I hope you make it through the jungle."

At 0500 the next morning, Landry and Nystrom sat with the other deck hands waiting for breakfast in the forward crew's compartment. The triple-tiered bunks had been pushed back and the men sat on their low lockers with their elbows on table tops that had been set up in the middle of the aisles. There were grunts of satisfaction when the food arrived from the galley. Nystrom took six pieces of toast along with his scrambled eggs and Vienna sausages.

"Don't know why you don't get fat," Landry said.

"Lots of exercise, just like when I was growing up on the farm," said the rangy Nystrom. "Funny. Every other morning we have breakfast after G. Q."

Landry nodded. "I think the captain smells trouble."

Nystrom laughed. "Some nose the old man's got. He leans on that bridge wing sniffing the breeze, don't he. Looks just like a horse nickering."

"You dumb farmer," Landry said. "Whickering is what the old man does."

"What's the difference?"

"Nickering is when horses talk to each other. Might be saying something like, 'Switch that horse fly off my shoulder,' or, 'You're standing on my hoof.' A horse whickers when he sniffs the air and twitches his nostrils."

"Sorry I asked." Nystrom took more Vienna sausages. "We had a tractor instead of horses. One good thing about a tractor."

Landry couldn't resist. "What's that?"

"Tractors cut down on the horse shit you Wyoming cowboys are so full of."

Even Landry had to join in the laughter. "Got me, Nystrom." Landry wondered what the kids who had called him an "Injun" would think if they knew he was now called a cowboy. He wasn't sure he liked it himself.

"Good Vienna sausages," Nystrom said.

Landry banged his coffee cup on the table top. "I damn near broke my back carrying all the boxes of those little bastards down below back in Manila. Now they're killing my stomach. I wish you'd throw those things at the Japs."

"Might do better with them than the .50 calibers," another deck hand said.

Minutes later, Landry headed topside for his station. At the first gray light, the *O'Leary*'s anchor was hoisted, and she threaded her way through the reefs and minefields that guarded the harbor. The destroyer steamed out to the open water of Makassar Strait and headed south at 20 knots with her antiaircraft battery manned and extra lookouts posted.

Fraser felt his knees weaken when the Japanese arrived at noon. Four single-engined carrier aircraft appeared over the distant land mass to the east. They orbited the *O'Leary* at a safe distance, as if taking measure of their adversary.

"I think we're in for it, now," said Durham as he watched the enemy through his binoculars.

"We've done all right so far," Fraser replied.

"Yeah. But these are carrier planes, not high-level Jap Army bombers. They'll be down a lot lower," Durham said.

"Will they dive bomb us?"

"Naw, if you'd been doing your homework instead of charming

Ilsa, you'd know those aren't dive bombers. The Japs use those babies for horizontal bombing and torpedo attacks."

"How can you tell they're not dive bombers?"

"Their dive bombers have fixed landing gear covered with streamlined fairings. Easy to spot."

"I guess you must have learned something at the Olongapo Tavern after all," Fraser said.

Durham ignored the gibe. "If you'd done your studying, you'd know that those Japs can carry a torpedo or three 500-pound bombs. Have machine guns on the nose and in the after cockpit. Only do about 225 knots. If I had a Wildcat fighter instead of this tub, they'd be dead ducks."

"Looks like it's up to the captain instead," Fraser said.

"Won't be so easy today," Durham muttered.

The enemy formation first tried a horizontal approach at 5,000 feet. Arkwright turned to port as the aircraft made their drop; eight bombs fell harmlessly to starboard.

"They'll try something else since we're such a small target," Durham said. "Each plane only has one bomb left. They'll pull out all the stops this time."

The orbiting attackers split into pairs, one off each bow. One pair began a horizontal bombing run at 4,000 feet; the other delayed slightly before beginning a shallow dive.

"Damn!" Durham said. "That second pair is going to glide bomb us. They'll come right down on the deck!"

Fraser suddenly realized the trap they were in; as soon as they turned to evade the bombs from the horizontal attack, the glide bombers would be on top of the *O'Leary*.

The captain reacted quickly. "All ahead standard. Tell the engineers to stand by for emergency flank in a minute."

The whine of the blowers and the vibration of the big turbines diminished. The hiss of water along the destroyer's side abated as the *O'Leary* lost speed. The first pair of aircraft droned toward their release point, their pale bellies and bright-red rising sun insignia vivid against the clear sky.

"All ahead emergency flank!" Arkwright barked.

The blowers howled and the ship shook as the steam sang

through the turbines. As the big screws bit into the water, the hull shuddered and the wake boiled up above the fantail. The destroyer accelerated quickly from 15 knots toward the 25 knots available with two boilers.

The horizontal bombers released their bombs just as the *O'Leary* accelerated. The falling silver bombs headed for the *O'Leary* as they were released, but began to drift astern as the ship gained speed. Arkwright had calculated well.

Fraser had already decided that the second pair, the low level attackers, were the only ones they had any hope of hitting with their limited weapons. "Air action starboard!" Fraser ordered his talker. "Three-inch, commence firing! Stand by on the .50-calibers!"

The 3-inch gun began firing, spent shell cases clattering on the deck. The projectiles were set to explode at 2,000 yards to form a ragged steel curtain through which the Japanese would have to fly. Black bursts blossomed in the sky ahead of the two approaching aircraft. Fraser and Durham cursed as the enemy came on, unaffected by the scanty barrage. Blasts shook the ship as the bombs from the horizontal attackers exploded harmlessly astern. The descending glide bombers neared their release point.

"Left full rudder!" Arkwright shouted.

The aircraft were near the effective range of the machine gun battery. "Fifty-caliber battery, commence firing!" Fraser shouted.

Just as the machine guns began to hammer away, the two Japanese aircraft released their bombs and pulled out of their glides. The *O'Leary*'s gunners kept firing as the pale-bellied bombers climbed away. Tracers streaked by the planes, but there was no evidence of serious damage. The first bomb blasted the ocean well short. As the destroyer's bow swung to port, the last bomb hit the water to starboard, twenty feet from the forecastle; the jolting explosion heeled the ship over and knocked men off their feet. Fraser clutched the railing in front of him and stayed upright.

On the bridge wing below, Arkwright picked himself up and

turned to the bridge talker who was putting his helmet back on. "Tell the forward repair party to check for damage. I want to know if we're taking any water forward."

The Japanese bombers re-formed and circled the *O'Leary*. Durham lowered his binoculars and laughed. "Damn vultures used all their bombs."

Fraser focused his binoculars on the Japanese. The last plane peeled off and turned toward the *O'Leary*, the pilot doing a snap roll as if to demonstrate his contempt for the destroyer's air defenses.

"He's going to strafe!" Fraser yelled. "Air action port!"

The 3-inch opened up but had no effect on the Japanese airplane, which bored in just forward of the port beam.

On the amidships deckhouse, Hank Landry swung his machine gun around to bear on the attacker. The water jacket around the barrel radiated heat from firing at the last attack, but the gun wasn't nearly as hot as Landry's anger. After months of harrassment by Mortland and two weeks of torment from Japanese attackers, he wanted to strike back. He had already failed to score any damaging hits during the first low-level attack. Now he focused his anger on the single approaching aircraft, determined to make the pilot pay.

The other machine gun on the port side opened up, but Landry knew the target was still out of range. The other gun suddenly stopped.

"Sombitch's jammed!" Shifflet shouted between bangs from the 3-inch.

As the plane neared the effective range of his gun, Landry squeezed the trigger and the gun bucked, spitting out a stream of bullets with an ear-splitting staccato roar. Spent cartridges clattered to the deck around him.

Flashes winked from the nose of the enemy plane. A line of splashes walked toward the *O'Leary* and hit just forward of Landry. Bullets whined and ricocheted. Landry just hunched his back and followed his tracers as they arced down to intersect the aircraft's path. The plane roared onward. Landry's stream of .50-caliber bullets shattered the aircraft's canopy. Shards of reddened plexiglass sprayed into the air where they caught the sunlight like pink drops of water. The plane flew relentlessly onward with its nose pointed right at Landry. He kept pumping rounds at the plane as his gut tightened. He heard shouts of fear and feet scrambling on the nearby deck. Barely 50 yards away, the Japanese aircraft lifted its nose and rose slightly as it bored in.

Christ! Landry's mind screamed. Is it going to clear us?

The plane was on them, its motor bellowing. It swooped overhead, barely clearing the stacks and radio antennas. The slipstream buffeted Landry, and he could smell the engine's exhaust. The Japanese plane rolled slowly, caught a wing tip in the water, and cartwheeled once before smashing into the sea and exploding in a ball of orange flame.

Some of the men on the amidships deckhouse ran to the starboard side for a better view of the wreckage as it receded astern. Landry's knees were still shaking, so he stayed behind his gun.

Shifflet shook his fist at the wreckage. "Good job, Landry! Scratch one Jap."

One of the men pointed to Shifflet's loader who had jumped from the amidships deckhouse. "Looks like the torpedomen got themselves a new striker."

"He'll fit right in," Shifflet said. "Rest of the damn torpedomen are hidin' under their mounts."

The loader climbed the ladder sheepishly. "Shifflet's gun was jammed. Wasn't nothing for me to do."

"Better jump over the side if you take off again," said Shifflet. "Next time you leave me will be your last."

Landry's loader thumped him on the heavy life jacket. "Great shooting!"

"Yeeeaahh!" Landry yelled. "Maybe that will teach them to leave us alone!"

Landry turned to wave at Ben Nystrom who was a loader on one of the machine guns along the other rail. Nystrom was sitting against his tripod, arms clasped across his belly. Slowly,

Nystrom rolled over on his side. Landry raced over to Nystrom and pried his moaning friend's arms apart. There was a rip in his life jacket and a small circle of blood over his belly. Landry knew it was serious. The pale Nystrom didn't look good. The hand that clutched Landry's arm weakened.

"Jesus, Hank. It hurts so bad."

"Stretcher! Get a stretcher up here!" Landry shouted.

When the Japanese strafer's machine guns had started to wink, Fraser had frozen with his hands clamped to the rail in front of him. The bomber's nose had seemed pointed right at him. Splashes ripped the water 75 yards off the beam and walked right at the bridge.

"Hit the deck!" Beringer shouted, and all non-essential personnel dove for shelter. Bullets clanged, whined, and ricocheted around Fraser, but he was too terrified to move. Just below him, Arkwright didn't even twitch.

When Fraser turned back from watching the enemy crash into the sea to starboard, he saw the captain frowning at a hole in his sleeve. On the wooden gratings of the wing, a lookout sprawled, blood gushing from his mouth and massive chest wounds. Chief Jablonski crawled over and tried to staunch the flow of blood, but it was hopeless.

Arkwright gazed at the dying man with a mixed expression. Fraser tried to read the captain's face. Was it compassion, sorrow—something else—even envy?

Moans came from the pilothouse. Arkwright snapped his head up. "Get a new man for the lee helm! Send for the stretcher bearers!" He turned to the telephone talker. "Instruct all stations to keep a sharp lookout! Report damage as soon as possible. Anything from the forward damage control party, yet?"

"No, sir," the telephone talker stammered.

Fraser unlocked his hands from the railing in front of him and scanned the sky to see if another attack was imminent. The remaining three Japanese aircraft seemed unwilling to follow their fallen companion and turned to leave the scene.

"Mr. Durham!" said Eckersly, Fraser's talker.

Fraser looked down where Durham writhed on the deck, one trouser leg blood-soaked. Fraser knelt and turned the groaning Durham over.

"Bull, what happened?"

Durham gritted his teeth. "Took one in my leg! Ah . . . Ah! Crap! I was watching the plane. I forgot to hit the deck."

"Lie still, and I'll get some stretcher bearers."

Soon, two stretcher bearers puffed up the ladder. They strapped Durham into the litter for the trip down the steep ladders to the wardroom where Doc Laster waited.

Damn, Fraser thought, I hope Laster isn't seasick today.

CHAPTER THIRTEEN

Laster looked around the wardroom; it was as ready as it would ever be. Sterile surgical instruments lay wrapped on the sideboard next to stacks of medical supplies. Laster took a deep breath to calm his nerves as two walking wounded arrived, dripping blood. Both men had superficial wounds, so Laster applied dressings and sent them to lie down until he had dealt with any serious problems.

The stretcher bearers banged the wardroom door open and carried in Nystrom, the centerfielder on the baseball team. Nystrom was pale; his pulse, rapid and weak; his blood pressure, ominously low.

"Get him on the table!" Laster said. He stuffed piles of blankets under Nystrom's legs so gravity would keep blood where it was most needed. The pharmacist's mate helped Laster cut Nystrom's clothes away. Laster's quick examination revealed no injuries other than a small entrance wound in Nystrom's belly.

"Jesus!" said Laster. "He's bleeding internally." He shook his head with frustration and wished he had the whole blood and plasma immediately available in a hospital or on a larger ship.

His thoughts were interrupted by Durham's arrival. Nystrom's prospects were so grim that Laster knew he had to check Durham first to make sure that a salvagable patient wouldn't bleed to death during the fight to save Nystrom.

Laster examined Durham rapidly. "You hit anywhere else?" he asked as he cut the leg of Durham's trousers away.

"No, that's it," Durham said, alert despite the pain. "Is it bad, Doc?"

"You're going to be in a hospital for a while." Laster was surprised to find that no major blood vessels had been hit in Durham's lower leg. The bullet had hit bone and left a nasty exit wound. The bleeding wasn't bad; Laster applied a pressure bandage and quickly administered a shot of morphine. While attending to Durham's wound, Laster gave instructions to the pharmacist's mate to prepare for an exploratory operation on Nystrom.

The assistant paled. "Jesus, Doctor, we're not equipped to do that. Besides—there's just you and me."

"I know that, but that kid is gone unless we do something. Everyone else here is under control, so I have to try to stop his bleeding. If I can do that, maybe we can get some blood from the crew and save him."

The pharmacist's mate put a mask over Nystrom's face and began dripping ether on it to put him under. Laster laid a tray of surgical instruments on the table and made a token gesture to sterile procedure by swabbing Nystrom's abdomen with a piece of gauze soaked with iodine and then donning a pair of sterile rubber gloves.

"Is he under?"

"He was unconscious when I started the ether," the pharmacist's mate said, still obviously shaken.

As Laster selected a scalpel from a pile of unwrapped instruments, he took a deep breath and tried to calm his nerves. He wasn't an experienced surgeon, having done only a year of internship after medical school. He had spent only three months on the surgical service where he had done nothing but routine operations. Laster had assisted and observed some of the more complex cases, but that was little comfort now. He knew he was about to tackle a problem beyond his limited experience, but he also knew it was Nystrom's only chance.

Laster turned to the patient on the table and made his first incision, running the scalpel from above the navel straight down the middle of the abdomen for almost a foot. This first incision went through the skin and a thin yellow layer of fat below. Laster was already down to the fibrous tissue which surrounded the abdominal muscles. Laster clamped a hemostat on one pulsing arterial bleeder and ignored some smaller bleeding vessels; he was in a hurry to find bigger game. Laster continued his incision down through the fibrous tissue and cut down between the two large muscles of the abdomen. Only the thin layer of the peritoneum remained between him and the abdominal cavity, which was ominously distended.

Laster shook his head and turned to his assistant, "Give him a couple of extra drops of ether and come down here and put on some gloves. I'm going to need some extra hands."

"Yes, sir," said the pharmacist's mate, moving quickly to the other side of the table.

Laster handed him some large metal instruments known as retractors, which were used to hold various organs in the abdominal cavity out of the way of the surgeon. "Be ready to hold these where I tell you."

When Laster made his final incision, he was amazed by the amount of blood that welled up as he entered the abdominal cavity. Laster grabbed a pile of sterile sponges and a syringe with a large rubber bulb.

"Jesus!" Laster's assistant said.

"Damn! Damn! Damn!" cursed Laster as he tried to deal with the blood so he could find the source of the bleeding. Part of the large bowel was damaged and the abdominal cavity was contaminated with its bacteria-laden contents. Nystrom was in deep trouble despite the availability of the new sulfa drugs. There was a high probability of a serious post-operative infection if Nystrom didn't die of shock first. Laster knew he'd have to find members of the crew with the same blood type or O negative. As Laster gained on the blood flow, he thought he could see a pulsation from the rear wall of the abdomen. He slid his left hand in and higher up, pressing hard on the aorta, the major vessel that came down from the heart. The influx of new blood stopped. He took a pile of sponges and mopped up the remaining blood in the abdominal cavity. As the blood cleared, he could see the bullet, which had lodged near the spine. It had perforated the large bowel, hit some loops of the small intestine, and nicked the aorta.

Laster stopped for a few seconds and planned his attack. First, he'd have to place some retractors to get enough room to work. Then, he knew he'd have to repair the leaking artery, patch the internal damage, and make a temporary bypass for the large bowel. There were still shock and infection to contend with, but he was determined to try.

Suddenly, Laster shook his head sadly as the nerves in the fingers of his left hand finally got their message through to his busy brain. The rapid, weak pulsations of Nystrom's aorta had gradually faded away, and he just died despite Laster's efforts.

"Ah . . . damn!" Laster said as he withdrew his hand.

The pharmacist's mate looked at Laster. "You did the best you could, sir."

"Hell, it wasn't good enough. We didn't have enough here to cope with this. Let's move him over to the corner so we can work on the others."

They lifted Nystrom off the wardroom table, laid him gently on the deck, and covered him with a blanket.

"That kid's arm won me a wallet full of cash from the *Holland*," the pharmacist's mate said.

"No more baseball," Laster said softly. "No more anything."

Laster bit his lip and turned toward the rest of the wounded. Suddenly he realized the deck was canted down toward the bow. The roll of the ship was sluggish, and they had obviously lost speed.

"What the hell!" Laster muttered.

The forward repair party was in water up to their waists, but their day had begun routinely enough. When general quarters sounded at dawn, Chief Hanlon had hustled to his station, where he worked with the forward repair party. Hanlon slipped on his life jacket and adjusted his helmet.

Two of the arriving deck hands cinched up their life jackets. "Pretty easy war so far," one said.

"We've paid for it, though," the other deck hand said. "That bastard Mortland has been running our asses into the ground for months with his drills."

Hanlon laughed. He had to admit Mortland had trained his men well. Hanlon was there to supervise another function of the repair party, passing ammunition from the forward magazine up to all but the after guns. Hanlon was also on call for emergency gun repairs or to take Fraser's place if the gunnery officer were disabled.

Within minutes, the other members of the repair party arrived. One was a metalsmith, who could weld and cut away damaged metal; another, a shipfitter, skilled in repair of piping, valves, and watertight doors.

Most of the repair party sat against the bulkheads during general quarters. Their box-like compartment was just aft of the wardroom. The hatches and ladders at the forward end of the space led down to the crew's forward living compartment. During general quarters, all the hatches and doors that opened off their compartment were dogged down tightly, like all other watertight closures throughout the ship. One of the two hatches up to the main deck was equipped with a small scuttle about two feet in diameter, which could be opened to pass up ammunition for the guns when the supply at the ready racks gave out.

The ammunition was stored in the main magazine below their station. Also near their compartment was one of the two main fuel tanks. The proximity of the two explosive areas, fuel tank and magazine, was something Hanlon had long since resigned himself to.

As he always did, Mortland paced back and forth—five steps each way. Hanlon, like the other members of the party, had learned to sit to one side in order to give Mortland room. There was nothing for the repair party to do when the attack began. Hanlon could only sit against the bulkhead wondering what was happening while Mortland paced back and forth.

"Mortland needs a crack at the Japs," one man whispered.

"Hell, I'd like to see the Japs get a crack at him," another muttered.

Mortland turned as he neared the forward bulkhead and fixed the group with a baleful stare as if he had heard the whispers. "Goddamn Japs better not mess up my topsides!" he muttered.

Hanlon felt the deck heave with the first series of bomb explosions, but he could tell the explosions were too far away to do much damage. A while later, the muffled thump of the 3-inch gun aft filtered down to their post. The staccato stutter of the .50-caliber machine guns joined in the noise of battle coming down the open scuttle.

"Coming down low," the shipfitter said.

"Must figure we're too fast to hit with high-level bombing," Hanlon said. "Means we got a shot at them, though."

Another explosion rocked the ship, closer this time. Mortland took three steps up the ladder and poked his head out the ammunition scuttle.

"What's going on, Chief?" asked the shipfitter, who got up and stood below Mortland at the bottom of the ladder.

Suddenly a tremendous explosion heeled the ship over and tossed Mortland down on the shipfitter; they crashed to the deck.

The shipfitter moaned. "Get the hell off my legs."

"Damn! The last one was close," Hanlon said as he helped the two men up.

Mortland jammed his helmet back on his huge head. "Too close."

The telephone talker pushed his talk button. "Forward repair, aye, aye." He turned to Mortland. "Captain wants us to check for damage and flooding. The last bomb hit twenty feet off the starboard bow."

Mortland lost no time. "You men know what to do. Check your assigned compartments."

The men fanned out and soon returned with their reports. The last was the metalsmith, who poked his head out of the scuttle down to the forward crew's compartment. "We're taking water. Several inches of water on deck already."

Mortland directed the talker to report the damage to the

bridge while the repair party gathered the equipment they would need to combat the flooding. Hanlon followed Mortland as he hustled down the ladder to find the source of the incoming water. The water at the foot of the ladder was over Hanlon's ankles and felt like bathwater.

Mortland sent the shipfitter and the metalsmith to check along the port side. "Come on, Hanlon, we'll check the starboard side."

The external waterline was about halfway up the side of the compartment, which simplified their search. They sloshed forward along the starboard side. Halfway to the forward bulkhead, they found water jetting through the hull. Two of the side plates had been sprung loose by the explosion.

"Look! Them damn rivets are gone," Mortland said. "This could get bad. We gotta shore them sprung plates."

The bow shuddered as they hit a wave, and there was a screech of protesting metal.

"Goddamn!" Mortland said. "If we don't slow down, the hull's gonna split from here to the fireroom!"

Hanlon felt a chill of fear. "If the whole compartment floods, we're in deep trouble."

They sloshed aft through water, now almost a foot deep. Before they reached the ladder, the 3-inch gun started to bark again. Soon, the machine guns began to chatter. Enemy machine gun bullets clanged against the hull.

"Comin' down low again!" Mortland said.

There was the roar of an aircraft engine and then an explosion. The telephone talker in the compartment above started to yell, "We got one! We got one!"

"Stop hollerin' and tell the friggin' bridge to slow down," Mortland shouted. "Only way we can stop the flooding."

Mortland ordered the rest of the repair party to bring down the shoring timbers and material needed to plug the damage. "And start rigging a hose and a pump down here so we can get this water out!" he bellowed.

"Bridge says they can slow down now," the talker reported. "They'll have to speed up if the Japs show up again."

"Tell the bridge they'll need a periscope if they go faster'n 10 knots," Mortland shouted.

While the men passed down shoring timbers, Mortland and Hanlon checked for other sources of flooding, especially those that might be hidden under the water which now was halfway to Hanlon's knees. Their search was negative, so Mortland led his men to the split in the *O'Leary*'s plating and directed the placement of the shoring timbers.

"Not there, you idiot!" Mortland yelled.

Despite some confusion, the shoring system began to take shape so timbers could be wedged into place to force the overlapping edges of the steel plates back together. The compartment reverberated with the sounds of the sledges pounding the timbers and wedges home. Their efforts were impeded by the water pressure generated by the ship's speed, which jetted water through the opening between the plates.

The water neared Hanlon's waist as he swung one of the heavy mauls. The compartment was filled with the racket of a portable pump, and the water level stabilized as the plates were forced closer together.

Mortland shouted toward the ladder. "Tell the bridge we got a lot of water down here. We could use another pump and some men from the after repair party, if they don't need 'em."

"Okay, Chief, they're on their way," the talker yelled a minute later.

Hanlon grabbed a nearby bunk as the *O'Leary* took a sluggish roll to port and recovered slowly. The deck was canted down toward the bow by several degrees. "Better get some of this water out of here," Hanlon said.

"You want me to drink all this and piss it out a porthole?" Mortland said. "Them pumps'll have to do that job."

"Okay, let's not waste any time." Hanlon remembered the four-stack destroyer wasn't a stable ship to begin with.

"Captain wants to know when can we speed up," the talker yelled.

"At least ten minutes," Mortland snapped.

The forward repair party wrestled with the shoring to close

the last of the gap. "Goddamnit! Get that shoring wedge in right," Mortland shouted at the men laboring in the waist-high water, which was sloshing from side to side with each roll. A pair of pants and a pillow floated between the lines of bunks. The repair party redoubled their efforts, but the last shore was wedged too loosely and slipped from its place. The rest of the shaky structure creaked ominously.

"Ask the bridge if we can slow even more for thirty minutes," Mortland shouted to the talker.

"Affirmative, but hurry up," the talker responded.

Mortland hammered part of the shoring loose. "Got to take most of this thing down and do it right!"

The repair party jumped to work and took the shoring structure apart and rebuilt it so more force could be directed against sprung plates to force the seam closed. They labored like madmen, cursing and straining as the water began to creep up again. Finally, the shoring structure was in place. Hanlon pounded home the last wedge, which slowly closed the end of the gaping seam. Each stroke with the heavy maul shot waves of pain through his aching arms and shoulders.

"That's got it," Mortland said. "You got her closed."

Mortland stepped back and shouted to the talker. "Tell the bridge we should gain on the flooding now. They can speed up some if we have to. Don't go no faster'n 15 knots." He inspected the hull where small streams of water still sprayed through. "That's about it. If we can hammer some caulking material into the joints and plug them rivet holes better, we should have her almost watertight."

Hanlon nodded. "Looks good, Mortland. I think the pumps have already lowered the level."

"Yeah, looks like we're winning this battle," Mortland said.

"If the Japs'll just leave us alone," Hanlon said.

Five minutes later the phone talker yelled, "Jap planes! We're gonna make a run for a rain squall."

Hanlon felt the ship begin to speed up and looked apprehensively at the thigh-high water. As the ship pounded ahead, the caulking they had just stuffed between the plates peeled back, and a spray of water shot into the compartment. The wooden shoring creaked as the damaged plates were hammered by the inexorable force pushing against them. Two of the plugs that had been jammed in the empty rivet holes popped out like champagne corks, adding new jets to the inflow.

"Stand clear of the shoring!" Mortland shouted. "We done all we can."

There was a sharp crack as another rivet gave way. Water sprayed across the compartment. The shoring groaned but still stood. Hanlon wondered if it would hold.

"Let's get the hell out of here!" Mortland shouted.

Fraser clung to the railing in front of the fire control platform. The *O'Leary* slammed ahead, the low-riding bow plowing through the growing swells as they neared the squall line that seemed tantalizingly near. The four approaching Japanese planes had fixed landing gear, surrounded by streamlined fairings. Durham had said the only Japanese aircraft like that were dive bombers.

They won't miss, thought Fraser. We're in for it now. He eyed the squall line. "Damn, it's going to be close," he muttered.

Fraser's right earpiece crackled. "The forward repair party reports the hull's leaking again. The shoring is holding, but the chief ain't sure for how long."

On the wing below, Arkwright looked ahead at the squalls as he listened to the talker's report. "We're going for broke. Lee helmsman, tell main control to give me all the power they've got for the next three minutes."

"Aye, aye, sir. Mr. Meredith says he can give you maybe 26 knots with the two good boilers."

Fraser felt the turbines pick up another notch of speed. The ship vibrated with the strain. The bow hammered through the waves, and the hull groaned ominously.

There was a clatter from the ladder at the back of the bridge. Chief Mortland bounced up, two steps at a time. The chief ran forward to where the captain was wedged into the forward corner of the bridge wing. "Captain, we ain't gonna have no bow unless you slow down."

Arkwright was watching the enemy through his binoculars. Without even taking his eyes off them, he pointed at the rapidly approaching aircraft and then at the nearing cloud mass ahead.

Mortland followed his gestures. "Sheeeit! Keep going. We'll hold her together." Mortland hustled back down the ladder.

The dive bombers were but a half-mile away when the rain embraced the *O'Leary* and hid her. The heavy drops spattered off the topside surfaces and drenched Fraser and the men around him. No one seemed to mind. The curtain of water had granted the destroyer a temporary stay of execution.

How long will this last? Fraser wondered as the *O'Leary* turned to run with the squall line to maximize the time under protective cover. They were heading due west, right for the Borneo shore line, so they would have to change course soon. But first Arkwright slowed them to 10 knots to take some of the strain off the bow, which was riding even lower as it slammed into a medium-sized wave and sluggishly fought its way back to the surface.

A half-hour later the talker reported the flooding was back under control and that the water level was dropping. That didn't keep them under the squall. Jablonski emerged from the pilot house and told the captain that the plot showed them nearing the coast. They turned south again, and fifteen minutes later, the last of the rain and protective cloud cover moved off to the west.

Fraser scanned the skies apprehensively looking for the tiny dots that might spell death. The sky was empty. "Guess they didn't have enough gas to wait," he mused.

By nightfall, the berthing compartment was almost free of water. Despite the repairs, water trickled in through the damaged plates. A small tide sloshed back and forth across the deck with each roll of the ship. Even though the compartment had been only partially flooded, none of the men who lived there had dry clothes because their lockers sat on deck.

Landry climbed into his bunk at the top of a triple tier. He wrinkled his nose at the damp mildewy aroma of the compartment. "Christ, this place smells worse than the after compartment, where those sweaty snipes live."

"Quit your bitching," groused the man in the lowest bunk. "At least you got a dry mattress."

"Yeah, you're right. I shouldn't be complaining," Landry said quietly, eyeing the empty bunk that had belonged to Ben Nystrom. Landry still couldn't believe Nystrom was dead. They had worked together on the deck force for over a year, and Nystrom had become one of Landry's few friends despite their different backgrounds. Together they had spent many hours in bars in Olongapo, Chefoo, Shanghai and Hong Kong.

"Ah, hell," Landry muttered, knowing there wasn't anything he could do except write a letter to Nystrom's parents the next morning. The decision seemed to ease his mind, and he turned over in his bunk.

"Hey, everybody," a deckhand said. "It's Christmas Eve."

"If Santa flies anywhere near this ship, he's gonna get his fat ass shot off," a tired voice answered.

Landry lay on his back staring at the bundle of thick wires a foot from his nose. He wished they were still in Manila and the war had never started. Hell of a way to spend Christmas, he thought. Running for my life and wondering if I'll ever see Teresa and my kid.

Landry took comfort from the familiar berthing compartment. Another two days and they would be safe in Java. Then he remembered he would have to face the punishment for his visit to Teresa. First there would be mast before the captain, and what then? Probably a court martial and a trip to a brig somewhere. He ran his hand along the metal rail at the edge of his bunk as he looked around the dark compartment. It wasn't much, but it was all he had. He didn't want to leave.

Fraser paced the bridge just after midnight, fighting to stay awake. He had been too keyed up from the action that day to fall asleep. He had dozed off just before the messenger woke him for the midwatch. Fraser sighed. When his relief arrived in almost four hours, there would be little more than an hour before predawn general quarters. Fraser knew he'd feel like hell the next day.

He was right. The next afternoon was even worse during his 12-16 watch. They plodded across the Java Sea at 10 knots, just fast enough to cancel out the following breeze, so they appeared to be in a dead calm. Now that they were south of the equator, the sun was high in the sky, far different from the low December sun Fraser remembered in Ohio. Sweat soaked his uniform, and Fraser prayed for a change in the breeze. Stack gases swirled around the bridge, irritating his burning eyes. A weary Fraser turned his watch over to Chuck Steiner and headed below to his stifling stateroom for a brief rest; his two off watches were the two-hour dog watches, so he would return to the bridge for another full watch in just four hours.

"A hell of a way to spend Christmas," he complained wearily as he headed below. He felt homesick as he thought of his family opening presents around the tree.

The next morning Fraser relieved Woody Korchak, who had taken over Durham's slot in the Condition III rotation. A low coast lined the southern horizon.

"Java?" asked Fraser.

"Close," Korchak said. "That's Madura—the long skinny island along Java's north coast. A few more miles and we'll be at its western end and the channel to Surabaya."

Fraser relaxed an hour later when the lookouts spotted a Dutch pilot boat coming out to meet them outside the Surabaya Channel.

Chief Jablonski looked up from the chart. "Nice to see the pilot, Captain. I've never been here before. No telling where the Dutch put their minefields."

"Yeah, it would be hell to come all this way and go aground or hit a friendly mine," the captain said.

The *O'Leary* slowed, and the pilot boat surged alongside. A stout Dutch pilot heaved himself up a rope ladder to the deck, where Fraser met him and escorted him to the bridge.

"Velcome to Java!" The pilot bombarded the captain with salvos of an effusive welcome.

Arkwright ushered the pilot to the chart table. "Would you please plot the minefields on our charts?"

The pilot laughed. "Vee don't tell you vare the minefields are. I know, and you don't haff to vorry. If you blow up, I blow up. I haff you in Surabaya in no time."

Fraser was aghast as he watched the pilot's navigation. The Dutchman refused to use the gyrocompass and gave only an occasional glance at the magnetic compass. He squinted at distant mountain peaks and other landmarks known only to himself. As they changed course back and forth in what Fraser hoped was the channel, the pilot said, "Don't vorry, ve chust trying to fool the Japanese submarines if they are vatching."

They finally left the minefields, crossed the harbor, and moored alongside the fueling pier. The Dutch pilot went over the brow with a cheery wave. "See you next time." The pilot was met on the pier by a colleague, and they exchanged greetings in rapid Dutch.

The other pilot looked up at the bridge and pointed at his friend. "Vas goot for first time, ja?"

Fraser could only watch with his mouth open as the pilots walked up the pier.

"Maybe he meant it was our first time," Arkwright said.

"I hope so." Fraser remembered the pilot's casual attitude toward the formalities of navigation. Despite the pilot, they had made it and escaped the Japanese. Fraser thought about Laster's prediction that the Japanese would try to conquer the Dutch East Indies for its oil and mineral resources.

And now the *O'Leary*'s right here in the middle of the bull's-eye, Fraser thought. How long do we have before the Japanese come? At least Ilsa Van Dorn is here—if she'll see me.

CHAPTER FOURTEEN

Thirty minutes after their arrival, a tall Dutch naval lieutenant strode briskly aboard. Fraser met him on the quarterdeck.

"I'm Dirk Jansen, your liaison officer."

"I'll show you to the captain," Fraser said after introducing himself. "When you're ready to leave, please have the quarterdeck messenger find me. I'd like to get some information from you."

Fraser appraised Jansen as a rival for Ilsa. But then Fraser saw the flash of gold on Jansen's left hand and realized that was impossible.

After Fraser introduced Jansen to the captain, he went to his stateroom and tried to catch up on his paperwork. He soon wearied of the administrative chores and picked up the box Ilsa had given him. He lifted the bagpipe chanter from its tissue paper bed. The dark wood seemed to glow. Fraser opened the instruction booklet and practiced the fingering for the different notes. He gave the instrument a tentative toot.

"Fraser!" the executive officer's nasal shout echoed down the passageway.

"Sorry, sir. Just slipped out." Fraser laid the chanter back in its box and went back to work.

The messenger knocked an hour later and told Fraser that the Dutch officer was ready to leave.

"You had some questions for me?" Jansen asked when Fraser arrived on the quarterdeck.

"Yes, I want to get in touch with a young lady named Ilsa Van Dorn. Her father is a captain in your Navy."

Jansen's mild blue eyes seemed to warm. "My wife is one of her best friends. Let me give you her phone number."

Fraser wrote the number down and thanked Jansen.

"I wish you luck," Jansen said. "Since Ilsa lost her fiancé, she hasn't let herself get close to anyone. She usually avoids single military men."

Fraser remembered their last night in Manila. "Maybe that will change."

"I hope so, for her sake," Jansen said.

Jansen roared off in an old Mercedes. Fraser's rising spirits were dampened when stretcher bearers carried the bodies of the *O'Leary*'s two dead across the quarterdeck and down to the pier. Conversations halted in mid-sentence, and men paused at their duties to give former comrades a moment of silence as the bodies were lifted into the waiting ambulance. As the vehicle coughed to life and rolled slowly down the pier, Fraser wondered if his time were growing short.

Fraser walked over to the pier to use a phone. He dialed the Van Dorns' number.

"Hello." Ilsa's familiar voice brought back memories of her warm body dancing against his.

"Ilsa, this is Ross Fraser from Manila."

"Yes." Her voice was reserved, cool.

"My ship just arrived in Surabaya today. I was hoping to see you. I have the duty tonight, but I'd like to take you to dinner tomorrow."

There was a moment of silence while Fraser wondered what was going through her mind.

"I can't let you do that . . ."

"But . . ."

"You'll have to come to our house for dinner. I know my father will want to discuss the war with you."

"Perhaps we could go dancing afterwards?"

"We'll see." She didn't sound enthusiastic.

After lunch the next day, Fraser changed into his white service uniform and joined the other officers on the pier. A night in port had eased some of the lines on their faces, but expressions were somber, and voices, muted. The enlisted ranks were quiet with none of the usual laughter and horseplay.

Fraser walked over to Jack Meredith. "Got your yard work schedule figured out?"

"I guess. Two or three weeks won't be a full overhaul. We'll steam out of here, but how far or how long is anybody's guess."

"At least we'll be able to rewire my number one gun," Fraser said.

They were interrupted by Beringer's nasal drawl. "Here comes the captain. Let's load the men."

Fraser slipped into a creaking seat at the front of a battered bus. The driver wrenched the gearshift into low gear, and they lurched off. The sweltering bus rattled over the rutted roads as humid, dusty air swirled through the windows. They rolled through the gates of a cemetery and squealed to a halt. Two wooden coffins covered by American flags sat by the graves. As Fraser walked toward the gravesite, he was struck by the scene. The freshly dug holes and the raw earth seemed to represent the violence of death; the neatly trimmed grass, shady trees, and flowering shrubs suggested a harmony beyond the ugliness of death.

The officers lined up on one side of the coffins; the chiefs, on the other. The crew formed ranks across one end. A stout Dutch Navy chaplain walked to the open end, cleared his throat, pulled out a prayer book, and began the standard service used for seaman and admiral alike. He started with a reading from the Bible and progressed through psalms and prayers for the dead. Fraser's eyes were moist at the chaplain's moving recitation of the Twenty-Third Psalm, which had special meaning for him now that he had passed through the "valley of the shadow of death."

The service ended with the Navy Hymn. The opening words seemed to hang in the air: "Eternal Father, strong to save, whose arm doth bind the restless wave."

Fraser thought the last lines seemed appropriate for their future. "Oh hear us when we cry to thee, for those in peril on the sea."

The chaplain signaled the rifle party, which responded with three volleys, shattering the silence of the surroundings. When the echoes of the last shots faded away, a bugler sounded taps, a mournful, yet somehow comforting conclusion to the simple and timeless ceremony. The eight sailors standing by each coffin folded the national ensigns covering the coffins. The petty officer in charge at each grave presented the folded ensigns to a somber captain for forwarding to each man's family.

The ceremony over, they filed back to the buses. Fraser turned back for a last look at the gravesite; the captain was still beside the coffins, staring at the raw holes in the earth. Arkwright finally lifted his head and turned toward the buses.

As his bus returned to the ship, Fraser was surrounded by silence. Each man rode alone with his thoughts. Fraser knew the Japanese would be coming soon for the oil and the other resources. Fraser considered the possibility that he might soon join his shipmates in this foreign ground or lie in the depths of the sea, unburied and unknown.

As they rolled up to the familiar shape of the *O'Leary*, there were a few murmurs of conversation.

"Damn," Simpson said. "I'd rather be buried at sea."

"Yeah, you'd make great crab bait," Shifflet said.

"Different kind of crabs will probably nibble you to death," Simpson said.

Shifflet laughed. "Take 'em a long time. I've got a lot for 'em to nibble on." Shifflet went on when the laughter subsided. "I think those boys would want us to hold a proper wake for 'em tonight."

"Good idea."

"What's a wake?"

"It's when folk's do a lot of drinking and carrying on after a funeral," Shifflet said.

"Sounds good to me. We're experts at drinking and carrying on."

"Yup," Shifflet said. "Look out Surabaya, here we come!"

Fraser shook his head and murmured a prayer of thanks he wouldn't be the duty officer that night. But he felt something more than relief—a sense of envy; Shifflet had obviously sampled most of life's pleasures. Fraser felt like he had missed most of the party.

Later that afternoon, Dirk Jansen knocked at Fraser's door and asked if he'd had any luck with Ilsa. "Excellent," Jansen said when Fraser told him of the dinner invitation. "I'll give you a ride when I leave."

Fraser met Jansen by the old Mercedes. The driver, an ancient Javanese sailor, saluted them. Jansen folded his tall frame and slid across the back seat ahead of Fraser. Soon they were out of the commercial shipping area and riding down a boulevard lined with stately trees.

"Beautiful city," Fraser said as he watched modern buildings slide by their windows.

Jansen's smile faded. "Yes, sad to think what the war may do to it."

"Been out here long?"

"I was born here. Many of the Dutch families have been here for generations."

"This is your home, then?"

"Yes, we expect to defend it to the last ship and man."

"Your navy won't retreat to Australia?" Fraser asked.

"There may not be much chance for that. We will try to stop the Japanese when they come from the north. Look at your charts and you'll see that Java is part of the Malay Barrier. There are only a few navigable straits offering an escape south to Australia. If the Japanese close them, we'll be trapped."

Fraser realized that the *O'Leary* could also be caught in the same trap.

Jansen looked depressed, so Fraser tried to find a happier subject. "You said you were married?"

"Yes. My wife is expecting our first child in March."

Fraser wondered if Jansen would survive the next three months to see his child.

A few miles farther, they reached the suburbs and entered a

curving gravel driveway in front of a large wooden house encircled by wide awning-covered verandas. Trees shaded the white-painted house, and tropical bushes and flowers filled carefully tended beds.

When Fraser closed the car door, Jansen leaned out the window and waved a lean hand. "Good luck!"

As the car crunched over the gravel, Fraser walked up the steps and tapped the large brass knocker. The door was opened by a smiling Javanese, barely five feet tall, whose mahogany-colored face was dominated by a pair of intelligent dark eyes and an expanse of white teeth. "Come in, sir. You must be Lieutenant Fraser. I am Mohammed, the house man."

"Thank you, Mohammed."

"Miss Van Dorn will be down in a minute."

Mohammed led Fraser to a broad porch, overlooking a tropical garden at the rear of the house. Flower beds and a lawn filled the spaces between tall trees.

Footsteps sounded behind him. "Nice to see you again, Lieutenant Fraser." Ilsa offered him a cool hand. Her smile was polite, even reserved; her green eyes, enigmatic. She wore a simple cotton dress, but Fraser was acutely aware of the firm body underneath.

"Would you like some refreshment? One of Mohammed's specialties?"

"I'll try a martini if you're having one," Fraser said hopefully, remembering their effect after Ilsa had switched to them in Manila.

"Ummm. I'm afraid I've given them up." Her expression was neutral.

"Mohammed's specialty will be fine, then."

Fraser sank into a wicker chair and stared at the profusion of tropical plants in the garden below. "This is a change from looking at nothing but blue water. It looks like I'm in paradise."

"Yes, this is beautiful. But the Japanese may not allow us to enjoy it much longer," Ilsa said pensively. She walked to the side of the porch and pressed a button. The smiling Mohammed brought out a tray with a pitcher and two frosted glasses. He poured two generous drinks.

Fraser took a sip of the amber liquid. "Mohammed, this is 'paradise enow.'"

"Thank you, sir. I see you are familiar with Omar Khayam."

"I'm afraid that's the extent of my repertoire."

"Ah, but you are honest about your limitations. Perhaps that will encourage you to learn more good poetry."

Fraser tasted his drink again. It was refreshing, but only mildly alcoholic—a poor substitute for a martini.

"How long will your ship be here?" Ilsa asked.

Fraser wondered if the question was more than just a polite one. "Two or three weeks while we get repaired."

"Your ship is damaged?"

Fraser told her about the air attacks.

"You were lucky to make it here. Let's go down to the garden until dinner's ready."

As they strolled down the pathway, Fraser was aware of Ilsa's body beside him. She seemed to sway as she walked, and he felt a rising physical passion. He was grateful when Ilsa suggested they sit in some lawn chairs. They talked of their recent experiences, and Ilsa said she was sorry to hear about Durham's injury and the loss of the two men. She promised to visit Durham in the hospital.

"Just don't get too close to him," Fraser said. "He has few scruples where women are concerned."

They talked quietly for another half-hour. The garden vibrated with life and insects hummed about their business. Fraser shivered slightly as he thought about the burial ceremony that afternoon. He wondered how much time any of them had left to appreciate the joys of life. He knew that if one of the enemy machine gun bullets had taken a different carom, he would be lying alongside the men in the cemetery.

Ilsa turned as Mohammed approached. "Is my father home?"

"No, Miss Ilsa. He just called and said there were problems at headquarters. He said to go ahead with dinner."

"Is the 'gulai ayam' up to your usual standards?"

Mohammed smiled. "That is for you to decide."

When Fraser sampled the chicken dish a half-hour later, his palate was tickled by the complexity of the flavor. "This is terrific. What am I tasting?"

"Coconut milk and a variety of spices in the curry paste—garlic, ginger root, coriander seed, fennel seed, cumin, sambal olek."

"No wonder they called these the Spice Islands."

"Much of the local cuisine has evolved slowly over the centuries," Ilsa said. "Europeans brought new ideas and then other vegetables and spices arrived from the new world—tomatoes, squashes, melons, and even chili peppers."

"This meal speaks well for the result." Fraser suddenly realized the Japanese might soon bring new additions to Javanese cooking.

After dinner, they sat on the porch and sipped spiced tea while Ilsa filled him in on some of the local history. The phone rang.

Minutes later she returned. "My father sends his apologies. He will be tied up the rest of the night. Can you come again tomorrow night?"

"Certainly."

"Let me drive you back to your ship. It's getting late."

They walked to the garage, and Fraser whistled when he opened the big double doors. The black Mercedes sedan wasn't new, but it was immaculate. Chrome gleamed in the dim light from a single bulb. The shiny fender was cool and smooth to his touch.

"You like cars?" asked Ilsa.

"Yes. I've been saving up for a red Ford convertible."

"This is not quite as sporty."

The exhaust burbled powerfully when Ilsa started the car. Fraser loved the sound. The soft leather seat held him comfortably. The Mercedes exuded a perfume of polish, leather, gas, and oil.

As they glided over the streets of Surabaya the breeze from

the open windows swirled Ilsa's sandy hair. She wasn't a blonde in a convertible, but Fraser didn't mind.

When the Mercedes rolled to a halt on the pier, Ilsa offered Fraser her hand. "I enjoyed the evening. I hope you weren't disappointed."

"Ahh . . ."

"That last night in Manila—I don't know what came over me. I really don't remember very much."

"You just had too many martinis."

"How did I get back to our suite?"

"I had to carry you. If you're concerned . . . nothing happened."

"You were a gentleman, then."

"Yes, but a part of me regrets that very much. I hope you'll take that as a compliment."

"Yes. Thank you. I'll see you tomorrow night then."

As Ilsa drove away, Fraser shook his head with frustration. The evening hadn't gone as he'd hoped. The warm, compliant girl who had danced against him in Manila that last evening was again the girl he had first met—cool, aloof, remote. As he boarded the ship, he wondered if he would ever find the other Ilsa again.

"Evening, Mr. Fraser," said Eckersly, the beagle-faced storekeeper, who had the watch.

"Evening, Eckersly. All quiet?"

"Yes, sir. A little early yet for the men on liberty. I'm sure it's going to get interesting before long."

When Fraser opened the door to the wardroom, he found the captain sitting at the head of the table. A cup of coffee sat at his elbow, and a pad of paper lay in front of him. Several sheets of wadded paper lay on the table.

"Evening, Captain. Late to be working."

"Just trying to write letters to the families of the men we lost."

"I don't envy you."

Arkwright crumpled another piece of paper. "Not having much luck, I'm afraid."

"Tough day today, with the funeral. Maybe it would be easier tomorrow."

"Could be you're right." There was a long pause while the captain stared at the bottom of his cup. "I haven't been to a funeral since I buried my wife and children." Arkwright's voice was barely audible.

Fraser searched for something to say as Arkwright's haunted eyes shifted to the green table cover.

"Tell me, Ross, did I fail our men, too? Would they still be alive if I had done my job better?"

"I don't think so, sir. You made all the right moves. I know the exec couldn't have done as well. Certainly I couldn't have. If anything, I think a lot of us owe you our lives."

"You mean that?"

"Yes, sir. I do. Captain, why don't you let me try to draft those letters. The two men we lost were Bull's. The exec has put his division under me. I think those letters would mean more to the families if I could dig up some personal details."

Arkwright seemed to brighten. "Thanks, Ross. That would be a load off my mind. I'll go take care of a few other things and turn in." The captain paused. "I guess you'll stand in as Landry's division officer when he comes to mast."

Fraser remembered how Landry had saved him from drowning the night Simpson went over the side. "You probably should pin a medal on him the same day you send him off to the brig. He's the one who shot down the Jap plane."

"Why would he jump ship?"

"Chief Hanlon told me Landry was having problems with his girl and didn't know she was pregnant. The chief told him about her pregnancy just before we left Manila."

"And he got caught coming back aboard?"

"I don't know exactly what happened, Captain. I do know two things. If Landry went, he had a good reason. More importantly, he came back."

"I'll hold off mast for another week while we think this over. We can't afford to lose a good man. The damn aviators and submariners get the cream of the enlistees, so we have to make do with the men we get. Fortunately, many of them turn into damn good sailors."

After the captain went to his cabin, Fraser poured a cup of coffee and scribbled a few preliminary notes for the letters to the families. But the words stopped coming. What can you say to replace a human life, he wondered. He struggled for some thoughts that would mean something. He shook his head and decided to tackle the job after a night's sleep.

He walked over to the captain's door and knocked gently.

"Yes?"

Fraser poked his head in. "Just wanted to know how soon you wanted these letters, Captain."

Arkwright laid his gleaming black .45 on his desk. "Two or three days will be fine." He saw Fraser looking at the pistol. "Just thought . . . I'd clean it."

As Fraser headed to his room he thought over what he had just seen. A clip of bullets had been in the pistol. Maybe that was understandable; they were at war. But the safety had been off. Fraser couldn't think of a reason for that.

Captain Van Dorn greeted Fraser warmly in his formal English the next evening. The tall Dutchman ushered Fraser to the porch. "Ilsa will be down soon. I have much to ask about your experiences against the Japanese, but that can wait until after dinner over some good brandy. Ah, here's Ilsa now."

What the previous evening's dress had concealed, Ilsa's dress now subtly emphasized. Her figure flared above and below her narrow waist. Tanned legs gleamed in nylon stockings. A light dusting of makeup emphsized her green eyes and enigmatic smile. In retrospect, the top-heavy Shirley McGee now seemed like an overstuffed pastry.

After a few of Mohammed's drinks, they moved to the dinner table which featured a pork saté—small pieces of grilled marinated pork served in peanut sauce.

After dinner, Fraser and Captain Van Dorn walked to the porch where Ilsa's father poured brandy. Fraser described his experiences in the Philippines and during the trip to Java. "Control of the air—that's becoming the critical factor in naval operations," he concluded.

Van Dorn's deepset blue eyes were serious as he lit a cigar. "I'm not sure your situation here is going to be any better. We Dutch have few modern aircraft. The British have some Hurricane fighters in the region, but their range is limited. Our best hope is your Army Air Force P-40 squadrons that are on the way to Java."

"P-40s are a sore subject with us," Fraser said. "The Japanese made short work of them in the Philippines."

"Maybe the situation is not as bleak as you think. By adding the Dutch, British, and Australian naval forces to your Asiatic Fleet, we can more than double your striking power."

"That's nothing compared to what the Japanese can muster. They'll have a big edge in air power."

Before Van Dorn could respond, Ilsa joined them on the porch, wrinkling her nose. "Even those awful cigars can only keep me away so long. Maybe we should try to forget the war for a while."

"If you'll hand me another bottle of Martell, I think we can manage that," Captain Van Dorn said. Ilsa's father opened the brandy and poured some for his daughter.

"I'm fine," Fraser said, his glass still half full.

Van Dorn poured a generous portion for himself and turned the conversation to their years in other places far from the island of Java. Fraser was surprised how much the Van Dorns knew of the United States from their two tours in Washington. He was fascinated by stories about Holland and Europe.

After finishing his second refill, Van Dorn yawned. "I hope you will excuse me. I had a long day today even though it was Sunday. I have to go in early tomorrow."

"Good night, Captain. I hope to see you again."

"That would be nice."

Ilsa watched her father weave off the porch. "I wish he wouldn't drink so much," she said softly.

"A problem?"

"Not yet. He never drank much until my mother died."

"That must have been hard on him."

"It was. Both before and after. The cancer took many months to kill her. She . . . she was in great pain. There just wasn't anything we could do to help her."

"I know how it feels to be helpless. I had to watch a lot of men die in the Philippines."

Ilsa looked at him for several seconds. "Yes, I thought there was something different about you."

"Death always seemed abstract," Fraser said. "I really hadn't seen much of death. Just my grandmother's funeral."

"That's the way it was with me, too. For all the years I was growing up, death seemed so remote, so unreal. Then my mother. Then Hans, my fiancé. He thought a war would be such sport—a test of his manhood. He lasted two days before the Germans killed him. Dead . . . gone. How many others will die before this war is over? My father will probably be one of them. Tell me, Ross, do you see war as some sort of game?"

"Not anymore, if I ever did. It's a rotten way to settle problems."

Fraser changed the subject, but the conversation had taken the spark out of Ilsa. She seemed to withdraw into herself. She held her arms as if protecting herself from the danger that must be growing closer, day by day.

When Ilsa drove the Mercedes back to the ship, he was afraid to ask her for another date, sure she would refuse.

"It was nice of you to look me up," she said politely.

Fraser tried desperately to think of something she wouldn't refuse. "Could I ask a favor?"

"Yes."

"Do you have any friends the two single officers from my ship could take out? They just haven't been able to meet anyone ashore."

"Perhaps I could get nurses from the military hospital. I've been taking training there, so I can help when the casualties come in."

"That sounds fine. Maybe we could all go out together," he said hopefully.

Ilsa paused for several seconds. Then she seemed to change her mind about something. "Yes, that might be fun. Why don't I make reservations at the Surabaya Hotel. They have a big *Rijsttafel* every Saturday night."

"What's that?"

"The Indonesian version of the Swedish smorgasbord. If you liked Mohammed's cooking, you'll like this too."

After making further arrangements and saying a polite good night, Fraser watched the red tail-lights of the Mercedes vanish into the humid night. Fraser boarded the ship, realizing he wouldn't see her for almost five days. But that was better than not at all.

Fraser saluted Torpedoman Tim Egan, who had the watch on the quarterdeck.

"Hope you had a nice evening, Mr. Fraser."

"Yes, I did, thank you. At least it was better than fishing Simpson out of Subic Bay."

It wasn't until the next afternoon that the Dutch reported the drydock was ready to receive the *O'Leary* for repairs to her hull.

Laster strolled out on the wing of the bridge just as the last of the water was pumped from the dock. Fish flopped, and crabs scurried on the floor of the dock.

"A lot of crabs," Fraser said.

"That's nothing," Laster said. "I used to see a lot more crabs at sick call after each stop in Olongapo."

The succeeding days reverberated with the clangor of air-driven chipping hammers and the harsh rattle of riveting guns the yard workers were using to repair the seams in the hull. Under the supervision of T. T. Simpson, the engineers worked around the clock in the after fireroom to repair boilers three and four.

"Keep at it," Simpson told his men one evening. "I'm going topside for a cup of coffee."

In the galley, he stirred a spoonful of sugar into the steaming cup and sipped the scalding mixture.

Hank Landry stepped out of the bridge structure and headed toward the galley. "Hey, Simpson. How're you doing? Fixed number two yet?"

"No time for her. Hell, it's going to take all the yard time just to get three and four fixed."

"Number two helped get us here, didn't she?"

"Yeah, but something ain't right. Speaking of problems, how's Mortland treating you?"

The deeply tanned Landry smiled wryly. "If I was a dog, they'd put him in jail."

"If you need a recommendation for mast, ask me. You did good work for me in the fireroom."

Landry shook his head. "That'd set Mortland off, me getting help from a snipe."

"Be a waste if they ship you off to the brig."

"Don't want that," Landry said softly.

Simpson watched Landry head back toward the forecastle. Damned shame, he thought. Seems like a good kid. Too bad that bastard Mortland is giving him a bad time.

Simpson put his cup back in the galley and decided to check the forward fireroom. He walked over and turned the wheel of the hatch to the air lock that led down to the deserted fireroom. As he started down the ladder, he heard a faint wail, which rose and fell. Simpson froze on the ladder. All the boilers were cold; they were getting services from the shore. There was no reason for any leak or noise from the fireroom. He listened for another minute. The noise continued to rise and fall and change in pitch. "Jesus! Number two boiler ain't jinxed! She's haunted!"

Simpson climbed down the ladder. There was silence. Just as he touched the wheel of the lower door, the ghostly wail started again.

Simpson jumped. "Damnation!"

After a minute of screwing up his courage, he opened the door. There was a figure in the dim light. Simpson looked closer. The khaki-clad ghost sat on a bucket, its back to Simpson. The wailing stopped. The ghost turned. It was Mr. Fraser.

"What are you doing here?" Simpson asked.

"Just learning how to play the bagpipes."

"Why here?"

"The exec can't stand to listen to me practice. I don't know why." Fraser looked down at the book on his lap and blew a string of wailing notes.

For once, Simpson thought he agreed with the exec.

"*Scotland, The Brave*. Not bad, eh?" Fraser said.

"Ummm . . . different," said Simpson, thinking all Scots must be brave if they lived with noise like that.

Fraser stood up and stretched. "Guess I've learned enough for one night. I'm going to hit my bunk. Good night."

After the door closed behind Fraser, Simpson turned and faced the number two boiler. "Dammit, it might have been easier if you were haunted. I'm going to fix you before you get me, you old bitch."

Simpson lowered himself to the grating and cushioned his head on an arm, staring at the boiler. "I'll figure the problem out. By God, I will!" Waves of weariness washed over him as he racked his brain for answers, but he found none. He couldn't keep his eyes from closing, and he drifted off to sleep.

That Saturday night, Fraser took Korchak and Steiner to the Surabaya Hotel, where they were to meet Ilsa and her friends. Because of the blackout, the lights had been turned out at dusk; only candlelight was allowed. The officers sat in the lobby in heavy Victorian chairs as they waited for the ladies to arrive.

"I hope this turns out better than the other blind dates I've had," Steiner said.

The chunky Korchak rolled his eyes and looked at the ceiling. "Know what you mean. The last one I had was a real disaster."

"No guarantees," Fraser said. "Just remember you weren't doing very well in this town on your own."

The main door opened and Fraser sucked in his breath. Ilsa wore a conservative blue silk dress, but she seemed to glow in the dim light. Her friends were almost as attractive. One was a blond Dutch girl; the other, a combination of Dutch beauty and Javanese sultriness.

After introductions the group walked to the dining room, where waiters in native Javanese attire bustled about. Potted tropical plants added the scent of their flowers to the aroma of the waiting food.

"All this foliage reminds me of the night we spent in Jolo Harbor under camouflage," Steiner said.

Korchak smiled at his date. "It's much nicer here."

The diners sat at long tables and the waiters brought a seemingly endless procession of exotic dishes to sample: soups, salads, satés, curries, sauces, and sambals; seafood, chicken, beef, lamb, and pork; vegetables, fruits and melons. Fraser's plate ended up a heap of exotically scented and spiced food. His palate worked overtime to sort out the contribution of the individual components.

"Woody, careful with that one sauce," Ilsa said.

"Don't worry, a Slavic stomach can handle anything." Korchak dipped a shrimp and popped it in his mouth. His eyes bulged and sweat beaded his forehead. "Remarkable!"

Fraser decided to skip that particular sauce, but he found the rest of the meal delightful. He found it almost impossible to gauge how Ilsa felt about the evening. One moment she was animated and full of life. A minute later and she would be quiet and withdrawn.

When the ladies retired to the powder room after dinner Korchak beamed at Fraser. "My girl's a knockout. She really seems to like Americans."

"I have the same feeling," Steiner said. "What luck! How are you and Ilsa getting along, Ross?"

Fraser could only shrug.

After dinner a small combo began to play and the officers danced with their dates. Ilsa maintained a polite distance during the slow numbers and Fraser was ready to admit the last night in Manila had been an aberration. Late in the evening, Fraser walked Ilsa out on a terrace overlooking the hotel garden. The smell of the exotic plants and flowers below drifted by on the breeze. A full moon hung directly overhead, just as it had a month before in the Philippines. He remembered the promise of that night in Manila, which had remained unfulfilled since his arrival in Surabaya.

Ilsa took his hand and leaned against him.

"Been sneaking martinis?" asked a surprised Fraser.

"No. Maybe it's the moon up there. Maybe it's you. Would you please just hold me."

Fraser wrapped his arms around her as she nestled against him. Her shoulders shook as she cried against his chest.

Fraser felt a surge of tenderness, love, and more than a little lust. Something was happening; he felt sure she would continue to see him. He wasn't sure what to do, so he just stood and held her.

CHAPTER FIFTEEN

The next morning, Fraser poured syrup on his waffles as Korchak and Steiner sat down.

"Your evenings turn out well?" Fraser asked.

Korchak's eyes narrowed above his high cheekbones. "Umm . . . okay."

"So-so," said Steiner.

"What happened? You guys were really happy early on."

"Don't want to discuss it," Korchak said.

"Just as well," Steiner said. "You'll never top my story. Things went great 'til the end of the evening when I tried to get friendly. She stopped me cold and said she was ready to make a serious commitment to her new boyfriend—one of her patients."

"Some hotshot P-40 pilot?" Fraser asked.

"Nope. None other than Bull Durham," Steiner said.

Korchak began choking on his coffee. He sputtered and coughed, his face crimson.

Steiner looked ready to punch Korchak. "I suppose you think it's funny."

Korchak finally cleared his throat. "Funny, hell! That's just what my date told me."

Steiner thumped the table with his thick fist, rattling coffee cups. "Durham! That two-timing little devil."

Fraser shook his head. "Two is probably conservative. I'll bet he has a girl friend on each shift. Wait'll he can move around to different wards."

"You'd better have Ilsa warn those girls," Korchak said.

At the foot of the table, Laster chuckled. "Once they find out, those nurses will prepare Bull's bedpan in the refrigerator."

Korchak glowered. "Maybe that will cool that little Romeo's balls off."

The two youngest officers turned to their breakfasts, morosely silent. A few minutes later, the captain walked out of his cabin and sat down, shaking his head. "Listen to that."

"I don't hear anything," Beringer said.

Arkwright frowned. "That's what I mean. Nobody's working in the whole yard. Last night Jansen told me that the Navy Yard doesn't work on Sundays."

Laster squeezed his tea bag. "Pearl Harbor should have taught the Dutch that the Japs fight on Sunday."

Arkwright sighed, looking resigned. "Might as well give the men some time off. They deserve it. Let's have early liberty unless there's important work to do."

"That means my men have to stay," Meredith said.

The captain nodded sympathetically. "Sorry, Jack. Your snipes work harder than anybody. I'll make it up to them."

"I can't figure out the Dutch," Meredith said. "Maybe they don't think the Japanese are going to come this far south."

Laster shook his head. "Maybe it's the opposite. If they think the situation is hopeless, it would make sense for them to spend as much time as possible with their families."

"Everybody see the message that just came in?" Korchak asked.

"No," Fraser said with a sinking feeling.

"We're to escort a convoy to Australia in ten days."

As soon as he finished breakfast, Fraser hustled to check the message. The only consolation was that they were supposed to turn around and bring another convoy back to Surabaya. That meant he would be away from Ilsa for at least two weeks, and there was no guarantee the war would allow him to return.

Three mornings later, Hank Landry knocked at the doorway to Fraser's room fifteen minutes before disciplinary mast was scheduled. Landry's mouth was dry and his stomach was jumping.

"Take a chair," Fraser said.

Landry had just shaved and put on his best uniform. He held his hat in his hands and twisted it through his fingers, wondering what the captain would decide. Sweat began to trickle down his sides.

"Jesus, Mr. Fraser, I'm sweating, and you don't even look warm."

"That's because I'm not going before the captain."

"Do I have a chance of staying out of the brig, Mr. Fraser?" Landry shifted his knees to one side to give the officer more room.

"It's a bad situation. Your only hope to avoid a court martial is to say nothing."

"I want to tell the captain everything."

"Chief Hanlon told me about your girl. I mentioned the situation to the captain, so he knows why you went ashore. If you explain that at mast, you'll be putting him on the spot. Leaving the ship in wartime is serious business." Fraser sighed, and his gray eyes seemed sympathetic. "You did save me from drowning. I'll go see the captain. I want to be sure we're doing the right thing."

Landry fidgeted while Fraser was gone. He looked around the stateroom. It wasn't much. Landry had seen bigger closets, but it seemed like a quiet refuge after living in the berthing compartment, where five or six men were crammed into the same amount of space.

Fraser returned a few minutes later looking discouraged and ran a hand through his dark hair. "The captain said it wasn't proper to discuss the case before mast. He seemed to hint that you shouldn't say anything."

"Okay, sir. I'll keep my mouth shut."

"Landry, seems like you're in a bad situation with Mortland. Ever think of striking for gunner's mate?"

"That's crossed my mind, sir. But I like working on the whaleboat. Sort of like I own it."

"You might find that kind of satisfaction on the guns."

"I'll think about it, but I ain't gonna let Mortland run me off the whaleboat."

"Nothing wrong with running as long as you're running toward something and not away," Fraser said.

"Probably like to stay where I am . . . if I don't get sent to the brig."

Fraser looked at his watch. "It's time. Let's go."

Landry followed Fraser up to the quarterdeck, where a small lectern stood in the sunlight. In a few minutes the captain emerged from the bridge structure.

"Attention on deck!" ordered the master at arms. "Mast reports salute!"

Landry and the other men before the captain saluted.

"Two," ordered the master at arms, and their arms snapped down smartly.

Landry listened while two other minor offenses were presented to the captain. Landry thought the captain handled the other two men fairly.

"Landry, step forward," said the captain, his glance taking in Landry's appearance.

Doesn't miss a thing, thought Landry. He'll nail me.

The captain riffled through the papers before him and looked up at Mortland, next to Landry. "Chief Mortland, you're the reporting petty officer. Tell me what you know about this case."

Mortland cleared his throat loudly. "Well, sir, I was making a patrol topside just before dawn to see if everything was shipshape so's to figure out what had to be done after reveille. On the day in question, just after I passed the galley—"

"I won't ask if you stopped there for a handout."

"No, sir, strictly duty. As I was saying, I headed aft. I heard dripping water and loud breathing."

"And what did you see?"

"I saw Landry coming over the side. I told him he was on report for being absent without leave."

"Is that all you saw?"

"Yessir, caught him red-handed. Told him to get his ass below, I did. Guilty as hell!"

"I'll decide that. You just stick to the facts. Did you see him leave the ship?"

"Well, nossir."

"Did you see him swimming back from the waterfront?"

"Ahhh . . . nossir."

"Do you know anyone who saw him ashore?"

There was a long silence. "Nossir." Mortland sounded like he was beginning to strangle.

Landry wanted to peek at Mortland, but he kept his eyes front and center.

The captain turned to the executive officer. "Bob, do we have any witnesses who saw Landry ashore?"

"No, sir."

Landry opened his mouth to say something. But then he remembered Lieutenant Fraser's advice. Landry swallowed and remained silent.

The captain examined the papers in front of him and rubbed the side of his nose. "Ross, as acting division officer, do you have anything to add?"

"Captain, Landry's a hard worker, and a valuable member on the gun crews. He shot down the Jap airplane. I do have one other piece of information. Shifflet had the watch that night and saw Landry go down to the whaleboat to do some cleaning. Landry told Shifflet he might sleep down there."

"Is that true, Shifflet?" the captain asked.

"Yessir! That's God's own truth. And I saw him lying on the cushions too. Sorry, Landry, I know the chief don't like anyone lying on them nice clean cushions. I'm sure Landry took his shoes off. That boy loves that boat. Reminds me of a young sailor back on the *Trenton*—"

"That's sufficient, Shifflet," the captain said. "We have no evidence Landry was actually AWOL and a reasonable explanation for his being over the side. I know those boats and ladders are slippery with morning dew. Chief Mortland, I know you have high standards for the boats, but I would suggest that you ease up until we are out of the war zone. It seems your men are going a bit . . . overboard. Case dismissed."

The master at arms coughed and found his voice. "Mast reports, salute! Two."

The captain turned and headed below as Landry let out a long breath. He thanked Shifflet and Lieutenant Fraser and headed for the forecastle. Chief Mortland was sitting on a mooring bitt, puffing on a cigarette. Landry nodded and turned toward the hatch.

"Landry, you'll damn well wish a court martial'd sent you to the brig before I get through with you. I'm happy you're not gonna be where the Japs can't get at you. If they get me, I can die knowing they'll get you too."

Fraser knocked on the captain's door a few minutes later.

"Come in and sit down," the captain said. "Sorry I was short with you before mast. It wouldn't be a good thing to let Landry or the crew think I approve of swimming ashore."

"I hope not," Fraser said. "Fishing Simpson out was enough for me."

"I hope you learned something about responsibility this morning," Arkwright said. "We have to protect the men from petty officers like Mortland who have all the leadership qualities of a mule driver."

"Why not transfer Mortland?"

"On destroyers we have to make do with the men we have. Professionally, Mortland is a damn good bosun. He helped save the ship by stopping the flooding from that Jap bomb. It's a bad situation, but we have to make the best of it. I tried to keep Landry out of the brig and let Mortland keep some face."

"You did, sir."

"What about having Landry strike for another rate? Maybe that would end the problem between them."

"I suggested that, Captain. But Landry wants to stay with the whaleboat. He takes great pride in it."

Arkwright stared at the .45 pistol at the end of the bookshelf. "Some problems you just can't fix."

Sunday morning, two days before their departure for Australia, Fraser took a cab to the Van Dorns' house. During the ride, he thought about the evenings he had spent with Ilsa since the party at the Surabaya Hotel. Ilsa had shown Fraser the night spots in Surabaya. Each night when he brought her home, they sat together on the living room couch with Ilsa's head on his shoulder. Fraser was content with kissing and holding her until the night before when he slid his hand up Ilsa's firm thigh. She gasped and grabbed his hand. But she didn't throw him out. When he left Ilsa had said she was looking forward to their picnic today.

Ilsa answered the front door when Fraser arrived. Her low-backed sun dress accented her firm arms and shoulders. "Are you ready for our picnic?" she asked.

"Yes. I guess I owe this day to the Dutch Navy because they don't work on Sundays."

"Some of us aren't so lucky. I've been in the kitchen because the help is off until this evening. You'd better like this picnic lunch."

"Do you cook as well as Mohammed?"

"Noooo. Would you rather take him on this picnic instead of me?"

"Certainly not. I'd take you even if you couldn't cook."

"That's more like it."

The Mercedes purred through the broad streets of Surabaya to the zoo gardens. Fraser carried the picnic basket to a shady spot by a small stream. As they ate lunch, he wanted to ask Ilsa what she had done to his sandwich, but he decided he'd better not.

"How is your sandwich? I remembered Americans like tuna salad."

"Maybe you forgot something?"

"I don't think so. I took it right out of the can. Maybe it wasn't the right brand. It's awfully oily looking. Was I supposed to drain the oil?"

Fraser tried to keep from laughing.

"What's so funny?"

"You're definitely supposed to drain the oil."

"Oh . . . I guess I don't know much about cooking. We've always had a cook."

"I won't tell anybody. Besides, I'm sure you can learn whenever you want to. Hmmm. I wonder what Mohammed is doing next Sunday."

Ilsa threw a roll at him and laughed. When they finished the meal, they lay back on the blanket, dappled by sunlight filtering through the branches overhead. The nearby stream bubbled quietly over its rocky bottom.

"Look," Ilsa said as two petals from a flowering tree fell to the surface of the stream. The petals danced across the water to a sheltered pool, where they circled lazily and finally touched. They were drawn back into the main stream, carried along by the irresistible force of the water. They found momentary refuges in their journey, but were always drawn forward, finally sweeping over a small waterfall and swirling into a whirlpool where they vanished. Fraser watched carefully, but the two petals failed to reappear. He felt an overwhelming sadness.

"They had a good trip," Ilsa said.

"Yes, maybe that's what counts."

After a pleasant afternoon wandering through the gardens, they returned to the Van Dorn home where Mohammed had resumed his duties.

While Ilsa was inside, Mohammed delivered a frosted pitcher to the porch. "Let me offer a few words from the Rubaiyat of Omar Khayam for you and Miss Van Dorn:

'Ah, my beloved, fill the cup that clears
Today of past and future fears.'"

"Thank you, Mohammed. No wonder the Van Dorns think so highly of you."

"Let me know if I can do anything for you, Lieutenant Fraser. I have never seen Miss Ilsa so happy. There has always been an air of sadness about her and Captain Van Dorn. I think they both miss her mother."

"I hope you'll try to see that no harm ever comes to Miss Van Dorn," Fraser said.

"You may count on that."

Ilsa's father arrived in time for dinner, and they sat down to a table that featured lamb curry and a sweet and hot pineapple "sambal."

When the two men retired for brandy, Captain Van Dorn seemed pensive. "I am sorry to hear your ship is leaving on Tuesday."

"I hate to go. But we should head right back with another convoy."

Van Dorn blew cigar smoke into the air. "The Japanese have landed in northern Borneo and may be on the move soon. Your ship may be diverted to challenge them. There is no way of predicting . . ."

"No," Fraser said. "What happens . . . happens."

Van Dorn took another sip of brandy. "Ross, I want to thank you for what you've done for Ilsa. Since she lost her fiancé . . . she hasn't allowed herself any romantic attachments."

"I hope I'm doing the right thing. I feel like I'm struggling against something I don't know how to deal with."

"I know the feeling, Ross. I . . . I'm not sure what to tell you to do if your ship returns. I would hate to see Ilsa make another commitment and lose you to the Japanese. On the other hand, there is no guarantee of her safety. She could die during a Japanese invasion or trying to escape from Java."

A chill ran through Fraser. He had never considered the possibility that Ilsa might be killed.

Van Dorn's blue eyes locked with Fraser's. "I do know that the first weeks of my marriage with Ilsa's mother were the best weeks of our lives. I wouldn't want my daughter to die never having known such joy."

Van Dorn lit another cigar and stood. Shoulders slumped, he paced the porch. "What I am trying to say . . . is that if your ship comes back for more than just a few days, you have my approval to find whatever happiness you decide to share together. Life is too precious to waste. We must enjoy what we have while we can."

Ilsa's father stopped and looked down at Fraser. "But I would ask you to wait until you return. If you don't come back it will be hard enough on Ilsa. Your two-week absence will also give both of you some time for reflection . . . and some perspective."

"Perhaps we're forgetting something," Fraser said. "We can't decide this for her. I think Ilsa will have to work out some of her feelings by herself."

Van Dorn nodded. "Of course. But I feel better now that you know where I stand."

The sounds of nocturnal insects in the garden were punctuated by Ilsa's footsteps. "You men have had enough time to talk about the war."

When Captain Van Dorn excused himself, Fraser was pensive as he thought of the *O'Leary*'s coming departure.

"Ross, I hope you can come again tomorrow night. Mohammed and I have planned a special dinner for you."

"Yes, I'd like to come," Fraser said, suddenly aware of the trust Ilsa's father had given him.

After breakfast the next morning, Beringer beckoned Fraser aside. "Ross, I want you to go ashore to extricate your man Shifflet and some others from incarceration."

"You mean jail?"

"Affirmative." Beringer lit his cigarette with his gold lighter and blew out a column of smoke. "Evidently there was a big altercation ashore last night. Damned ruffians."

Altercation? Fraser thought Beringer had spent too many years in expensive prep schools.

At the city jail, Fraser discovered that bureaucracy moved slowly in Surabaya. Few spoke English, so an interpreter had to be found. Fraser got results when one elderly official discovered that Fraser knew Captain Van Dorn.

"A fine man, Captain Van Dorn." The florid Dutchman beamed

as he completed the forms required to release the *O'Leary*'s men. The official lost his smile when they found the destroyer's battered and bruised sailors, their uniforms dirty and torn.

Shifflet smiled broadly, revealing a new gap in his teeth. "Mr. Fraser, I told the boys you'd probably be the one to get us out!"

"Don't think you can get away with this again," Fraser said. "The authorities have decided to look the other way this time. I told them you'll behave yourselves from now on."

Shifflet looked as if that wasn't what he had in mind.

Egan, the red-haired torpedoman, spoke up before Shifflet could protest. "It was just a temporary misunderstanding, sir. Some Dutch sailors at the bar told us we were cowards for leaving the Philippines."

Shifflet laughed. "There were twice as many of 'em. That didn't stop us from changin' their minds about that!"

"Yeah," Egan said, "once we settled that, we all got along great in jail. They told us to come back for a beer whenever we felt like it."

"That Heineken and Amstel—that's good beer," said Shifflet. "Worth fighting the Japs to keep our hands on that. Hell, the Japs already got our San Miguel. You'd think that would hold the greedy bastards."

Fraser was happy to see someone else had a vital interest to defend in Java.

That afternoon, after leaving the dry dock, the *O'Leary* shifted to one of the commercial piers that lined the Mas River across from the Dutch naval base. There, the destroyer was moored among civilian ships that were seeking refuge from the war. As Fraser looked at the different home ports lettered on the sterns, he realized that most of the vessels, like the *O'Leary*, were far from their countries. They all had dismal prospects of ever making it home again.

Fraser returned to the Van Dorns' that evening. Mohammed brought Ilsa and Fraser a tray of cold drinks. As Mohammed poured, Fraser stared down at the garden from the porch.

"You like this place, don't you?" Mohammed said.

"Yes, Mohammed. I don't want to leave tomorrow."

"Perhaps there is more than the beautiful garden here for you. As our Muslim poet Labid wrote:

'Beside the garden flowed the Nile,
Often have I steered my boat there,
And landed to repose awhile,
And bask and revel in the sunny smile,
Of her whose presence made the place so fair.'"

Fraser applauded. "Mohammed, your choice of poetry is as good as your bartending."

The Javanese smiled in response to the praise and diplomatically returned to the kitchen.

When they finished their drinks, Ilsa led Fraser to the dining room. He wondered how Mohammed could possibly top the meals he had already produced, but he was dumfounded when he saw the table.

"I wanted to remind you of home," Ilsa said. "After all, what's more American than hot dogs?"

"But those aren't hot dogs."

"We thought Vienna sausages would be close enough."

Fraser's stomach rebelled. He had been eating Vienna sausages several times a week ever since the *O'Leary* left Manila. Six of the hated objects reposed in a bed of vegetables in a large tureen in the middle of the table. The vegetables had been cut to represent flowers. Surrounding the central dish were sixteen small dishes containing the condiments and relishes for sixteen-boy curry.

"Mohammed wanted to dress things up," Ilsa said.

Fraser sighed, took a roll and one of the sausages, and looked through the condiments.

"What are you looking for?" Ilsa asked.

"Mustard."

Ilsa laughed. "Mohammed is a wonderful cook, but he doesn't know much about you Americans."

"Never mind. I'll eat them Javanese-style."

Fraser smothered his sausages under piles of condiments, hoping they would obliterate the familiar flavor.

Mohammed poked his head out the kitchen door.

"You like your American dinner?"

"I don't know when I've tasted better-cooked Vienna sausages," Fraser said truthfully.

Mohammed displayed a half-acre of white teeth. "I can do them everytime you come."

"Don't do that," Fraser said hastily. "I must confess I've developed a taste for your Javanese cooking. Our American food pales in comparison."

Mohammed smiled and retreated to the kitchen.

After a leisurely brandy on the porch, Ilsa led Fraser to the living room couch where she leaned against him and looked up into his eyes. Her arms encircled his neck and her mouth moved to his, her tongue probing. Fraser slid his hand down Ilsa's back and across her hip and down her leg. Another kiss and he brought his hand up and cupped a breast as she moaned softly. Her hands began to roam over his body, pulling at his shirt, his pants.

Fraser felt a surging heat between his legs and finally pulled away as he felt ready to explode. Ilsa sat back and shook herself as if to restore her self-control.

She seemed dazed, stunned. When he finally put his arm around her again, she was unresponsive. "Maybe I'd better drive you to the ship," she finally said.

It wasn't that late, but Fraser realized they had suddenly reached a point where decisions had to be made—decisions that he had promised Ilsa's father to delay until the *O'Leary*'s return.

When Ilsa pulled the Mercedes to a halt at the pier, they sat together in the darkness.

"We should be back in two weeks," Fraser said, but he realized the Japanese might have something to say about that. He remembered Captain Van Dorn's assessment that the enemy was on the move.

A single tear slid down Ilsa's cheek. "If you don't come back, it has been nice . . ."

"No ifs. I'll be back. Maybe it won't be two weeks, but I will be back."

He kissed her again, not one of the passionate kisses they had exchanged on the couch, but softly as one would kiss a child. He finally slid across the seat and stepped out of the car. As he watched the Mercedes vanish into the night, he felt as if part of him were driving away.

CHAPTER SIXTEEN

The morning after the *O'Leary* left Surabaya, the convoy turned south and entered Lombok Strait to pass through the Malay Barrier. The island of Bali was off the starboard beam. Fraser leaned on the starboard wing, ready for a slow morning on the bridge. The signal bridge was lined with off-duty signalmen and quartermasters, taking turns peering ashore through the signal bridge telescope. After the proprietors of the instrument took their turns, they allowed other crewmen to look, but only if they paid five dollars.

Arkwright walked out on the bridge wing. "What's going on?" he asked Fraser.

"They're looking for the bare-breasted babes on Bali."

Arkwright smiled. "The girls on Bali put on blouses twenty years ago."

Fraser tilted his head toward the angry grumbles from the signal bridge. "I think some customers are finding that out."

There was a burst of laughter mixed with a cry of outrage. "Whad'ya mean my time's up? I ain't seen nothin' yet."

"Sorry, snipe. You pays your money and takes your chances," said one of the signalmen. "Five bucks'll get you another minute."

"Sheeit no! Find another sucker."

Arkwright raised an eyebrow at Fraser. "Who says people don't live and learn."

As Fraser stared at the distant island, he was lulled by the clear water and a gentle breeze that brought a tantalizing suggestion of Bali's fragrance. Then a shark fin cut the water nearby, reminding Fraser that the strait might become a death trap. It would be easy for the Japanese to blockade Lombok Strait and the other passages through the Malay Barrier. Escape to Australia might become impossible.

As they left Bali behind, the *O'Leary* zig-zagged ahead of the plodding merchant ships. The monotonous routine forced Fraser to fight to stay alert. During the last hour of his watch, his head began to pound. The ping of the sonar seemed to shoot through his skull and the light reflecting off the water was almost unbearable.

When Chuck Steiner relieved the watch, he frowned at Fraser. "You don't look so hot."

Fraser headed below for his bunk, skipping lunch. Within an hour, chills shook him, and he asked a passing steward to bring Laster. The doctor took his temperature and examined him.

Fraser lay back on his bunk. "Doc, my eyes feel like they're going to fall out."

"How about your back and legs?"

"They ache like hell."

"Looks like dengue fever," Laster said. "You ran into the wrong mosquito ashore."

"How soon will this be over?"

"Depends. Mild cases are back on their feet in three days. The classic case gets better after two or three days and then has a relapse. Count on being in your bunk for a few days."

Laster was right. Fraser was rarely sick in bed, but dengue fever was another matter. The severity of his case only allowed him a short glimpse of Darwin, the dusty, primitive northern Australian port. Fraser was back in his bunk while the *O'Leary* steamed to a rendezvous with part of the Asiatic Fleet. Laster told him they were preparing to stop the predicted Japanese invasion of Balikpapan, the Borneo oil port the *O'Leary* had visited on her escape from the Philippines.

Fraser wasn't ready to stand bridge watches until the American force headed north to slip through the Malay Barrier. They were entering Sape Strait when Fraser relieved the watch after breakfast.

"Good to see you back at work," said Korchak, who briefed him on the formation. There was bad news: one of the two light cruisers with them, the *Marblehead*, had suffered a turbine casualty and had been forced to withdraw along with an escorting destroyer.

"Just the *Boise* and six four-stackers now," Korchak said. "Hell, intelligence is predicting we're going up against a Jap cruiser and a dozen destroyers."

Fraser didn't like those odds, but there was nothing he could do about them. They were still a day and a half from Balikpapan; he hoped the attack would be canceled.

Fraser relieved Korchak and took his position on the port wing. He raised his binoculars and inspected the *Boise*, exactly the kind of duty he wished for. In contrast to the *O'Leary*, the cruiser was solid, modern, and safe looking. She had the speed of the *O'Leary* but eight times her weight. She had armor plate to protect her instead of thin rusting steel. The *Boise* was classified as a light cruiser because her main armament consisted of 6-inch guns, which were mounted in five triple turrets. Fraser envied the secondary battery of eight 5-inch guns which could be used against aircraft. Float planes perched on the cruiser's catapults, ready for long-distance scouting or spotting the fall of shot during battle. A bedspring-like contraption rotated on the Boise's foremast. Fraser thought the apparatus had to be radar equipment. If so, the *Boise* was the only ship in the Asiatic Fleet to have the system.

The *Boise* looked like she had been invited to the wrong party. The destroyers escorting her belonged to an earlier era. Fraser shook his head as he looked over the five identical sisters of the *O'Leary*. The four-stack destroyers were woefully equipped compared to newer American or Japanese destroyers. However, if they could close the enemy as a group and launch their torpedoes, they would be a lethal force because each ship carried twelve torpedoes. Fraser hoped they'd get a chance to use those torpedoes against Japanese merchantmen rather than an enemy battle line.

Fraser leaned against the bridge wing, ready for a dull morning. Suddenly, messages began to flash between the *Boise* and the destroyer force commander aboard the *Ford.*

"Captain, *Boise* reports she's hit bottom," one of the signalmen shouted.

Arkwright leaped out of his bridge chair. "Copy all their signals. I want to know what's happening."

"What next?" Fraser muttered.

An hour later the *Boise* reported that she had suffered major underwater damage. The force turned back through the strait and steamed south to rendezvous with the crippled *Marblehead* before heading for nearby Warorada Bay.

Arkwright's face was grim. "Probably means the *Boise* will have to go back to the States for repairs."

There goes our only radar, Fraser thought, and our only new ship.

"So much for our attack," Arkwright said softly, almost regretfully.

The captain was wrong. Headquarters ordered them to prepare a sortie to Balikpapan with five destroyers. The *Boise* with one escort was ordered to southern Java for temporary repairs. The *Marblehead* and another escorting destroyer were ordered north to support the attacking destroyers when they retired southward from Balikpapan.

Two days later the column of five American destroyers steamed north toward the southern entrance of the Makassar Strait. Fraser paced the bridge after lunch, knowing this part of the trip was critical. Success would depend on surprise. If they were spotted during their approach, the Japanese defenders would be forewarned. Japanese air power would hammer them.

The American destroyers entered the 200-mile wide opening to Makassar Strait in the early afternoon. Commander Talbot, the force commander riding the *Ford*, ordered a course change toward Mandar Bay on the opposite side of the strait from Balikpapan.

Arkwright nodded approval as Fraser paced by his chair. "If a Jap plane spots us before dark, the Japs may not think we'll be headed for Balikpapan tonight."

"Let's hope these clouds hold up," Fraser said.

Fraser got his wish—and more. Strengthening northerly winds pushed ever larger swells at them. The *O'Leary* and her sisters dug their bows into the growing masses of green water, and the wind whipped spray up to the bridge wings.

As Fraser's watch continued that afternoon, the wind and seas picked up even more. The column of destroyers labored through 10-foot waves at 25 knots. The seas surged over the bow of the *O'Leary*, inundated the forward 4-inch gun, smashed into the base of the bridge structure, and showered spray over the fire control platform. Water sloshed under the gratings as Fraser held onto the chart table. He wondered if the critical fire control circuits for the forward gun would be able to function during the attack that night.

When Steiner relieved him, Fraser stopped at the captain's chair for any instructions. Fraser knew he had a lot to accomplish because he would have only the 2-hour dog-watches off before returning to the bridge.

"We'll change course after dark and head straight for Balikpapan," Arkwright said. "Should get there about 0200 when they're nice and sleepy." Arkwright ran his finger down the tactical instructions from Commander Talbot. "This sounds good. Hold our gunfire until the force has expended its torpedoes. Avoid action en route so as to get in close to the transports—our main target. Use discretion in picking targets and use the appropriate number of torpedoes. When out of torpedoes, we close with guns, using initiative and determination."

"Sounds like a good plan, Captain, but I wish we had the two cruisers and extra destroyers we had a few days ago."

Arkwright appeared untroubled. "That's life."

And maybe death, Fraser thought.

Fraser left the bridge to look for Chief Hanlon to ensure that all their equipment was ready for the expected battle. Fraser didn't have far to look. As he headed down the ladder behind the signal bridge, Fraser saw Hanlon on the amidships deckhouse supervising work on the 4-inch gun by the starboard rail.

"Anything serious, Chief?" Fraser asked.

"No, sir. Just another piece of wiring needed replacing. Otherwise, both of these guns check out fine."

"What about number one?"

"Your guess is as good as mine." Hanlon grabbed the gun barrel for support as the *O'Leary* shuddered through another wave and spray whipped over the rail. "We won't know if there's a problem up there until we stop taking water over the bow. The gun was fine this morning, but . . ."

Fraser said, "As soon as the seas die down, let's get up there and check it out. I'm afraid all that salt water may have screwed things up again."

"Likely," Hanlon said.

"We'll have to do the best we can," Fraser said. "We've got until midnight to set things right, but you won't be able to show any lights up there if you're working."

"I've been working on 4-inch guns long enough to fix them in the dark," the stolid Hanlon said.

Shortly after dinner, Fraser held a meeting with his gun crews. He looked around the forward berthing space crowded with the assembled men. There was electricity in the air as the men exchanged nervous taunts and laughter.

Fraser quieted them. "All right, I know you've been waiting for this. Something different—we'll man both amidships guns tonight."

There were murmurs of excitement. Usually a single gun crew took care of both guns, manning whichever gun faced the target.

Fraser continued. "We might steam right among the enemy

transports tonight. We may want to shoot to both sides at the same time. The regular gun crew will man the port gun. Chief Hanlon will act as gun captain of the starboard gun. Landry, I want you to move over to the starboard gun as the pointer. Morales will replace you on the port gun."

"Mabuhay! Hoo-ray! I get to shoot the Japs!" shouted the Filipino steward who had been begging Fraser for months for a promotion from his general quarters station as a loader. Morales began jumping up and down as his shipmates cheered.

Fraser finally quieted them and filled out the new gun crew with men from the ammunition passing party. There were murmurs of satisfaction as he announced the names. "You men in the new crew haven't had a chance to work as a team, but you've all been trained as replacements for these slots. Keep cool. Chief Hanlon and Landry will steer you straight."

"Sir, there ain't many men left to pass ammunition up from below," Shifflet said.

"The captain and I decided that the rounds in the ready racks would probably be enough. We'd rather pump rounds out of the extra gun at the beginning of the battle. If we need a lot of ammunition from the magazines, Chief Hanlon will send his crew below."

"Need a whip to get 'em off the gun," Hanlon said.

Laughter rippled around the compartment.

When it quieted down, Fraser outlined the plan of attack for the expected battle. "Any questions?"

"Be enough Japs to keep me happy?" Shifflet asked.

"I don't think you'll run short," Fraser said. "Any other questions? Chief, when we go to general quarters, I want a bucket of hand grenades up on the director platform."

"Expecting some action at close quarters, sir?"

"You never know. I don't think grenades have been used in a ship action since the Civil War. We may need everything we have before the night's over."

Fraser was interrupted by the clatter of feet on the ladder. Two dripping torpedomen joined the group.

"You guys been swimming?" Shifflet asked.

"Might as well have been," Egan said, his red hair matted. "Been topside charging the air flasks and setting the torpedoes for straight fire. The damn waves and spray were hell."

Fraser realized that all their peacetime routines were being discarded. An elaborate simultaneous torpedo attack was out the window. They wouldn't need the torpedoes to make a 30-degree turn to parallel the ship's course.

"I think that shows you what's in store for tonight," said Fraser. "Forget a formal attack. It'll be brass knuckles and knees in the dark. I want you gun crews ready to go to local control if we get among the transports."

"Hot damn!" Shifflet said. "Gonna be like a free for all in a whoo-ore house."

As the evening wore on, Landry and the other off-watch men in the forward berthing compartment prepared for battle. Landry had already showered and scrubbed with soap, a pre-battle ritual that was supposed to minimize wound infections. Despite the heat, Landry pulled on a long-sleeved shirt to reduce the possibility of flash burns. He checked his life jacket for the Dutch money, fish hooks, and lines he had sewn into watertight packets. Landry knew that south of Balikpapan the island of Borneo offered nothing but 300 miles of jungle.

Landry glanced at his watch. Still two hours to midnight. The boisterous atmosphere had long since evaporated, and men had seemed to withdraw into themselves. Landry didn't feel much like talking anyway, so he hauled himself up to his bunk and closed his eyes. His roast beef dinner felt like a heavy lump in his belly. A few of the men around him appeared to be dozing, but Landry didn't know whether to envy them or not. Who wanted to spend the last hours of his life asleep? Landry turned restlessly in his bunk and thought of the days and nights he had shared with Teresa in Manila. He wondered if all was well with her and the child growing inside her. Had she made it to the hills safely with Maria? Landry wished he could roll back the clock to be with Teresa in their Manila apartment. He wondered how he could have been so stupid to waste most of their last week together.

Chief Hanlon was too busy that evening to have more than a few minutes to think about better times in the Philippines. When the *O'Leary* stopped taking heavy water over the bow, he and Shifflet checked the 4-inch gun on the forecastle. Their initial tests were discouraging: the readout dials on the gun didn't match the orders from the director. Because the weather was moderating, Hanlon decided to wait an hour for the spray to die down. Then, when they opened the electrical boxes, there would be hope of drying them out to eliminate the electrical grounds and shorts caused by the salt water.

Hanlon climbed to the bridge and reported to Fraser, who took off his hat and ran a hand through his black hair. His gray eyes looked concerned. "Even if you can't fix the problem, we can still use the gun in local control."

Fraser walked over to the captain's bridge chair, where Arkwright was slouched down. Arkwright lifted his head from his chest. "Just been resting my eyes. I heard you and the chief. Sounds like you're doing all you can. Chief, I know you'll do your best. Keep up the good work."

"Thank you, Captain." Hanlon felt gratified that the captain seemed to understand the situation. He resolved to find the problem, encouraged by Arkwright's positive attitude. Hanlon had seen a few captains who never seemed to understand the problems of their ship's equipment.

As expected, the wind and seas moderated further. Hanlon and Shifflet felt their way along the dark forecastle. The *O'Leary* was charging into the wind so the air on the forecastle tore at them with a force of over 40 knots, flapping Hanlon's trouser legs. Before they reached the gun, Hanlon had to grab his cap as it started to blow off.

"No admirals around to gig you for not wearing a hat," Shifflet said. "Whoeee! Ain't seen nothing this dark since I took Betty-Sue down in the old coal mine!"

All Hanlon could see of the *Ford* just ahead was a tiny blue light at her stern and her white wake. When they ducked behind the metal gunshield it broke some of the wind. Hanlon pulled out a screwdriver and wrench and went to work, following wires from boxes and terminals as they traced the faulty electrical circuits. They finally had to drape a tarpaulin over the gun so Hanlon could use a small penlight to inspect some of the junction boxes. The tarp flapped around Hanlon's head in a frenzy.

"Hold that tarp still," Hanlon said patiently. "Gonna beat my brains out."

"Doin' my best," Shifflet said.

"Just making sure. You have a strange sense of humor."

"Yeah, Mr. Fraser don't always appreciate it neither. I tell you, it ain't easy gettin' these young officers broke in right. But he's okay for an officer. Maybe we'll make a destroyerman out of him yet."

Hanlon had to smile. That was high praise from Shifflet. The chief almost lost his patience when he dropped one of his favorite screwdrivers, and it rolled over the side. "Been using that for eight years," Hanlon said.

"Nothin' lasts forever," Shifflet said. "You can always find another screwdriver."

"Good thing you didn't fall over," Hanlon said. "We'd never find another Shifflet."

"Mr. Fraser might not mind that."

After two hours of intense labor, Hanlon's back was aching and his hands shook with fatigue. He finally grunted with relief.

"That one do it, Chief?" Shifflet asked.

"I think so. Let's give it another test." Hanlon watched anxiously as the dials spun and settled to the desired position.

"Hot damn! That last box was it!" Shifflet said.

Hanlon sighed. "Yep. This gun is back in business. Close it up while I tell Mr. Fraser and the captain."

As the 20–24 watch wore on, Fraser paced from wing to wing, keeping a sharp eye on the *Ford*, just ahead of them in the five-ship column. The weather had moderated, and the *O'Leary* sliced through the swells at 27 knots. The clouds were still thick overhead, so there was no light from the stars or the first quarter moon, which would set near midnight.

"Should be plenty dark for the attack," Fraser said.

"Just so it's not too dark to find the Japs," the captain said.

An hour before midnight, Arkwright called Fraser over.

"Let's go to G. Q. now. I want the men to have plenty of time to test their equipment and to adapt their night vision."

Fraser rolled down his long sleeves as the gong-gong of the general alarm brought men running to their stations. He turned the deck and the conn over to Woody Korchak and climbed the ladder to the fire control platform, where he pulled on his bulky kapok life jacket and donned his headset and helmet.

Because there was no immediate threat of combat, Arkwright secured the cooks from their battle stations to distribute sandwiches and coffee to the men who still felt like eating. Fraser wasn't interested; his stomach felt like the final hours before a football game at the Naval Academy. He recognized the familiar symptoms and knew he could cope with them. He sympathized with the men who'd never performed under intense pressure before.

"Damn waiting is getting to me," Eckersly muttered next to Fraser.

The seas continued to die, easing their passage. Shortly before midnight, Mortland bellowed from the crow's nest. "Flashing light off the starboard bowwww!"

"Jesus," Eckersly said, "I forgot Mortland took Mr. Durham's spot up there. They probably heard him all the way to Balikpapan."

"Maybe they'll think he's a foghorn," Fraser said.

As the destroyers pounded ahead at 27 knots, Fraser studied the light Mortland had reported. The glow flickered in his binoculars but definitely wasn't the regular flash of a navigation beacon. "Looks like a burning ship, Captain," he shouted down to Arkwright on the bridge wing below.

"Maybe our bombers finally hit something."

The burning ship slid by several miles to starboard, and darkness surrounded them again. The solid cloud cover eliminated any light from the stars or the setting quarter moon.

Two hours after midnight, they began their final approach to Balikpapan, now about 30 miles to the west. A reddish-orange glow lit the horizon ahead. Fraser remembered the portly Dutch governor's promise to burn the oil facilities. Fraser realized that as long as they could stay to the east of the Japanese, the enemy would be silhouetted against the light, but too much light might expose the four-stackers to the defenders.

Fraser paced his station on the fire control platform. The glow to the west beckoned them on as the five old ships hurtled through the humid night. An acrid stink from the fires ashore burned Fraser's nostrils; what a difference from Ilsa's subtle perfume. At that moment he would gladly have relinquished his chance to be a hero for the safety of Surabaya.

A thickening haze drifted across their path. They ripped through several banks of smoke. Suddenly a large Japanese destroyer shot out of the night and hurtled by to starboard, no more than 300 yards away.

"Hold your fire," Arkwright shouted. "We want the transports!"

Fraser relayed the order to his gun crews.

"Goddamn! He didn't see us," Eckersly said.

"Maybe he thought we were Japs," Fraser replied.

"Jap destroyers! Bearing three four zero. Range—three oh double oh!" a lookout shouted.

Fraser swung his binoculars and picked up the enemy—four ships in a column, heading across their bow from port to starboard. The *Ford* swung left, taking them astern of the enemy and into a nearby bank of smoke. One Japanese destroyer blinked a challenge before the Americans slipped into the smoke.

"Hold your fire," Arkwright ordered.

The Japanese must have thought the Americans were a group of their own ships because there was no sign of an alarm.

"Jeeesuss," said a voice from the signal bridge. "I wish I knew some Japanese so I could tell what he wanted to know."

Maybe we should tell them we're the UCLA Alumni Association collecting dues, Fraser said to himself.

Minutes later, the *O'Leary* followed the *Ford* out of the smoke. Fraser sucked in a deep breath. "This is it."

Just ahead was their quarry, the enemy transports. The Japanese ships seemed to be at anchor, or at least stopped in the inky water. Two lines of ships ran from north to south several miles offshore, silhouetted against Balikpapan's fires. Fraser gritted his teeth with frustration, knowing his gunners would have to wait until the torpedomen did their job. Below on the port wing, Fraser heard Steiner at the torpedo director, setting up to fire at a nearby Japanese transport.

Fraser scanned the night for the Japanese defenders. If Japanese warships spotted them and opened fire, the element of surprise would be gone. Fraser and his men had to be ready to return fire immediately. While Fraser was searching aft, the *Parrott* unleashed a salvo of torpedoes. The *O'Leary*'s two triple tube mounts on the port side had already swung out. The range was so short and their speed so high that the mount captains were probably having a tough time keeping up with the rapidly changing director orders.

"Fire two!" Steiner shouted.

There was the muffled explosion of the impulse charge, a whine of the starting torpedo machinery, and the swish of the propellant gases escaping from behind the emerging torpedo.

"Fire four!"

Another torpedo splashed into the water. "Go, baby, go!" Chief Robustelli's raspy voice shouted behind the amidships deckhouse.

The second weapon popped to the surface once and then dove, trailing bubbles of steam as it steadied on its run toward the target. Fraser watched the two wakes. The first looked as if it would miss astern, but the second arrowed straight for the middle of the transport. Fraser grabbed the rail in front of him, anticipating the explosions of their own torpedo and of those fired from other destroyers.

Nothing happened. Muffled curses floated up to where Fraser

was standing. Fraser clenched his fists. What was wrong? Their second torpedo had headed right at the target. They had come so far, surmounted so many problems, and now—complete failure.

Their course had taken them by the northern corner of the anchorage, so the *Ford* led the column around to starboard and steadied on a southerly course. The Japanese ships were now off the starboard side, still outlined against the fires of Balikpapan to the west. Just as the destroyers settled on their new course, the night erupted with blinding, crunching explosions.

Some of the torpedoes are working, Fraser thought as he searched the night for enemy destroyers and cruisers. Nothing. He hoped the defenders wouldn't return from out in Makassar Strait. If they did, the Japanese would find the Americans outlined against the blazing skyline, just like the transports were.

The destroyers made a long run to the south. Steiner fired torpedoes from the starboard mounts as targets loomed out of the smoky gloom. Fraser grunted with satisfaction because the destroyers were perfectly positioned to attack the transports, which began to show signs of life. A signal light blinked. Random shots were fired into the darkness, but there was no indication that the Japanese had located the Americans or even understood the nature of the threat.

A blinding flash erupted from a nearby transport, then another from the same ship, and another. The intense light bathed the scene in a yellow twilight. Seconds after each explosion, shock waves drove the air from Fraser's chest and left his lungs laboring for air.

"One of those torpedoes was ours!" Steiner shouted.

Their fifteen-minute race southward was punctuated by the explosions of more torpedoes. When they passed the last of the targets, the destroyers followed the flagship around in another loop. Before the column headed back north, the *Pope* and *Ford* fired torpedoes at a small enemy escort. For tense seconds, the torpedoes ran their deadly course. Then two violent explosions ripped the escort as the *O'Leary*'s waiting gun crews cheered. The enemy ship jackknifed; the bow and stern sections almost touched as she went under.

Another transport exploded and appeared to be sinking, a victim of American torpedoes from the ships *Ford, Jones*, and *O'Leary*. As they raced north, the water was full of swimming Japanese, and the high-speed wakes from the passing destroyers overturned several lifeboats.

Ahead, the *Ford* suddenly turned westward to steam across the center of the anchorage. Fraser glanced aft; the destroyers astern were beginning to straggle from their stations in the column. The high speeds and sudden maneuvers were difficult and dangerous under the best of circumstances. Now the trailing ships had to contend with enemy vessels and the clouds of smoke that swirled over the water.

As the *O'Leary* came around in a skidding arc to follow the *Ford*, she passed dangerously close to one of the sinking transports. Fraser looked astern again. The trailing destroyers were maneuvering radically to avoid collision with the transport and each other. They faded into the smoke.

The *O'Leary* followed in the wake of the *Ford* as she continued westward toward the fires of Balikpapan. They were now out of torpedoes. The gun battery was ready for action. Fraser had already ordered his director to track a large Japanese merchant ship to port. Although the *O'Leary* passed the other ship rapidly, the gun director was able to stay on target. The guns followed obediently—even number one. Still no orders to open fire; when they came, it would be shooting from the hip. In these tight quarters there would be no time for firing ladders and the formal procedures of peacetime exercises. Like the torpedo firings, the gun battery was dealing with targets that were so close that the ship's high speed and violent turns made target tracking by the director extremely difficult.

The radio telephone speaker crackled as Commander Talbot ordered his ships to use their guns and to withdraw independently.

"Commence firing!" the captain shouted.

Fraser wasted no time. "Rapid salvo fire! Commence firing! Commence firing!"

The deck jolted under his feet and concussions shook him as

the first salvo roared out. Tracers arced toward the merchant ship. The projectiles hammered the transport, barely a thousand yards away. The target disappeared in the smoke as their second salvo shattered the night. "Cease firing!" Fraser shouted, unwilling to fire blindly into the smoke because the other American destroyers were out there somewhere.

Fraser searched the smoke-filled night for another target, but his night vision had been impaired by the torpedo explosions and the flashes of their own guns. He had lost his orientation now that he'd been forced to focus on individual targets. He felt he was in the middle of hell itself. They were surrounded by smoke, flames, and the terrible red glow from Balikpapan.

A large ship loomed through the smoke. "Target just off the port beam!" he barked to his director personnel.

"On target!" shouted the director pointer and trainer simultaneously.

"Surface action port! Match pointers!" Fraser ordered the guns through Eckersly.

As soon as the guns were following the director, Fraser shouted, "Rapid salvo fire! Commence firing!"

Three salvos punished the enemy ship. Four-inch projectile explosions blew deck plates and debris in all directions, but the hits were too high to cause flooding.

"Lower your aim to the waterline!" Fraser shouted to the director pointer.

The next salvo roared from the *O'Leary*'s guns just as the enemy ship was about to vanish into the smoke. Two flashes erupted near the waterline. On the Japanese ship, men scrambled over the side as it listed.

They raced past the western limit of the anchorage. The fires of Balikpapan were dead ahead, so the *O'Leary* followed the *Ford*'s sweeping turn, taking them back toward the anchorage. Suddenly, there was the flash of a small explosion ahead. The *Ford* had taken a hit from one of the transports. Flames spouted from the destroyer's after deckhouse, but they died as burning debris was jettisoned.

The *O'Leary* had fallen behind the *Ford*, which was barely visible in the smoky darkness ahead. A massive black shape loomed ahead to port. "Right full rudder!" Arkwright shouted. The *O'Leary* heeled over as they narrowly missed colliding with the enemy transport that had gotten under way. "Left standard rudder! Steady on zero nine zero!" ordered the captain, taking them back to their eastward course. They only got one salvo off at the black shape before the smoke obscured it, but one projectile hit home amidships with a tremendous explosion.

When the *O'Leary* emerged from a thick patch of smoke, there was no sign of the *Ford*; they were alone. Slicing through another layer of haze, they were suddenly in the middle of four enemy transports. Fraser judged that this was no time for director-controlled fire. "All guns local control! Fire at targets of opportunity! Commence firing!"

"Get on that target just forward of the beam!" Chief Hanlon shouted. The long barrel swung rapidly as the trainer cranked his wheel. Landry hunkered down in his pointer's seat and found he only had to elevate the barrel slightly because the target was so close.

This was what Landry had been waiting for, a chance to shoot the enemy himself. Until now, all he had done was to keep his readout dial matched with the order dial from the gun director. Now he could watch what they were shooting; he fixed his sight on the waterline.

"On target!" the trainer yelled.

"On target!" Landry shouted.

"Commence firing!" Hanlon shouted.

Landry jabbed the firing pedal under his foot. The gun bucked, and a yellow flash engulfed him as a giant hand seemed to shake his body. Landry's ears were overwhelmed by the familiar blast, and powder smoke filled his nose.

Landry watched his tracer arc over to the Japanese hull, where it blew pieces of steel plate skyward. He felt Chief Hanlon yank the breechblock open behind him, and the shellcase clanked on the deck. The steel seat vibrated as the next round was inserted, and the breechblock slammed shut. Landry sent the next round on its way with the feeling it was somehow bringing his return to Manila that much closer. As fast as his loaders supplied him with ammunition, Landry poured rounds into the night. His efforts were rewarded with several hits on the Japanese vessel.

"Good shooting!" Hanlon shouted. "Keep it up!"

While they were shifting to another target, Landry heard the port gun hammering away, punctuated by the high-pitched shouts of Morales, the Filipino steward. Landry knew he wasn't the only one who wanted to return to the Philippines.

With the guns under local control, Fraser and the men on the fire control platform were spectators. As they raced by a Japanese transport at a range of no more than 40 yards, Eckersly reached down for two of the grenades that Fraser had ordered brought to the platform. Eckersly pulled the pin and heaved a grenade to the deck of the enemy ship as the *O'Leary* swept past. He added a second for good measure. Two explosions lit the Japanese decks.

"Great arm!" Fraser shouted.

"I'm saving one for the *Holland*'s dugout," yelled the third baseman on the *O'Leary*'s team.

Fraser had a few seconds to reorient himself and assess the panorama around him. The view was intermittently obscured by the heavy smoke that was now coming from burning ships as well as the flaming facilities ashore. The flashes from the *O'Leary*'s guns lit up the night for a half-second at a time. The guns of the other American ships and the impact of their projectiles created a violent pyrotechnic display far removed from the Fourth of July fireworks that Fraser had witnessed as a boy. Burning Japanese ships cast a flickering light on the scene; ships flared as ammunition or volatile cargo exploded.

One of the Japanese troop transports resembled an anthill under attack by a rival colony. The decks and side of the listing ship were thick with bodies scrambling for the dubious safety of the water where patches of flaming oil awaited swimmers. Fraser wondered if the Americans and Japanese were any more civilized than mindless ants.

Minutes later, the *O'Leary* reached the eastern edge of the anchorage again.

"Right full rudder! Come to two seven zero," Arkwright shouted, ordering them back the way they had just come.

The guns were momentarily silenced by the hard turn. Evidently the pointers and trainers couldn't stay on their targets. During the lull, it was obvious that most of the gunfire had died away.

Fraser looked down at the bridge wing where Beringer approached Arkwright. "The rest of our ships have cleared out, Captain."

"We're not done yet," Arkwright said. "I want another chance."

Halfway through their sweeping turn, Mortland's voice rattled the earpiece over Fraser's right ear. "Jap warship, maybe a cruiser, off the port beam, 3 miles, headed this way."

Fraser ordered his director to track the target and tried to find the enemy with his binoculars. He scanned the dark horizon out in Makassar Strait.

"Shift your rudder to left full," the captain barked.

There! Somehow a long corridor of clear air had opened between the walls of smoke. Fraser picked out the white bow wave and focused on the enemy—bigger than a destroyer, with a high slab-faced bridge and a pagoda-like foremast. It was a *Sendai*-class light cruiser with more than twice as many guns—all much bigger.

It's time to get the hell out! Fraser thought, waiting for the captain to head south for safety, but the bow continued to swing toward the enemy. A series of yellow flashes blossomed from the Japanese cruiser. Fraser hunched his shoulders as he realized enemy shells were in the air, heading for the *O'Leary*. The seconds crawled by as he waited for them to hit. Towering columns of water shot out of the sea 50 yards to starboard.

The gun director reported on target; Fraser ordered the guns to open fire as they continued their swing. Two salvos roared out. When the captain settled them on a course due east, directly at the enemy, only the gun on the forecastle was unobstructed as they charged at the Japanese cruiser.

Fraser looked down at the bridge wing. The captain's mouth was fixed in a grim line, his face lit by the red glow from ashore and the flickering flames from Japanese ships nearby. Beringer grabbed the captain's upper arm, but Arkwright shook him off with a cold stare.

"We have no torpedoes left!" Beringer shouted. "Our guns are no match for a cruiser!"

Arkwright turned back toward the enemy and ignored Beringer.

Beringer kept trying. "It'll be daylight in a few hours. We'll all be dead if we stay."

Arkwright didn't answer.

Fraser forced himself to lean out to port to look behind for any other sign of danger. He was tossed back by a tremendous blast as shrapnel peppered the ship. Water cascaded down on Fraser as he lay on the deck. His chest ached. His arm and face felt like they had been stung by bees. He staggered up and felt under his life jacket. There was no blood, but his chest hurt. Blood began to drip down his neck, and there was blood on his left arm. In spite of his injuries, he could function normally, so he went about his job, finding out if there were any casualties in the gun battery. Miraculously, there weren't; the fire control party was shaken but still doing their jobs, firing at the enemy cruiser.

Fraser looked ahead. They were still racing eastward, directly at the cruiser. The forward gun barked again. Another enemy salvo screamed overhead and burst astern. Fraser tried to swallow, but his throat was dry. If the cruiser zeroed in, they were doomed. The *O'Leary* was in a terrible position. The fires of Balikpapan gave the Japanese a tremendous advantage: the *O'Leary* had to be outlined against the blazing horizon.

Fraser tried to focus his binoculars on the enemy ahead, but the cruiser's white bow wave was fading from sight. What was happening? Fraser suddenly noticed the breeze against his left cheek had increased. The wind was shoving a thick bank of smoke across their path, blotting out the cruiser. He could smell the pungent stench as the first wisps swept over them. It was better than any smokescreen they could have made.

What would the captain do now? Fraser waited for an order. Arkwright stood like a stone figure, leaning on the bridge as they pounded straight ahead. Fraser tried to do some quick calculations—a combined closing speed of 60 knots, two miles to go—two minutes. If the smoke would just hold. Fraser tried not to think of a head-on collision—they'd hit the bigger ship like a bug splattering on a windshield.

Fraser looked at his watch and counted the minutes—one, one and a half, two. A noise to starboard: the whine of blowers, the thrash of screws? Was it his imagination? Three minutes went by. Five. Seven. Ten.

Down on the bridge wing, Gerald Arkwright shook his shoulders as he disengaged himself from the corner of the bridge wing. "Come right to one eight zero."

"My rudder is right standard, coming to one eight zero," repeated the helmsman, relief in his voice. He seemed well aware the new course would take them south to Java.

Ten minutes later they left the thick smoke behind. Fraser scanned the dark night with his binoculars but could see no sign of friend or foe. Now they had a chance, but Fraser knew they were a long way from safety. The captain's move had taken them out of immediate danger. Fraser tried to reconstruct what had just happened. Fraser's instinct had been to turn the ship south for home as soon as they spotted the cruiser. Had they done that, the *O'Leary* would have been broadside to the enemy, silhouetted against the fires of Balikpapan like a target in a shooting gallery. Moreover, they would have outrun the protective wall of smoke that the wind had pushed down from the north. Arkwright's bold move had obviously outfoxed the Japanese and caught them by surprise.

The captain had saved them; there was no question of that. But Fraser remembered the look on Arkwright's face. What had been his real intent? Fraser wondered if Arkwright had plunged head-on toward the enemy looking for another kind of escape.

As the *O'Leary* continued her lonely sprint southward, there was no sign of the other American destroyers. It was after 0400, and the sky soon began to brighten to the east with the first pre-dawn light. Fraser started to feel naked as the protective darkness lifted.

"Tell the engineers to give us all the speed they've got," Arkwright ordered.

CHAPTER SEVENTEEN

"They want more steam," Simpson said in the forward fireroom. He put his foot against the number two boiler where the vibration was worse than ever. He wished he'd had time to fix her while they were in Surabaya. "What the hell! Let's go for broke!"

Ten minutes later main control called and told the forward fireroom they were making just over 32 knots, the fastest the *O'Leary* had gone in Simpson's eight years aboard. For over an hour, they maintained their maximum speed.

Simpson watched the number two boiler and its piping carefully, ready for another disaster. Simpson hoped the boiler was in better shape than the men around him. They had been sweating at their stations ever since the ship went to general quarters almost six hours before. Some of the men in the fireroom looked close to heat exhaustion, not surprising because the temperature had hovered around 140 degrees. Despite the heat, they had carried out their jobs flawlessly, steaming the ship throughout the battle without any serious problems.

Simpson's nerves were still jangling from the long battle. It had been hard not seeing anything outside the steel confines of the fireroom. He had felt the ship twisting and turning. Each torpedo firing had caused them to heel slightly as the heavy weight no longer burdened the ship. The thudding explosions of the torpedoes and the sharp jolts of the recoiling 4-inch guns had been only hints of what was happening outside Simpson's little world. He'd been forced to go about his job, knowing that an enemy torpedo or projectile could come crashing through the thin hull at any time.

Now that the battle seemed over, the bridge was asking them to strain the old boilers to the limit—perhaps beyond the limit. Simpson wiped a sweat-soaked sleeve across his face and hoped they would slow down soon.

Fraser searched for signs of Japanese pursuit as the sky lightened to a pale gray. He lowered his binoculars and gazed at their boiling wake and the empty northern horizon beyond. Where were the Japs?

Every two minutes took them another mile farther from Balikpapan and closer to Surabaya—and Ilsa. Fraser wondered if she had heard about their mission. Events had made a lie of his promise of a safe trip to Darwin and back. How would she react to the news that he'd been in action?

"Smoke off the port bow!" shouted Mortland from the crow's nest.

Fraser's stomach tightened, but then he realized it must be the other American destroyers. He caught the smudge of smoke in his binoculars. Soon, the characteristic silhouettes crawled over the horizon. After a long chase, the *O'Leary* slipped in astern of the column and slowed to 25 knots.

Signal flags fluttered from the yard arm of the *Ford*, in the lead. "Well done," the signal read, the traditional accolade. Fraser was elated, but Surabaya was still 500 miles to the south. The Japanese would want revenge for the losses they suffered during the night. The men around Fraser seemed to have the same apprehension because they were content to remain at their posts as if they expected action any minute.

"Mast on the horizon, dead ahead!" shouted Mortland.

Anxious minutes passed. "Looks like the *Marblehead* and *Bulmer*," Mortland reported.

Before long, they formed up with the old light cruiser and her escort. The *Marblehead*'s four slender smoke stacks gave her the same silhouette as her escorting destroyers. The *Marblehead*'s armament was also antiquated: only four of her ten 6-inch guns were encased in turrets. The cruiser did have modern 3-inch antiaircraft guns, so the formation wouldn't be as defenseless from the air.

Eckersly, his long face concerned, walked over to Fraser. "Sir, you'd better have Doc Laster take a look at you."

After Chief Hanlon climbed up to take over the fire control platform, Fraser headed for the wardroom. He found Laster dozing on the deck with his head on a life jacket.

Laster woke up quickly. "Get on the table so I can examine you."

When he finished his inspection, Laster straightened. "You were lucky. All I can find is a laceration on your cheek and a wound in your arm."

"I can't believe I only have a bruise on my chest," Fraser said.

Laster lifted Fraser's kapok life jacket off the deck and probed under a heavy metal buckle that was bent and scarred. The doctor pulled a 2-inch piece of steel shrapnel out of the kapok. "You're lucky. This could have ripped through your chest just like it tore up your life jacket. All you got was the nasty bruise when it hit the buckle."

Fraser let out a low whistle.

"You didn't get off scot-free," the doctor said. "There's a piece of shrapnel in your upper arm. I'll have to get it out before I sew you up. You were only grazed on the cheek. A scar there will match that bent nose of yours. All you need is a pair of cauliflower ears to look like a real pug."

"Thanks. Make it quick. Jap planes may be here soon."

"No sense rushing and doing a half-assed job. There isn't a hell of a lot we can do against air attack, with or without you. The men on the few pitiful guns we have are capable of getting along fine without you. If I don't clean you up right, there's risk of infection."

"Okay, do it right. If the 4-inchers start to shoot, it means surface targets. I'll be gone."

Laster set to work, scrubbing with disinfectant and irrigating the wounds with distilled water. Fraser gritted his teeth as Laster probed the wound in his left arm.

"Ah-ha! Nothing to it!" Laster held up a shred of steel in his gleaming forceps.

"Easy for you to say," mumbled Fraser, soaked in sweat.

After sprinkling sulfa powder on the wounds, Laster sutured them carefully. "At least we have sulfa to fight some of the infections. There's a new magic drug called penicillin, but I don't expect to see any for a while."

Fraser thanked Laster and climbed to the fire control platform, ready for Japanese retaliation from the air. All morning, the gun crews stayed at their guns, and extra lookouts scanned the empty sky. The crew ate in shifts at their battle stations. An hour before noon, the captain secured them from general quarters. Fraser stretched his aching legs and remembered he would have to go to the bridge for the last part of the 08–12 watch. But he was glad not to be facing the full four-hour watch that afternoon. His adrenalin had long since worn off, and he felt exhausted.

During his abbreviated watch, Fraser paused at the captain's bridge chair. "Captain, we don't have enough fuel left to reach Surabaya if we stay at 25 knots."

Arkwright nodded. "You're starting to think like a destroyer captain. The formation will slow down soon to save fuel. If the Japs haven't caught up by now, they won't."

"Captain, what's your estimate of the damage we did?"

"Tough question. It was a mess with all that smoke. We crisscrossed that anchorage several times. It seemed like we sank seven or eight ships. But we may have been seeing the same ships more than once. I'd say our force sank one escort and four to seven merchant ships. We certainly damaged some more."

"Not bad," Fraser said.

"Should have been better. Not enough torpedo hits."

"What went wrong?" Fraser asked.

Arkwright ran a finger over one thick eyebrow. "I've been trying to figure that out. Maybe we were going too fast and the targets were too close for good fire control solutions. Maybe some torpedoes hit the shallow bottom before stabilizing in depth. Maybe our torpedo officers made some bad estimates about target motion. It was hard as hell to see anything."

"I swear our second torpedo headed right at one transport," Fraser said.

Arkwright sat up in his bridge chair. "Could mean it failed to explode—or it went under the target. Damn crime if there's something wrong with the torpedoes. But it wouldn't surprise me. We never tested any against real targets."

"Too expensive, I guess." Fraser eased the binocular strap that was biting into his neck.

The captain's jaw muscles bulged. "Going to cost a lot more than money now that we're at war. We were lucky. Men are going to pay with their lives if there's a torpedo problem."

Fraser broke a long silence. "It wasn't a bad night's work."

"Yes, our men can be proud of what we accomplished. Especially since we had about half the force we originally planned to take."

"Why didn't the Japs detect us early on?" Fraser asked. "They had enough escorts to shoot our force to pieces."

Arkwright rubbed his Roman nose for several seconds. "Interesting question. All that smoke from Balikpapan was a factor. Holding our gunfire until we finished with our torpedoes was a smart move. Their escorts probably thought they were under submarine attack until we finally opened up with our guns. But the key may have been those four Jap destroyers we saw on the way in. Anyone who saw us probably thought we were a group of Jap destroyers."

Fraser shifted his weight from one aching foot to another. "I still can't believe we all got away."

"According to the messages, only the *Ford* was hit." Arkwright stared out the bridge windows. "By all rights a lot of us should be dead now."

Arkwright's expression reminded Fraser how close they had come to destruction under the guns of the enemy cruiser at the end of the battle.

Just before Fraser turned over the watch, Meredith came up to the bridge and reported that the number one boiler was showing signs of distress. Arkwright gave him permission to shut it down because they could easily keep up with the formation using the remaining three boilers.

"Let me know what the problem is as soon as you can," Arkwright directed.

Meredith looked like a wilting plant. He took a red bandana out of his pocket and wiped his grimy face. "Captain, we took a bad jolting from the near misses at the end of the battle. We'll have to wait until number one cools down before we can get inside."

"Maybe it'll just be superficial damage like Ross's," the captain said.

Fraser joined in the laughter, but as he walked out on the bridge wing, he shuddered. Only the buckle of his life jacket had saved him from serious injury. He was thankful to be alive and realized they were less than a day away from Surabaya.

When Chuck Steiner relieved him, Fraser dreaded the thought of going below to his oven-like room. He went back to the top of the after deckhouse and found shade near one of the ammunition ready boxes. Fraser slipped off his life jacket and laid it on the deck for a pillow. A cooling breeze swirled around him, smelling of salt water and gun oil. As he lay down, the stubble on his cheek rasped against the coarse life jacket.

The steel deck vibrated under his back like some kind of a massage machine. He tried to recall Ilsa's face, but he had trouble concentrating. He opened his shirt and the wind coursed down his chest. Fraser closed his eyes and let his hands fall to the deck as sleep overcame him.

The next morning Fraser stood on the after deckhouse with his men when the *O'Leary* made her approach to the pier in Surabaya. Crowds of Dutch workmen cheered their approach and hustled fresh food aboard as soon as a brow rolled into place. The Dutch hauled over hoses for refueling and began passing boxes and supplies aboard, refusing to let the tired Americans do any work.

Fraser joined the other officers in the wardroom. "How much fuel did we have left?" he asked Meredith.

"Barely made it. Just over a thousand gallons."

Fraser whistled. That was about one percent of capacity.

"Jack, what's the story on the number one boiler?" the captain asked.

"We need to rebrick it and replace some tubes. That's not the only problem. Just before we entered the channel, number two started acting up. Captain, we may not be going anywhere for about two weeks unless you want to steam without the forward fireroom."

Arkwright slid the brass ash tray from one hand to the other across the table cloth. "You were right about needing a full overhaul."

"At least the boilers got us to Balikpapan and back," Meredith said. "Good thing none of them broke down up there."

Before the stewards could serve lunch, there was a frantic knock on the wardroom door, and the messenger of the watch poked his head in.

"What's the matter, son?" the captain asked. "Are we having the second coming?"

"No, sir. The first coming, and he's headed this way."

Arkwright frowned. "Who is?"

"Admiral Hart, sir."

The captain bolted from his chair and ran for the door. Fraser and the other officers crowded out the wardroom door and almost trampled two stewards headed in. They clattered up the ladder to the main deck and onto the quarterdeck.

Followed by several aides, Admiral Hart strode down the pier toward the bottom of the brow. Hart's trim body was immaculately attired in a high-collared white service uniform. The admiral was short, with narrow but erect shoulders. He had a large, intelligent-looking face. The gray-haired admiral was over sixty, but his alert eyes seemed to miss nothing.

Fraser fidgeted, remembering the admiral's reputation as a

strict disciplinarian. Fraser knew his men had not had the time or energy to begin cleaning their guns or spaces after the battle. Half of them were probably unshaven and asleep in shady spots about the decks. From where Fraser stood, he could see debris and litter.

The admiral paused at the bottom of the brow and looked the *O'Leary* over with a puzzled look, as if wondering how such a battered veteran could have beaten the Japanese.

Fraser groaned when he saw that Shifflet had the quarterdeck watch. Ships always put their sharpest personnel on watch when important visitors were expected; Shifflet was the last man Fraser would have picked for the quarterdeck. A large bulge distended Shifflet's cheek, a post-victory wad of chewing tobacco. Fraser winced as he thought of Shifflet spitting over the side with the admiral on the quarterdeck, so he gave Shifflet a warning look. Shifflet met Fraser's eye and blinked as his Adam's apple bobbed up and down. The chaw was still there, but at least Shifflet hadn't spat over the side.

The admiral smiled and strode up the brow. At the top, he faced aft, saluted the colors, turned, and saluted Shifflet. Hart asked the time-honored question, "I request permission to come aboard, sir."

"Permission granted, sir," replied Shifflet, saluting smartly, something Fraser had never seen him do before.

Arkwright stepped forward and greeted Hart. "Welcome aboard, Admiral. We're honored by your visit."

"Sorry not to have given you proper notice. I'm here to congratulate you and your men for the fine job at Balikpapan. I'd like to walk around your main deck, if I may, and talk briefly with your men."

"Certainly, sir, but you won't find us up to our pre-war standards. The decks are littered and dirty. We've been taking on fuel and supplies. I intend to give my men a well-deserved rest before we clean up."

"I respect your priorities, Captain," Hart said.

As the group walked away from the quarterdeck, Fraser heard

a hawking noise. Shifflet spat his cheekful of tobacco over the side. It hit the water with a splat.

Admiral Hart started. "What was that?

Fraser ended an awkward silence. "Could have been a fish jumping, Admiral."

Hart spent a half-hour walking about the upper decks, stopping to exchange remarks with members of the crew. As he approached the amidships deckhouse, he looked up at the augmented machine gun battery. "How did you manage that? You've got twice as many machine guns as anyone else."

Arkwright looked guilty. "We're not supposed to have them. Maybe you'd better forget the question, Admiral."

Admiral Hart smiled. "What question?"

After Admiral Hart left to inspect the other ships, Arkwright declared a twenty-four-hour holiday for his exhausted men. Liberty was postponed until the next day, but Fraser heard no complaints. The men just seemed to want to sleep. The main problem seemed to be the competition for shady spots topside, away from the stifling heat of the berthing compartments.

When Fraser saw Dirk Jansen driving down the pier, he picked his way to the quarterdeck, trying not to step on the bodies that were sprawled in the shade.

"Congratulations! You are big heroes!" Jansen eyed the bandage on Fraser's cheek and the bulge of the dressing on his upper arm. "Looks like the Japanese did some damage."

"Nothing serious."

"What shall I tell Ilsa about your wounds? She wants to know if you're all right."

"Tell her I'm fine. I'll be out to see her tomorrow night. They're not letting anyone ashore tonight." Fraser nodded at the sleeping men. "For good reason, too. Sleeping's all I feel like doing right now."

For Fraser, the next day crawled as he waited until he could leave the ship to see Ilsa. The *O'Leary* shifted to another pier to replenish expended ammunition and supplies. The stock had been left by the destroyer tender *Black Hawk*, now south in safer waters. The *O'Leary* could have used the facilities of the tender and the expertise of her crew to help remedy the boiler problems.

As Fraser supervised the loading of ammunition, he wondered how Ilsa would react to his return. He thought of calling her, but he was afraid she might have had a change of heart and refuse to see him. He was determined to see her even if he had to kick the front door down.

When his cab crunched over the gravel driveway, Ilsa ran down the steps. She stopped short and stared when she saw the bandage on his face.

"Don't worry. Doc Laster said a small scar might draw some attention away from my nose."

"As long as you're all right."

"I have stitches in my arm, but Doc promised I'll be okay in a week."

"Thank God!" She ran into his arms.

Fraser held Ilsa and stroked her sandy hair. She smelled of soap and a subtle perfume. Ilsa finally disengaged herself, took his hand, and led him inside. "My father will be at Allied headquarters in Bandung for the next two days. Would you fix us some martinis? I gave Mohammed and the help the night off."

Fraser finally found his voice. "Of course." It sounded as if he were gargling.

Fraser's hand shook slightly as he poured the Beefeater's gin into the shaker. He suddenly realized he was about to make a commitment affecting the rest of his life. Then he smiled wryly. Rest of my life might be days or weeks, he thought. Besides, what more could I want in a woman. Hmmm . . . a Shirley McGee chest maybe . . . no, that's too much. Shirley's a cow. Ilsa's a racehorse. And there's a lot more than just the physical part. Hell, this is it. Full speed ahead.

He gave Ilsa a martini with a steady hand.

She patted the couch, and he sat beside her. "Tell me about your battle."

Fraser gave her a brief account of the night off Balikpapan.

"How does it feel to be considered a hero?"

"I don't feel much different. Frankly, we were very lucky. The Japanese haven't made many mistakes in this war, but they made some the other night."

"You don't sound thrilled by your experience."

"I wasn't. There were times when I thought I'd never see you again."

"And seeing me was important to you?"

"Yes. More important than anything else." Fraser broke a long silence. "Ilsa, your father told me just before I left that we'd be foolish to waste the time we could have together."

"He told me the same thing."

"He did?"

"I agree with him," she said. Ilsa put her empty martini glass on the coffee table.

"A refill?" Fraser asked.

"No."

"Oh," Fraser said with a stab of disappointment.

She smiled at him. "I don't need any more. I have some Vienna sausages for hors d'oeuvres, but maybe we should get to the main course." Her green eyes bored into his, and she raised her face. Her kiss was at first gentle, then fierce and demanding. Her body pressed against his, and Fraser could feel her firm breasts against his chest. The evening breeze sweeping in from the garden added the scent of tropical flowers to Ilsa's delicate perfume.

Ilsa finally pulled away, took his hand, and led him up the broad staircase to her bedroom. The dim twilight filtered through opaque curtains, which billowed in the breeze. Fraser took her in his arms. They stood together as he stroked her hair and back gently. Her subtle perfume teased his nose. Finally, Ilsa stepped back and unbuttoned her silk dress and let it slide to the floor. Her bra and blue panties followed. Fraser was aching with desire; the body he had admired at the beach on Corregidor was even more beautiful with nothing on. Her high, pink tipped breasts rose and fell with each breath.

She turned to the bed and pulled the sheets down. As she bent over, Fraser admired the flare of her hip and rounded bottom. She slid onto the bed as Fraser moved to the other side. He fumbled with his shoelaces and popped two buttons in his haste. He slid his underwear off and turned to face Ilsa.

"Oooh! That big purple bruise on your chest. Does it hurt?"

"It's throbbing. So is my arm. So is everything."

"Enough talk," she said as she pulled him down to the bed. Her mouth covered his.

Several hours later, Ilsa lay cradled in his arms. The large blades of the overhead fan turned lazily and sent cooling currents across Fraser's damp skin. Fraser lowered his gaze and looked around the room. A battered brown teddy bear sat atop a full bookcase that lined one wall. Make-up on top of the dresser and a small jewelry box seemed to be the only concession to feminine needs.

Ilsa rose on one elbow and pointed at the book shelf. "I forgot to introduce you to my teddy bear. I hope you won't be jealous, but he was my first love."

"I think I can share you with him."

"Funny. All my favorite books are in those shelves, but none of them ever gave me as much comfort as that bear did when I was a child."

"Shows we need emotional fulfillment to be complete. I found mine tonight."

"So have I."

Fraser knew he wanted to make their relationship permanent. "How soon can we get married?"

"Sunday at four o'clock in the garden," Ilsa said. "The minister didn't like the idea of such a short engagement, but my father will talk him into it when he gets back."

Fraser chuckled. "You have everything planned."

"I realized we'd already wasted too much time."

"I feel the same way. Hmmm, with such short notice, I hope you don't expect my family to drive here from Ohio."

"With a war on I'll settle for you. I hope they won't be upset at missing the wedding."

"No," Fraser said, "I'm sure they'll be happy to hear I'm married, especially my mother. My older brother's still single, and her letters sound like she's getting nervous."

Ilsa laughed and nestled against him. "How much longer before your stitches come out?"

"About a week. Why?"

"It will be nice not to have to worry while we're making love."

"You were holding back?"

Ilsa blushed. "We'll see. Just wait until I've had more practice. Speaking of which . . ."

It was two hours before midnight, and both boilers were cold, but it was still over 100 degrees in the forward fireroom. The sun had baked the steel hull all day. The air temperature outside was still in the mid-eighties, so the fireroom would swelter until almost dawn.

T. T. Simpson glared at the front of the number two boiler. I'll damn well fix you as soon as we take care of number one, he thought. His shirt was covered with tiny pieces of soot. He had just made the mistake of wiping his brow with his sleeve, so he grabbed a clean rag to wipe his face.

Simpson turned to the number one boiler and sighed as he prepared to crawl back inside. "I'd just as soon crawl up an elephant's ass. It might be cooler and cleaner," he muttered.

He dragged himself through the opening into the boiler, stood up, and regarded his fire-blackened surroundings. Fire brick lined the walls and floor of the boiler chamber. Rows of boiler tubes stretched above him. The tubes were the heart of the boiler and held the water that was turned into steam by the fire that would burn where Simpson stood. In principle, the boiler operated like a giant teakettle, but it was far more complex. The rows of tubes provided a vastly expanded surface area for the exchange of heat, but they complicated maintenance and repair. The soot that built up on the outside was easier to clean than the accumulated mineral deposits on the inner surfaces of the tubes. Simpson knew the men working in the boiler had a long job ahead of them. Damaged tubes would have to be removed and replaced. Even the good tubes would have to be cleaned inside with air-driven brushes.

Simpson shifted his position to see how his men were doing. Suddenly, soot rained down. The man next to Simpson let loose a string of profanity. "I'd rather be cleaning out a privy back home. At least I wouldn't have all this crap falling on my head."

"I hope not," Simpson said. "But if you did, you could just reach up and pay the bastard back."

"No such luck here. We just have to stand here and take it," muttered the engineer, shaking soot out of his hair.

"There's worse to come. We've just started on this boiler." Simpson knew once they finished the tubes, they'd have to replace the fire brick and mortar. "Those Jap near misses shook a lot of bricks loose."

"I'll be glad when we're done."

"Yeah," Simpson said. "Then we get to do it all over again with number two. I don't mind that so much because when we go inside, I'm gonna find out what's wrong with her. Then we get to take a break and fight the Japs again."

The sailor sighed. "The Japs'll seem like a vacation."

CHAPTER EIGHTEEN

Fraser received a raucous cheer in the wardroom the next morning when he announced the wedding. As he went about his business, he met nothing but grinning sailors. Back in the wardroom just before lunch, he asked Jack Meredith to be his best man.

"I'd be honored." Meredith then frowned. "Maybe I'd better decline. I have so many problems aboard, I can't guarantee that an emergency won't keep me away from the wedding."

"I understand," Fraser said. "If you can make it to the wedding, fine."

The wardroom door opened and Meredith turned his head. "Here comes Doc. Why don't you try him?"

When Fraser asked him, Laster beamed. "Happy to do it. Relax, you're in good hands. I've been a best man several times."

Woody Korchak looked up from the cribbage board between him and Chuck Steiner. "I almost forgot to tell you guys. I was going through our routine dispatches this morning and found the latest promotion lists. Ross, you and Jack are full lieutenants! Durham, too. Chuck and I are now 'jay gees.'"

"About time," Meredith said. "But I'd trade my promotion for a set of orders. Anything for me?"

"No, Jack. Sorry."

Fraser realized that the war had produced one positive result. He had expected to wait two more years for his promotion. Soon the Navy would expand tremendously, and the promotions would come even faster—for those who survived.

Beringer looked up from his seat with an annoyed expression. "Anything about a promotion for me?"

"Not yet," Korchak said. "Looks like you and the captain have to wait for selection boards."

Fraser wondered how any selection board could promote Beringer, but the war and the executive officer's uncle in Congress probably made his promotion inevitable.

A few minutes later, Simpson poked his grease-streaked head in the wardroom door with a smile. He came in and presented Fraser and Meredith with collar pins bearing the two silver bars of a full lieutenant.

"I didn't want you to be out of proper uniform." Simpson explained how he had made the insignia from silver Dutch coins by filing them down and brazing the bars to safety pins.

Fraser felt genuinely flattered. "Thank you, Simpson. We'll pass our old insignia down to the new 'jay gees.'"

Simpson said, "I have a set for Mr. Durham, but I don't have time to go to the hospital."

"I'll take them to him," Korchak said. "Better yet, I'll let one of the nurses surprise him."

Steiner rubbed his thick hands together. His broad face seemed to light up. "I know just the one. I'm sure she'll find a good place to pin these, and I don't mean his pajamas."

When Simpson left the wardroom, Fraser followed him out. "Just wanted you to know someone appreciates how hard you snipes have been working. If your boilers had broken down the other night, we'd never have made it back."

"Would've spoiled the whole night," Simpson said. "Damn, I feel so good about finally getting back at the Japs! I think I'll do a victory dance." The balding Simpson broke out in an impromptu jig.

The stewards looking out the nearby pantry door clapped. "Not bad," Morales said. "Just like a bear in one of our circuses."

Simpson stared at Morales coolly. "You don't have a sister in Olongapo, do you?"

"No. Why?"

"Never mind. I've got work to do."

For Fraser, the rest of the afternoon was a blur. He took off early so he could take Ilsa to a jeweler where they picked out engagement and wedding rings.

When they arrived back at the Van Dorn house, Fraser was amazed by Mohammed and the assistant cook. They vowed to put together the best wedding reception ever seen in Surabaya and seemed in constant motion.

Ilsa tried to calm them. "This won't be a very large wedding and reception. I'm going to keep the guest list down."

"No matter how many," Mohammed said. "It will be the best."

Later that evening, Ilsa insisted on wearing her wedding ring on a chain around her neck. "Having this ring makes our time in bed seem legal." The gleaming band of gold dangled between her breasts.

Fraser kissed the ring and then the rest of her in ever expanding circles.

After lunch the next day, Chief Hanlon lingered over a cup of coffee with Jablonski, who stared at the deck, his deepset eyes remote behind his glasses. Hanlon realized that Jablonski had appeared distracted for several days. "Something bothering you?"

"Not worth discussing."

"Come on. Get it off your chest."

Jablonski finally looked up. "I just don't know. I may be way off base, but I'm worried about the old man."

"Why?" asked Hanlon. "He has his moods, but he knows his stuff. He should be the least of our worries."

"You haven't seen him under fire," Jablonski said.

"Hell, anyone can look shaky under fire."

"That's not it. From what I've seen, he looks like he . . ."

"He what?" Hanlon asked.

"Like he wants to get hit."

There was a long silence which Hanlon finally broke. "Are you sure?"

Jablonski's long fingers stroked his prominent brow. "Hell, how do I know? I'm no psychiatrist. Just a feeling I have. I couldn't say it wasn't something temporary. Maybe it won't happen again."

"No sense worrying about it. There aren't any replacements out here. We could do worse."

"Like Beringer?" Jablonski said.

"I'll take the old man any day."

"Yeah, me too."

"Maybe we shouldn't discuss this with anyone else," Hanlon said. "That kind of talk is the last thing we need."

"Yeah, you're right. Nobody else seems worried. Let's get back to work."

Later that afternoon, Landry and Egan walked into one of the bars the crew had discovered.

"Hey fellas! Come on over!" yelled Shifflet from his table. A striking Eurasian girl perched on his lap. "Still some beer left for y'all."

"Worked up a thirst loading torpedoes today," Egan said.

"How many'd we get?" Shifflet asked.

"Just two. Don't have any here. The *Barker* and *Whipple* split up theirs with the rest of us."

"Christ, why are you so tired looking?" asked Shifflet.

Egan ran a hand through his wiry red hair. "The chief had me check each one three times. He wasn't happy with the results the other night."

Shifflet belched. "Good stuff, this Heineken."

"Little on the bitter side for me," Landry said.

"So are you. Come on, cheer up," Egan said.

"I wish we were back in Manila drinking San Miguel."

"Yeah, I know," Egan said. "You miss Teresa."

Shifflet patted the girl's leg. "Nothing better'n a good woman. Unless it's a naughty one!"

The girl returned his smile, displaying a set of even white teeth. Her tongue slowly licked her lips as Shifflet's hand caressed her.

"Landry, you should try some of the local talent," Shifflet said.

"Naw, I feel like I'm married, with a kid on the way."

Shifflet shook his head. "Nothin' more faithful than a man who wants to get married. Then look what happens to a lot of 'em. They get what they want and then start to fool around worse'n they ever did afore gettin' married."

"Maybe folks like that don't have a woman like Teresa," said Landry.

Shifflet nodded. "Maybe not. Sure was a pretty little thing."

Landry could see why Shifflet was satisfied with the girl on his lap. He had evidently met her in the bar just after they returned from Balikpapan. Landry wondered if she would keep Shifflet from his wild ways.

The girl sipped her drink. "Jake, how long your ship be here?"

"Don't rightly know, babe. As long as you and Heineken hold out, I'll vote for staying."

Their quiet conversation was interrupted by a khaki-clad figure who loomed over the end of the table. "Excuse me, sailor, but that lady is taken for the evening."

They looked up at an Army lieutenant, who had silver pilot's wings on his chest. Shifflet put his beer down. "I think you oughta ask the lady herself 'bout that."

"Sir!" the pilot snapped.

"Yes, permission granted for you t' speak," Shifflet said.

The pilot quivered like a taut bowstring. "Sailor, I meant I expect you to address me as 'sir.'"

"That your first name? Mighty nice of you. Had a dog named 'Sir' once. No, I take that back. I guess we called him 'Cur.' Young fella, You can call me, 'Mr. Shifflet.'"

The girl laughed as the officer reddened. "Sorry, Stanley," she said. "I busy tonight and any night Jake want."

"Sir Stanley. That sounds nice. I wonder what his middle name is. Smedley would fit nice," Shifflet said.

The Army officer reached in his pocket and held out a wad of cash at the girl. "Does this change your mind? Flight pay talks, swabbie."

"Not tonight," the girl said. "Jake twice man you are."

The officer's eyes widened. "That's a load of crap! Swabbie, I'm ordering you to take a hike."

Shifflet rose slowly, "Excuse me, Sir Stanley. Them wings—you a pilot?"

"Yeah, P-40s."

"Figures," Shifflet said. He shot a left to the pilot's jaw. The pilot catapulted backwards against the bar and slid to the floor with one leg hooked over the brass rail. He lay on the floor like a pile of beached seaweed.

The bartender leaned over the bar and looked at the figure sprawled at the foot of his shiny mahogany bar. He shook his head and went back to polishing his glasses. The other patrons of the bar had looked up when the officer had fallen, but most were already back to their drinks.

Landry was relieved when no one complained. "Nice work, Shifflet, but you'd better get out of here."

Shifflet rubbed his knuckles. "Dumb donkey of a lieutenant. 'Fore long he'll be a full-fledged jackass, and they'll make him a general."

The girl pulled at Shifflet's sleeve. "We go to my sister's place. She out of town."

"Now you're talkin,'" Shifflet said.

As the girl gathered her purse, Landry caught her eye and nodded toward Shifflet. "Twice the man?"

The girl giggled. "Not quite—but three times as often."

Shifflet smiled modestly.

Landry and Egan turned back to their beers. A few minutes later, the pilot disengaged his leg from the brass rail and staggered to his feet. "Where's that damned sailor?"

"Don't know, sir. He just left," Egan said.

"What ship's he from?"

"Ummmm . . . he was talking about the *Canopus* earlier," Landry said truthfully.

"Good! I'll get that bastard. Wait'll I find the shore patrol. I'll have his ass yanked right off that ship tomorrow. That bastard will be in the brig forever."

Landry watched the pilot stalk out of the bar. "I hope he finds the *Canopus*. She's still back in Manila Bay."

At quarters two days before his wedding, Fraser was informed that Shifflet had not returned the night before. Fraser shook his head ruefully as he realized Shifflet had reverted to form. Fraser figured he'd turn up in a day or two. It almost seemed comforting that the war hadn't changed everything.

Later that day, a shore patrol party returned a battered Shifflet to the quarterdeck in handcuffs and leg irons. The gray-haired chief in charge of the shore patrolmen was steaming. "If there wasn't a war on, this man would be in the brig for a year. I'd better not see him ashore here again."

Fraser studied the list of charges the chief handed him with a straight face. "Shifflet really did all this?"

"Yes, sir, and more. We just got tired of writing."

"Shifflet, I guess you know this means losing your second class stripe again." Fraser tried to look stern.

"Yessir, Mr. Fraser, I know that." Shifflet looked almost contrite.

Apparently satisfied that Shifflet would be properly punished, the chief turned and led his men ashore.

"What happened, Shifflet? I heard you had a steady thing going with some girl."

"I did 'til she caught me with one of her friends. That ended that. Thought I should celebrate my bein' independent again. Well, one thing led to another."

"Was it worth it?"

Shifflet's battered face broke into a huge grin. "Hell yes! Mr.

Fraser, I ain't had that much fun since I lost two stripes in Olongapo three years ago."

"Maybe I can convince the captain to keep it down to one stripe this time. You're restricted to the ship until he holds mast."

"Just as well, Mr. Fraser. Wore out my welcome here."

Sunday morning, the day of the wedding, Laster felt pleased with his work as he took out Fraser's stitches. "You're now fit for action. However, if you'd like me to stand in for you tonight . . ."

The pink scar on Fraser's cheek puckered as he smiled. "I think I'll be able to handle it myself, Doc. Noble of you to volunteer though."

"What's a best man for?"

"Wait there a minute will you, Doc?" Fraser went out the forward door and reappeared a minute later. "The exec's ashore, so I can test my bagpipe chanter on you."

Laster eyed the foot-long instrument. "Test?"

"I thought I'd serenade my bride tonight." Fraser launched into a wailing rendition, cheeks bulging. His grey eyes widened and his face reddened.

"My God!" Laster said when Fraser finished.

"That's known as the '72nd Regiment's Farewell to Aberdeen.'"

"No wonder they had to leave," muttered Laster. "Doesn't quite seem appropriate for a honeymoon."

"Yeah, you're right. Too bad. That was my best number."

"Ummmm," Laster muttered. "You may have stumbled on a solution to one of mankind's great problems. Wives are often less interested in sex than their husbands. If a man were to give his wife a choice between a bagpipe serenade and sex, most women would probably rip their husbands' pajamas off."

"Very funny. I'll see you at the wedding."

Laster decided to start getting ready. In his cabin under the bridge, Laster pulled out his best uniform and tried the pants on. "Damn, I've been eating too much." Laster sighed, opened his black bag, and pulled out a pair of scissors. "Good thing I learned to sew in medical school," he muttered. "I'll have to fix this for the wedding."

The Van Dorns' garden was already humming with conversation when Laster arrived. Potted plants lined the stairs leading down from the porch. Guests dotted the grass, and the *O'Leary*'s officers wasted no time in joining them. Captain Van Dorn, aided by Dirk Jansen, was a nervous but gracious host as he greeted them. It didn't take long for Laster to find the bar, which featured pitchers of exotic drinks. Laster filled a glass with an amber fluid. He decided the drink was rum with a mixture of papaya, orange, and pineapple juices. He topped off his glass and headed for his white-uniformed colleagues.

"Better not eat or drink too much, Doc," Meredith said. "That uniform is ready to explode."

Laster ignored the comment. As he looked around the garden through his thick glasses, he was amazed. "Look at all these strange plants and herbs."

Even Korchak, the forestry major, admitted he was baffled by some of the plant life. He rattled off the Latin names for some of the ones he recognized.

After a glance at his watch, Laster excused himself and walked to the house, where he found the bridegroom pacing a bedroom.

"Doc, I forgot to get the wedding ring from Ilsa." Fraser scribbled a note and folded it. "Please take this to Ilsa. Then you'd better check with her father and Dirk Jansen to see that everything's ready."

"Will do. Not getting nervous, are you?"

"I hope not. I haven't had much time to think about this. It just hit me all of a sudden. This is for keeps."

"Don't worry. I haven't lost a patient at the altar yet. But I suppose there's a first time for everything."

"Thanks for the vote of confidence. Just don't forget the note for Ilsa."

Laster chuckled. "I'm on my way."

Fraser had just finished dressing when there was a discreet knock on the door. "Come in."

"I'm here to deliver the ring," Marta Jansen said. The petite blonde wore a dress that almost disguised her pregnancy, depite the fact she was due in two months. Ilsa had insisted that her friend take part even though Marta pointed out that pregnant attendants weren't proper for weddings. Marta had relented when Fraser told her that the best man's stomach was larger than hers.

"We'll look like a pair of bookends," Marta had said.

Fraser took the ring from Marta. "Ah . . . thank you. I thought Ilsa would bring it."

"It's bad luck for you to see her before the ceremony."

"I forgot about that."

"Don't be embarrassed. I approve of the fact that you and Ilsa have made the most of the time you've had together."

"You do?"

"Yes. The Japanese are so near. Who knows how much time any of us has," Marta said, suddenly pensive. "One night I had a dream I would never see my baby."

"Come now, that was just a dream."

"I hope so. Anyway, I decided to enjoy every minute with Dirk and our baby." She patted her stomach as if to reassure herself that the baby was still there.

"I'm sure your baby will be fine, especially if he—or she—is like you and Dirk."

"Thank you. You may not believe this, but in my dream I knew the baby would be fine."

"I'm sure it will be. I just hope Ilsa and I can be as happy as you and Dirk seem to be."

"I hope so, too. But you should realize marriage is not always easy. You will have many problems to solve, even in the best of circumstances."

"I guess the first problem will be to survive the celebration today," Fraser said.

"Don't worry about today. I'd better get back to Ilsa. She will think I deserted her."

A few minutes later, Laster returned and told Fraser that all was ready. Fraser handed Laster the ring, and they walked down the broad staircase to the main floor and out to the porch. The guests sat on folding chairs in the garden below. In a few minutes, Marta appeared. Then the guests stood as a radiant Ilsa walked out of the house on her father's arm. The minister seemed hesitant, as if remembering the somewhat precipitous notice he had received. A stern look from Captain Van Dorn and a glance at the pregnant matron of honor seemed to stimulate the minister's enthusiasm.

The vows were alternately in Dutch and English. Fraser felt like the words were being burned on his mind. As Fraser looked down at Ilsa, her presence filled his being. When he heard the words, "until death us do part," the reality of the war crawled back from a dark corner of his mind and prowled the edge of his consciousness like a hungry animal circling a campfire. Ilsa's eyes had misted as if she were wondering how long they would have together.

Then it was time for the ring. Laster reached in his pocket and brought it out, but the band of gold slipped from his fingers and fell to the floor. As Laster bent to retrieve it, there was a loud ripping sound. Laster straightened and handed Fraser the ring as his pudgy face turned red. From the audience on the grass below, there were gasps and titters. Laster tugged the sides of his white service tunic down over the back of his trousers.

As Fraser slid the ring on Ilsa's finger, her eyes cleared, and she smiled as if she knew his sudden thought that no matter what happened, they would now share the joy, laughter, and heartaches that life would bring them.

After the minister pronounced them man and wife, Fraser lifted the veil and kissed Ilsa gently.

"You can do better than that," she chided him under her breath.

"Not in front of an audience."

Champagne corks popped as Fraser and Ilsa walked down the stairs to greet their guests in the receiving line. Afterwards, they circulated through the garden talking to their friends. They reached a large group of *O'Leary* people talking with the Jansens.

"How did things look from the audience?" asked Fraser.

Meredith's tired-looking eyes warmed. "A picture wedding. A beautiful bride, a glowing matron of honor, an almost handsome groom, and the best man . . . a heck of a show, Doc."

"I can't understand it," said Laster. "I used my best surgical stitch on these trousers this morning."

As the laughter died away, Fraser heard Meredith whisper to Laster, "Thank God your underwear held."

Amen to that, thought Fraser. Surabaya society would have never been the same. Fraser turned to Dirk and Marta Jansen. He enjoyed talking with the Dutch couple as Marta held the arm of her much taller husband.

Marta seemed to glow with the prospect of motherhood. "It's nice to know there's a doctor here in case my little one decides to come early."

"I hope he holds onto babies better than he does wedding rings," Korchak said.

Meredith took a glass of champagne form a passing waiter. "Laster specializes in the use of gentian violet. You might wind up with a purple baby."

Marta laughed warmly. "Come now, Ross says Doctor Laster is very competent."

"I just hope the stitches he put in Ross hold better than the ones he put in his trousers," Meredith said.

Laster seemed to puff up. "I have faith in my work. Those stitches will get the ultimate test tonight."

Fraser felt Ilsa tugging at his elbow. "We should go talk to my father."

Fraser craned his neck and looked around the crowded garden. "There he is, talking to our captain."

"Congratulations, Ross," Arkwright said when they walked up. "You have a beautiful bride." Fraser could see wistful envy in the captain's eyes.

They chatted for a few minutes. Ilsa's father drained his glass. "I'll be right back," he said. "Gerald, can I get you something?"

"No, thank you, sir. I'm fine."

Ilsa smiled at Arkwright. "I'd like to thank you for bringing Ross back to me, Captain Arkwright."

There was a long pause. "As much luck as my doing."

"I've heard your men really respect you. They're counting on you. I want you to know I'm counting on you, too."

"I'll do my best," Arkwright finally said.

Ilsa smiled innocently as Fraser tried to think of a way to change the subject. "That's a promise?" she asked.

Arkwright gave her a long look. "Yes . . . yes it is."

"Here we are," Ilsa's father said. "Fresh champagne for the bride and groom."

After a few minutes with the two senior officers, Ilsa took Fraser off to meet some other friends. Several hours later, the party showed no signs of winding down so Fraser and Ilsa decided to sneak away to the hotel room they had rented for the night. "Let's not tell anyone. It'll just break up the party," Ilsa said.

After they slipped upstairs for their bags, they walked unsteadily out the front door to the shining black Mercedes parked on the gravel driveway. Ilsa giggled. "Here's the key."

Fraser dropped it and leaned against the car. "Whoo. Maybe I had a little too much to drink."

A quiet voice said, "Maybe you'd better let me drive. I don't drink anymore."

"Oh, Captain Arkwright! We couldn't impose," Ilsa said.

"No problem. I have an international driver's license. It will save me from waiting for a cab. You two hop in the back."

In a champagne fog, Fraser watched the streets of Surabaya slide by as darkness fell. He couldn't believe he was letting the captain drive them. When they arrived at the hotel, Arkwright deftly slid the car into a parking space.

"Thank you, Captain," Ilsa said. "I guess we had a little too much champagne."

"No problem. I wouldn't have slept well if I'd let you drive off." There was a long pause. "I hope the two of you find the happiness my wife and I knew."

Before they could thank him, Arkwright turned and walked away. Fraser and Ilsa watched the solitary white-uniformed figure stride off toward the waterfront.

When they were in their room, Ilsa smiled. "At last, we're alone."

Fraser sat on the bed. "I'm really tired. I had no idea a wedding could be so exhausting."

Ilsa pulled back the curtain and looked out the window. "Look at that full moon coming up. It makes me feel romantic. But if you're tired, I'll let you sleep."

"I'm not that tired."

An hour later, it was Ilsa who yawned.

"Ah. I have just the thing to revive you."

"Not more champagne. I'm falling asleep."

Fraser walked over to his bag and pulled out his bagpipe chanter. "The present you gave me in Manila. I've been practicing."

Ilsa's eyes were sleepy.

Fraser flipped through his instruction book and found a tune he liked.

By the time he finished Ilsa's eyes were wide. "Dear God! That's incredible . . . and I gave you that."

"Let's see—that was 'Flower o' the Forest.' That seems a nice description of you."

"Thank you. The thought is beautiful."

Fraser looked down at the music. He felt a chill when he read a note that told him the tune was a funeral song. The war and all its horror rushed back into his mind.

"Something the matter?" Ilsa asked.

"No," he mumbled. "Let me find you another song. How about 'The Campbells Are Coming?'"

Ilsa rose from the bed, walked over to him, and leaned her naked body against his. She took the chanter and dropped it in his suitcase. "Maybe later. I'm more interested in the Frasers . . ."

The chanter seemed to revive Ilsa miraculously. It was three hours before they agreed to sleep. As Fraser closed his eyes with Ilsa cradled against him, he thought of Gerald Arkwright. Fraser realized he had discovered a part of what the captain had lost. He hoped he would never lose Ilsa and tried not to think of the oncoming Japanese.

CHAPTER NINETEEN

Two mornings after his wedding, Fraser sat in the captain's cabin waiting for Arkwright to finish reading the latest messages. The engineers wouldn't have the forward fireroom ready for four or five more days. Fraser wasn't sorry. He wasn't ready to trade his nights with Ilsa for anything, much less the sortie against the Japanese that was being prepared. The possibility for action had developed during the last two days, and Fraser had read the message traffic carefully. A Japanese invasion force had been spotted heading toward targets near the southern end of Makassar Strait. Admiral Hart had ordered the creation of a striking force composed of the available American and Dutch forces—four cruisers and seven destroyers. Admiral Doorman of the Dutch Navy had been placed in command of the force, which had been ordered to rendezvous at Bounder Roads, almost 100 miles to the east of Surabaya.

Arkwright flipped the message file on his desk. "I told headquarters we were ready to fight on two boilers but they turned me down."

"I wish we'd had all those ships at Balikpapan," Fraser said. "We could have stayed and wiped the Japs out."

Arkwright toyed with the torpedo tubes of his partially completed model of the *O'Leary*. "Be lucky to get close this time. Jap aircraft will be out searching."

"How're our ships going to work with the Dutch? We don't use the same signals or speak the same language."

Arkwright frowned for a few seconds. "That'll be a hell of a problem, especially at night. I guess that's for headquarters to figure out."

"Speaking of problems, the after gun has a leak in the recoil cylinder. I'd better go see how Chief Hanlon is doing."

As Fraser started to rise, the captain gestured him back to his chair. "Ross, I'd like your opinion about something."

"Certainly, Captain."

"I've been thinking about what Ilsa said—how she was counting on me to get you back to her. I realize I have the same responsibility for all the men. I . . . I'm not sure I'm fit to keep the promise I made her. I told you about losing my family. There . . . there are times when the pain seems too much to bear. There are other times when the anger wells up—when I'm tired . . . during the heat of battle." The captain cradled his head in his hands. "I just can't guarantee I won't do something I shouldn't."

Fraser didn't know what to say. Some of his worst fears were confirmed. He considered the alternatives. If Arkwright stepped down, Beringer might get command. At best the executive officer would lean on his subordinates. Jack Meredith was near exhaustion and clearly unable to assume a greater burden. Fraser swallowed as he realized he was the next senior officer aboard.

Fraser took a deep breath as he realized he was making a decision which might determine the fate of the *O'Leary*. "Captain, aside what you've told me, we couldn't ask for a better commanding officer. From what I hear, we're short of officers out here. Commander Talbot's heart attack forced the *Parrot*'s C. O. up to the division commander's slot. If you leave . . . they'll probably put the exec in command. I'd rather stick with you. I think most of the officers and men would agree."

"I was afraid that's what you'd tell me." Arkwright stared at the green linoleum deck. The long silence was broken by the strident gong-gong of the general alarm. "What the hell?" the captain said.

Fraser bolted from his chair and ran for his general quarters station. As Fraser climbed the ladder to the fire control platform, he heard the distant wail of airraid sirens. He grabbed his binoculars. The familiar vees of twin-engined Japanese bombers were almost overhead.

Oh, no! Oh, no! Fraser thought. I've just been married two days. Fraser was suddenly conscious that Ilsa was ashore; fortunately, the Van Dorn house was nowhere near any military installations. But that didn't give him much comfort. The Japanese were there in the air. Their Navy and Army wouldn't be far behind.

The captain released some of the men from their general quarters stations to ready the *O'Leary* for getting under way. There was a screech of scraping metal from the quarterdeck as the brow was shoved onto the pier. Two engineers threw a spewing fresh water hose ashore as deck hands ran down the pier singling up the mooring lines.

"All stations ready," the phone talker said on the bridge wing just below Fraser.

"Cast off all lines except number two," said Arkwright, who then twisted the stern away from the pier.

"Cast off number two!" the captain ordered.

The deck hand on the pier tossed the line into the water, dived after it, grabbed the line, and hung on as his shipmates pulled him aboard.

The *O'Leary* cleared the waterfront just as the first bombs fell. The nearby Dutch airfield erupted in flames as columns of black smoke towered into the cloudless sky. The rest of Surabaya's military facilities were hit but escaped the devastation that had leveled Clark Field and the Cavite Navy Yard. That was small consolation for Fraser, who realized his joy of the last few days might be short-lived.

The next evening the *O'Leary* returned to her berth after a second day of air raids. Dirk Jansen joined the destroyer's officers in the wardroom while they pored over dispatches and pieced together what had happened to the Allied strike force that had sortied to hit the Japanese. The Allied ships had been hounded by Japanese air attacks. The light cruiser *Marblehead* had been severely damaged, and the heavy cruiser *Houston* had taken a bomb in her after turret. Admiral Doorman had been forced to abandon the attack, retire south through Lombok Strait, and make for Tjilatjap on the south coast of Java.

Jansen put his coffee cup down. "I forgot to tell you. The sortie was almost delayed because of an incredible foul-up yesterday. Interpreters scheduled to ride your ships were supposed to leave here yesterday. But they sat at the pier until almost too late because of a mix-up in orders."

"Getting there in time was about the only thing that went right," Laster said.

"Thanks only to your little auxiliary ship *Isobel*," Jansen said. "She had to go full speed through the minefields to make it."

"Hardly a miraculous endeavor," Beringer said.

"It was after dark and during a rainstorm," Jansen said.

"Oh, I suppose," Beringer said.

Fraser shuddered as he thought of steaming blindly through strange minefields at high speed. Visibility during a tropical rainstorm would have been down to zero at night.

"Sounds like the *Marblehead* will have to go back to the States," Meredith said enviously.

Jansen frowned. "Headquarters will be thankful if she makes it as far as Tjilatjap to start. Her rudder is useless, and she is flooded badly up forward."

"That means the *Houston* will be the only American cruiser left out here," Steiner said. "But she's damaged. Where are some ships from the Pacific Fleet?"

"Good question," Laster said.

Fraser wondered why the Navy hadn't sent them any reinforcements as he flipped through the pile of messages, one of which caught his eye. "Look at this. Many of the *Houston's* 5-inch antiaircraft shells were duds."

"Hell of a time to find that out," Steiner said.

"Friend of mine told me the *Houston* figured that was probable before the war started," Laster said. "They requested permission to test the ammo, but they were turned down."

"Incredible!" Fraser said.

The captain seemed to realize the morale of the wardroom was plummeting. "Gentlemen, we have an idea of what we're up against. Let's either get back to work or get some rest."

As the other officers filed out of the wardroom, Fraser knew that the odds against them had grown even worse. The old *Marblehead* wasn't much, but she had been better than nothing. The disastrous Allied sortie and the arrival of the Japanese bombers had destroyed the euphoria that had persisted since the victory at Balikpapan.

Arkwright beckoned Fraser aside before he left the wardroom. "Ross, I'm going to let you go ashore because you're newly married. Make sure you get back an hour before dawn. Stay by a telephone at the Van Dorns' so we can reach you."

"Thank you, Captain," Fraser said. "There's a phone by Ilsa's bed."

A smile flickered across Arkwright's eyes. "We'll try not to bother you. Enjoy yourself. You're a lucky man." The smile was replaced by a haunted look. Arkwright turned and headed for his cabin.

Fraser shook his head and wondered why such a competent and compassionate man had suffered the disaster that had overtaken his family. Fraser felt no one deserved that fate, especially not the captain. After his week with Ilsa, Fraser was beginning to realize the magnitude of Arkwright's loss.

The Van Dorns' Mercedes rumbled to a stop on the gravel driveway in front of the house.

Ilsa smiled up at him. "I wonder if abstinence will make our love seem better."

"A night of waiting is one too many for me," Fraser said.

"Lieutenant, I hope you are ready for some heavy action."

"I'm always ready where you're concerned."

An hour later, a sweaty Fraser stood in the shower in the

bathroom next to Ilsa's room. She pulled the curtain aside and stepped in beside him.

"I thought you were asleep," he said.

"I was just resting my eyes. The night is young." She handed him the soap. "Don't stand there, get to work."

He started by soaping her back and then moved down to her firm bottom and the backs of her legs. Her body felt smooth and slippery, and her skin glistened in the dim light. She turned around and he continued his work, devoting a lingering and gentle attention to her firm breasts.

"Let me do you now." Her green eyes were amused as she took the soap.

Fraser groaned with pleasure as her hands slid slowly over his body and then brought him to a full state of readiness. They rinsed off quickly, not even pausing to dry off, and ran back to the bedroom to release the almost electric charge that had been built up between them.

"Are you hungry?" Ilsa asked later.

"I could use something to keep up my strength."

"Let me see what I can whip up."

Fraser lay back and wondered what Ilsa would bring from the kitchen. Perhaps Mohammed had already taught her some of his exotic recipes. When Ilsa returned bearing a tray, Fraser lifted the cover off a dish. up on one elbow. "Vienna sausages!"

"I know you like these, so I bought them just for you."

Fraser looked for some mustard to smother the familiar flavor but there wasn't any. He forced a smile and dug in. He debated telling Ilsa he hated Vienna sausages, but one look at her smile stopped him. He wasn't about to spoil their night together. He wondered how many more of them they would have.

Three days later, as the *O'Leary* cruised off Surabaya, Hank Landry stood behind his machine gun watching the Japanese bombers pound the city with the regular morning air raid. The blowers picked up speed and smoke belched from the two after stacks as the bow pointed toward the eastern channel through the minefields. Landry watched the coastline of Madura slide by. The wake was boiling behind them and it felt like they were doing the 25 knots that the two good boilers would permit.

"Ol' man's in a hurry to get somewhere," Shifflet said behind his gun.

When they cleared the eastern tip of Madura, four hours later, a light breeze ruffled the tops of the 2-foot swells that rolled the *O'Leary* gently. The general quarters alarm began to sound. Off-watch men scrambled for their stations as Landry scanned the empty sky for enemy aircraft.

Ten minutes later, Lieutenant Fraser climbed the ladder and called the gun crews over. "We're going out to hunt a Jap submarine. We're also supposed to pick up the survivors from the ships this bastard has already torpedoed. The second ship stopped to pick up survivors and got torpedoed, too."

"What's to stop them from doin' that to us?" asked Shifflet.

"The captain's been thinking that over," Fraser said. "We're going to put the whaleboat in the water well clear of the survivors. Landry, you'll be part of the boat crew. The boat will take Doc Laster to help any injured while we hunt for the sub. We are going to need every pair of eyes we have topside to look for that sub's periscope. He has to stick it up to shoot his torpedoes . . . but only for a few seconds at a time. Each of you men has to keep watching the sector I'm going to assign you. If you dope off or look somewhere else for a few seconds, that scope could be up and gone."

"And next thing we know, we'll be swimmin'," Shifflet said.

Fraser's grey eyes were grim. "Exactly."

After outlining the responsibilities of each man, Fraser left to brief the torpedomen and the after gun crew.

Landry had mixed feelings about leaving in the whaleboat. He wanted to be a part of the hunt for the submarine, but he welcomed the chance to put his boat in the water. Then he remembered Doc Laster was going. "Oh, hell!"

"What's the matter?" Shifflet asked.

"Doc Laster's probably gonna puke all over my boat."

Landry's nerves tightened another notch when Mortland bellowed a report from the crow's nest that boats and rafts were six miles ahead. Landry grabbed his machine gun as the *O'Leary* heeled over in a turn and circled with the survivors still miles away.

"Looks like the old man's sniffin' around with the sonar 'afore puttin' your boat in the water," Shifflet said.

Minutes later, word was passed to man the whaleboat. The destroyer headed back to the center of the area that had been searched. Landry boarded the whaleboat with the rest of the boat crew, a signalman, and Doc Laster, who paled and clutched his seat as the boat swayed under the davits.

"Easy, Doc, we'll be in the water in a minute," Landry said.

The hiss of water along the destroyer's side lessened as she slowed to 5 knots. "Put the boat in the water!" the captain shouted from the bridge.

Landry tensed. They had drilled many times before, but there was always danger while launching a boat under way. The falls squealed through the blocks as the boat slid toward the water. A swell kissed the bottom of the boat, and the next one received the whaleboat with a thump. Landry stood by the forward fall waiting for the coxswain to release the after one first. A stout line known as a sea painter was towing the bow of the whaleboat, so the falls could be slacked. The after fall swung free.

"Let go the forward fall!" shouted the coxswain.

Landry disengaged the heavy hook from the boat and ducked as it was hoisted away. The boat shook as the engine roared, and the sea painter went slack as the propeller bit into the water. Landry scrambled to cast the line off the bow. Thirty seconds after the captain's order, the whaleboat turned away from the *O'Leary*'s side. The destroyer's blowers whined and her wake boiled behind her. The *O'Leary* pulled away with an ever increasing surge of power as a light haze rose from her after stacks. The whaleboat bounded over the gentle swells as it headed toward the distant survivors. The burble of the exhaust was accompanied by Laster's retching.

He'd better not miss that bucket, Landry said to himself.

As the *O'Leary* accelerated back to her maximum sonar search speed of 17 knots, the unrelenting pings of the sonar floated out of the charthouse, where the sonarmen manned their controls. Fraser listened for the telltale echo that would indicate the enemy, but he heard nothing suspicious.

On the port wing just below Fraser, the captain scanned the horizon ahead with his binoculars. Fraser knew the captain faced a difficult problem. Their sonar had a maximum range of about 2000 yards under normal water conditions. A submarine outside sonar range still had a good chance of torpedoing them, particularly if the *O'Leary* remained at the speed required to use her sonar; any speed over 17 knots generated too much turbulence over the sound head projecting from the bottom of the hull. They had accepted a dangerous trade-off: to have a chance of detecting the submarine, they had abandoned their best defense—high speed.

Recovery of the survivors would be even more dangerous. Stationary in the water, the *O'Leary* would be an easy target. Fraser knew it would be foolhardy to steam up to the survivors and stop, as one rescue ship had already found out.

Arkwright ordered Chief Jablonski to prepare an expanding search pattern centered on the survivors. Laid out on the chart, it would look like a square-sided spiral. The first leg took them within 500 yards of the survivors. Two battered lifeboats, three rafts, and debris dotted the water. Over a hundred life jacketed swimmers surrounded the two rafts. There were far too many swimmers to fit in the whaleboat, but Laster would be able to treat any wounded or injured. Survivors waved frantically as the *O'Leary* steamed past. Arkwright had the signalmen flash a message in plain English, telling the survivors they would be rescued soon.

The men on the fire control platform each watched an assigned sector for a periscope. "Jesus, I feel like a target in a shooting gallery," muttered the computer operator. "I hope you guys are watching behind me. I feel like that Jap's looking right at my back."

"Quit yapping and make sure you're taking care of my back," Eckersly said.

The *O'Leary*'s search consisted of a succession of left turns, each leg longer than the last. The bow cleaved through the gentle swells, and a breeze ruffled the surface of the water. Fraser realized the scene was deceptive; they were hunting fifty or more men who, if given a chance, would destroy the *O'Leary* and her crew.

As turn followed turn and the legs became longer and more boring, Fraser's initial excitement faded. The warm sun sapped his concentration. His drifting mind relived the nights he had spent with Ilsa. He shook himself out of his reverie when he heard Beringer step out on the wing below.

"Captain, we've spiralled out for several circuits now," the executive officer said. "It would seem a logical deduction that the submersible has decamped."

Arkwright shook his head. "One more time around before we quit."

"But the survivors may require our assistance," Beringer said.

Arkwright stared at the empty sea. "I have a feeling that bastard's still out here."

Ten minutes later, Fraser was sure the captain was wrong and lowered his binoculars to wipe the sweat out of his eyes. "Periscope!" a lookout shouted. "Zero five zero relative. Two miles!"

"Right full rudder!" Arkwright barked. He bent over the pelorus. "Steady on one nine zero. Fantail, stand by to drop depth charges."

The *O'Leary* settled on her new course and charged toward the enemy.

"Sonar contact! Bearing one nine five. Range two two double oh! Slight up doppler. Possible submarine!" a sonarman shouted from the charthouse.

"Come right to one nine five," the captain ordered. "Tell the fantail to set the depth charges for 200 feet."

Fraser realized it was Gerald Arkwright's skill against the enemy captain's. Fraser tried to put himself in Arkwright's head. The captain would have to determine the submarine's course and speed. The sonarmen could help there by evaluating pitch changes in the returning echo—the doppler effect. Combining bearing drift with the doppler, an astute conning officer could estimate what direction the submarine was headed and how fast. Sonar could also hear the submarine if it tried to move rapidly. To these mental calculations Arkwright would have to guess the submarine's depth and add the time it would take the depth charges to fall through the water. Fraser took a deep breath as the range wound down.

"Lost contact!" reported sonar as the range hit one hundred yards, too close for the sonar to work.

Arkwright bided his time. "Release six depth charges!"

Seconds later the heavy can-shaped weapons rumbled down the tracks on the fantail and tumbled into the boiling wake. Nothing happened for many seconds. Then the sea behind suddenly became opaque, and towering columns of white water erupted. The shock waves shook the *O'Leary*. Fraser grabbed the railing to keep his feet.

"Bet those babies fixed that Jap," shouted the computer operator.

"Don't be too sure," Fraser said, clutching the rail as the *O'Leary* wheeled around in a hard turn. The sonarmen resumed their pinging. Fraser focused his binoculars on the water roiled by their depth charges but found no evidence of any damage.

Now they would have to find the submarine again. The sonarmen had been out of contact for minutes now, ever since the destroyer had closed in for her attack. Now the sonarmen's task was complicated by the turbulence left by the depth charges. Fraser heard the solitary pings as the sonarmen made their time-consuming search. The sonar only examined a 20-degree wedge of water with each ping. Sound traveled five times faster in water than air, taking about two seconds for an impulse to travel out a mile and return. A complete search around the *O'Leary* would consume almost a minute. If the first search missed the sub, the Japanese would have that much more time to sneak away—or to attack.

Pinnggg . . . pinnggg . . . pinnggg. Nothing. Pinnggg . . . eep!

"Sonar contact!" shouted a sonarman from the charthouse. "Bearing zero two five. Range nine double oh. Down doppler. Probable submarine!"

Arkwright turned the *O'Leary* toward the submarine for another attack. Sonar continued its reports as they closed in. Fraser realized the captain would have to outwit the submarine captain. Arkwright would have to make a series of guesses for which there were no obvious clues. One guess was the submarine's depth, which could range from 60 feet to over 300 feet or more for a well-built submarine with a captain willing to risk the crushing pressure on his hull. More guesses concerned the evasive tactics of the other captain. As soon as the *O'Leary* lost contact 100 yards from the submarine, the enemy captain had a short grace period to maneuver. Arkwright would have no way of knowing what the enemy was doing.

The contact was drifting right so Arkwright altered course to lead the target. The range wound down and the pings came more rapidly as the sonar operator shortened his scale. "Range two double oh. No doppler. Lost contact."

After Arkwright completed the attack, more columns of water blasted skywards. The *O'Leary* wheeled back to the hunt, but no echo answered the ping of the sonar. Arkwright took them over the center of the last attack, but there was no debris.

The captain pounded his fist on the bridge wing. "Damn!"

Hank Landry stood in the bow of the whaleboat as they motored toward the cluster of survivors. A ragged cheer arose from the oil-soaked men.

"When will your ship be here?" one man shouted.

The rumble of depth charges seemed to answer the swimmer.

"Damn! Mate, tell your ship to take it easy," yelled an Australian voice from the water. "Those bloody depth charges're rattling my balls."

The coxswain stopped the whaleboat near the lifeboats, and Laster told the two captains he wanted to shift the wounded and injured over to the whaleboat for treatment. After the transfers, some of the swimmers then had room to climb up to the empty slots in the lifeboats. Almost a hundred men remained in the water when the boats were full again.

"We'd better not take any more right now," Laster said. "I need room to work."

"Don't have to worry about any one freezing to death in this water," Landry said.

"Just sharks," said one survivor who had been pulled from the water.

Laster set to work. Landry gritted his teeth as one of the injured men groaned while Laster splinted a broken leg. Landry looked over at one of the other boats and saw a tiny bundle in a woman's arms. A high-pitched cry sounded, and Landry realized it was an infant rather than some prized possession. Tiny fists waved in the air as the baby expressed a loud protest. Landry's thoughts were suddenly back in the Philippines. His own child would have to come into a world that was tearing itself apart. He thought it was bad enough that grown men were killing and maiming each other.

A man in the water began to thrash. "Something bumped me!"

Landry watched in horror as the man screamed. A gray fin sliced the water, and a pale belly flashed. Landry grabbed the Springfield rifle in the bottom of the boat. He worked the bolt to chamber a cartridge. Another flash of gray—a gaping mouth opened to show rows of white teeth. Landry sighted on a dark eye and pulled the trigger as the swimmer screamed again. The butt slammed against Landry's shoulder as the rifle roared. The 8-foot shark bucked sideways and began thrashing aimlessly, trailing blood in the water. They hauled the moaning swimmer into the whaleboat, where Laster put pressure dressings on his mauled leg and shoulder.

"Goddamn!" the coxswain said as jets of blood spurted into the bilges of the boat.

There was a babble of excited foreign voices. Landry looked up and spotted a gray fin a hundred yards away and heading for them. Then another—and another. The wounded shark was thirty yards away, still thrashing. The big body was jolted half out of the water as the first newcomer hit like an express train, shaking the wounded shark's body as it ripped out a mouthful of flesh. Then another shark hit. The water boiled with white froth and blood.

Men in the water screamed.

"Jesus! Signal the ship we need help! And quick!" Laster ordered the signalman in the whaleboat.

They pulled ten of the frantic men into the whaleboat, and a few more piled into the other boats, but the water was still thick with men. A stout Dutchman next to Landry swung his legs over the gunwale.

"Where are you going?" Landry asked.

"My heart not gutt for much longer. You get two young skinny fellows up here instead." The gray-haired Dutchman slid into the water.

Landry reached out to grab the Dutchman, but he just shook his head and kicked away from the boat. As they pulled two more men aboard, the overloaded whaleboat rocked, and a swell slopped water over the gunwale. A gray form flashed alongside the boat, its dark eye looking right at Landry. The seat jolted under him as the shark bumped the boat. More water sloshed in.

"Bail!" Landry shouted.

A signalman raced up to the captain. "Flashing light from the boat, sir. 'Help. Sharks attacking. Can't get all the swimmers out of the water.'"

"Sonar contact!" shouted a voice from the pilot house. Bearing one two five. Range one eight double oh. Slight up doppler. Probable submarine!"

"Jesus!" Fraser said as he watched the captain.

"Left full rudder! All ahead flank," Arkwright ordered, turning away from the submarine and toward the survivors.

Beringer popped out of the pilothouse. "Captain! The submarine! If we stop, he'll torpedo us. We'll be swimming with the sharks, too." Beringer's voice took on a note of panic. "He'll be shooting at the broad side of a barn!"

Christ, thought Fraser, the exec is right for once. Sharks! What a way to die.

Arkwright turned and looked up at Fraser.

"Ilsa," Fraser said softly.

Arkwright stared at him and then nodded and turned back to Beringer. "Have the boatswain rig our cargo nets so we can get those survivors on board as fast as possible."

"The captain zig-zagged as he headed toward the survivors. Fraser's mouth dropped as they neared the boats because Arkwright appeared to be going by them.

Left full rudder! Port stop! Port back full!" the captain ordered. The *O'Leary* heeled over sharply in the tightest turn she could make. As the destroyer turned back toward the submarine and neared the survivors, Arkwright backed the starboard engine full. The destroyer shuddered to a halt thirty feet from the survivors struggling in the blood-tinged water.

"Sonar contact, bearing one four zero, range two one double oh."

He's still out there, thought Fraser. But he understood what the captain had done. The U-turn had put them bow on to the submarine. Not only was the *O'Leary* presenting the minimum target, but Arkwright had avoided leaving the submarine directly astern where the sonar was blind.

"Loud screw noises," reported sonar.

Fraser began to sweat as he listened to the subsequent reports which indicated the submarine was moving off to starboard for a better shot. Jesus, get these people aboard, he thought.

As the *O'Leary* had raced toward them, Landry wished they'd hurry up. There were sharks all around them. He fired his Springfield again and again, hitting several sharks as they came near enough to the surface for the bullets to penetrate the water. Two wounded sharks thrashed as others began to feed on them. In a nearby raft, blood from a mauled survivor dripped down through the slats. A shark butted the bottom of the raft and chewed at the bloody wooden slats.

When the *O'Leary* shuddered to a halt, the whaleboat engine roared, and the coxswain nosed the boat alongside. Landry grabbed the forward falls and hooked them to the boat. The whaleboat and its load of injured were hoisted to the main deck. Life jacketed swimmers swarmed up the cargo nets slung over the destroyer's side just forward of the boat. Landry hopped out of the boat as Mortland and two deck hands climbed down the cargo net and began assisting men too weak to climb by themselves.

Mortland's legs were submerged up to his thighs. He looked up at Landry. "Get your ass down here and help!"

Landry clambered down the net and grabbed a man and pushed him up toward the deck, where other men pulled him over the side. Only a few men were left in the water. The gray-haired, elderly Dutchman floated 50 feet away.

"Get over here!" Landry shouted.

The Dutchman groaned and ignored the line that had been tossed next to him.

"Somebody's gotta go get him," Mortland said, his uniform coated with a mixture of water, oil, and blood. You man enough Landry, or am I gonna have to do it."

Gray bodies flashed between the Dutchman and the destroyer. Mortland was still hip deep in the water and his eyes mocked Landry.

Landry had to admit the bastard had balls. He wasn't about to let Mortland think he was afraid. He wished the hell he'd asked Mortland the same question first. Landry leaped from the net and stuck out for the Dutchman. He heard the thrash of the *O'Leary*'s screws. Christ, he thought, they were leaving him here with the sharks. He churned through the water and hooked one arm through the Dutchman's life jacket and grabbed the line with both hands. The line tightened and began pulling him toward the ship. He knew the destroyer would soon be moving too fast for him to hang on; he thought he was as good as dead. But the pressure on the line remained constant. Then he was at the cargo net, and he pushed the Dutchman up. As the old man was pulled from the water, Landry gagged. Both legs were ragged stumps. Something bumped against Landry's leg and he scrambled up the cargo net and collapsed on the wet steel deck, his lungs heaving.

While the deck hands had been hauling the whaleboat and the survivors aboard, the submarine had continued to work its way from dead ahead to a position off the beam. Fraser had felt his knees wobble as he listened to the screams from the water. How can the captain just let us sit here and get torpedoed, Fraser wondered.

"Right full rudder," ordered Arkwright. "Port ahead one-third. Starboard back one-third." The destroyer shuddered as her screws twisted her around to face the Japanese submarine's bearing.

Relief washed over Fraser. They still had a chance. "Periscope! Dead ahead, range one five double oh," shouted a lookout.

Fraser focused his binoculars on the black finger, which remained above the surface for a minute as if the other captain couldn't believe what he was seeing. Fraser wondered what the man on the other end of the instrument was thinking. The *O'Leary* was only 31 feet and 8 inches across the beam, a narrow target for a torpedo. The submarine's high-speed run for a better firing angle had been for naught.

"Landry and the last swimmer are aboard!" shouted the talker.

"All ahead standard. Indicate turns for 17 knots," the captain ordered. "Here we come you bastard."

"Torpedoes!" shouted two lookouts simultaneously.

Fraser tried to swallow, but his mouth was dry. Arkwright held their course because they were already presenting the minimum possible target. Even so, Fraser didn't find it easy to rush headlong toward their fate. His heart began to pound, and he leaned forward and watched the faint wakes arrow toward them. "Oh, hell," he breathed, trying to stay calm. The two deadly weapons bored on; their speed plus the *O'Leary*'s meant a closing speed of over 50 knots. They were now seconds away. Then the deadly wakes were on them. The closest flashed down the port side barely 10 feet away. The glinting, unpainted steel shape was clearly visible beneath the surface.

The *O'Leary* continued her charge toward the submarine. The range wound down. Six more depth charges blasted the ocean, but with no apparent result. The destroyer wheeled around and started the hunt again.

"Sonar contact. Bearing two six five, range one two double oh. Slight up doppler. Probable submarine."

"Captain," the bridge talker said. "Fantail reports six depth charges left."

Fraser knew the next attack would be their last.

As they began their last run, Arkwright paced the bridge wing. Fraser tried to review the results to see if he could discern any pattern in the submarine's movements. Whatever the submarine captain had done had outfoxed them so far. Fraser knew it was up to the captain now. Arkwright would have to outwit the Japanese captain. It was down to something almost as simple as the childhood game of rock, paper and scissors. Arkwright would have to anticipate what evasive tactics the Japanese captain would take, or the attack would fail again. The range decreased as the destroyer charged after its prey. Arkwright paced back and forth restlessly, rubbing his nose as the reports from sonar continued in an unbroken stream. The pings came more rapidly as the sonar operator shortened his scale.

"Tell the fantail to standby to drop six depth charges. Set them for 150 feet."

The range wound down and the last six depth charges tumbled into the wake. More columns of water erupted, and the *O'Leary* circled again. The sonar resumed its search. Arkwright conned the destroyer over the site of their last attack, but there was no debris or oil to indicate success.

Beringer came out on the wing. "Captain, do you want a course to return to Surabaya?"

Arkwright looked out over the Java Sea. "I just know that bastard's out here somewhere."

"Captain, we don't have any more depth charges."

"He's got to come up for air and charge his batteries tonight."

"If we hang around, he could torpedo us before it gets dark." Beringer's voice rose in pitch. "He'd be hard to find in the dark. Besides we have over a hundred civilians aboard. A gun battle would probably get a lot of them killed."

Arkwright set his jaw and stared at the horizon.

Again, Fraser had to agree with Beringer. Even if they regained contact, the submarine would soon realize they had no more depth charges. Then it could bide its time and wait for a good shot. Even a night gun battle seemed unattractive. A surfaced submarine would present a small target. She might have two deck guns. The *O'Leary* could only fire three guns to one side and presented a far larger target. Fraser shuddered as he thought of one of the submarine's shells bursting among the survivors, who would have to be packed below decks.

While the captain continued staring at the horizon, a high-pitched cry sounded from the galley. The baby that had been brought aboard sounded like it needed to be fed.

The captain lowered his head, and his shoulders slumped. "Give me a course for Surabaya," he said softly.

As they neared Madura, the crew was secured from general quarters. Landry left the amidships deckhouse and climbed into the whaleboat to clean up the blood in the bilges. He shuddered as he remembered the men who had been attacked in the water. His job complete, he jumped to the deck and scanned the water nearby for any sign of sharks. A dark flash cut the water in their wake. A fin—or an illusion?

"What the hell are you doing standing around?" shouted Chief Mortland.

"Looking for sharks, Chief."

"You want to see sharks, I'll kick your useless ass over the side." Mortland's lips drew back, showing his teeth. "Almost fed yourself to the sharks today, Landry. Another damn-fool move like that and I'll be going back to Manila some day to comfort little Teresa."

Landry ground his teeth together.

"Just don't stand there, get to work!"

As Mortland turned on his heel, Landry realized he had the Springfield in his hands, ready for return to the gunner's mates. Fury at Mortland boiled up. A red-hot heat seemed to flare up his neck and into his skull. Landry yanked the bolt open and the spent cartridge clattered to the deck and rolled to the scuppers. Landry's hand itched to chamber another round and give Mortland the same dose of lead he had given the sharks.

Mortland froze. He slowly turned and looked Landry in the eye. Landry refused to drop his gaze. Mortland finally lowered his eyes to the deck.

"Just getting rid of the spent cartridge case," Landry said softly.

When Mortland turned and hurried away, Landry felt he had just won a small victory over the chief. But he knew he had won a bigger victory over himself. Teresa was worth the brig. Mortland wasn't.

CHAPTER TWENTY

Two days after their return to Surabaya, Fraser paced his station on the fire control platform as the *O'Leary* steamed in the roadstead during the daily airraids. While more bombs fell on Surabaya, he thought of Ilsa. Fraser watched helplessly as the Japanese continued to pound the city.

A light haze of smoke rose from the first two stacks indicating the newly repaired boilers were functioning normally. Fraser didn't know whether to be happy or not that the *O'Leary* was ready for action. They could expect orders at any time, orders that could take them far from Surabaya. How far was another question; Fraser had encountered a discouraged-looking Simpson earlier that day. Simpson had told him that during their repair of the number two boiler, the engineers had found nothing inside to explain the vibration problem.

The sun was low in the western sky when a radioman brought a message to Arkwright on the bridge wing. Fraser looked down from the fire control platform and wondered if it were orders for the *O'Leary*. He had been hoping for an opportunity to see Ilsa that night, but he feared the message would send them away before he could go ashore.

As soon as they secured from general quarters, Fraser read the message file with hands that trembled slightly. "Damn!" he muttered when he found orders for the *O'Leary* to depart in the morning with a convoy headed for Australia.

At dusk they returned to a pier to take on supplies and fuel. Fraser was summoned to the captain's cabin.

"You wanted me, sir?"

"Ross, I assume the gunnery department has no problems—at least none that Chief Hanlon can't handle."

"Sir, everything's in good shape."

"I'd like you to go ashore tonight and confer with Captain Van Dorn about the situation in Java. I expect we'll head back here with the next convoy, so I'd like to get some idea of what we can expect."

"Doc's not having any success reading all the coded message traffic?"

"No, he's not sure what's going on. Doc doesn't have friends ashore to pump for information like he did in Manila. I'd like to hear how things look from Van Dorn's viewpoint."

"What if Captain Van Dorn isn't home?"

"Then wait for him to show up. Do the best you can to ascertain what local conditions are like." The corners of the captain's mouth twitched upwards.

"Aye, aye, Captain. Maybe Ilsa can help me."

One of Arkwright's bushy eyebrows lifted. "I hope so. Be back by 0430."

Fraser turned to leave, but he stopped. "Captain, even though we didn't get that sub, I think those survivors and our crew owe you their gratitude. Your thinking saved a lot of people from the sharks the other day."

A series of emotions swept across the captain's face. "We might still be out there if I hadn't heard that baby crying," Arkwright said softly. "It reminded me of my children."

The captain rubbed the side of his nose and closed his eyes for a few seconds. "That baby has made me do some thinking the last two days. I always thought war would be a noble business. Warrior against warrior—something I could take pride in. That kind of war is dead—if it ever existed. We're probably going to kill a lot of women and children before this war is over."

"At least that woman and her child will live another day," Fraser said.

"I suppose that's something."

Fraser finally broke the silence. "At least we didn't start this war, if that's any consolation."

"Not much. You'd better get going for the Van Dorns'."

After one of Mohammed's better dinners, Fraser and Captain Van Dorn retired to the dimly lit porch. Ilsa's father poured generous portions of brandy, lit one of his large cigars and stared out at the dark garden for a moment before answering Fraser's question about the course of the war. "You must understand what I am about to tell you is secret and sensitive information, or else my opinion about controversial issues."

"You can count on my discretion."

Van Dorn seemed to take a few seconds to translate his thoughts into his formal English. "The war is a disaster. The Japanese are victorious everywhere . . . and closing in on Java. They have just started landing at the southern end of Borneo."

Lord, thought Fraser, the Japanese were only a few hundred miles away.

"We aren't the only ones in trouble," Van Dorn said. "Your forces are barely holding out on Corregidor and Bataan."

Fraser felt a surge of anger. "The whole region is fighting on a shoestring. Why aren't we getting any help?"

Van Dorn shrugged. "Roosevelt and Churchill have decided that the European theater has the priority on men, equipment, and ships. More importantly, your Navy isn't willing to risk valuable ships out here."

Fraser drew a deep breath and forced himself to ask the next question. "How soon do you think the Japanese will attempt an invasion of Java?"

"That depends on whether we can slow them down. We need another victory like Balikpapan . . . but it must come before the Japs send their troops ashore." Van Dorn's expression hardened. "If the war continues badly, they might be here in a month or two."

"That seems hard to believe."

"If you saw what I see every day, you would believe it," Van Dorn said, his angular face grim. "We are having difficulties coordinating forces from four different countries. There are language problems . . . communications problems. All of this should have been worked out before the war."

Van Dorn shifted in his chair and looked uncomfortable. "Many of my countrymen want to replace Admiral Hart and put a Dutch admiral in command of the naval forces. Our leaders know these waters intimately. The Dutch Navy believes that the Japanese must be hit with a decisive blow before they arrive on our doorsteps."

Fraser winced at the implied criticism of the American Navy. "Admiral Hart did everything humanly possible to get us ready for the war. He made sure his forces weren't caught like those at Pearl Harbor and Clark Field."

Ilsa's father shrugged. "From what I've seen, he's a fine man, but Dutch headquarters would like a more aggressive approach."

"Will a change really do any good?" Fraser asked.

"I'm not sure. Even a tactical genius couldn't do much without air cover. Too much aggressiveness might be foolhardy. Perhaps Admiral Hart is taking a longer range view. Your old ships may not be worth much, but the veteran crews are a priceless asset."

Fraser realized Van Dorn was right. When new ships slid down the ways back home, they would be useless without veterans to teach the new draftees how to run them.

Van Dorn paused to savor his cigar, as if reluctant to let the grim conversation diminish his pleasure. He blew a large cloud of gray smoke into the night. "Keeps the bugs away. Daughters and wives too, if you want peace and quiet."

Van Dorn looked at his watch. "We'll have to continue this discussion another time . . . if we get the chance. I have to go back to the office tonight."

Van Dorn started to rise from his chair but then sighed and sat down heavily. The dim light caught the lines of fatigue and sorrow that etched his face. "Ross . . . I think you should convince

Ilsa to leave for Australia as soon as possible. There may not be much time left."

Fraser put his brandy down, afraid he might drop it.

Van Dorn was silent, as if unwilling to discuss something. He finally drew a ragged breath. "Japanese troops are sometimes doing unspeakable things to European women in the areas they've conquered. If they discover she is married to an American naval officer, it . . . it might be especially bad."

Fraser realized his hands were aching from squeezing the arms of his chair. He stared out at the dark garden, where he had celebrated his wedding. He finally turned and looked Ilsa's father in the eye. "Yes, sir, I agree she should leave. But convincing her might not be easy."

Van Dorn nodded. "She can be very stubborn. Perhaps if we both work on her, we can succeed."

"I wouldn't bet on it. She seems to have a mind of her own."

Van Dorn chuckled. "At least you know what you've gotten into. Her mother would have liked you." He rose and gave Fraser a firm handshake and an understanding smile before heading for the door.

Fraser had a sudden premonition he would never see Ilsa's father again.

Ilsa joined Fraser on the front steps, where they stood arm in arm as an official car pulled away.

"Ready to go upstairs?" Fraser asked.

"I've been ready for hours."

A sweaty Fraser lay back on his damp pillow and watched the fan blades turning over Ilsa's bed. He tried to figure out how he could persuade Ilsa to leave for Australia.

"You seem awfully preoccupied." Ilsa nibbled at his ear. "Have I worn you out already?"

"Oh, no. A Marine regiment would be showing the white flag, but I'll be ready to go again in a few minutes."

Another hour and Fraser lay back panting. "We have to talk."

"Talk? Now?"

"Now."

"Well, hurry up and get it over with," Ilsa said.

"Ilsa, both your father and I want you to think about leaving for Australia while you still can."

Ilsa sat up in bed, her mouth set. "That's out of the question. I'm staying here with you and my father."

Fraser tried to think of another tack. "There's a chance we both might retreat to Australia at the last minute, leaving you here alone."

"Ummm. You have a point. I'll think it over, and then we'll see how the war goes."

"After we sail tomorrow, I'm not sure when . . . or if the *O'Leary* will return. Please listen to your father and use your common sense. He's so busy with the war, he doesn't need you to take care of him. Think how much easier his mind—and mine—would be if you were safe."

Ilsa's green eyes clouded. "If I'm trapped here, it might be years before we could be together." She nestled against his shoulder. "That's a long time to wait for more of this."

Fraser suddenly realized they might never have another night together. Despair hit him. Their chances seemed hopeless with the Japanese heading at them like a tidal wave. He felt himself wilting. Fraser was so discouraged, he wondered if he could perform again that night.

Ilsa raised up on one elbow. "Something else the matter?"

Fraser wondered if he should burden her with his fears about the war and the *O'Leary*. The war had driven her into a defensive shell once before, and he didn't want to upset her. "No . . . just tired I guess."

"It's the war isn't it?" Her voice was calm. "You know, we have to die someday. Let's talk about it and then we can get on with living this night."

Fraser let himself go. He told her about his frustrations aboard the *O'Leary*, and how he had spent months wishing he were aboard a cruiser or battleship. "Actually, that's not true—I'd rather be a civilian working back in Columbus so I could come home to you every night."

Ilsa sighed. "I wish we could make the war go away. Is the fighting terrible?"

"It is when people around you are hurt or dying. If you know them, it's even worse."

"Are you ever afraid? I don't see how you couldn't be unless you were stupid or crazy."

"Yes, often. Waiting before a battle is usually the worst. When the fighting starts, I'm usually too busy to worry. Even so, it's tough to watch the enemy guns point at you and go off. You know the next few seconds before the shells arrive could be your last."

Ilsa nestled against him. "The next few hours are ours. Nothing can take them away."

"No, nothing can." But Fraser was still limp.

"There must be something else on your mind. Don't worry. Your captain is so competent. He promised to bring you back to me."

Fraser groaned to himself. The captain. How can I tell her. She's counting on the captain to get me back.

"You must talk to me. I don't want any secrets in our marriage."

Fraser told her about the captain.

"Oh, God," she said.

Fraser felt as if he had dropped a load from his shoulders. Then he realized Ilsa couldn't carry it for him. No one could. It was a load he would have to carry himself.

"What can you do?" she asked.

"Nothing, really. All I can do is hope the captain can hold together. I'll just do the best I can. Talking to you has made me feel better."

"I wish I had some answers for you," she said.

"Sometimes there are no answers."

"Shhh," Ilsa said. "Look. On the ceiling."

Above the fan crawled a gecko. The small chameleon-like lizard hit a spot of peeling paint and fell. The gecko bounced off a slowly rotating fan blade but righted itself in midair before hitting the floor. The lizard crouched for a few seconds, emitted a loud "geck-oh," and scurried over to the wall and climbed toward the ceiling.

Fraser felt Ilsa's gentle hands bringing him back to life. If the gecko could rise above his problems, Fraser thought, so could he.

"Looks like you won't have to call the Marines after all," Ilsa said.

Two hours before dawn, they sat in the Mercedes at the base of the pier. Fraser gave Ilsa a final lingering kiss and held her. He walked reluctantly along the pier to the brow and boarded the ship. Fraser watched from the rail as Ilsa drove into the predawn darkness.

The destroyer was already alive with men about the decks. The *O'Leary* was scheduled to gather the merchant ships just after dawn in order to depart before the first Japanese air raid. Fraser hustled down to the wardroom and took his seat.

Morales placed a cup of coffee at his elbow. "Real eggs today, Mr. Fraser."

"Thanks, I'll take one of your cheese omelettes with toast."

Fraser picked up his napkin and removed it from its stainless steel ring. He gazed at the inscription on the napkin ring: "GUNNERY OFFICER." He turned his eyes to the simple gold wedding ring on his left hand. He knew that however long he stayed in the Navy, he could never care for his profession as much as he cared for his wife.

Three days after their departure from Surabaya, Laster decided the weather seemed calm enough to get out of his bunk. As he tied his shoelaces, his door rattled with a harsh knock.

"Come in."

Red faced, Beringer appeared in the doorway, holding a shoe. "Look at this!"

"What's the matter? Foot fungus rotting the shoe? You want me to treat you with gentian violet?"

"Look in the shoe!"

Laster peered inside. A flattened cockroach oozed on the instep. "That's a big one! Sorry, I'm not a veterinarian. I can't treat one of your pets. You'll have to be more careful when you take them for walks."

Beringer ripped the shoe out of Laster's hands. "You're responsible for ensuring the health and cleanliness aboard this ship! The roaches are out of hand!"

"Ah, but in your case, not out of foot." Laster stood and faced the quivering Beringer. "No problem—as soon as the insecticide we ordered gets here from the States. But bullets and bombs should have a higher priority—unless some idiot decides we should try spraying the Japs."

"Don't give me a lot of excuses."

Laster felt his patience ebbing. "Why don't you try telling the crew not to drop any crumbs when we feed them sandwiches at general quarters. They'll laugh you off the ship. They know their job is to fight the Japs."

Beringer set his long jaw. "Korchak was a forestry major in college. He must have learned something about insects. I want the two of you to find some way of eradicating these pestiferous creatures. I expect some good ideas in a week."

"Sailors have been trying to get rid of roaches for thousands of years. You expect success in a week?"

"Affirmative." Beringer stalked out.

Laster sat down and pondered the cockroach problem, but no immediate answers came to mind. Before he could decide what to do, the general alarm began to sound. "Ah, hell! I thought we were going to have a few easy weeks."

"What's going on?" Laster asked the pharmacist's mate when he reached the wardroom.

"Dunno, Sir."

The rumbling boom of depth charges shook the wardroom. Laster's palms dampened as he remembered the wardroom was just above the water line. A torpedo could change that fast. Laster paced the deck near the wardroom door ready for a quick exit. A boatswain's pipe twittered securing the crew from general quarters.

"Maybe a false alarm," the pharmacist's mate said.

"This stuff is hard on my nerves," Laster said. He headed for the door to discover what the excitement had been about. He found that the sonar contact had been a school of fish. The back-up whaleboat crew was already out recovering a fresh dinner for the ship. The *O'Leary* circled, and when the boat crew was ready, slowed to 5 knots. The boat surged alongside. The inexperienced boat crew performed their difficult task creditably. Boat, crew, and fish were soon aboard.

"Doc, we need you," shouted a man near the boat.

Laster's stomach did a flip-flop. He had handled a fair number of medical emergencies in his short career, but he still had a fear of running into something he couldn't handle.

By the dripping boat, Laster could only shake his head. "A clear case of multiple concussions. No treatment possible," he announced gravely as dozens of silver-scaled fish writhed on deck. Laster turned to a nearby cook. "Since there's no chaplain aboard, I commend these souls to your hands. Personally, I like mine baked Filipino-style."

"Those aren't soles. They're wahoos," the cook said.

"Close enough," Laster said.

For Fraser the voyage was a numbing succession of boring watches, sleep, and meals, several of which featured Vienna sausages. The *O'Leary* zig-zagged with her sonar pinging for Japanese submarines. Part of Fraser was bored, but he welcomed a chance to recover from the hectic first two months of the war. He realized that even the time in Surabaya had been a strain. A serious courtship and marriage hadn't been a rest cure.

The convoy bound for Java finally arrived at the rendezvous, and the *O'Leary* led the merchant ships toward Tjilatjap, a port on Java's southern coast. Fraser inspected one of the ships through his binoculars. She was a large American freighter with crates of P-40's on her weather decks. Fraser could see the faces of the young pilots who lined the rails, lounging in the sun. "I hope those guys are enjoying themselves," he muttered. Some of his resentment evaporated when he realized the pilots would soon take to the sky against overwhelming odds. Many of them looked younger than he was. Fraser reflected that the cocky fliers in the Philippines had been victims of their leaders.

The remainder of the voyage was even longer and more boring, but Fraser heard few complaints; evidently all hands were well aware the only alternative was an unequal fight with the Japanese.

The day before their arrival at Tjilatjap, Laster winked at Korchak and knocked at Beringer's door.

"Come in," the executive officer said.

"Are you busy, sir?" Laster asked.

"Well, yes. I'm drafting some suggestions for some new reports. The ones we make now are too damn skimpy. They don't give the decision makers enough information, or frequently enough."

Jesus! thought Laster. Just what the Navy needs. "In that case, we won't bother you about the roach problem."

Beringer gave them a toothy smile. "Sit down. I knew the two of you could do it."

Laster gave Beringer his best professional look. "I want you to appreciate that we've applied the latest scientific techniques. For the last week my pharmacist's mate and I have captured the enemy and traced their movements. Surprisingly, we found few roaches in the after part of the ship."

Korchak broke in. "My theory is that the roaches can't stand the sweaty snipes who live aft. There's another possibility. The snipes will eat anything. They don't leave many crumbs for the roaches."

"It sounds like we may need to get tougher about cleaning up the forward part of the ship," Beringer said.

Laster pulled out a notebook. "That occurred to me, too. I've been inspecting the living areas every day. All were shipshape except for one space which had the following problems: day one, crumbs on desk with unfinished cup of coffee; day two, half-eaten sandwich next to bunk; day three, pieces of cracker on floor; day four, apple core and bread crusts on desk."

Beringer frowned. "Slovenliness personified! Who's the culprit?"

Laster paused and gave Beringer his most malicious smile. "I found all that right here in your room."

Beringer pushed a half-eaten sandwich under some paperwork and cleared his throat. He drummed his fingers on the desk. He looked like a horse who'd been given a moldy carrot. "Frankly, I think you're obfuscating the primary problem. The main issue is how you're going to exterminate the roaches."

Obfuscating? mused Laster. He shrugged his shoulders. "The only guaranteed solution is insecticide, but none is available."

"Damnation, you two had an entire week to come up with alternatives. Perhaps you two scientists will have to forget going ashore until you produce a solution."

"Well, we do have something we'd like to try," Laster said.

Beringer sniffed. "That's more like it."

"You should understand we haven't had time yet for field tests. Bring it in, Woody."

Korchak reappeared in a minute with a large shallow bowl which he laid on the deck. The metal bowl was full of white powder.

"I thought we didn't have any insecticide," Beringer said.

"It's not insecticide," Laster said.

"What good will it do then?"

"It's flour mixed with plaster of Paris from sick bay," Laster said. "If the roaches go for it, we're hoping they develop terminal constipation."

Beringer's long jaw dropped open as he stared at the bowl. His mouth finally snapped shut. "Ingenious! Absolutely brilliant! I've underestimated you. By God, I'll guarantee you both some extra time ashore."

"Is that a promise?" Laster asked.

"Of course. Are you questioning the word of a Beringer?"

"Oh, no."

"Go have a cup of coffee in the wardroom."

"Thanks," Laster said. "That's big of you."

Beringer smiled expansively. "Don't take too long. We do have a war to fight."

Then why the hell are you worrying about roaches and reports, Laster wondered.

In the wardroom, Korchak shook his head as he sat down and stirred his cup of coffee. "What are you going to do with the roaches you collected?"

"Hmmmm." Laster said. "I may find a use for them."

Korchak nodded toward Beringer's room. "Think our trap will work?"

"Oh, yes," Laster said. "I have great expectations."

"Why?" Korchak lowered his voice. "A roach can find better things to eat. I'll bet their digestive systems can probably handle the plaster of Paris."

"Actually, that trap is designed for larger game."

"A rat?"

"A fair description."

Korchak frowned. "I still don't understand."

CHAPTER TWENTY-ONE

The afternoon sun broiled the men standing the Condition III watch on the amidships deckhouse. Landry swapped places with Shifflet's loader, so he could look at a different piece of the ocean. Landry looked around the empty horizon. "Nice change over here. Got naked mermaids to port. Just got tired of looking at them."

"Don't be puttin' ideas in ol' Shifflet's head now. I'm havin' enough trouble waitin' until we get in port this afternoon."

"Yeah, it'll be nice to go ashore—if Mortland lets me."

"That prick still givin' you a bad time?"

"Yeah."

"Why the hell don't you put in a chit to strike for gunner's mate?"

"I've thought of that, but I'd have to give up the whaleboat."

"So?"

Landry clenched his fists. "Don't you start in on me too. Hell, nobody understands. I never had a damn thing as a kid. The other kids had toys, clothes, cars. That boat is something I can call my own. Like it's mine. Where I lived not even the rich kids had boats."

Shifflet nodded. "Yeah, I grew up dirt poor, too. Hell, stick in there."

"Thanks. Nobody else seems to understand."

They were silent for a half-hour as the *O'Leary* continued her zig-zag patrol ahead of the merchant ships.

Shifflet stretched and yawned. "Good thing we're puttin' into a new port. They won't let me go ashore in Surabaya no more."

"Don't worry," said Landry. "This place is on the south coast of Java. No one will know about you."

"What's the name of this port?"

"Tjilatjap."

A frown creased Shifflet's weathered face. "Musta changed plans then. The Plan of the Day said we were goin' to a place called . . ." Shifflet wrinkled his brow with concentration. "Tuh-jil-at . . . damnation, what a mouthful."

Landry smiled. "It's the same place—Tjilatjap."

"You ain't sayin' the same name."

"Sure I am. Tjilatjap. 'Chil' like in 'chili.' 'A' like in 'at.' 'Chap' like in chaps cowboys wear."

"I don't know, boy. That moniker may be mor'n I can handle."

"Forget what you saw on paper. Try saying 'Chil-a-chap.' "

"Chil-a-chap. I think I got it." Shifflet beamed like a child with a new toy. "Chil-a-chap, Chil-a-chap. Look out Chil-a-chap, here comes Shiff-a-let!"

Landry looked ahead. Land had emerged from the haze. "You won't have long to wait."

Near the coast, the first merchant ship picked up a pilot and led the column of ships in. The *O'Leary* prowled for submarines and turned to follow the last ship. The destroyer twisted and turned through a tortuous channel that skirted numerous sand banks.

When they reached the inner harbor Shifflet snorted disgustedly. "This ain't no Surabaya."

Allied shipping, military and civilian, jammed the piers. Heat waves shimmered off the tin roofs of the warehouses, and a fitful breeze swirled dust from rutted roads. Piles of freight and equipment littered the piers. Partially stripped vehicles dotted the waterfront.

Landry saw a familiar shape. "Hey, Shifflet, there's the *Black Hawk*!"

"Hot damn! We'll be able to get some more torpedoes. Been feeling downright naked with only two aboard."

Landry felt reassured by the sight of the *Black Hawk*, the destroyer tender that had ministered to them before the war. The tender carried parts and supplies for most of their needs. She also had machine shops, specialized repair facilities, and trained specialists who could fix almost any problem the *O'Leary* had.

"Been waiting to see the dentist on the *Black Hawk*," Shifflet said. "He was gonna make me some false choppers so's I can impress the ladies."

"Hmmmm. Wouldn't be the real you with a full set of teeth. How the hell could a dentist match those tobacco stains? You'd look like an old piano with a couple of new keys."

"Maybe you're right. Better give the ladies a break. I'm overpowerin' enough as it is."

The next afternoon, Ross Fraser sat in the wardroom and stirred his coffee while the officers waited for the captain, who was due back from a conference aboard the *Black Hawk*. Fraser hoped Arkwright would bring them orders to return to Surabaya, but he wasn't optimistic. All the recent news had been bad. Japanese landings at the southern end of Makassar Strait had been successful. Fraser felt his stomach tighten as he remembered the Japanese were only a few hundred miles away from Ilsa, almost as close as he was.

That wasn't the worst news. The British bastion of Singapore had fallen on the 15th of February, three days before. Fraser had always heard Singapore described as the "Gibraltar of the Far East." The Japanese had also invaded the large island of Sumatra just to the west of Java. Their target, the city of Palembang, was the center of half the oil reserves in the Dutch East Indies. An Allied force of five cruisers and nine destroyers had steamed west to break up the invasion. However, they had to turn back after they were hit with an all-day air attack just short of their objective. Most of the Allied ships survived and returned to Java ports, but one Dutch destroyer was lost running aground. Two

American four-stackers, the *Barker* and the *Bulmer* had suffered serious damage from near misses.

"Ross, you look pretty glum," Doc Laster said from the end of the table.

"Just trying to digest all the bad news. I wonder where the Japs will hit next."

Laster released a perfect smoke ring. "My money's on Bali."

"Bali! That's ridiculous," Beringer said. "The Japs have already bitten off more than they can digest."

Ten minutes later the captain returned. At the head of the table, he grasped the gleaming brass ashtray with his stubby hands. "I know some of you were hoping for a couple of weeks alongside the *Black Hawk*."

Meredith slumped. "Don't tell me we're leaving. Simpson has experts from the tender coming to examine the number two boiler tomorrow. It's still vibrating."

"Sorry, Jack," the captain said. "We've been added to a strike force departing tonight. The Japs are expected to land on Bali today or tomorrow."

Laster smiled as Beringer flushed.

Arkwright continued. "Our airfield on Bali has allowed P-40s to refuel and fly here from Australia. In Japanese hands, it will be a threat to Allied shipping south of the Malay Barrier."

Arkwright paused and looked around the table. "We leave tonight to try and break up the invasion. Admiral Doorman has ordered a three-pronged attack on the landing area at Bali tomorrow night. Our force, leaving here, will consist of two Dutch cruisers, two Dutch destroyers, and three of our destroyers. We'll steam east along the coast of Java tomorrow and hit the Japs before midnight. Several hours later, another Dutch cruiser and four of our destroyers now in Surabaya will hit the Japs again. After they clear the area, Dutch PT boats will move in and mop up."

Laster let out a low whistle. "I thought the wise military commander always tried to concentrate his forces."

"I won't disagree with you. Wait until you hear the plan for our group," Arkwright said. "Admiral Doorman will go in first with the cruisers and open fire on any targets. The destroyers will follow three miles astern. We're expected to fire torpedoes at the enemy ships the cruisers reveal."

"Lord!" the mild-spoken Chuck Steiner said. "If the Japs get stirred up and start to maneuver, it'll be almost impossible to hit them with torpedoes."

"Unnhh!" Fraser grunted. "We'll be shooting gallery targets making our approach for a torpedo attack. The sky'll be full of star shells. We should sneak in and use our torpedoes first like we did at Balikpapan."

"Come now," Beringer said. "You're being too pessimistic. We'll probably have a field day. I'm sure the admiral knows exactly what he's doing. After all, he is an admiral."

"And MacArthur's a general," Laster said.

Beringer tapped the table with his forefinger. "Ah, you've proven the point."

Arkwright turned to the tactical and technical problems they would have to solve. Fraser was happy to hear they were supposed to retire to Surabaya. After a half-hour of discussion, the captain looked around the table. "Any more questions?"

"I predict this expedition will be a smashing success," Beringer said. "Much better than Balikpapan."

"Wait, there's one more thing." Arkwright ran a hand over his close-cropped hair. I'm sorry to report that Admiral Hart has been relieved, supposedly because of ill health. Admiral Helfrich of the Dutch Navy will replace him in command of ABDA-FLOAT."

There was a shocked silence.

"Let's get ready," said the captain. "We don't have long. We'll be under way at 2200."

Two hours before midnight, Fraser had the watch as officer of the deck. The *O'Leary* groped through the dark channel to the open sea. Their pilot seemed to know the waters well. The navigation was almost impossible, and the usually unflappable Chief Jablonski admitted that some of his fixes were questionable. Ahead of them, the Dutch destroyer *Kortenaer* ran aground.

"New sandbar," said the pilot who guided them well clear. "At least the minefields stay put."

Fraser hoped so as he realized their force had already lost one ship.

When they cleared the last minefield, Fraser escorted the pilot down to the boat that would take him ashore. "Great job," Fraser said.

"This is my last day. I'm leaving with my family for Australia tomorrow."

Fraser thought of Ilsa and wished she'd made the same decision.

The pilot looked at the *O'Leary* and shook his head. "Good luck. You'll need it."

Just before midnight, the Dutch light cruisers steamed out the channel with Doorman's flagship, the *DeRuyter*, leading the *Java*. The destroyers took their stations, and the formation turned east for Bali. Fraser turned over the watch to Chuck Steiner and headed below for some sleep. Fraser was dreaming of Ilsa when the general alarm went off before dawn. He jumped down from his bunk, sure he had just gone to sleep. He stumbled up to the fire control platform and waited for dawn. The wind had picked up as ever larger swells marched northward from the Indian Ocean.

As soon as the sky lightened, the four destroyers were ordered to a semi-circular antisubmarine screen in front of the Dutch cruisers. The *O'Leary* turned and pounded through waves to her new position. When she reached her station, the swells caught her on the beam and rolled her heavily. Fraser clutched the rail in front of him as he heard pencils and equipment clattering to the deck in the pilothouse.

Eckersly, Fraser's talker, looked at him soberly. "This is nothing compared to riding one of these babies in the North Atlantic."

"I'll skip that thrill." Fraser hoped the *O'Leary* would be his last four-stack destroyer.

When they were secured from general quarters, Fraser went below for breakfast. He sighed as he realized he was due to take over the forenoon watch as soon as he ate. When he opened the wardroom door, Fraser was surprised to see Laster at the table. "What are you doing eating in this weather?"

Laster was pale but he smiled. "I have my reasons." The doctor lowered his head over his cornflakes as the other officers filed in.

The *O'Leary* began to roll even more heavily. The stewards poured water on the table cloth to create more friction to hold the utensils and plates in place. A metallic clanking began in one of the forward staterooms.

Beringer looked irritated. "Woody, go check your room. They never teach you reserve officers how to keep your belongings from going adrift."

"Aye, aye, sir." Korchak was back a few minutes later. "No problem with my room, sir. But it sounds like something's loose in yours."

"Impossible. I always keep everything shipshape. A place for everything and everything in its place."

Laster coughed and Fraser saw him give Korchak a long look. "You must have been wrong, Woody," Laster said.

Korchak frowned and suddenly smiled. "Yes . . . I guess I could have been wrong."

Fraser was puzzled by the exchange and then amazed when Laster hung on through breakfast despite the heavy rolling. The clanking grew even more obnoxious up forward.

"Ross, you'd better check your room," Beringer said.

As Fraser entered the passageway forward, he realized the metallic noise was coming from Beringer's room. He dutifully checked his own room and poked his head back in the wardroom. "It's definitely your room, sir."

Beringer shook his head and patted his mouth with his napkin. "Impossible. Oh, very well. I'll check."

Fraser stood back to let the executive officer stride by. Laster and Korchak were right behind Fraser as Beringer slid his door back. A cloud of fine white dust billowed into the passageway.

"I'll be a son of a bitch!" Beringer shouted.

"I won't argue with that diagnosis," Laster said softly before he ran aft holding his sides.

Fraser walked down the passageway and peered in Beringer's

room. An overturned metal bowl slid along the deck with each roll, stirring the white dust that coated the deck and filled the air. A fine powder was settling on every exposed surface.

"Where's Laster?" Beringer roared.

"I think he's under the weather again," Fraser said.

"Yes," Korchak said with a straight face. "He was practically doubled over when he left."

The small fan in chiefs' quarters hummed as it stirred the humid evening air. The expected battle was only hours away. Hanlon felt his dinner sitting in his stomach like a heavy lump.

"How about a game of backgammon?" Chief Jablonski asked.

Hanlon looked across the table at his friend. "Now?"

At the end of the table, Mortland tilted his chair back. "What's the matter, Hanlon? You nervous?"

"Sure. The Japs might blow the hell out of us before the night's over. I guess that puts me a little on edge."

"Mortland, you don't get nervous?" Jablonski asked.

"Naw. I ain't no chicken shit."

"If you say so." Jablonski adjusted his wire-rimmed glasses. "Just make sure you don't monopolize the head like you did before Balikpapan."

"Musta been something I ate that night."

"I guess we had the same menu tonight," Jablonski said. "You've already been to the head twice."

"Okay, okay!" Mortland said. "So my gut gets a little nervous. How would you like to be up in that crow's nest with shells whistling by your nose. Ain't nowhere for me to run and hide."

"I'd rather be up there than in a fireroom," Hanlon said. "Take a hit down there and you get cooked."

"Serve them damn snipes right," Mortland said.

Hanlon turned to Jablonski. "Let's play backgammon."

Mortland said, "I don't know why you two don't play acey-deucy like real Navy men."

"Backgammon takes more skill—not as much luck involved," Jablonski said.

"Says you!" Mortland stalked into the chiefs' head and the doorknob rattled as he slammed the door.

"At least his gut is human," Jablonski said.

"That's about all," Hanlon said. "Let's see how well you play backgammon tonight."

"Don't expect much." Jablonski's brown eyes clouded behind his glasses. The chief quartermaster's long hands trembled slightly as he distributed the pieces about the board. "I don't think this is going to be as easy as Balikpapan."

Halfway through the game, Jablonski smiled wryly. "You aren't concentrating very well, either."

Hanlon stared at a cracked linoleum square on the deck. "No, I keep thinking about Maria."

"I hope you know you were lucky to find her."

"I know. I had a pretty bad marriage back in the States."

Jablonski sighed. "Me too. My wife hated men. She said God had screwed up when he created Adam. Then he made the necessary corrections when he created Eve."

"How did you answer that?"

"Hell, I told her that if Eve was anything like she was, the result probably scared God out of the creating business altogether."

Hanlon laughed and shook his head. "A good woman can be just about the best thing in a man's life."

"Yeah, consider yourself a fortunate man, Byron. A lot of folks have marriages that aren't so hot."

"I know—and Maria's church won't even let us get married."

"You're still a lucky man."

"Maybe that's all life is, chance and luck. I hope there's more to it than that," Hanlon said.

After a minute of silence Jablonski laughed and nodded toward the head. "I finally figured out why Mortland takes so long to take a crap in there."

"I'll bite," Hanlon said.

"Because Mortland's so full of it."

Hanlon laughed and felt some of his tension ease until the general quarters alarm catapulted the chiefs out of their chairs.

"Aww Sheeit!" Mortland bellowed from the head. "Not now!"

As the light faded from a blood-red western sky, Fraser buckled on his phone set and put on his heavy steel helmet. The men around him manned their stations but with none of the relaxed chatter present during routine calls to general quarters. The men on the fire control platform tested the director with quiet efficiency. They seemed well aware the main battery would see action before the night was over. The communications were terse; the voices, tense.

The manned and ready reports flowed in quickly. Then, there was nothing to do but wait as the last gray light was consumed by darkness. The expected battle was still three hours away, but that was only a prediction based on tenuous intelligence. Without radar, they might stumble upon Japanese forces at any time. They were already up to 27 knots, and the destroyers had peeled back to allow the two Dutch cruisers to surge 3 miles ahead. The newly formed destroyer column was led by the Dutch destroyer, *Piet Hein*. The *Ford*, *Pope*, and *O'Leary* followed obediently behind, each ship steaming in the wake of the one ahead.

Fraser raised his binoculars and picked up the tiny blue lights burning at the sterns of the destroyers ahead. Other than that, the Allied ships were darkened so as not to give them away to the enemy.

The waiting continued. One hour. Two hours.

"Land off the port bow!" reported Mortland from the crow's nest.

"Definitely Bali—Tafel Hook," called Jablonski from the pilothouse. No reefs or shallows to worry about."

Just Japs, thought Fraser. He scanned the dark horizon with his binoculars and barely made out the blacker shoreline. It would be difficult to pick up any ships against the dark background. As he lowered his binoculars, Fraser shuddered. He knew it was an illusion, but it seemed like their destroyer column was steaming in daylight. The four-day-old moon and the stars glinted in the cloudless sky, their pale light illuminating the open water. The slender moon was down in the western sky behind them. If the Japanese were tucked against the Bali shore, the Allied force would be silhouetted against the moon.

"It feels like the whole Jap Navy must be watching us," muttered Eckersly beside Fraser.

Fraser turned to the men at the director. "Be ready. If the Japs haven't seen us yet, they'll spot us after the Dutch cruisers wake them up."

A few minutes later, the *Piet Hein* turned north to enter Badung Strait between Bali and the smaller island of Nusa Besar about ten miles to the southeast. The captain paced the port bridge wing just below Fraser and peered toward the dark shore of Bali. Arkwright lifted his Roman nose to the breeze as if he expected to smell the enemy presence. "Alert all stations we expect action soon," the captain ordered.

Seconds ticked by. Minutes.

A searchlight flashed from one of the Dutch cruisers in the middle of Badung Strait and probed the Bali shoreline with a luminescent finger. Seconds later yellow fire leaped from the cruiser's guns as she opened fire to port. The Japanese along the shoreline responded immediately with searchlights, star shells, and rapid salvos, which lit the night with yellow tongues of flame. The distant booms rolled across the water as if from a summer thunderstorm.

The destroyer column forged ahead, rapidly closing the battle. The *Piet Hein*, at the head of the column, made several course changes while the Americans played follow the leader. Arkwright cursed as he adjusted their speed to maintain proper station at the end of the destroyer column.

Fraser steadied himself as they raced ahead. Smoke swirled across the strait, obliterating the gun flashes. Evidently the *Piet Hein* had spotted something, because she opened up with her guns and sent a torpedo off to port.

"Can't see a thing in that smoke," muttered Fraser.

Neither the *Ford* nor the *Pope* was firing torpedoes or guns, so they were equally blind. Ahead, the *Piet Hien* made more quick turns and belched black and white smoke from her two stacks, further obscuring the view ahead.

Arkwright thumped his fist on top of the bridge wing. "Damn it! That's all we need!"

The *O'Leary* steamed blindly through the pungent smoke, which bit at Fraser's nostrils. When they finally emerged from the thick pall, Arkwright had to increase speed to regain their station behind the *Pope*.

"Ship off the port bow!" shouted a lookout.

Arkwright took only seconds to make his decision. "Give him three torpedoes," Arkwright ordered Steiner. "Surface action port! Guns, open fire when ready!"

Fraser heard Arkwright and ordered the director toward the target before the bridge talker could repeat the captain's order.

"On target!" the gun director trainer shouted.

"On target!" echoed the pointer.

"Range five oh double oh. Standby to fire an up ladder," shouted Fraser who knew his estimate was a rough one, and he cursed their worthless range finder.

"I have a solution," the computer operator reported.

"Match pointers," Fraser ordered.

"Pointers matched," said Eckersly.

"Rapid salvo fire! Commence firing! Commence firing!"

The salvo buzzer rattled, and the *O'Leary* jolted sideways as the first salvo went out. Seconds later the first torpedo chuffed from one of the port tubes. The Japanese had found the range already. Geysers of water erupted around the leading Allied destroyers. Gunflashes indicated the Japanese were off both bows.

Fraser focused his binoculars to port trying to pick up the *O'Leary*'s red shell splashes. Steiner clattered from one wing to the other as he responded to the captain's order to send three torpedoes at the gunflashes to starboard. Fraser wondered how the captain could handle so many problems at once. He felt like all hell was breaking loose, yet the captain was working like some kind of master juggler.

Fraser kept searching for their red-dyed shell splashes. Swirls of smoke and flashing guns confused him. He thought he saw their final ladder salvo hit short. "Up four double oh! Continuous salvo fire!"

Torpedoman Tim Egan cranked the forward starboard mount out and matched his dial with the orders coming from the director. The mount bucked as the first of his three torpedoes leaped into the night. Powder smoke from the impulse charge swirled around him and burned his nostrils. He fired his last two weapons in quick succession. The metal beasts splashed into the water with their counter-rotating propellers whining.

Egan cranked his mount back inboard and leaned out to see what was happening ahead. Japanese shells rained around the *Piet Hein*. The Dutch destroyer slowed to a halt, suddenly enveloped in flames that ate along her length. The three American destroyers raced by the sinking Dutch vessel close enough for Egan to catch a glimpse of survivors scrambling over the side. The *Piet Hein* was already deep in the water as she settled stern first. Men were jumping into the water, but their lifeboats and rafts were caught in the blazes aboard.

"Poor bastards," Egan muttered. "I hope thay can swim."

Egan heard curses from the the men on the mounts along the port rail. He jumped down from his mount and ran across the deck. Ahead, the *Ford* heeled over in a turn to port. A Japanese searchlight transfixed the *Ford*'s bridge. A salvo smashed down, almost obscuring her with a wall of water. Black smoke billowed from her stacks as she attempted to hide from the enemy. More salvos thundered down, and the shell splashes were so thick they blotted out the probing rays of the searchlight. The *Ford* seemed to disappear.

Egan groaned. "She's gone!"

But the *Ford* emerged from cascades of white water apparently unscathed. The *O'Leary* heeled heavily as she followed the *Ford* and the *Pope* in a long circle to port to escape the fire that had nearly engulfed the *Ford*. The enemy redoubled their fire at the lead destroyer. Sheets of white water again surrounded the *Ford*, but she kept on going.

Fraser had been completely preoccupied with the difficult job of trying to spot the fall of shot. He realized they had completed a full circle and were headed after the Dutch cruisers which had exited toward Lombok Strait as planned.

But enemy ships were waiting in that direction and greeted the destroyers with a blizzard of gunfire. The *Ford* veered to starboard, heading east for the dark mass of the island of Nusa Besar, 10 miles away. The last of the *O'Leary*'s port torpedoes leaped into the night as the destroyer heeled over in a hard turn to follow her two sisters.

"Only three torpedoes left, all on the starboard side," shouted Steiner.

As they headed away, with the enemy to port, another searchlight flicked on. The terrible white eye swung by the *O'Leary*, stopped, returned, and caught them in its glare. Yellow flashes lit the night. Seconds later enemy shells whistled down, raising geysers alongside as the near misses shook the ship. A cascade of water rained down on the fire control platform, almost knocking Fraser off his feet. More salvos splashed around the old destroyer.

No orders from the captain. Fraser knew they had to do something or they were dead. "Shift target to searchlight!" Fraser shouted to the men on the director.

"On target!" shouted the director trainer.

Fraser's mouth went dry. They needed an accurate range estimate and they needed it fast. There was no time to fire a ladder and spot the fall of shot.

"On target!" shouted the pointer.

Fraser made his decision. "Range, five two double oh! Add two hundred after each salvo!" He knew it wasn't by the book, but there wasn't time. To hell with the book, he thought. I'll do whatever it takes to get out of here and see Ilsa again.

"Ready!" the computer operator yelled.

"Match pointers!"

"Pointers matched!"

"Rapid salvo fire! Commence firing! Commence firing!" Fraser shouted.

The first salvo jolted the deck under Fraser's feet just as another flight of enemy shells crashed alongside. The enemy searchlight continued its unwinking stare; the harsh light seemed to have become a part of the *O'Leary*'s paint work. Their second salvo roared its defiance at the enemy. Seconds later, there was a winking orange flash and the search light died to a sickly yellow and disappeared. Scattered cheers sounded from the topside stations, and Fraser felt like shouting with relief. They had a chance.

The third salvo had already left, but Fraser quickly ordered the range corrected to repeat the successful second salvo.

More *O'Leary* salvos ripped the curtain of darkness apart for a second at a time, but without the enemy searchlight, the night mercifully cloaked them between salvos. On the other hand, the director lacked a fixed aiming point, but Fraser wasn't about to complain. The Japanese were falling astern and no longer were bracketing the *O'Leary*.

Between salvos, Fraser heard a repetitive thudding. He looked aft where the whaleboat dangled over the side from its forward davit and battered against the *O'Leary*'s side. The headphone crackled in Fraser's right ear. "Captain wants the starboard gun crew to cut the boat loose."

Fraser passed the order through Eckersly. Two minutes later the boat vanished into the night.

As they continued their flight east toward the dim island ahead, one of the enemy ships to port started to drift toward the *O'Leary*'s stern. Arkwright dashed from the port wing and reappeared on the other side. "Right full rudder!" the captain barked.

Fraser's stomach dropped, and he looked down in alarm, wondering what the captain was doing. They had just escaped the vortex of enemy fire, and the *Ford* had led them near the dark background of Nusa Basar. Now, Arkwright appeared to be turning back toward the enemy.

"Steady as she goes!" the captain ordered when the enemy was off the starboard quarter. Arkwright turned to Steiner. "Give that Jap astern your last three fish!"

Steiner was soon ready. "Fire seven!" he ordered. "Fire nine! Fire eleven! All torpedoes away, Captain!"

Fraser held his breath waiting for the captain's next order. "Left standard rudder," the captain ordered, swinging them back behind the *Pope*, which then sheared out to starboard to duplicate the *O'Leary*'s torpedo firing. As soon as the torpedoes were away, the *Ford* turned, crossed astern, and made smoke to cover their retirement. As the thick smoke blotted out the last of the enemy ships, Fraser gave his final order, "Cease firing! Cease firing!" The guns fell silent. Fraser was suddenly conscious of the whine of the blowers, which had been obliterated by their gunfire and the incoming enemy salvos.

The *Ford* turned south and the other two destroyers fell in behind. Fraser realized the Japanese had cut off their retirement through Lombok Strait. The prospect of an immediate return to Surabaya looked dim.

Eckersly's eyes were wide under his helmet. "That was a near thing."

"Too near for me," Fraser said.

The phone circuit crackled in Fraser's ear. "Have all stations make a quick inspection for damage."

Fraser passed the word on through Eckersly and waited for the reports to come in. The solemn Eckersly frowned as he listened to his line. "Mr. Fraser, the only damage is the whaleboat—it's gone. Landry's missing too. No one has seen him since his gun crew cut the boat loose."

"Ah, hell" Fraser said. If Landry had fallen overboard, they could do nothing. Finding a man at night under ideal conditions was difficult. Landry might be dead anyway; there was no way to justify turning back and endangering the rest of the men and the ship. Fraser remembered how Landry had saved him from drowning in Subic Bay. His mind pictured Landry decking the *Holland*'s fat catcher.

Astern, yellow flashes lit the horizon. The rumble of gunfire reached them many seconds later. Fraser looked at his watch. The second wave of the Allied attack wasn't due for two hours. "That has to be the Japs shooting at each other," he told his men.

"Let's hope they don't miss this time," Eckersly said.

Fraser hoped so, too. His relief at their escape turned to frustration as he realized they hadn't stopped the Japanese invasion.

They had also been cut off from their withdrawal to Surabaya—and Ilsa. Now they would have to return to Tjilatjap. The Japs are closing in, he thought. What's going to happen to my wife?

When the Japanese searchlight caught the *O'Leary*, Hank Landry had been sitting in the pointer's seat of the starboard gun on the amidships deckhouse. The Japanese ships had been to port, so he was forced to sit and do nothing as the enemy salvos rained down. Shrapnel rattled off nearby metal surfaces. The glare of the enemy searchlight was blinding. There was a crash aft as the stern of the whaleboat dropped loose and bounced over the side. The enemy light suddenly died, and Landry watched helplessly as his boat banged against the side.

"Let's go!" Chief Hanlon shouted. "We have to cut the boat loose!"

Landry jumped off his seat on the gun and ran down the ladder to the main deck. "I'll cut the belly band first!" he yelled. He pulled his knife from the sheath at his belt and sawed at the canvas strap. It parted and the boat sagged. "Cut the falls!"

Chief Hanlon swung a fire axe at the thick lines. They parted with a snap, and the lines sang through the block at the head of the davit. The bow of the whaleboat splashed into the water, and the boat slid down the side.

"Back to the gun!" Hanlon shouted.

Regret surged through Landry. He'd saved his boat from being pounded to pieces against the side, but now it was gone. The rest of the gun crew clattered up the ladder to the top of the deckhouse. Landry had to take one last look at his boat. He leaned out over the side and tried to find it in the wake but could see nothing in the dark. He leaned farther. He heard a sudden snap as the stanchion next to him gave way. Landry grabbed for the sagging lifeline, missed, and toppled into the water. The starboard screw slashed the water as the ship roared by him. The turbulent wake tumbled him over and over before his life jacket buoyed him to the surface. Coughing and sputtering as he bobbed in the gentle swell, he finally remembered to look for the whaleboat, but he saw nothing.

Minutes later, the night was ripped by yellow flashes as two nearby ships exchanged rapid salvos. Booming concussions rolled across the water and hammered Landry's ears. An orange flash indicated a hit. One ship ceased firing and flashed lights on her mast. The other exchanged more signals with her temporary adversary.

Landry pounded the water with satisfaction as he realized both ships were Japanese. "Come on! Go at it again!"

As the Japanese turned and steamed into the night, Landry was relieved to see them go, but he was sobered by the realization that there were no Allied ships around. Immediate rescue seemed unlikely. Landry kicked his feet hard as the swell lifted him, and he searched the dark water ahead. He turned around and repeated the process with another swell. Nothing. He settled back in the water and a wave slapped his face. He sputtered and spit out a tepid mouthful of salty water. His lungs still burned with the water he had inhaled in the *O'Leary*'s wake, and he coughed until he retched.

Landry was thankful for his kapok life jacket, but he realized he was alone. A chilling fear ran through him. He calmed down as he remembered his ship had been close to Bali, so he had a chance of making land. Then he remembered the sharks. His mind burned with a picture of the savaging of the survivors only two weeks before.

Landry closed his eyes and leaned his head back against the rough life jacket as he tried to think of Teresa. He remembered how she had looked on the clean white sheets the last night he had been with her. He wondered why he was serving as shark bait thousands of miles away. As if in answer, the vision of the white sheets under Teresa gave way to a vivid image of the battle—the sheets of white water which had enveloped them when they had been caught in the harsh glare of the Japanese searchlight. The purity of the white light against the foaming columns of water had been almost unbearable. Death had whistled by and missed him then, but it seemed close now. He wondered how much longer he would have before the sharks came.

When Landry opened his eyes and looked around, the smoke of battle had drifted off. The moon had set, and high overhead was the familiar constellation of Orion—the Hunter. Canis Major and Sirius, the dog star, glittered nearby. Back home they had always appeared in the southern sky in the winter. It seemed strange to see them almost overhead, but he realized he was just south of the equator.

Landry remembered who had first shown him the constellations—his father. Sadness surged through him. Landry's father had not come home one day. Now Landry's ship—the home he had lived aboard for the last two years—had left him, too. He longed for the confines of the crowded forward berthing space, even with the unwashed bodies and snores. He yearned for the hard life of the deck hand. But he didn't miss Mortland; at least there was one consolation. Then he thought of the sharks and even Mortland didn't seem so bad.

As he bobbed in the swells, Landry remembered the Dutch destroyer that had been sinking as the *O'Leary* had steamed by. If he could find other survivors, his chances would be better. He kicked hard with his feet to take another look. Toward Bali, there were distant flickers. Burning oil? Landry set out with a steady breast stroke. He had to stop frequently to rest and get his bearings.

The night suddenly erupted in another gun battle as the horizon lit up with intermittent flashes. Landry couldn't tell what was happening, but it was obvious that some hits were scored by both sides during the running battle, which died away temporarily and then flared again to the north.

"I paid for a ringside seat and can't see worth a damn," Landry sputtered, spitting out another mouthful of water.

The silent darkness reasserted its claim. Landry felt more alone than ever as the gentle swells lifted him. Landry set off again. His arms began to ache, so he rolled over on his back and floated with the collar of the life jacket supporting his head. Orion had moved over to the western sky. Landry listened for sound of human activity, but all he could hear was the slap of the water against his life jacket. He was weary and wanted to quit. He knew if he did, he'd never see Teresa again. Their child would never know him. At least he had known his father. Landry wondered if his child would feel the same sense of abandonment. Landry didn't want to die. A sudden realization struck him. His father hadn't had any choice either. His father had been on his engine shoveling coal to feed a family, doing his job when the engine derailed. It was as simple as that, but Landry had never been able to accept it.

Landry looked up at Orion the Hunter. His father had given him that knowledge. He was determined to give his own child something, if only a letter that could be delivered after the war if the Japs finally killed him.

Landry struck out again but soon tired. As he floated he thought he heard a swirl in the water behind him. He turned to look but could see nothing. Something large and hard butted against his thigh. Thrashing his legs, he pushed away with his fist. His knuckles grated against a rough surface that felt like sandpaper. Landry stopped his flailing and waited, resigned to the death that seemed so close. "Father, forgive me," he whispered.

CHAPTER TWENTY-TWO

Two days after the battle in Badung Strait, Fraser sat in his room, updating his ammunition inventory. The *O'Leary* had arrived in Tjilatjap that morning, and they had spent hours refueling and loading ammunition in the muggy heat. Fraser shoved the papers aside and thought about Ilsa. If she hadn't left for Australia, there was now a chance he might see her in a few days. The destroyers in Tjilatjap had been ordered to steam south that afternoon for a rendezvous with the tender *Black Hawk* to rearm with torpedoes. The destroyers were then to head north for Sunda Strait off the western tip of Java and return to Surabaya to join other Allied warships gathering there.

Fraser desperately wanted to see Ilsa, but part of him hoped she was on her way to Australia. He wondered what he should tell her to do if she were still in Surabaya. Fraser threw his pencil against the bulkhead and headed for the wardroom for coffee.

A disgusted-looking Laster sat at the wardroom table, blowing smoke rings in the air. "Heard the latest news?" he asked.

"Our orders to Surabaya?"

"That's old news," Laster said. "A message came in while you were loading ammo. It ordered Beringer detached immediately."

"When's his relief coming aboard?"

Laster jammed his cigarette in an ash tray. "It didn't say. Beringer just packed up and left."

"Hell, he hasn't been aboard six months. What about Jack Meredith? He's been here over two years."

"Jack doesn't have an uncle on the Appropriations Committee to bail him out of here," Laster said. "That bastard was out of here so fast, he must've known what was coming."

"Thought you'd be happy to be rid of him."

"Hell, up to now I've been able to console myself thinking if the Japs get me, they'll probably get Beringer too."

"They say rats always leave a sinking ship," Fraser said.

"I gave that rat a little going away present."

"You gave Beringer a present?"

Laster rubbed his hands together. "I had a can full of roaches left from the research I had to do for him. I sprinkled them in that bastard's suitcases. I may never make it home, but I feel comforted by some measure of immortality."

"Immortality?"

"Ah, yes. I have visions of those roaches and their offspring overrunning the Beringer plantation when he gets home. Generations of Beringers will be plagued by those little devils."

That thought only relieved Fraser's concern about Ilsa for a few minutes. He decided to see if the captain could give him any advice.

"Come in," the captain said when Fraser knocked.

Fraser stepped in. On the captain's desk, the wooden model of the *O'Leary* gleamed with a coat of gray paint.

"Your model is beautiful."

"It's not really finished. I need to redo some mistakes. It needs some more details—the right ones—to give it real life. Go ahead and pick it up."

"I might drop it." Fraser leaned over the desk and inspected the model. Guns, torpedo tubes, piping, signal halyards—almost everything was there. There was even a miniature captain's chair inside the pilot house.

"I wanted to see you for a minute anyway," Arkwright said. "You've heard the exec's gone?"

"Yes, sir."

"Life might be easier without him. We can forget about our administrative reports until we finish fighting the Japs."

"What about the navigation?" Fraser asked.

"Officially, Jack will take over, but Chief Jablonski will continue to do the job as he was already doing. Jack will take command if something happens to me, but I want him to stay down in main control during G. Q. The engineering plant has so many problems, I want him available down there."

"I heard Simpson is still unhappy with the number two boiler."

The captain nodded. "Evidently the vibration was pretty bad the other night."

During the captain's pause, Fraser wondered how much longer they could steam before number two caused more trouble.

"If I get hit you might have to take over temporarily until Jack gets up to the bridge."

Fraser took a deep breath. The thought of having to command the *O'Leary*, especially during combat, seemed more responsibility than he could handle.

The captain tapped the message board. "The attack the other night turned out to be a complete fiasco. According to these messages, the second group had problems, too. The *Stewart* and the Dutch cruiser *Tromp* took some serious hits."

"Certainly wasn't like Balikpapan."

"No. It looks like the Japanese know how to fight at night after all. But that's not the only bad news," the captain said. "The Japs bombed the hell out of Darwin. They sank the *Peary* and several other ships."

Fraser winced. They had lost a sister ship. He wondered whose turn would be next.

Arkwright paused. "It gets worse. Many of the attackers at Darwin were carrier aircraft."

Fraser jerked upright in his chair. "That means a Jap carrier group is operating south of the Malay Barrier."

Arkwright nodded.

Fraser felt like a trap was ready to close around them. He had been worried about escaping through the Malay Barrier. Now, even if that gauntlet were run, they might have to face carriers roaming south of Java before they could reach Australia.

"Have you thought about sending Ilsa to Australia?"

"Easier said than done." Despair seemed to well up from Fraser's gut.

The captain's scarred forehead furrowed. "If those carriers head east, it may be too late already. Merchant ships will be easy pickings for Jap planes and surface units."

"My thoughts exactly, sir."

"It might be smart for her to make arrangements to depart from Tjilatjap. If she hears the Japs are to the south, she could always cancel out at the last minute."

"I guess that would be best," Fraser said.

"You seem to have problems with that."

"It's just that Ilsa can be so strong-willed. If she makes up her mind to go, there'll be no stopping her."

"I don't envy you," Arkwright said, his gaze on the picture of his family.

The *O'Leary* steamed south for a day to rendezvous with the *Black Hawk* in the lee of Christmas Island. Tim Egan sat by his torpedo tubes, waiting for motor launches from the tender to begin delivering torpedoes. Egan was depressed as he thought of the friends the war had claimed: first Ben Nystrom, and now Hank Landry. They'd had good times together in ports throughout the Far East. Landry had been tough to make friends with, but Egan had come to feel a real bond with his catcher. Egan wondered if Teresa would ever hear how Landry had been lost.

"Come on, Egan," said 'Beerbarrel' Robustelli, the chief torpedoman. "Here come our new babies."

Egan got up as a boat from the *Black Hawk* approached. The torpedoes were not fully assembled. The large warheads were lying separate from the afterbodies, which contained the air flask, fuel tanks, and machinery. As the motor launch eased alongside the *O'Leary* under an empty set of boat davits, Chief Robustelli joined Egan at the rail.

"My God!" Robustelli bellowed. "Those torpedoes look like they've been in a train wreck."

A *Black Hawk* torpedoman looked up from the boat and shrugged. "Sorry, Chief, they've been out in the open in Australia for months. The Army must've screwed 'em up. Hell, we did the best we could to fix 'em up. They ain't much, but they're all we got."

"That's great!" Robustelli shouted. "The things don't work worth a damn when they're in perfect shape."

As the torpedoes were hoisted up on deck by sweating men heaving on lines rigged through the boat davits, Robustelli became more agitated as he inspected each arrival. "Egan! Look at these two afterbodies!"

When Egan inspected the afterbodies, he knew they were going to have a tough time trying to join them with the warheads. The forward edges of the air flasks were badly bent. Normally, the edges mated exactly with the after edges of the warheads, allowing for the insertion of thirty-two small bolts.

As the last warhead was lowered to the deck, the rotund Robustelli bounced up and down on his toes. "Look at this elephant turd!"

Egan and Steiner, the heavy-set torpedo officer, walked over to look at the last arrival. Steiner bent his broad back over the warhead. "Son of a bitch!"

Egan was amazed. He'd never heard Steiner use profanity.

Steiner stood up. "I don't believe this."

When Egan took a closer look and ran his hand over the bulging mating flange of the warhead, he knew why Steiner was so upset.

Robustelli looked at the warhead a few seconds longer and stalked over to the side and poured profanity on the torpedoman in the boat below. "And take this worthless piece of crap back and bring me a decent warhead."

The *Black Hawk* torpedoman held up his hands. "That's it, Chief. That's all there is."

"You must be kidding me."

"It's true. I swear on my mother's grave."

"You'd better get that boat the hell out of here, or I'll be swearing over your grave," shouted Robustelli.

As Egan followed Robustelli back to the warhead, he remembered there was almost 500 pounds of high explosive packed inside the rounded nose. The explosive normally required the firing of a detonator to set it off. The detonators were not installed until the torpedo was assembled and ready to shoot, so the warhead was considered safe and stable under normal conditions. But Egan knew stability was a relative term; the warheads were handled and stored with care by the torpedomen. He had never seen a torpedoman abuse one.

Robustelli bit his lower lip as he looked down at the warhead. "Mr. Steiner, this bastard worries me. I don't mind banging those damaged afterbodies. There's nothing to blow up inside. But this one warhead's going to need some major work."

"What kind of work?" asked Steiner.

"Gonna have to bang it with a sledge," said Robustelli. "I don't much like the idea of hammering on that bastard. But I don't want to be short a torpedo fighting the Japs."

Steiner stared at the warhead while Egan's mouth went dry. Egan didn't want to be around if they started banging on that much explosive.

Steiner broke the silence. "Get the men started on the other torpedoes. I'll go discuss this with the captain."

Two hours later, all the torpedoes except one had been mated and inserted in the tubes. "What now?" asked Egan.

"Let me get the captain," Steiner said. "He wanted to take a look at the bad warhead before we started."

When the captain arrived, he removed his sunglasses and stared at the warhead. It sat on a wheeled dolly lined up with the last afterbody.

"What do you recommend?" Arkwright asked.

Chief Robustelli wiped his perspiring face. "Captain, we've done the best we can to adapt the last afterbody to this sorry sombitch of a warhead. The top of the joint misses mating by about an eighth of an inch. I've been able to connect the bottom and part of the sides with eighteen of the thirty-two bolts. That should hold the bottoms while we hit the top of the warhead to bring it in line."

Arkwright eyed the large sledge hammer standing nearby. "And you think that will do the job?"

"It had better. That's the largest one they had in the repair locker."

Arkwright stooped over the torpedo and looked at the warhead. He ran his hand over the distorted edge as if he were greeting an old friend. "That warhead is going to get a hell of a jolt if you use that sledge."

Robustelli scratched his jaw. "I know, but I'm willing to take the chance. That explosive is supposed to be stable stuff. I hate the thought of being short a torpedo."

The captain set his mouth. "Me, too. Let's fix this weapon." Arkwright turned to Steiner. "Tell Jack to keep a man in the steaming fireroom and move the crew to the bow."

"Most of the men seem to be there already," Steiner said. "Word got around pretty fast when we started banging on the afterbodies."

"Let's get all nonessential men out of here," Arkwright told Robustelli while they were waiting for Steiner to return.

Egan headed for the amidships deckhouse.

"Egan!" Robustelli's voice rasped. "You stick around. This should just take the two of us."

Egan's stomach did a flip-flop. "Aye, aye, Chief."

In a few minutes Steiner returned. "The ship is cleared, Captain. Simpson volunteered to stay in the fireroom."

"Thank you, Chuck," the captain said. "You go on up to the bow."

Steiner hesitated. "Captain, I can't leave. This is my responsibility."

Arkwright looked at him for a few seconds and then said gently, "Yes, it is. But it's also mine. Go forward. That's an order."

When Steiner had retreated, Arkwright turned and looked at Robustelli and Egan. "Just the three of us . . . and our friend here. What are the odds of this warhead going up?"

Robustelli frowned. "I dunno for sure, Captain. Maybe one in a thousand . . . one in a hundred. Who can say?"

Egan noticed the captain didn't even blink. If anything, he seemed a little disappointed.

Robustelli fixed his eyes on Egan. "You're our man on the sledge." Egan felt the sweat running down his body as he realized what he was about to do. He hefted the heavy sledge and eyed the chalk-marked "X" on the rim of the warhead. He bunched the muscles in his shoulders and started to lift the sledge.

"Ah, Captain," Chief Robustelli said quickly, clearing his throat. "Do you mind if I take some of my cough medicine first?"

Arkwright shrugged. "Go ahead."

Robustelli hurried to a nearby locker used for torpedo alcohol and yanked out a large bottle of clear fluid. He unscrewed the top and took several healthy swallows and coughed heavily.

"You'd better be careful, Chief," the captain said. "That's a nasty cough."

"I'm all right now, sir. Okay, Egan. Have at it."

Egan took a deep breath and braced himself against the edge of the dolly as he fixed his grip on the smooth wooden handle. He hoisted the sledge, and started it down toward the edge of the warhead. Halfway down, his mind rebelled. He pulled back and took most of the force out of his blow. The sledge still hit the warhead with a bell-like clang.

Arkwright and Robustelli bent over the torpedo and looked at the edges. "That didn't do it," Arkwright said. "It's going to need more force than that."

Robustelli looked at Egan. "Looked like you pulled back."

"Yeah, I did."

"Let's see your best shot this time," Robustelli said.

Egan looked down at the warhead and shuddered. He lifted the sledge overhead, but he just couldn't force himself to bring it down. "Jesus! I'm sorry!"

The captain stepped forward. "That's okay. Let me give it a try."

Robustelli frowned, obviously worried that the captain was violating the unwritten rule that officers weren't supposed to get their hands dirty.

Arkwright nodded. "Don't worry, Chief. I won't tell anyone."

"Okay, Captain have a go. Would you like to try some . . . cough medicine first?"

Arkwright shook his head. "No thank you, Chief. I don't touch the stuff anymore."

"Here's the sledge, sir," Egan said apologetically. "Watch your back, Captain. It's heavy."

Arkwright took the sledge, almost fondly, and hefted the heavy tool. The captain braced himself, and hoisted the sledge until his arms were fully extended. The heavy tool hung in the air over the warhead. Arkwright brought it down with a furious grunt that exploded into a reverberating clang as the sledge hit the warhead.

Egan watched in horror as the warhead jumped under the force of the blow. "Jesusss!" he hissed.

Arkwright trembled slightly and the scar on his forehead reddened. A wide-eyed Robustelli let out a low whistle and bent over the warhead. He ran his fingers over the edge. "That did it, Captain. If you'll let me take a couple of little taps, the job'll be done."

When Arkwright seemed reluctant to surrender the sledge, Robustelli took it gently from his hands. He turned and gave two careful blows to the edge of the warhead and put the crude instrument aside. "Check them bolts now, Egan."

The torpedoman picked up the rest of the small bolts used to secure the warhead and tried them by hand. "Couple may take some forcing. I wouldn't want to have to take them out."

"I don't think you'll have to worry about that," a drained-looking Arkwright said. "I expect we'll be firing that fish soon." He held out his hand to Robustelli and then to Egan.

"Sorry about the grease," the chief said.

"No problem," the captain said. "I'm honored to shake the hands of men brave enough to stand here. Why don't you take some of that cough medicine down to the fireroom? I'm sure Simpson could use a little help with his cough too." Arkwright turned and made his way forward toward the bridge.

"Damn! Ain't afraid of nothing, is he?" Robustelli said.

Two days later, just before noon, the *O'Leary* followed the *Ford* and *Pope* through the minefields that protected the western approach to Surabaya. Fraser found it hard to believe that almost two months had passed since first seeing the city. As they steamed toward one of the fueling piers, Fraser was depressed by the scars the Japanese bombers had inflicted upon the beautiful face of Surabaya. The waterfront was dominated by blackened warehouses, and shattered hulks sat alongside many of the piers. The Dutch Naval Club, a handsome building where American naval officers had socialized with their Dutch comrades, had been painted a depressing camouflage gray. Many of the club's windows were broken.

After the *O'Leary* moored alongside a pier, Dirk Jansen met with the *O'Leary*'s officers in the wardroom to expedite arrangements for water and fuel, but he advised them not to expect any parts, ammunition, or food. He also had bad news about their sister destroyer, the *Stewart*. Put in dry dock for repairs to battle damage, she had toppled because of faulty bracing. Japanese bombs had then finished her off.

After Jansen completed his official duties, he talked with Fraser. The Dutch officer's face was creased with lines of fatigue and worry. "This is the last time I will be working with your ship. I have orders to one of our destroyers, the *Kortenaer*."

"The last time I saw her she was aground in the Tjilatjap channel. I hope you bring her better luck," Fraser said. "We'll miss you."

"I expect we'll be operating together against the Japanese in a few days."

Fraser tried to find a more pleasant subject. "Do you know where Ilsa is?"

"Probably at the military hospital. She's working evenings as a nurse's assistant on the same ward with Marta."

"Dirk, what are you going to do about Marta? The Japanese will probably invade Java soon."

Jansen smiled. "Ilsa solved that problem for me. Our wives will be evacuated on one of the next ships taking wounded to Australia."

Fraser took a deep breath and tried to think of what to say to Jansen. "But Marta is almost due with your baby."

"She still has over a month to go. That's all the more reason for her to get out. They could be in Australia in a week," Jansen said.

Fraser finally summoned the courage to explain the probability that Japanese carriers could be operating south of Java in a position to decimate ships heading for Australia.

Jansen groaned. "My God! I must report aboard the *Kortenaer* this afternoon. I don't know if I will have the time to talk this over with Marta. If you have a chance to see her and Ilsa, could you explain the situation? I would appreciate it."

They walked to the quarterdeck where Fraser tried to think of some answer to their mutual problem, but he could find none. Air raid sirens began to wail. The crew of the *O'Leary* bolted to their stations, so the ship could get under way for the safety of open water. Jansen gave Fraser's hand a final grasp and hurried down the brow just before the deck gang shoved it ashore.

As Fraser watched the Dutch officer jog up the pier-side, dodging forklift trucks and native workers, he realized how much he had come to like Jansen and his wife. Fraser hoped they would survive the war. Fraser ran for the fire control platform wondering how much of a chance any of them had.

The air raids continued throughout the afternoon. As dusk neared, the *O'Leary* steamed back to the naval base. As soon as they were secure alongside their pier, Fraser and Laster piled into an ancient taxi and rattled through the streets to the military hospital. They found Bull Durham sitting by his bed, swatting at flies with his crutch. His white pajamas were covered with red hearts.

"Hey, Ross! Doc! Didn't think I'd see you guys again."

Laster smiled. "Nice pajamas."

"A gift from one of my admirers."

After an exchange of news and an account of the *O'Leary*'s experiences, Durham told Fraser Ilsa was working in the ward next door.

"How'd you know where she was?" Fraser asked.

"I know where every good-looking woman in this hospital is."

"I don't doubt it," Laster said.

In the next ward, Fraser found Ilsa taking a thermometer from the mouth of a man swathed in plaster casts. The thermometer fell to the bed and she ran to his arms. Most of the patients applauded.

"It's all right," Fraser said. "We're married."

"It's all right even if you aren't, mate," responded one patient with a thick Australian accent.

Ilsa finally pulled away. "How did you find me?"

"Bull knew where you were. Have you had any trouble with him?"

Ilsa laughed and shook her head. "I haven't, but the nurses say he seems to make better time on one leg than healthy men do on two."

"Nice to hear I'm famous." Durham leaned on his crutches in the doorway. "Nothing's broken but my leg. You two need some time alone." He pulled a key from his bathrobe and flipped it to Fraser with a wink. "That's for the examination room. The doctors don't use it at night."

"How did you get that?" Ilsa asked.

"A resourceful naval officer has his ways. You two can have a good time there without riling all these spectators."

Ilsa took Fraser's hand. "Thank you, Bull. We appreciate your thoughtfulness." She led Fraser to the end of a dim hallway, where Fraser fumbled with the lock in his haste. Ilsa closed the door to the tiny office and locked it.

Fraser smiled. "Just what do you have in mind?"

"Everything we can do during my half-hour break, my Lieutenant. I don't intend to waste this time."

And they didn't.

During a brief lull in the action, they exchanged news.

"My father's been transferred to Admiral Doorman's staff aboard the *De Ruyter*. That should make him happy since he's been so frustrated ashore." Her voice quavered, and she held him tightly. "Now I can look forward to losing you both."

Fraser felt he had to reassure her although he wasn't optimistic. "Come on now. We'll have a go at the Japs and then escape to Australia."

She held him even tighter. "I hope so, because that's where I'm going to be." She pulled away with a determined tilt of her head. "I know that's the only way we have a chance to be together. I've volunteered to go with the next group of wounded they send to Australia. We'll take a train to Tjilatjap and leave by ship. I'm glad you talked me into it."

Fraser was silent. He had to force the words out. "I'm not so sure you should go now," he said softly.

"Of course, I should. Besides, Marta Jansen is going because it's such a good idea. I can't let her go by herself. I promised Dirk I'd look after her."

Fraser felt trapped in a snare of his own making. He tried to explain the danger from the Japanese carriers.

Her green eyes were clear. "Why should I worry about Japanese ships that might not be there. There's no doubt you men will be fighting the Japanese. Who has the better chance?"

Fraser felt powerless to refute her logic, especially since she had become interested in other activities again. "Ilsa, I think you . . . should . . . ohhh . . . ahhhhh . . . God!"

When they finished, he held her and stroked her sandy hair, wondering how the same world could offer so much joy as well as so much pain and anguish. He realized their time was almost up. "All I ask is that you not do anything foolish. If you hear the Jap Fleet is to the south, don't try it. All right?"

She looked at him for several seconds. "Oh, all right. Time for me to get back to work." She rose from the doctor's examining table and buttoned her rumpled white dress. "Don't forget your hat, Lieutenant. I wouldn't want you out of uniform."

"You weren't worried a few minutes ago."

She gave him a lingering kiss. "See you in Australia."

He wished he shared her optimism.

CHAPTER TWENTY-THREE

Well after midnight, Byron Hanlon realized he couldn't sleep. Memories of Maria and Manila wouldn't leave his mind. He crawled out of his bunk and pulled on his pants. He padded softly out of chiefs' quarters and up the ladder to the forecastle, where he sat on a mooring bitt. The decks were silent; all but the essential watchstanders had retired to their bunks. The bow of the ship was at the head of the pier, pointed toward the facilities of the Dutch Naval Base, which were partially obscured by the haze generated by the day's air attack. Wisps of smoke wafted past the ship, and flames flickered in the distance.

"Looks like hell itself," Hanlon muttered.

At the limit of Hanlon's visibility, a figure floated through the gloom toward the ship. It was dressed in Navy dungarees, but Hanlon knew that no enlisted man should have been ashore at that hour. The figure looked familiar, and Hanlon leaned forward for a better look. He had long since discounted his Irish grandmother's tales of leprechauns and spirits, but now he felt a niggling doubt. The approaching form resembled Hank Landry.

The figure halted opposite the bow and looked up. "Is that you, Chief Hanlon?"

"Yes." Hanlon realized Landry was scratching his crotch vigorously. Either Landry's alive, Hanlon thought, or he's got a case of eternal jock itch. Only Mortland deserves that.

"Chief, think there are there any leftovers in the galley? I'm hungry as hell."

Hanlon laughed and stood up. Landry was definitely alive. "If there aren't, I'll cook something myself. Welcome back."

Hanlon met Landry at the quarterdeck where Tim Egan had the watch. "What the hell happened to you?" Egan asked. "We all thought the Japs had you—or the sharks."

Landry's eyes narrowed. "I'd just as soon we don't talk about sharks. I had a bad night in the water. I'd about given up when some *Piet Hein* survivors found me."

"How?" Egan asked. "From what I saw, the poor bastards didn't have time to get any boats or rafts in the water."

"The wind blew our whaleboat over to them."

"I figured that boat of yours was beaten to pieces," Hanlon said.

"It was in bad shape, but it got us to Java. Somebody else jettisoned some gas cans so we had more than enough fuel."

"I hope you realize how lucky you are," Hanlon said.

"Hell," Egan said, "if he had any real luck, he sure wouldn't be back here."

Landry yawned. "Better go get some sleep."

"Gonna be some surprised folks when they see you in the morning," Egan said.

"Jesus, I'd love to hide. Then I could sneak around and haunt Mortland for a few days."

Hanlon had to laugh. "Don't push your luck. I'm sure life with Mortland will be tough enough as it is."

The next day brought more air raids, and Fraser spent most of the morning on the fire control platform. There was a conspicuous addition in the Surabaya roadstead. The *Houston*, the last American cruiser in the region, swung from her anchor, where her 5-inch antiaircraft guns blasted away at the Japanese. Her black bursts blossomed around the high-flying Japanese bombers and disrupted their formations. Many of the bombs were dropped early as the bombers scattered to avoid the *Houston*'s barrage. Columns of water rose all around the proud-looking cruiser, but no bombs hit her.

Fraser heard the *Houston* was using 5-inch ammunition left behind by the damaged *Boise*. There was no evidence of the duds that had plagued the *Houston* several weeks before. Fraser paced back and forth on his fire control platform watching with admiration as the *Houston*'s secondary battery hammered away, her amidships area a mass of smoke and yellow flame.

After the first attack was over, word was passed to make preparations for an Allied sortie scheduled for that evening. When Fraser checked the message board, he found that Japanese invasion forces had been sighted heading south toward Java.

"This is it," Fraser muttered. He knew that unless they could turn the Japanese away, Java was doomed. He wondered if Ilsa had already left. Then he thought of the carriers that might be waiting between Java and Australia. "Damn!" he said softly.

Between attacks, the crew of the destroyer worked to make sure their weapons and equipment were ready for the expected battle. The air attacks continued throughout the afternoon. Fraser swore as one Dutch destroyer was bombed and put out of action. Several merchant ships were sunk or seriously damaged, their burning hulks casting a pall of smoke and gloom over the waiting combatants. Even a Dutch hospital ship was hit despite its large red cross markings. It was obvious that Surabaya's usefulness as a naval base was nearing an end.

Fraser stared at the burning Surabaya waterfront as the last air raid ended. He felt discouraged, depressed, and trapped. The *O'Leary* and her crew seemed to have little chance of surviving.

As they steamed slowly across the harbor, Fraser heard something—the thump of a drum, a soaring trumpet, the bleat of a clarinet. He looked up and saw sailors clustered around the nearby *Houston*'s quarterdeck, where they cheered and clapped as their band broke into "Bugle Call Rag." Fraser felt his spirits lift. Shouts of approval sounded from the *O'Leary*'s decks where men were readying their weapons for the scheduled sortie.

Hell, Fraser thought, these guys aren't giving up—I guess I can't either.

As they passed the *Houston*, Fraser envied the officers aboard the proud heavy cruiser that had carried President Roosevelt on several cruises. She was heavily armed, with a main battery of 8-inch guns in three triple turrets. She also had eight of the 5-inch guns that were effective against enemy aircraft or surface forces. Around her topside were four 1.1-inch quadruple machine gun mounts and several .50-caliber machine guns for short-range air defense.

Fraser knew the *Houston* had problems, too. Her bombed, fire-blackened after turret would never shoot again without major repairs. The *Houston* was eleven years old and lacked some of the recent developments in naval equipment such as radar. Because she had been built under treaty limitations, her armor plating was skimpy, leaving her vulnerable to enemy shells.

Fraser realized that before the war, or even a month ago, he would have given several months pay for a transfer to the *Houston*. As he looked around the *O'Leary*, he realized he wasn't so certain about his feelings now. Besides, the *Houston* would now be the focus of any Japanese attack. If nothing else, the *O'Leary* was a small target.

Fraser looked down as Jack Meredith approached the captain on the bridge wing. "Captain, we've got problems," said Meredith. "Two of the steam line joints in the forward fireroom are starting to leak. I'd guess the vibration from the number two boiler is the culprit there. There's also a problem with one of the main condensers. We need twelve hours for repairs."

"Damn!" Arkwright said. "There's nothing you can do?"

"Sorry, sir. I'm flat out of miracles. There's no way we can steam at high speed tonight. We can be ready to go again tomorrow, but I'm not sure for how long. Number two will probably cause the same problems in the steam lines again."

Fraser realized the engineering plant might have just granted them a stay of execution. The odds facing the defenders of Java seemed that bad.

The wheel of the hatch to the main deck gleamed above T. T. Simpson. He turned the wheel and shoved the hatch back until it clanked against its stop. He pulled himself out into the night breeze, which evaporated some of the sweat from his soaked dungarees. Four of his men followed him out the hatch.

"Buy you guys a cup of coffee before you turn in?" asked Simpson.

"No thanks," one man said. "I'm heading right for my sack."

"Me too," said another.

"At least we got the steam line fixed," Simpson said.

"Sorry we couldn't find the problem with number two," said one of Simpson's helpers.

"I'll find it sooner or later," Simpson said grimly.

As his men headed aft, Simpson stepped into the galley for coffee. Hank Landry was there pouring a cup.

"What are you doing up?" Simpson asked.

"Just got off the midwatch on the quarterdeck."

"Mind shooting the bull for a few minutes?" Simpson asked. "I need to get my mind off that number two boiler. She's driving me crazy."

After Simpson filled a cup with the steaming black liquid, they stood by the life lines in a night breeze scented with the exotic aromas of Java. They talked over their experiences in the Philippines.

"I'd give a lot if they'd just forget this war ever started," Simpson said.

"Yeah, we had a nice life back in Manila," Landry said softly, a faraway look in his black eyes.

"Hey, I'm sorry," Simpson said. "Didn't mean to get you worrying about your girl."

"That's okay."

Simpson noticed the dull ache that had started in his midsection several hours ago now felt worse. "Christ, this coffee is strong tonight. Thanks for talking about old times. At least you stopped me thinking about number two for a few minutes."

"What's the problem?"

Simpson told Landry about the vibration. He recounted how he had carefully examined everything inside the boiler when they'd had it open for repairs two weeks before.

Landry frowned for a few seconds. "Then it must be something outside."

"We just went over every inch of the piping and all the joints tonight."

"Then it must be something you didn't look at," said Landry.

"Something else . . ." Simpson ran his hand across the fringe of hair at the back of his head. "Something else . . . Come on! I need some help."

Simpson led Landry down through the interlocking hatches and into the forward fireroom. Simpson yanked open the tool locker and hauled out an enormous wrench.

"Grab that drop light," Simpson said. "Pass me this stuff when I jump down in the bilges."

"What are you going to do?"

"The boiler stands on four feet—or at least the fittings look like feet. They're bolted to the beams framing the ship's bottom. Could be some of the bolts are loose. Only way to find out is to test each one."

Landry leaned over the edge of the grating. "Whooee—those bilges stink!"

"I'm used to it," Simpson said. "Thank God I pumped them almost dry this morning."

Simpson stepped down off the grating and squirmed along the front corner of the boiler. He slid the wrench under the boiler and onto one of two large nuts. He braced his feet and heaved against the 3-foot wrench. "Unnhhh!" he grunted as the ache in his stomach racheted up a notch. The second nut was just as solid. "Nothing wrong there."

Simpson crawled back along the boiler's edge, dragging the drop light and the wrench after him. The bolts holding the foot at one rear corner were tight, as were those at the other rear corner. His dungarees damp with the greasy slime that coated the bottom plating, Simpson shuffled forward to the other front foot. The pain in his belly was sharp now; it had moved down and to the right.

Simpson looked up where Landry stood on the lower grating. "Hell, I thought you gave me a good idea."

"Still one more corner to go?"

Simpson felt anger well up along with the pain in his belly. "Yeah. Might as well give it a try. I can't think of anything else to do."

Lying on the bottom plates, Simpson played his drop light over the bolts and nuts, which were covered with layers of paint. They didn't look loose. Simpson cursed and flipped his wrench aside where it clattered on the bottom plating.

"Aren't you going to test them?" Landry asked quietly.

"Okay. If it'll make you happy."

Simpson slipped the head of the wrench around one of the nuts, braced his feet against a girder and heaved. His hands jerked back and pain shot through his midsecton. He slammed back against the bottom plating, and his glasses slid off. The wrench bounced off his chest and clanked into the bilges. Simpson grunted with satisfaction and pain.

"You okay?" Landry asked.

"I'll be goddamned," Simpson muttered as he retrieved his glasses with a hand that dripped slime and sweat. Once he could see again, he found his wrench and examined its jaw. "Look at this! The bolt shaft's broken."

"Did you just do it?"

"Hell, I ain't that strong. The paint and rust were holding the bolt head and nut in place. Let me check the other one."

"You don't look so hot. Want me to do it?"

"I'll make it. I been looking for this problem for months. Ain't gonna quit now."

The second nut came off with part of the bolt shaft just as the first had. Simpson ran a blackened finger over the jagged fracture line and held it up for Landry to see.

"Means the foot on this corner was loose so the boiler was free to vibrate. It started vibrating just before I took my swim in Subic Bay."

"Why'd the bolts break?"

Simpson shrugged. "Who knows? Age, corrosion, rust, shooting the guns. Maybe all of those." Simpson reached up and patted the steel under-belly of the boiler. "Sorry, old girl. No wonder you've been a bitch."

Simpson gathered his equipment and Landry grabbed his hand and pulled him up to the lower grating where Simpson sat down, pain stabbing his belly.

"Sure you're okay?" Landry asked.

"Think I'd better go see Doc Laster as soon as I get those new bolts in. I should have figured this out before now. Been so many other damn problems, I just didn't have the time to find it."

"Must be satisfying."

"Yeah. It's a bitch working down here, but there are times like this that make it worth while. I wouldn't trade this for anything—right now."

"How about a good woman?"

"Well, yeah. But only if she was a good dancer." Simpson tried to find a dry piece of sleeve to wipe his forehead.

Landry handed him a clean rag from a nearby bundle.

"Thanks," Simpson said. He unraveled the rag, which turned out to be a pair of women's underpants. "Might be a while before I see a pair of these again."

Landry's tanned face looked sober and his black eyes were distant. "Japs might have something to say about that."

"At least I beat this old bitch of a boiler," Simpson said. "She's been a lot of trouble. Thanks for giving me the clue I needed. Next time we're ashore I'll buy you and your friends a round of drinks. Hell, I'll even buy Mortland a drink, if you ask."

"Not likely."

"Didn't think you would."

As they cruised the Surabaya roadstead during the first air raid the next morning, Fraser looked around at the Dutch and American ships that had returned from their night at sea, having failed to find any Japanese. So much for the *O'Leary*'s stay of execution, thought Fraser. We're ready for the next sortie.

Fraser was surprised to see Laster arrive on the bridge wing below.

"Good morning, Captain," said Laster. "Are we going alongside a pier this morning?"

"We're supposed to refuel as soon as the air raid's over."

"Good. I need to send Simpson to the hospital. Looks like a classic case of appendicitis. He doesn't want to go, but there's no choice. If it ruptures he'll be sick for a long time—if he doesn't die."

"No doubt about your diagnosis?" Arkwright asked.

Laster took off his glasses and wiped them. "It's never 100 percent certain. A white cell count at the hospital will just about clinch it. Simpson has most of the classic signs and symptoms. It's not even a tough call as far as I'm concerned."

"Okay," the captain said. "Send him to the hospital. I'll be down to say good-by and make sure he doesn't give you an argument. You're taking too many of our men, Doc."

"Both men last week were in bad shape—Malaria and a bad skin infection. I'm just doing my job."

"Sorry," the captain said. "I wasn't criticizing you."

Fraser shook his head as he watched Laster go. They were getting thin on men. The *O'Leary* had been forced to transfer almost a dozen men in the last month. Fortunately, they had just picked up some of the *Stewart*'s men as replacements.

"No justice," said a doleful-looking Eckersly next to Fraser. "Simpson gets that boiler fixed so we can go get ourselves killed. Then he gets off here scot-free."

"His chances aren't much better than ours," Fraser said. "If we don't stop the Japs, they'll be ashore soon."

The air raids continued as the Japanese kept pounding Surabaya with high-altitude attacks by twin-engined bombers.

Early that afternoon, Fraser spotted gray shapes entering the harbor from the western channel. He lifted his binoculars and realized the ships weren't American, but they weren't Japanese either. Then he made out the proud flags.

"The British and Aussies are here!" he called down to the bridge wing.

Fraser focused his binoculars on the lead ship and realized he was looking at a legend—the veteran heavy cruiser *Exeter*. She was one of the three cruisers that had defeated the German pocket battleship *Graf Spee* off the coast of South America in 1939. The *Exeter* was small for a heavy cruiser; she mounted only six 8-inch guns in three double turrets. In all other respects, she looked a modern ship of war. Next came the equally proud Australian *Perth*, a modern light cruiser mounting eight 6-inch guns. Three sturdy destroyers followed the cruisers through the minefields.

Those look like fine ships, Fraser thought. Why the hell hasn't our Navy sent any reinforcements?

A signal light began to flash from Admiral Doorman's flagship, the *DeRuyter*. Minutes later a signalman ran up to the captain. Arkwright looked up from the message. "Doorman's holding a pre-sortie conference in an hour. Now that the British are here, maybe we'll stop fooling around."

Arkwright returned from the conference several hours later and sat down at the wardroom table where Fraser and the other officers were gathered. He tossed his hat in his cabin and undid the neck of his high-collared white service uniform. "Hate these formal uniforms—but I didn't want the Limeys to show us up."

Meredith cleared his throat. "Captain, we developed a problem with one of the feed pumps while you were gone, but it should be fixed in an hour."

"Good work," said the captain. "The *Pope* has been forced to sit out this evening's sortie because of an engineering problem."

Fraser found himself envying their sister ship. She'll miss the battle and have a chance to get away, he thought. If Simpson hadn't fixed the number two boiler, we'd have a chance too. Lucky *Pope*.

Arkwright looked around the table. "The ABDA Command has been dissolved. The British and American ships in Surabaya have been put at the disposal of the Dutch. Admiral Doorman aboard the *De Ruyter* is in tactical command."

"How is Doorman going to communicate with us and the British?" asked Meredith, concern in his dark-rimmed eyes.

Arkwright explained a complex setup using liaison officers aboard the Dutch flagship and the use of several radio channels to relay signals. "If all else fails, the flagship will signal by flashing light in English."

There were mutters of disbelief.

Laster shook his head. "Might as well use smoke signals. That system's bound to fall apart in the heat of battle."

Arkwright shrugged. "Doorman's made the best of a bad situation."

"What do we know about the Japs?" Fraser asked.

Arkwright's fingers tightened around the brass ashtray in front of him. "At least two invasion forces are heading south to Java. Each group is escorted by cruisers and destroyers. Admiral Doorman plans to attack the eastern group tonight and break through to the transports. After we dispose of them, we'll head west for the other force."

Laster rattled his cup of tea. "And then we'll steam up to Tokyo Bay and accept the Japanese surrender."

The corners of Arkwright's mouth rose. "We may decide to wait on that until next week." Arkwright outlined Doorman's battle plans. Their formation that night would have the British and Dutch destroyers screening ahead of the column of cruisers. The American destroyers would follow in a column at the rear. If they found the Japanese, the lead destroyers would immediately head for the transports and attack with guns and torpedoes. The cruisers were supposed to stand off and inflict as much damage as possible with their guns. The American four-stackers would sneak in and use their torpedoes after the other destroyers were clear.

"What if there's a daylight battle tomorrow?" asked Fraser.

"In that case, we can expect a long-range gun battle," continued Arkwright. "Our American destroyers are to stay on the disengaged side of the cruiser line until we're ordered to make a torpedo attack."

Laster blew out a large smoke ring. "As good a plan as any under the circumstances. We'd better hope for a night battle. A general melee in the dark might give us a chance."

Arkwright frowned. "Our experience at Balikpapan would support that idea, but after Badung Strait, it looks like the Japs might be excellent night fighters."

Meredith lowered his coffee cup with a thin hand. "Captain, what did you make of Admiral Doorman and the British."

"I know we disagreed with Doorman's tactics at Badung Strait, but I found the admiral a thoughtful man. He was aware of all the engineering problems and will attempt to accommodate them. He was well organized and prepared, but a trifle optimistic. He suggested we might get some air support."

There was a chorus of coughs and snorts.

"Having trouble swallowing that one?" Arkwright looked down the table and continued. "The Dutch are ready to defend Java to the last ship and man. The British captains seemed equally determined."

"How about our torpedoes?" Steiner asked. "Are we going to set them for straight fire like we've been doing?"

Arkwright nodded. "Straight fire—that would be best for a melee tonight. For a daylight attack against the enemy battle line, we'll have to fire off one side, change course, and fire off the other side."

Fraser shook his head as he thought of all the hours they'd spent before the war practicing straight-ahead attacks using 30-degree firing offsets for the torpedoes. He realized many of the techniques practiced for gunfire also had been discarded in the heat of battle.

Steiner's broad face paled. "That type of torpedo attack against a main force will make us a lot more vulnerable to counter fire."

The captain didn't even blink. "Next question?"

Fraser remembered the account he had heard of the captain using the sledge on the torpedo warhead. He suspected part of the captain would like nothing better than making a torpedo attack in the teeth of enemy fire.

Arkwright cleared up some other problems and finally looked around the table. "Any further questions? Then let's get to work. This is going to be the biggest battle at sea since Jutland in 1916."

"Maybe we'll be famous after tomorrow," Steiner said.

Laster shook his head. "Yeah, just like General Custer."

CHAPTER TWENTY-FOUR

Fraser paced the bridge early that evening as the Allied force weighed anchor for the sortie. The Surabaya roadstead bustled as ships exchanged signals and jockeyed for their assigned stations for departure.

"Look at the *De Ruyter!*" the captain said next to Fraser on the bridge wing.

The Dutch flagship's whistle shrieked five short blasts, the danger signal, and water boiled under her stern as she backed down to avoid a tug and barge. Despite her maneuvering, the cruiser hit the barge and capsized it. The scene was punctuated by frantic toots of ships' whistles, flashing lights, and fluttering signal flags as ships tried to avoid more collisions.

"Christ! What a Chinese fire drill!" Arkwright said as the *De Ruyter* backed away from the wreckage of the barge.

Fraser leaned wearily on the bridge wing and wondered how the Allies would ever be able to fight the Japanese. He remembered that Ilsa's father was aboard the *De Ruyter* as a member of Admiral Doorman's staff. "I'll bet Captain Van Dorn isn't happy about that mess," he told Arkwright.

"A hell of a way to start things off," muttered the captain.

By the time the Allied ships steamed clear of the minefields, the last light had faded. The five cruisers and their escorting destroyers aligned themselves into the prescribed night-attack formation. Fraser hauled himself up to the fire control platform as the rest of the crew manned their general quarters stations.

Admiral Doorman turned the Allied force to the east, paralleling the long coast of Madura Island. The calm Java Sea was illuminated by a bright moon only a few days short of full. Thousands of stars added their light from the cloudless sky. Fraser knew they would have no trouble seeing the invasion force if it were out there, but springing a surprise attack seemed out of the question. The Japanese were coming; the only question was where along the 600-mile northern coast of Java would they land? Fraser realized they might as well be trying to defend the American coast from San Diego to San Francisco.

As the evening wore on, Fraser maintained his vigil even though his eyelids kept drooping. His body ached, and he tried to ease his throbbing feet by shifting his weight from one to the other. Only the prospect of action kept him going. As he searched the dark horizon, he knew the night was just beginning.

The hours ground on, minute by minute. There was no sign of the enemy as they continued to steam east. An hour after midnight, Doorman reversed course. After more hours of searching, they passed Surabaya off their port beam just before daybreak.

Beside Fraser, Eckersly kept nodding off and catching himself with a start. "I'm so damn beat, Mr. Fraser."

"Could be worse. Most of the other ships spent a night out here while we were getting fixed." Fraser's voice felt thick with fatigue.

"Those guys can't feel any worse than I do," Eckersly said. "Wish the Japs'd hurry up."

There was no invasion force to be found. Daylight brought occasional Japanese bombers that pestered the Allied force. The ships with modern antiaircraft weapons responded with a spirited defense, which seemed to discourage the Japanese, who failed to do any damage.

At mid-morning, Doorman ordered his force to turn back toward Surabaya for refueling and replenishment of antiaircraft ammunition. Early that afternoon, as another air raid threatened, Fraser focused his binoculars on the channel to Surabaya. Three days had passed since he'd seen Ilsa. He wondered if she'd left for Tjilatjap and the voyage to Australia. Fraser swung his binoculars to the sturdy Dutch destroyer *Kortenaer* steaming nearby and felt comforted, knowing that Dirk Jansen was returning, too. The Dutch officer would know how to find out about their wives.

While they were in the channel to Surabaya, the *De Ruyter* wheeled out of line and reversed course with her wake churning. A light flashed a message to the rest of the force.

A signalman ran forward to the bridge wing and handed the captain the message form. Arkwright read it aloud as Fraser peered over the rail. " 'Follow me. The enemy is ninety miles away.' " Arkwright looked up at Fraser. "Looks like we finally got good reconnaissance information. So much for refueling. We won't need much fuel if the Japs are that close."

Fraser knew Doorman had just made a tough decision. That's what admirals get paid for, Fraser said to himself.

Like firemen responding to an alarm, the Allied ships turned and followed the flagship out the channel. Once in clear water, they scrambled into the daylight battle formation that Doorman had prescribed the day before. The three modern British destroyers raced ahead into screening positions several miles in front of the cruiser column. The two Dutch destroyers lagged off to port, barely able to keep up because of engineering problems. The five old American destroyers brought up the rear in a column, with the *Edwards* leading the *Alden*, *Ford*, *Jones*, and *O'Leary*.

Fraser watched the line of cruisers as they steamed into the open waters of the Java Sea. They were a mixed lot, the results of different eras and philosophies of naval design. Leading the column was the unusual-looking but graceful *De Ruyter*. Her 6-inch armament was arranged unconventionally: one twin turret on the forecastle, an open single mount just below the bridge, and two twin turrets aft. Her single smokestack resembled a tall, squared-off mushroom. Modern twin Bofors 40-millimeter antiaircraft guns were clustered in a circular array amidships.

Second in line, the British heavy cruiser *Exeter* was a sensible-looking result of a no-nonsense school of naval architecture. Built in the early 1930s, her squared-off lines were trim and efficient-looking. Her smart appearance expressed the solid competence of her crew. The *Exeter*'s only obvious weakness was having but six guns in her 8-inch main battery.

At the middle of the line, the American heavy cruiser *Houston* had a more rakish look, as if embodying the flamboyant attitudes of her country of origin. The largest of the cruisers, she had a pointed clipper bow. Two bulky triple 8-inch turrets just forward of the bridge gave her a broad-shouldered look.

Next came the Australian light cruiser *Perth*. She was an obvious relative of the larger *Exeter* and looked equally crisp and competent. Her 6-inch guns were arranged in four twin turrets, which were training and elevating as their crews tested them for battle.

Last in column was the other Dutch light cruiser, *Java*. Stout and elderly looking, she had a low bridge and two thick stacks. Her 6-inch main battery was scattered about the ship in old-fashioned single mounts. The *Java* seemed a stately dowager, serving as a chaperone for the younger, flashier cruisers.

Fraser frowned as he realized the smaller-gunned light cruisers weren't grouped so they could maneuver separately from the longer-shooting heavy cruisers.

Fraser searched each Allied cruiser for catapult-launched observation aircraft. Cruisers usually carried several, but there were none to be seen. Fraser leaned over the rail. "Captain, where are our scout planes?"

Arkwright looked up. "They were off-loaded yesterday because a night battle was expected."

Fraser leaned back and thought about that decision. Aboard in battle, the planes were a fire hazard. An enemy shell could turn one into a flaming beacon, a disaster in a night battle. A spotting plane aloft in a daylight battle, however, was an invaluable asset. If the Japanese had planes aloft, they'd have a tremendous advantage.

With no enemy yet in sight, Arkwright had the cooks pass out sandwiches and coffee. Fraser munched on a dry Spam sandwich as the Allied formation steamed doggedly to the northwest.

An occasional Japanese plane darted out of the partial cloud cover to release its bomb load in the face of vigorous Allied antiaircraft fire. The Allied formation was once thrown into disarray, but the Japanese attacks were otherwise unsuccessful. As he searched the sky, Fraser noted three specks trailing the Allied ships. Bulky floats underneath the wings and fuselages indicated the trailers were spotting planes from Japanese cruisers or battleships nearby.

Almost two hours after the force left the channel to Surabaya, one of the British destroyers 3 miles ahead was surrounded by white shell splashes. She turned about, heading for the protection of the main body with her signal light winking a report of what she had discovered on the horizon.

A signalman ran up to Arkwright. "Captain, the *Electra* reports, 'One cruiser, unknown number of large destroyers.' "

Fraser told himself there'd be a lot more where those came from. He looked at his watch—1615. They had less than three hours before dark. Fraser wondered if it would be smarter to avoid action and tackle the Japanese at night, when the smaller Allied force might be able to capitalize on enemy confusion as they had at Balikpapan. Certainly the four-stackers would be best employed in a sneak torpedo attack on the Japanese transports. But Fraser realized there was a problem with that idea; the destroyers' fuel was running low. Some quick calculations told him they had another ten hours of high-speed steaming at best.

The *O'Leary*'s blowers whined louder as the Allied force increased speed to 26 knots. Doorman appeared determined to answer the critics who had complained that he lacked aggressiveness on previous sorties. Fraser hoped Doorman wasn't going to do anything foolish just to redeem his reputation.

Mortland's voice crackled in the earpiece over Fraser's right ear. "Two big ships off the starboard bow—battleships or heavy cruisers!"

Fraser swung his binoculars just to the left of the first group of Japanese ships and spotted puffs of smoke marking enemy gunfire to the north. Pagoda-like masts of the Japanese heavy ships were rising over the horizon. They had obviously seen the Allied cruiser line because their first salvos blasted geysers just short of the *Exeter* and *Houston*.

The forward 8-inch turrets of both Allied heavy cruisers were trained toward the enemy and the gun barrels elevated for maximum range—about 14 miles. Minutes later, the *Exeter* belched clouds of cordite smoke from her forward guns. The booming reverberation took almost three seconds to cross the half-mile that separated the American destroyers from the cruiser line. The *Exeter*'s after turret was unable to bear on the two enemy ships which were just off the starboard bow of the Allied column.

The *Houston* followed with plumes of yellow flame from her forward guns, her after turret silent because it was still a shambles from the bomb hit sustained weeks before. The *Houston*'s smokeless powder produced only a light haze of brown smoke, a contrast to the billowing clouds of cordite smoke that poured from the *Exeter*'s guns.

"Them two big Japs look like heavy cruisers," reported Mortland over the phone circuit.

Fraser focused his binoculars on the two large Japanese ships whose bridges were now visible above the horizon. Scarlet spouts leaped high in front of the second Japanese cruiser. Fraser deduced the red-dyed columns of water belonged to the *Houston* because of the salvo pattern—two sets of three. It looked as if the ocean itself was sending up fountains of blood. Fraser squeezed his binoculars. "Come on! We need some quick hits!"

Fraser scanned the panorama in front of him. He was perfectly situated to watch the battle. He had little to distract him because the American destroyers were steaming on the disengaged side of the cruisers with no Japanese within range.

Damn! Fraser said to himself. Admiral Doorman was in a difficult tactical situation. He needed to head toward the enemy to bring the Japanese heavies within gun range of his light cruisers. But if Doorman steered his cruiser column at the enemy, the

Japanese would be in position to cross the Allies' "T." Fraser recalled his tactics lessons at the Naval Academy. Crossing the "T" was the dream of naval tacticians. The force at the top of the "T" could fire all its weapons down the length of the opposing column, which was handicapped because it could not respond with its after guns. Also, long and short shots still had a chance to hit a ship other than the intended target.

"If only Doorman could maneuver the light cruisers separately," Fraser muttered. But he knew it was too late to rearrange the formation. As a consequence, the *Perth* and the two Dutch cruisers were wasted because there were no targets within their range.

Fraser remembered that the famous naval battles had always seemed so clear back at the Naval Academy. Simple marks on the blackboard had represented ships or whole formations. Instead of the dry aroma of chalk dust, Fraser now smelled the biting tang of gunsmoke drifting down from the cruiser line. Fraser grabbed the steel rail in front of him. It wasn't a chalky abstraction. It was sun-baked metal and hot to his touch. The hands on the rail were his—the same hands that had caressed Ilsa. A single enemy shell could turn those hands and his whole body into hamburger. Abstract concepts had been replaced by the reality of life—and death.

The Japanese concentrated their fire on the two Allied heavy cruisers and the *De Ruyter*, the flagship. The towering Japanese shell splashes rose slowly, almost as if in slow motion, hung suspended, and collapsed back to the surface of the sea. There were ten splashes in each tightly grouped salvo, indicating the Japanese ships had twenty 8-inch guns compared with the Allies' twelve.

The Allied cruiser line steamed on, seemingly unperturbed by the accuracy of the enemy fire, but a more careful look revealed that the individual cruisers were weaving slightly about their assigned stations to throw off the Japanese aim.

The *Exeter* and *Perth* had unfurled oversized national flags from their masts, a British tradition dating from the earliest days of sail. Watching the huge flags whip in the breeze, Fraser was stirred by the sight as he realized that similar battles at sea had taken place for centuries. It occurred to him that this might be one of the last daylight gun battles, now that aircraft had apparently changed the nature of naval war.

The *Houston* seemed to dominate the Allied battle line. She was the biggest of the Allied ships, and her partially mechanized guns fired at the enemy about every ten seconds, almost twice as often as any of the other cruisers. Fraser knew it had to be difficult for the *Houston*'s gun crews to load their 250-pound projectiles and bulky powder bags in the heat. Conditions in the gun turrets were probably getting worse than those in the engineering spaces.

Fraser was suddenly thankful he was out in the breeze. Even so, his throat was parched. He took his canteen out of the holder on his belt and downed several swallows of aluminum-flavored water. It wasn't much, but it moistened his throat. He realized he was hungry and nearly exhausted. Fraser blinked his eyes to clear the fatigue. Knowing it would be a long time before he could close his eyes for more than a few seconds, he took a deep breath and concentrated on the scene around him.

The opposing forces were headed to the west on roughly parallel courses. Doorman was edging to the north, working his battle line closer to the enemy so his light cruisers could join the action. One of his light cruisers, the proud Australian *Perth*, had to endure consecutive straddles—near-misses from the same salvo, slamming into the sea both long and short.

"A hell of a waste of a fine ship," Fraser muttered. He knew the frustration of having to remain a mere spectator, but he was thankful that the *O'Leary* wasn't under similar fire.

Fraser winced as a sheet of sparks burst from the forecastle of the *De Ruyter* indicating that she had been hit; there was no explosion, so the Japanese shell had been a dud. The flagship plowed ahead, apparently unaffected. The other Allied cruisers were straddled again and again by enemy salvos but remained magically untouched.

Fraser scanned the sky. The Japanese spotting planes orbited the Allies like huge vultures, in perfect position to radio the results of each salvo back to their cruisers. The airborne spotters had better angles and could maneuver to avoid the gun smoke that often obscured the view from sea level. Fraser knew the spotting planes gave the Japanese cruisers a tremendous advantage, one the Allies could ill-afford to concede.

"Mr. Fraser! Aircraft off the port bow!" Eckersly reported.

Fraser swung his binoculars around, fearing the worst. "Okay! Those are ours!" The aircraft in the distance were a small flight of Allied bombers escorted by more than a half-dozen P-40s. If one of the fighters came to their assistance, it would make short work of the ungainly Japanese spotting aircraft. But the fighters flew on, obviously unaware that they could affect the battle.

"Damn! Damn! Damn!" Fraser hammered the rail in front of him as the friendly aircraft droned on their way.

Mortland's voice boomed in his earpiece. "Jap destroyers approaching just forward of the starboard beam! Looks like a torpedo attack!"

Fraser lifted his binoculars and found the enemy heavy cruisers and the first light cruiser and her eight destroyers. He swung aft of the first two groups. There! Another six destroyers led by a light cruiser. Fraser realized the Japanese now outmatched the Allies in all but light cruisers. The Japanese had the advantage in heavy guns, and their destroyers were not only more numerous but heavier and more modern.

The upperworks of the advancing Japanese destroyers stood out on the horizon in chilling detail. Their laid-back stacks gave the impression that they were going faster than the 30-plus knots they were probably making. After a few minutes, Fraser could make out the six destroyers clearly; sheets of white water flew back from their flared bows.

The Japanese were led by an old light cruiser that looked identical to the one that had nearly caught the *O'Leary* at Balikpapan. The first of her four funnels was taller than the others, and the third was almost twice as thick. The bridge reared high above the main deck, and the cruiser's guns were scattered about the upper decks in single mounts. The Japanese cruiser looked as if it had been assembled from a warehouse of leftover parts.

"Ugly bastard," Fraser said.

The Japanese pressed implacably onward, closing the range to under 10 miles. The Allied light cruisers hammered away at the approaching Japanese, their defensive fire rapid and accurate. Towering white splashes rose all around the enemy.

Fraser fidgeted nervously as he realized the torpedo attack could decimate the Allied force. He watched the Japanese, hoping that the Allied gunfire would reduce the enemy numbers before they fired torpedoes. One Japanese destroyer took a hit and faltered for a moment, but it rejoined the attack. In another minute, at a range of about 8 miles, the Japanese began their launch. The sun glinted off the silvery Japanese torpedoes as they left their tubes and hit the water with huge splashes. One by one, the Japanese attackers wheeled away and began spewing heavy black smoke from their stacks. The smoke swirled between the battle lines, intermittently obscuring the Japanese heavy cruisers and complicating the Allied job of spotting the fall of shot.

Fraser realized Admiral Doorman now had a serious problem: he needed to maneuver his ships out of the path of the oncoming torpedoes, but that would disrupt the fire of his heavy cruisers. The Allies could ill afford that loss because they were desperate for some hits on the Japanese cruisers.

"Torpedoes should arrive in about ten more minutes," Chief Jablonski shouted from the pilothouse.

The *De Ruyter* plowed straight ahead. Arkwright pounded the bridge rail. "Why doesn't he turn?"

"Maybe communications problems," Chuck Steiner said, next to the captain.

Arkwright said, "If he doesn't turn soon to evade those torpedoes, he'll be communicating with Saint Peter."

Fraser had to agree with the captain's assessment. He could almost feel the tension around him as the minutes ticked away. Arkwright again banged his fist on the bulwark.

"Three minutes," Jablonski called.

With only two minutes remaining before the expected arrival of the torpedoes, the *De Ruyter* heeled over in a sharp turn away from the enemy. Some of the cruisers astern tried to follow in column, but others turned to parallel the *De Ruyter*. The maneuver was not neat, but it took the large ships out of the way of the oncoming threat, but not before Fraser spotted torpedo wakes nearby. As the destroyers turned away, Fraser let a low whistle of relief escape from his compressed lips.

"Jesus!" Eckersly pointed to the south.

Two miles away, a towering column of water hung in the air. Ten seconds later there was another. Fraser was puzzled by the enormous random explosions that continued in the same area.

Minutes later, Doorman turned his ships back to the west to parallel the Japanese again. The opposing heavy cruisers continued to slug it out with long-range salvos from their big guns. Fraser winced as salvo after salvo straddled the *Perth*, but she was undamaged. The *Java* and the *Houston* were not so lucky; they suffered hits but continued steaming in line, their fighting ability unimpaired. As more salvos rained down, Fraser gave up trying to count how many times the Allied cruisers had been straddled by shell splashes. With the gun battle over a half-hour old, he knew the Allies were lucky not to have suffered any major hits.

Fraser was hard pressed to judge the effect of the Allies' fire on the two Japanese heavy cruisers. For a while, the second Japanese heavy cruiser appeared to be on fire aft and turned away from the action. However, she returned to the fray a few minutes later and began to belch regular salvos at the Allies again with no evident loss in her fighting power.

Fraser trained his binoculars aft of the last cruiser in the Allied line. He was amazed how quickly the sea had begun to repair the ravages of the boiling wakes and the towering splashes that had ripped the surface. Aside from some white water and a few pockets of bubbles, there was little to indicate the violence that had roiled the Java Sea. When Fraser looked farther astern, the gently rolling ocean seemed to have completely healed its wounds.

Fraser lowered his binoculars and turned back to the Allied cruisers. It seemed as if he were watching a heavyweight boxing match where the fighters traded blow after blow but failed to stagger each other with a vital punch.

Suddenly, heavy black smoke and clouds of white steam billowed from the *Exeter* amidships, engulfing her proud battle flags. The British cruiser slowed and sheered out of the battle line to port. The cruisers behind the *Exeter* heeled over and imitated her turn, leaving the *De Ruyter* the only cruiser still steaming to the west along with the British destroyers. The Dutch and American destroyers were now in the path of the turning cruisers. There was no time for coordinated maneuvering.

"Left full rudder!" Arkwright shouted as the menacing steel bows of four Allied cruisers pointed their way. The *O'Leary* and the other destroyers scampered for safety.

"Torpedoes astern!" Mortland shouted from the crow's nest just as they settled on a southerly course. "One approaching the starboard quarter."

Arkwright leaned out over the wing and peered aft. He responded immediately. "Left full rudder!"

Seconds passed before the *O'Leary*'s rudder bit and finally began to swing the ship. "Rudder amidships!" Arkwright ordered. "Steady as you go."

The destroyer paralleled the torpedo, which was rapidly overtaking them.

Hank Landry slipped out of the pointer's seat on his 4-inch gun and watched the torpedo lance toward the stern. "Shit! That bastard's gonna be close."

Even though the *O'Leary* was doing over 26 knots, the torpedo overhauled them quickly. "Must be doing 45 knots," Chief Hanlon said calmly at Landry's shoulder.

The torpedo slid along the starboard side not more than 15 yards away. Its unpainted steel body and churning counterrotating propellers flashed by in the cobalt-blue water.

"That baby ain't leaving a bubble wake like ours do," Landry said, realizing the Japanese weapon was much bigger than any American torpedo he had ever seen.

"That was close," Hanlon said as the torpedo pulled ahead and cleared the bow.

A nearby Dutch destroyer erupted with a tremendous explosion that hurled debris high. The men around Landry's gun cursed as the shattered Dutch destroyer broke in two, and the stern section went down quickly. Part of the up-thrust bow section remained above the surface like a grave marker planted in the ground. Several men from the forward gun mount hung by the life lines high above the water. One waved at the Americans just before he fell.

Landry shuddered and raised his arm in an admiring salute. "Poor bastards! I hope they get picked up."

"Could have been us," Hanlon said softly.

A few miles to the south, another huge explosion blasted a geyser of water high in the air. Then another and another. The single columns of water were much bigger than those thrown up by the Japanese cruiser shells.

"What the hell are those?" Landry asked. "Battleship shells?"

Hanlon frowned under his gray helmet. "A battleship would be shooting salvos. Those must be the Jap torpedoes blowing up at the end of their runs."

Landry felt relieved that the explosions weren't from a Japanese battleship. That was the last thing they needed. He remembered the torpedo that had passed only yards away. If it had reached the end of its run alongside, it would have blown in the side of the *O'Leary*.

Landry's sense of relief quickly changed to irritation. "Dammit! When are we going to do something? I'm tired of watching."

Hanlon nodded toward the bow of the Dutch destroyer as it finally slid under. "Don't be too eager."

Fraser felt a wave of nausea as he watched the bow section of the *Kortenaer* disappear. Dirk Jansen had joined the ship only days before. There weren't many survivors in the water, so Fraser feared the worst had happened to his friend. He remembered his wedding and how Dirk and Marta had seemed so content together in the garden. Fraser lifted his binoculars and tried to find Jansen, but even with binoculars, the heads in the water were nothing but oil-stained dots.

The Allied formation had disintegrated. A few of the Allied destroyers scurried around apparently looking for submarines because there was no obvious source for the torpedoes that had just arrived. Admiral Doorman turned the *De Ruyter* and the British destroyers around and joined the other ships steaming in a southerly direction, away from the enemy.

"Look at that," muttered Fraser, as the *Perth* charged to the aid of the lagging *Exeter*. The Australian cruiser was making about 30 knots with her battle flags streaming in the breeze. Her main battery fired at Japanese destroyers that were closing in for the kill on the *Exeter* like a pack of jackals. Black smoke billowed from the *Perth*'s stacks as she passed the *Exeter*, screening the damaged British cruiser.

A flashing light winked on the *De Ruyter*'s signal bridge. " 'All ships follow me,' " a signalman reported.

The Allied cruisers and destroyers maneuvered in ragged disorder, trying to regain their positions. Doorman headed in a southeasterly direction, keeping his milling force between the *Exeter* and the enemy. There was a flurry of blinking lights between the flagship and the crippled British cruiser. The signal gang relayed the information to the bridge wing, telling the captain that the *Exeter* could only make 15 knots. Doorman's final signal ordered the British cruiser back to Surabaya. When Fraser overheard the last messages, he realized the Allies had just lost half their 8-inch guns.

Fraser lifted his binoculars and tried to find the enemy on the smoke-swept seascape. The Japanese heavy cruisers had closed and turned to the east, paralleling the Allied line, and it was obvious that the enemy destroyers were gathering for another torpedo attack.

Doorman ordered the three British destroyers to counterattack, although they were widely separated. The *Electra* in the lead, the British turned smartly and charged into the smoke that swirled between the opposing forces. A series of brief but furious exchanges of gunfire echoed through the smoke.

"Those Limeys ain't afraid of anything," Eckersly said.

Only the *Jupiter* and the *Encounter* returned from their mission on the other side of the wall of smoke. A rift in the gray curtain revealed the shattered hulk of the sinking *Electra*. The two surviving British destroyers joined the Dutch destroyer *Witte de With* guarding the withdrawal of the *Exeter*. Whenever a Japanese ship poked through the smoke looking for the crippled cruiser, it was turned back by the hot defensive fire of the destroyers.

When Doorman completed the reorganization of his remaining ships, he ordered the two surviving British destroyers to rejoin him as the Allies continued steaming eastward. The formation approached the wall of smoke that separated it from the Japanese. The wisps of dirty gray smoke enveloped the *O'Leary* briefly, and then she burst into the clear. The cruisers reengaged the enemy as the sun neared the horizon on the smoky sea scape. The Allies were now minus the guns of the *Exeter*, and the *Houston*'s rate of fire was diminished, indicating a low ammunition supply or exhausted gun crews.

The Japanese responded with accurate gunfire, again assisted by their spotting planes. When Japanese torpedo launchings were spotted, Doorman turned his ships south and avoided disaster. The *O'Leary* and her sisters doggedly followed the cruiser column in its maneuvers. After the turn south, a signal lamp winked on the *De Ruyter*'s bridge.

Arkwright looked back toward the signal bridge. "What did he say?"

" 'Counterattack,' sir," a signalman yelled over the angry rumble of the battle.

Immediately, signal flags ordering a torpedo attack leaped to the yardarm of the lead American destroyer, the *Edwards*, which turned to lead the column on its mission.

The *De Ruyter* began to flash additional signals at the American destroyers. The signalmen gave rapid-fire reports to the captain. " 'Cancel counterattack. Make smoke.' " Then, " 'Cover my retirement.' "

Fraser shook his head, wondering exactly what Admiral Doorman was ordering them to do. Commander Thomas Binford, the American destroyer commander, evidently decided the conflicting signals justified a continuation of the torpedo attack. The earlier signal hoist was repeated by the *Edwards*, which steamed on toward the enemy.

Arkwright looked up at Fraser and nodded his head grimly. "Better do something before we run out of fuel."

Fraser's mouth went dry as he realized their long wait for a role in the battle had ended. The American destroyers had been little more than spectators. However, they weren't heading for a crack at the fat transports; they were steaming directly at the two Japanese heavy cruisers. Fraser's knees felt weak as he realized just one 8-inch shell could blow the heart out of the *O'Leary*.

The five obsolete American destroyers raced north toward the enemy cruisers, which were about 10 miles away and still outside the 8-mile range of the American torpedoes. The *O'Leary* vibrated and shook as she strained to maintain her position at the end of the column; her blowers whined at a higher pitch as they revved up near their maximum speed to force more air into the boilers.

Eckersly hunched his shoulders and his eyes were wide under his helmet. "Listen to those shells!"

Fraser shared the talker's amazement. The destroyers were steaming between the two battle lines, and salvos from both sides rumbled overhead like flights of berserk freight trains. Fraser looked up and caught the flash of a salvo of projectiles. He also saw Mortland clutching the metal rim of the crow's nest as he peered through his binoculars. As a salvo roared over, the boatswain ducked. Fraser realized that Mortland, tough as he was, must feel fear too.

Gun smoke and remnants of smoke screens swirled across the water, temporarily obscuring the sight of both friend and foe. Despite the limited visibility, the little American ships raced on at 28 knots toward the enemy. While they were engulfed by a dense patch of smoke, two of the destroyers ahead in the column almost collided in the choking gray haze. When they emerged from the smoke, the two destroyers maneuvered smartly and regained their proper stations for the attack.

Fraser let out a long breath. "Close! No place for a collision."

He looked down where Chuck Steiner crouched behind the torpedo director on the starboard wing of the bridge. Fraser suddenly remembered the torpedoes were set for straight fire; they wouldn't be able to fire simultaneously off both sides while heading directly at the enemy. He groaned as he realized they would have to turn almost broadside to the enemy twice, a dangerous maneuver. Fraser tried not to think how vulnerable they were going to be.

Onward steamed the destroyers, apparently unnoticed by the enemy. Fraser realized that both the success of the attack and their survival depended on the judgement of Commander Binford, riding the *Edwards* at the head of the column. Binford would have to weigh the situation and decide when to launch their weapons. Their chances of hitting the enemy cruisers would be better in close. If they waited too long, enemy fire might hammer the fragile destroyers to pieces before they could launch their torpedoes, wasting the weapons, the ships, and many of the men who manned them. Fraser gritted his teeth as the range decreased.

The captain stood on the wing below, staring out at the two enemy cruisers, which were growing closer every second. Fraser felt like Arkwright's will was pulling the *O'Leary* toward a destiny that part of the captain's mind craved.

The two identical Japanese heavy cruisers, which had been distant specks on the horizon for so much of the day, were growing ever larger in Fraser's binoculars. He focused on the leading one. Like the modern Japanese destroyers, it was a rakish-looking ship with a high flared bow and a tall bridge. The funnels were tilted back, and the front one was twice as thick. Plumes of yellow flame leaped from the cruiser's main battery of 8-inch guns, which were mounted in five twin turrets with three on the forecastle.

Fraser realized they had closed to about 8 miles—the maximum range for their Mark VIII torpedoes. How much longer would they wait before firing? Two more minutes passed and Fraser estimated they were down to 7 miles. An enemy salvo blasted water into the sky a half-mile ahead. They had finally been spotted. It wouldn't be much longer before the full fury of the Japanese defenses was turned on them.

Ahead, the *Edwards* heeled as she turned to port. She waited until the others had followed in her wake, and then signalled the order to launch the starboard torpedoes.

"Salvo fire! Fire one! Fire three! Fire Five! Fire seven! Fire nine! Fire eleven!" Steiner shouted into his microphone.

The last of the six starboard torpedoes splashed into the water and headed toward the Japanese. The destroyer column followed the *Edwards* around to starboard to unmask the port tubes. As Fraser waited for the second phase of their attack, the Japanese reacted to the American attack. Projectiles of different calibers began smashing into the water around the old destroyers, threatening to tear the fragile ships apart. Fraser flinched as the shells arrived, but he spotted a Japanese destroyer that was almost in range of their 4-inch guns. "Get on that destroyer to port!" he told the director crew.

Fraser took another look in his binoculars. It was still too far for their 4-inch guns. He watched the enemy's forward 5-inch mount swivel toward the *O'Leary*. The guns elevated and then belched yellow flame. Fraser hunched his shoulders and waited for the salvo to arrive. Shells screamed overhead and exploded 500 yards to starboard. Fraser realized he was holding his breath, and he gulped for air. Another flash from the Japanese destroyer.

"On target!" reported the pointer and trainer.

"Crank in our maximum range!" Fraser told the computer operator.

"I have a solution."

"Captain says go ahead and open fire at your discretion," the bridge talker said in Fraser's earpiece.

"Match pointers!" Fraser ordered.

"Pointers matched!" Eckersly said.

"Rapid salvo fire! Commence firing! Commence firing!" Fraser shouted.

The *O'Leary*'s 4-inch guns went off with a jolting roar, and some of Fraser's fear seemed to evaporate. Red splashes leaped up short of the enemy. "Stay at maximum range!" Fraser ordered. More salvos blasted out. There was an orange flash as the Japanese destroyer charged right into the *O'Leary*'s fourth salvo. The Japanese destroyer heeled over in a sharp turn and vanished into a patch of smoke while the *O'Leary*'s gun crews cheered.

By then the last of their port torpedoes had leaped into the sea. The *Edwards* had already turned to starboard, away from the enemy. Each of the other destroyers turned in succession to follow in her wake. The *Jones*, just ahead of the *O'Leary*, was just clearing the turning point when an avalanche of enemy shells burst behind her, obliterating the swirl of water that her turn generated.

"Left full rudder!" barked Arkwright.

"Left full rudder," echoed the surprised-sounding helmsman. "The rudder is left full, sir."

Slowly the bow of the *O'Leary* began to swing north toward the Japanese cruisers as the other American destroyers headed to the southeast and safety. Fraser's legs felt rubbery. His worst fears seemed to be coming true; Arkwright was turning toward the enemy and sure destruction.

Suddenly, the sea exploded in the set of wakes they had just left. The turning point that each destroyer had used in succession was ripped by a series of salvos. A few long shots plowed up the sea nearby. Fraser swallowed as he realized the captain's maneuver had just saved them from obliteration.

The *O'Leary*'s bow continued to swing inexorably toward the enemy cruisers. Arkwright stared out toward the ships that were still blasting salvos at the Allied main body. Fraser tensed, knowing part of Arkwright probably wanted to head right at the enemy. Arkwright straightened as the bow neared the bearing of the enemy cruisers. Fraser waited for the order that would stop the swing and send them at the enemy.

The captain remained silent as the the bow swung past the cruisers. The *O'Leary* continued to spin around in a complete circle, seemingly confounding the enemy gunners.

"Continue left to one two zero," Arkwright ordered in a thick voice, heading them after their retreating sisters who were retiring toward the Allied main body.

Fraser looked back at the Japanese cruisers. They had turned away, standard practice for avoiding torpedoes. The minutes went by and there was no sign of any torpedo explosions. The American destroyer attack had succeeded in forcing the enemy heavy cruisers to turn away from the beleaguered Allied cruisers, but that was the extent of their success.

After the *O'Leary* regained her station at the end of the destroyer column, the Americans continued to retire through the twilight under a curtain of black smoke that spewed from the four stacks of each vessel. Fraser was happy to see their smoke billow around them; the Japanese were already out of their limited gun range.

They found the other Allied ships as the last daylight faded from the western sky. The flagship's signal light blinked, "Follow me." The column of American destroyers swung in beside the cruisers, and then doggedly maintained its station as Doorman searched through a night lit by a bright moon. By this time the Japanese had broken off the action and disappeared to the north.

"Did the Japs run away?" Eckersly asked.

Fraser shook his head. "I think they're just trying to get closer to the transports so we can't sneak by in the dark. The Japs know they can beat us whenever they want to, but if we get a free shot at the transports, we can really hurt them."

"Hell," Eckersly said softly. "We didn't do so hot."

Fraser had to agree with that assessment. They had lost the destroyers *Kortenaer* and *Electra*, and the *Exeter* had been knocked out of the battle. While the Allies had scored hits on the Japanese, Fraser hadn't seen any of them sinking or stopped for long. Then he realized things could have been a lot worse: the *O'Leary* was undamaged, and he was still alive.

A radioman emerged on the wing below and showed some messages to the captain who read them with a disgusted look.

Fraser leaned over the rail. "Bad news, Captain?"

"Doorman's been asking headquarters if they know where the convoy is, but headquarters can't help him."

"What about those planes that flew over during the battle?" Fraser asked. "They must have seen something."

"Didn't tell anyone if they did."

While Doorman led his battered force in search of the enemy tranports, the exhausted men of the *O'Leary* remained at their battle stations. Fraser's body and mind screamed for sleep. Then he remembered the men who had been at their stations in the sweltering engineering spaces for just as long. At least there was a cooling breeze on the fire control platform. Fraser had already heard reports that two men had passed out in the inferno below. They had been carried to the wardroom for treatment.

The steam generated by the dogged engineers drove them northward across the darkened sea. The Allies encountered elusive segments of the enemy force several times and exchanged sporadic gunfire. Allied star shells and Japanese parachute flares partially illuminated the night, but there were only glimpses of the enemy. During two skirmishes, the dim flashes of Japanese torpedo launchings were visible. Doorman ordered quick course changes to avoid disaster. The Dutch admiral finally headed south toward the coast of Java.

Fraser wasn't sure what the Admiral had in mind. Perhaps Doorman had deduced the Japanese convoy was nearing the coast of Java, or maybe he was preparing to circle around the Japanese defenders. There was, however, little chance of eluding the Japanese because the enemy observation planes continued to dog the Allies even though it was dark. The bright moon, a relatively cloudless sky, and the phosphorescent wakes that trailed behind the Allied ships made it impossible to shake the enemy overhead. Every time Doorman settled on a new course, a line of bright-green parachute flares blossomed overhead indicating the Allied position and direction of advance. Each set of winking flares floated down slowly, casting an eerie light on the Allied ships.

"Wish those damn planes would go away," Eckersly said.

"Wouldn't be there if our fighters had come to help us," Fraser said bitterly.

As they neared the Java Coast, the radiotelephone in the pilot house crackled with a request from Commander Binford for fuel reports from his American destroyers. Arkwright informed Binford they had fuel for just a few more hours of steaming. The other destroyers were equally short, so Binford ordered them to head for Surabaya when they neared the Java Coast.

Doorman turned the other way and took the four cruisers and two British destroyers to the west along the Java coast in search of the enemy. Fraser looked astern as the courageous Dutch and British faded into the moonlit night. He wished them well, knowing he might never see any of them again. Fraser shook his head wearily, leaned against the rail in front of him, and gazed at the wake of the *Jones*, just ahead. He knew that the role of the American destroyers in the battle had ended. The *O'Leary* had survived for the moment, but what would happen next?

Fraser looked down at the captain, who leaned against the bridge wing. There was no doubt the captain had saved them from destruction that afternoon. But Fraser noted the weary slump of Arkwright's shoulders; he wondered how close the captain was to total exhaustion. Fraser was ten years younger, and he felt ready to drop. He wondered whether the captain would have the strength to control his personal demons.

CHAPTER TWENTY-FIVE

Fraser rubbed his burning eyes as the five American destroyers steamed toward Surabaya through the humid darkness. The men on the fire control platform drooped with exhaustion and leaned against the director. Fraser felt his adrenalin wearing off as the gentle rolls of the *O'Leary* lulled his brain.

Suddenly, the *Edwards*, at the head of the column, reversed course and began to lead them back to the west. "What the devil?" muttered Fraser, shocked back into alertness.

The radiotelephone speaker on the bridge sputtered as the American destroyer commander informed his ships that they had been ordered west to the Java port of Tandjung Priok where torpedoes were available. A succession of reports over the voice circuit indicated that most of the destroyers didn't have enough fuel for the trip.

Fraser was relieved when the *Edwards* turned back toward Surabaya. Just before midnight, outside the Surabaya minefields, they met the *Pope*, which had missed the battle because of engineering problems. Their sister ship joined the column, and the old destroyers entered the channel as a parachute flare from a Japanese aircraft illuminated the scene. The flickering yellow-green light cast an eerie glow on the *O'Leary*'s fire control platform, where the helmeted and life jacketed men looked like misshapen creatures from another planet.

In the harbor, they found the battered *Exeter* and a Dutch destroyer already at the fueling pier. The *O'Leary* had to wait until a few hours before dawn when she eased alongside a berth just vacated by one of her sisters. Fraser had the watch on the bridge and leaned wearily on the wing bulkhead as the engineers prepared to refuel. The Javanese workmen were gone. Exhausted *O'Leary* sailors dragged the heavy black hoses aboard. On the pier just below Fraser, the chief machinist and several of his men clustered around the control valves trying to figure out how to operate the Dutch pumping system.

Chief Mortland walked to the life line. "Are you gonna take all night? Jap planes'll be here before you snipes get through farting around."

The chief machinist looked up. "Stuff that shit up your snot locker, Mortland! If we screw this pumping system up, we ain't going nowhere."

"Okay, okay," Mortland said. "Take your time, and do it right. You can even spill a little oil on deck."

"That's damn big of you, Mortland."

Mortland's face reddened. "Just don't make a habit of it."

A few minutes later the chief machinist stepped back from the maze of valves. "I think everything is lined up. I wish the hell Simpson was here. Let's give it a go."

Fraser hoped the chief was right and knocked the bridge wing for luck. Seconds later, the black hoses pulsed as oil flowed into the *O'Leary*'s nearly empty tanks. Many of the watching men headed for the nearest patch of open deck and curled up for a few minutes of sleep.

There was a burble as the forward fuel trunk overflowed for a few seconds. Chief Mortland watched the black oil run down the scuppers and over the side. He seemed to vibrate with rage but finally turned on his heel and stalked up the forecastle.

The captain leaned against the wing beside Fraser. "Ross, we don't know if our men in the hospital were sent to Australia. I want you to go ashore and bring back anyone who's fit to return."

"Glad to, sir. I can find out what happened to Ilsa too."

"That occurred to me. Good luck. Be back before dawn."

Fraser rushed down to the pier and trotted up the street between the yard buildings. The streets were littered with glass and other debris blown out of the warehouses by the Japanese bombings. Open boxes lay on the pavement, their contents strewn along the gutters.

Behind a row of buildings, Fraser found a battered pickup truck. A key was in the ignition; the engine turned over and wheezed to life, rattling the body. Fraser guided the creaking pickup to the yard entrance, where the once-smart sentry box stood deserted. One of the massive yard gates had been torn off its hinges and leaned by the roadside. Outside the yard, Fraser threaded the truck between bomb craters, pieces of metal, and shards of glass.

At the hospital he ran up the front steps. The entryway was deserted, and the desk telephone dangled off its hook, swaying in the breeze coming through shattered windows. His footsteps echoed in the empty corridors. He looked in Durham's old ward, but except for the faint aroma of antiseptic, it was deserted. He picked up a phone and tried the Van Dorns' home, hoping Mohammed could tell him something. The phone rang on, mocking his anxiety. Fraser replaced the instrument in its cradle and walked back to the truck. A few blocks from the yard, two of the tires blew out, and the truck jolted against the curb. Exhausted and despondent, he walked the rest of the way to the ship.

As Fraser approached the *O'Leary* in the predawn light, he realized his ship looked almost as bad as he felt. She seemed to lean against the pier, like an old race horse ready for the glue factory. Her hull was marred by rust and oil streaks, and her steel plates seemed to sag against the underlying framework. A weary-looking wisp of smoke rose from the number two stack. There were few signs of life topside as Fraser approached the brow. Men were curled up on open patches of deck with heads pillowed on grease-stained life jackets. Tim Egan and another red-eyed sailor had the watch on the quarterdeck.

"No luck, Mr. Fraser?"

"None at all, Egan."

"We could use Mr. Durham now. He's usually good for a laugh."

Fraser wondered if even the irrepressible Durham could have improved his spirits. Farther down the pier, a Dutch patrol boat was disembarking oil-soaked sailors. The men shuffled down the pier, supporting wounded comrades. Fraser realized that he had no idea what had happened to Ilsa's father or Dirk Jansen. "Do any of you speak English?" Fraser asked the passing men.

One limping petty officer stopped. "Yes, sir."

"What ship?"

"*Kortenaer*, sir."

"Lieutenant Jansen, was he picked up?"

The man looked down at his feet. "No, sir. I'm afraid he went down with the ship."

"What about the *De Ruyter*?" Fraser asked.

"We heard she and the *Java* were sunk last night. Very few survivors."

"Did you see any of them?"

"No, sir. They were picked up by another ship."

"Thank you." Fraser was certain that Jansen was dead, and he had little hope for Ilsa's father. He lifted his hands to his head and tried to control his swirling emotions. Fraser wondered why such fine men had to die.

An automobile engine murmured. The morning light glinted off the windshield of a familiar black Mercedes, which drove along the pier. Fraser felt his hopes leap, but as the car drew nearer, he saw both occupants were male. When the Mercedes pulled up by the brow, Mohammed jumped out and assisted Bull Durham from the passenger's seat. Fraser rushed down to meet them.

"Hello, Lieutenant Fraser," Mohammed said. "Miss Ilsa told me to get Lieutenant Durham to your ship."

"Mohammed, where's Ilsa?"

Durham smiled. "Don't worry. She and Marta left for Tjilatjap two days ago. They should be on their way to Australia."

"Why didn't you go with them? You're still in no condition to fight."

Durham smiled sheepishly. "Hey, I was worried an Aussie

patient would feed me to the sharks on the way to Australia. The crazy bastard was sweet on one of my nurses. He was no problem as long as he was in his body cast, but they were ready to turn him loose."

"I should have known," Fraser said. "I thought you were here for more noble reasons."

"You know me better than that. I was hoping I could go underground here, but Mohammed found out you'd come in."

"Miss Ilsa told me to get him to the *O'Leary*," Mohammed said firmly, as if he were well aware that Durham was a threat to the morality of the community.

"You're a man of your word, Mohammed," Fraser said. "I'm afraid I have bad news. Captain Van Dorn's ship was sunk last night. He may be dead."

Mohammed's smile dissolved, and his eyes misted. "That is terrible news. Captain Van Dorn was a fine man. He understood that my people were becoming ready to run their own affairs."

"Goodbye, my friend," Fraser said, extending his hand.

The diminutive Javanese took his hand and shook it firmly. "Please take care of Miss Ilsa. I know you will be very happy together." Mohammed gave them a final wave and jumped in the car. The transmission whined as he backed the Mercedes down the pier. The car turned and weaved through the littered streets.

Durham still had a bulky cast on his leg, so Fraser helped him up the brow. Laster waited at the rail. "Bull, what happened to Simpson?"

"Appendicitis. They popped him out of the operating room and onto the last bus. I'll bet he was mad when he woke up."

Laster eyed Durham's leg. "Bull, if the Japs sink us, you'll go down like a stone with that cast."

Durham just smiled. "Doc, keep in mind I'm going to have both hands on your neck, so we'll sink together. You'd better figure out a way to get this cast off in a hurry."

By mid-afternoon the *O'Leary* swung from her anchor off Surabaya during a lull in the air raids. Hank Landry walked by the quarterdeck where Shifflet had the watch. The gunner's mate nodded wearily from the small patch of shade cast by a piece of dirty canvas. Landry stepped into the galley and picked up a stale cheese sandwich.

He went aft to the torpedo deck hoping to find some shade, but all the choice spots under the torpedo tubes were taken. Landry sighed, slumped down against a bulkhead, and munched his dry sandwich.

Landry heard a metallic rattle and looked up. Chief Hanlon shuffled from man to man with a bucket and a ladle, dripping water on their heads, almost as if in a baptismal rite. The proud chief wore a clean uniform and was freshly shaven.

"Water?" Hanlon asked.

"Thanks. This sandwich is going down like sawdust."

"It'd taste a lot better if we were back in Manila," Hanlon said.

"Gotta get out of here, first."

"Yeah. May not be easy," Hanlon said. "Gonna be a long time before we kick the Japs out of the Philippines."

Landry shook his head. "I miss the hell out of Teresa. I hope I can make it back to see my kid. I can barely remember my own father. It ain't right for a kid to grow up without a father."

"Sometimes there's nothing a father can do."

"Yeah, I found that out the hard way." Landry remembered his long night in the water and the shark that had circled him. "I guess my old man didn't have any choice either."

"If it'll make you feel any better, I can guarantee Maria'll do her best for Teresa and the baby. That woman has been itching to get her hands on a child for years."

"Thanks, Chief, it's good to know Teresa's not all alone like my mom was. But I still get discouraged thinking about how long it's going to take to see them."

"Yeah. Me, too. We've got to keep on going." Hanlon shook his head and looked down at Landry. "What are you going to do if we get out of here? You could strike for gunner's mate instead of staying on the deck force."

"Thanks, Chief. But I've been hoping we'll get a new whale-boat soon."

"You can't spend the rest of your career taking care of a boat, son."

Landry felt a flare of anger. "Don't call me 'son.' You ain't my father."

"No, I'm not. Doesn't mean I can't give you good advice."

"Yeah. Maybe you're right. A new boat won't be the same as the old one."

Hanlon nodded. "Think about working somewhere that will give you some satisfaction."

"Okay, I'll keep it in mind. Chief, if we get back to Manila, will things be the way they were before?"

Hanlon looked over the rail for a long time. "This war's going to change a lot of things, even if we win. The Asiatic Fleet doesn't even exist on paper anymore."

"Who the hell are we?"

"United States Naval Forces in the Southwest Pacific."

The name was too long for Landry's tired brain. "I'll always be an Asiatic Fleet sailor. Nothing will ever change that."

"Feel the same way," Hanlon said. After a few seconds of silence, even Hanlon appeared to admit his weariness. He disappeared into the amidships deckhouse like a condemned angel returning to hell.

An afternoon air raid jolted Fraser out of his bunk after a few hours of sleep. When it was over, he climbed down to the bridge, where Arkwright slumped in his chair, his red-rimmed eyes staring out of his lined face. A cooling mist of salt water drifted through the open bridge windows from a fire hose Landry was playing over the main deck to cool it off.

"Christ, that feels good!" Arkwright said.

For an instant, Fraser thought of better times—the community swimming pool in Columbus, the beach on Corregidor with Ilsa. But his memories evaporated as quickly as the mist. Sweat rolled down his body as the midafternoon heat pressed around him.

"Any orders yet?" Fraser asked.

"Nothing."

"Why won't they tell us anything?"

" 'Ours not to reason why,' " the captain said.

"I hope they haven't forgotten us."

"That would be embarrassing," Arkwright said. "But I expect we'll get orders to head for Australia. We lost about half our force yesterday. The *Houston* and *Perth* survived the night, but they're 400 miles away. There's no way to put together another strike force."

Fraser considered the problem of steaming to Australia. The Japanese carriers were probably roaming south of the Malay Barrier. First, the *O'Leary* would have to escape through one of the straits that were sure to be guarded by Japanese surface ships. Fraser wondered if they would head east for Bali Strait or Lombok Strait—or west for Sunda Strait off the other end of Java.

A radioman clattered across the wooden gratings and handed the captain the message board. Fraser's spirits lifted when it was his turn to read the message. It ordered five of the American destroyers to head for Australia via Bali Strait that night. He saw the *Pope* wasn't going with them. Engineering problems had kept her out of the battle the previous day, so their sister ship still had a full load of torpedoes. The message ordered her to go with the crippled *Exeter*, which was going to try to sneak around the Japanese invasion forces. The *Pope*'s group was supposed to steam north that night, west along the south coast of Borneo the next day, and then south through Sunda Strait the next night.

Fraser remembered how he had envied the *Pope* the day before. He wasn't sure how he felt now. Only time would tell how Simpson's work on the boiler had altered their fate. Fraser said, "It might be nice to have the *Exeter*'s big guns along with us."

"The *Exeter* can only do 25 knots now," Arkwright said. "Sure you'd like to have her along?"

"I guess not. I want to be able to go like hell."

Arkwright was silent for a while. "If I still had my family, I'd want to go like hell too," he said softly.

As dusk neared, the *O'Leary* prepared for her final departure from Surabaya. When she steamed by the battered *Exeter*, the crews exchanged cheers of respect and encouragement. Fraser was moved as he stood at attention, wondering why it was that war could somehow bring out both the best and worst in mankind.

"Unnhh. Where am I?" T. T. Simpson's mouth felt like the firebox of one of his boilers. Sunlight streamed through a row of portholes. He tried to sit up, but there was a sharp pain in his side. "Oohh."

"It's about time for you to wake up."

Simpson looked up from his mattress which lay on deck.

A sandy-haired young woman smiled at him. "I've been taking good care of you because you're from my husband's ship."

"Your husband?"

"Lieutenant Fraser. I'm his wife, Ilsa."

"Nice to meet you Ma'am. I heard your wedding was very nice. Did you have any dancing?"

"No. It was a garden wedding."

"Too bad. I love to dance. I would have been honored to dance with such a beautiful bride. The garden wouldn't have stopped me. We still could have done a nice tango in the tulips."

"If your dancing is like your flattery, I would have enjoyed it. You're not another Lieutenant Durham are you?"

"Definitely not! I have my standards." He looked around the large room where rows of wounded men lined the deck. "Just where are we?"

"You're in the dining room of a merchant ship that just left Tjilatjap for Australia."

Simpson tried to sit up and felt another stab of pain in his side. "Are you sure it's all right to get up?"

"Yes," Ilsa said. "The doctor said we were to get you up and around as soon as possible."

"Do you need some help?" A short blonde, obviously pregnant, walked over to join Ilsa.

"I think I can do it myself," Simpson said, too proud to ask for help from a pregnant woman. He gathered one leg under him and pushed himself up. Pain shot through his side, and the room seemed to swirl around. Hands grabbed his arms, and the room steadied. "I'm okay now."

Ilsa introduced Simpson to Marta Jansen, and they walked him out to the main deck for some fresh air.

"Look at all these people," Marta said. "Ilsa, I told you not to worry."

Ilsa frowned. "Ross seemed worried about Japanese carriers to the south. Mr. Simpson, did you hear anything before you left the *O'Leary*?"

"Nothing but rumors, Mrs. Fraser. I doubt if anyone knows for sure where the Japs are."

"See," Marta said. "We did the right thing. Dirk and Ross will probably get to Australia before we do. Besides, the wounded men need us."

"I feel responsible for you and the baby," Ilsa said.

Marta shook her blonde hair. "The Japanese wouldn't bomb a ship full of wounded."

Simpson looked around the decks, which were crowded with people. "Don't be too sure of that, Ma'am. Besides, there aren't any Red Cross markings so they'd know."

"Oh." Marta suddenly rubbed her stomach.

"Are you all right?" Ilsa asked.

"Fine. Just the baby kicking me."

"Tell it to stay there until we get to Australia."

"I think we'd better get our patient back," Marta said. "We have others who need some attention."

Simpson spent a restless few hours lying on his mattress. Ilsa and Marta went to work with a doctor, three nurses, and some civilian volunteers. They moved from patient to patient, changing bandages and ministering to men with serious wounds. Simpson found he couldn't stand the inactivity, so he struggled to his feet and shuffled over to Ilsa.

"I'm feeling better now, Mrs. Fraser. I don't know anything about medicine, but I've fixed just about everything else there is to fix. Maybe I could help out, if you ladies will show me what to do."

"As long as you don't overdo it. Marta needs some time to rest."

An hour later, Simpson had learned a lot about bandaging wounds. He had also seen firsthand how war could maim the young men who went into battle.

"Maybe you'd better let me do this next one alone," Ilsa said quietly.

"I think I can handle anything now," Simpson said.

The patient was a young Dutchman, who had little more than peach fuzz on his cheeks. Ilsa murmured a greeting and introduced Simpson. The man smiled wanly. Simpson sucked in his breath when Ilsa pulled the sheet back. One leg had been amputated near the hip, the other at the knee. Bandages swathed the stumps and the man's groin.

Oh, God! Simpson said to himself. Not there!

Simpson's worst fears were confirmed when they changed the bandages. Ilsa's gentle hands did most of the work.

"Maybe I'd better get some fresh air," Simpson said when they dumped their load of old bandages in the trash.

"Take a break," Ilsa said. "We've caught up."

Simpson stepped out on the main deck and clutched the rail with hands that refused to stop shaking as he thought about the young Dutchman. The ship plowed through the gentle swell. The door creaked behind him, and Ilsa joined him at the rail, where the breeze fluttered her sandy hair.

"I remember crossing the Atlantic with my family," she said. "Somehow, the ocean didn't seem as large then."

Simpson looked around the empty horizon. "Guess it makes a difference when you have to worry about being sunk."

Ilsa hugged herself tightly. "I just wouldn't want to be alone out here. It's so empty."

Simpson hoped it would stay that way. The merchant ship looked like it might be able to make 12 knots on a good day, so she couldn't outrun any Japanese warships. She had no antiaircraft weapons. There would be little hope if the Japanese found her.

Simpson straightened as the ship changed course to starboard.

He looked off the port quarter and saw a black smudge on the horizon.

"What's happening?" Ilsa asked.

"Probably another merchant ship out there. I'll bet the captain doesn't want to take chances."

The minutes passed and the dark plume slowly diminished.

"Guess that guy didn't want to find out who we were either," Simpson said.

Late the next afternoon Simpson felt the deck vibrate as the reciprocating engine picked up speed. The distant drone of an airplane engine and anxious shouts came through an open door. Simpson hurried out to the main deck. A single Japanese carrier dive bomber orbited slowly. The pilot broke out of his lazy circle and dived but pulled out without dropping his bomb as if he were a cat playing with a crippled bird. The pilot was evidently checking to see how maneuverable they were; the merchant ship's turn to port had been painfully slow. Apparently satisfied that he had an easy target, the pilot turned again and lined up for another run as the passengers cowered on the crowded decks. The aircraft hurtled down. The bomb fell free as the aircraft pulled out of its dive, its pale belly highlighted by the afternoon sun. Simpson felt the deck shudder as the engine went into reverse. The ship heeled as they turned to starboard. The large bomb whistled down and exploded just off the port bow, shaking the ship.

The Japanese plane circled, turned, and roared in low above the water, machine guns winking. Simpson scrambled through the door behind him and hit the deck. There were cries from the main deck as machine gun bullets clanged off the ship's side and superstructure. Bullets shattered glass portholes near Simpson, showering glass shards across the deck. Shouts of fear and pain filled the room. As soon as the angry whine of bullets and the sound of falling glass ended, Simpson raised his head. Several of the wounded were writhing with new injuries. One of them lay motionless, and Simpson knew the man would never move again. Simpson heard a low moan behind him and turned to see Ilsa's dress covered with blood. She was cradling Marta's bleeding head in her lap.

Simpson crawled over. "Oh God! Is she dead?"

"She's still breathing." Ilsa's tears mingled with the blood of her friend. "Please find the doctor."

"Here I am," a weary voice said. The gray-bearded doctor examined Marta's ugly head wound, checked her pulse and blood pressure and examined her for any other signs of injury. He listened to her abdomen with his stethoscope.

"The baby is still all right. Marta's vital signs are almost normal, but that won't last long when her brain starts to swell from the wound."

"Can't you do anything for her?" Simpson asked.

"It would be bad even in a big hospital," the doctor said. "Here, it's hopeless. How far along is her pregnancy?"

"She's due in five weeks," Ilsa said.

The doctor sighed as if reluctant to bring another innocent child into the chaos of their war-torn world. "She's your friend. Will you be responsible for the baby?" The doctor's bloodshot eyes watched Ilsa for an answer.

Simpson was suddenly aware of the commitment the doctor was asking for. This wasn't a puppy Ilsa was about to buy. He remembered the long hours his own exhausted mother had worked to take care of her children. He suddenly felt guilty about not writing to her very often.

"Funny," Ilsa said. "My husband and I thought it would be better to wait a few years for children."

"Few of us get what we expect," the doctor said softly.

"Yes, I'll be responsible," Ilsa said in a firm voice.

The doctor stood. "Let me see what else we have to contend with. Come get me if her vital signs change for the worse."

He returned a few minutes later splattered with blood. "Six dead and five wounded. The wounded can wait." The doctor massaged his brow as he stared at the deck. "One of the dead was a six-year-old girl. Madness! War is madness! Let's bring this child into this world before it's too late."

Simpson helped carry Marta down the passageway to a small

office that had been set aside for treatment and surgery. They lowered her gently to the improvised operating table. The doctor cut away her clothes and exposed her distended abdomen. He pinched Marta's skin but there was no reaction. "Seems strange not to have to worry about anesthesia or sterile procedure." The doctor picked up a scalpel.

Simpson swallowed as the doctor made a long cut down the middle of Marta's belly. He handed Simpson a pair of metal instruments. "Just hold the edges of the wound back away from the uterus when I cut through to the abdominal cavity. Okay, I'm going between the stomach muscles—now the peritoneum and into the abdominal cavity."

Simpson sucked in his breath as what looked like a red basketball appeared.

"That's right—hold the retractors there so I can open the uterus."

The doctor made another long incision, reached inside, and pulled a baby boy out of his dying mother's body. The infant was a dusky reddish-blue color, covered with his mother's blood and a whitish substance. This was the first newborn child Simpson had ever seen. He was alarmed at its appearance, but the tiny baby responded to his sudden birth with a lusty cry of protest.

The doctor smiled wearily. "He'll be fine. He looks normal and healthy, although he's small because he's a little early. I'm sorry I can't do anything for Marta." He snapped two pairs of surgical clamps on the cord and severed the infant's last connection with his mother. The doctor wrapped the baby in a piece of clean blanket and handed the bundle to Ilsa. He checked Marta's blood pressure and shook his head. "I don't think she'll last much longer. I'd better get back to the other wounded."

"Can you do without us for a while?" Ilsa asked. "Maybe when she dies, somehow she'll know her son is here, and he's all right."

"Surely. More of the passengers have volunteered to help out. I don't know if they'll be as capable as you two, but we'll make out."

After the doctor left, Simpson sat next to Ilsa as she cradled the little bundle in her arms and wept. Simpson reached over and wiped the blood off Marta's face, but a gash on her forehead kept renewing the trickle down her temple.

Ilsa shuddered. "This is what war is, isn't it?"

Simpson thought for a minute. "Doesn't seem much different from murder when you get right down to it."

"That's exactly what it is." Ilsa's voice was low. "I guess that's why they have bands and the handsome uniforms to make it seem like something else. How many men would fight if they knew this was what they would do."

"Not many." Simpson took off his glasses and wiped them, suddenly thankful that his country hadn't started this war.

As Simpson slid his glasses back on, he noticed that the roll of the ship seemed sluggish. The thump of the reciprocating engine died away. "I'd better go see what's happening."

When he reached the main deck, passengers were shouting angrily. One of the ship's two lifeboats was pulling away.

"What the hell is going on?" Simpson asked a nearby man.

"Whole damn engine room crew just came up and abandoned ship! The captain was yelling at them to stop, but it didn't do any good."

"Oh, shit!" Simpson said softly. He searched the horizon hoping for a friendly ship that could rescue them. Nothing. The sky was empty, but there was still another hour of daylight for more Japanese aircraft to find them and finish the job.

CHAPTER TWENTY-SIX

The five destroyers bound for Bali Strait steamed away from the Surabaya waterfront. Fraser had the watch on the *O'Leary*'s bridge as she followed the *Ford* toward the western channel and the Java Sea to confuse any Japanese reconnaissance aircraft. As soon as the sun neared the horizon, the two destroyers reversed course and raced to catch up with their sisters that had headed out the eastern channel.

Fraser turned the watch over to Chuck Steiner and leaned against the starboard bridge wing as the once-beautiful Surabaya faded into the twilight. He realized he was leaving part of his life behind and wondered if he would ever return. What would become of the Van Dorns' house, that quiet oasis, which had offered a refuge from the ravages of the war? He wondered whether he would see Ilsa again.

The *Ford* and the *O'Leary* caught up with the other destroyers just before dark, and they formed a column with the *Edwards* leading the *Alden*, *Ford*, *Jones*, and *O'Leary*. Before Fraser left the bridge, he stopped at Arkwright's chair. "When are we going to general quarters, Captain?"

"About an hour before midnight. I think we can wait until we're near the eastern end of Madura. There haven't been any reports of Jap ships between Java and Madura."

Arkwright shifted wearily in his chair and massaged his temples. There were dark circles under his blood-shot eyes, and his shaggy eyebrows seemed about to fall off his lined forehead. "Ross, you and the men deserve to make it home. But I'm so damn tired I can't give you any guarantees about . . ."

"Your best is all we ask, Captain."

"I just don't know . . . I'm so tired."

Three hours later Fraser and the rest of the men were back at their general quarters stations. Near the tip of Madura, the silence was broken by one of the lookouts. "Small ship! Zero nine zero. Three miles!"

Fraser peered into the night off the starboard beam where he picked up a familiar silhouette in the moonlight. "Looks like a Dutch patrol boat," he reported into his phoneset.

Fraser relaxed, but he knew they wouldn't have much longer to wait before real opposition would appear. Flexing his neck, he settled his life jacket and tried to shift his steel helmet, which felt as if it weighed 30 pounds. Fraser scanned the dark horizon ahead with his binoculars. He felt a tap on his shoulder. It was Durham. "I knew you could use a fresh lookout. I'll just sit on the edge of the platform."

"How'd you make it up here?"

"The stretcher bearers helped. I had plenty of practice getting around the hospital meeting my nurses."

"Why the extra life jacket?"

"Doc figured two of 'em would hold me up. If we sink, I'll just float off." Durham frowned. "I hope Laster knows what he's talking about."

Fraser knew kapok life jackets would become water-logged after much time in the water, but he decided not to tell Durham that.

As Durham settled himself on the forward edge of the platform, Laster's round face appeared at the top of the ladder. "Where the hell's my patient?" he whispered.

"It's okay, Doc," Fraser said. "The Japs won't hear you. How'd you find him?"

"He left a trail of plaster chips. Bull, what are you doing here?"

"I'm helping the lookouts."

"If you can help, so can I." Laster paused and looked around. "Nice moon tonight."

"Some military expert you are," Durham said. "That moon is just what the Japs need to see us."

"I focus on the strategic plane. Mere tactical details don't interest me."

Laster and Durham added their eyes to the lookouts', but there was nothing to see. Just after midnight, the column increased speed to 27 knots, and headed south toward Bali Strait. The bright moon, just a few days short of full, was past its zenith and starting down in the western sky.

"Doc, maybe you'd better get back to the wardroom," Fraser said. "We could find the Japs anytime now. You won't do wounded folks any good up here."

The ships hugged the western shore of the strait, keeping their distinctive outlines against the coastline of Java. Fraser cursed the bright moon and knew their column would be visible in silhouette to any Japanese forces further out in Bali Strait.

The *O'Leary* followed at the end of the column while Fraser swept his binoculars over the moonlit water, trying to find the enemy who had to be there. He spotted the triangular lateen sails of a Madura prau. The raked stem of the slender vessel sliced through the water as it hurried by on an opposite course. As they neared the southern end of the Strait, Fraser began to hope there were no Japanese.

"Ship! Three two zero! Four miles!" shouted a lookout.

Fraser swung his binoculars off the port bow and sucked in his breath. A high-bowed Japanese destroyer, with one 5-inch twin mount forward and two aft patrolled the southern exit of the strait. Fraser ordered the director to start tracking. The bridge talker's voice sounded in his right ear. "Put the guns on the target, but hold your fire until the captain gives the word."

The fire controlmen and the gun crews were soon tracking the target. Fraser agreed with the decision not to shoot. There was no sense in stirring up the Japanese before they had to. Out of the corner of his eye, Fraser saw the gun barrel of the number one 4-inch gun elevate slightly as it followed the computer's orders.

He instructed his computer operator to be ready to use a continuous rocking ladder. Each salvo would be adjusted up or down 500 yards around the base range until Fraser ordered otherwise. Fraser kept feeding new range estimates to the computer operator.

Five minutes later, the Japanese destroyer's bow began to swing.

"Uh-ohhh," Durham said, as the destroyer paralleled their course and picked up speed.

"I think he's spotted us," Fraser said.

"Flashing lights three one zero," the port lookout reported.

Two more Japanese destroyers steamed out of the night on their way to join the first one.

"Wish we had some torpedoes," Fraser said.

"Christ, I don't like this," Durham said. "We have a few more guns, but theirs are bigger . . . and they have torpedoes."

"May be more Japs where those came from," Fraser said.

The American column continued to skirt the shoreline of Java. The *O'Leary's* director tracked the first Japanese destroyer, and Fraser kept feeding the computer operator range estimates. "Range six five double oh."

Yellow flame suddenly blossomed from all three Japanese ships.

"Commence firing!" Arkwright shouted.

"Rapid salvo fire! Commence firing! Commence firing!" echoed Fraser.

The *O'Leary*'s guns barked a response as the first Japanese salvo hit only 200 yards short. The Japanese salvos were amazingly accurate considering they hadn't used any star shells to illuminate.

Salvo after salvo lit up the night around them. All five American destroyers blasted away at the Japanese, so the blinding sequence of their flashing guns made accurate spotting impossible. Fraser did his best to estimate the fall of shot and kept his men pumping out rounds. The Japanese continued to charge after them and seemed to be closing the gap slightly. "Christ," Fraser muttered, "we'd better do something."

The captain evidently concurred with that judgement. He shouted to Steiner, "Torpedo battery simulate fire."

Steiner shouted the orders over his phone circuit.

Behind the amidships deckhouse, Tim Egan watched another torpedoman crank the forward port torpedo mount out to face the enemy as spray whipped over the rail.

"Forward mount, fire your impulse charges!" shouted Chief Robustelli.

Dull flashes lit up the side. Egan and another man picked up bundles of empty shell cases and hurled them over the rail to mimic the splashes of torpedoes entering the water. A minute later, they repeated the charade with the after mount. Egan realized they had done what they could; it wasn't much, but he hoped their fake torpedoes would do a better job than the real ones the Navy had given them.

Fraser lowered his binoculars and felt like cheering. The three Japanese destroyers had turned away, obviously fearing that torpedoes were on their way. "Those bastards will have a hell of a time catching us now."

The American destroyers continued to fire at the Japanese with their after guns even though the range had opened up to 12,000 yards. The Japanese fired back, their salvos less accurate at long range. Suddenly, a stray salvo whistled down around the *O'Leary*. Columns of water erupted along the port side and an explosion shook the ship. Fraser grabbed the rail in front of him as he almost lost his feet. A shrieking plume of steam jetted from a hole in the port side.

The lee helmsman shouted a report to the captain. "Main control reports damage in the forward engine room. Steam pressure from the after fireroom is dropping."

Fraser could feel the *O'Leary* slowing. The four destroyers ahead were already drawing inexorably away like a passenger train leaving a station. Fraser felt like a forlorn relative standing on the platform as his family pulled away.

The radiotelephone speaker in the pilothouse sputtered as Commander Binford acknowledged Arkwright's damage report.

Fraser heard Arkwright's voice in the pilot house. "Recommend you proceed at top speed. I will sheer out to starboard so the Japs can't chase both us and your formation. Over."

"Roger," the flagship acknowledged after a long pause. "Good luck. Out."

Arkwright turned the lagging *O'Leary* to starboard. The captain returned to the port wing and gazed back at the flash of the Japanese guns. Fraser looked down at the captain as the yellow flame of an outgoing salvo froze Arkwright's face for a second. The picture etched itself on Fraser's mind; the lined face was haggard, almost wild—a man at the end of his resources.

Fraser's mind raced. He's going to turn back at the Japs.

Another salvo.

Fraser waited for the captain's next command.

Another salvo.

Christ! The Japanese must see us falling behind now, Fraser thought. They'll come after us for sure.

"Cease firing! Make smoke!" the captain ordered.

"Cease firing!" Fraser said. Thank God! he thought. Maybe the Japanese won't see we're crippled.

Seconds later, black smoke billowed from the first two stacks, obscuring the sea behind them. The next damage report indicated the forward engine room would be repaired in an hour. Nobody was answering in the after fireroom.

Fraser realized they were down to two boilers and one propeller. Before the *O'Leary* had been hit, the American destroyers had been drawing away from the Japanese. Fraser hoped the enemy had already given up the chase. If the serious damage was limited to the after fireroom, the engineers should soon be able to give the *O'Leary* 25 knots. Even that wouldn't enable them to outrun a determined Japanese pursuit. Fraser peered astern, but their smoke was impenetrable. All he could do was wait.

An hour later, the forward engine room was repaired and they edged back to 25 knots.

"Cease making smoke," the captain ordered.

Fraser stared astern as the thick cloud slowly dissipated. If the enemy had followed at high speed, they could be close behind. The last wisps finally slid away. The moonlit seascape behind them was empty. There was no sign of the Japanese or the rest of the American destroyers.

The captain leaned against the bulwark of the bridge wing just below Fraser and stared aft. Arkwright's expression seemed one of pain and regret, as if he were leaving behind something he didn't expect to find again.

Distant gun flashes lit the northern horizon as if Java were flickering a final farewell.

The latest damage report from the lee helmsman indicated one man was dead and two men were burned badly in the after fireroom. Jack Meredith and another man had sustained serious burns pulling men out of the fireroom.

"Very well," Arkwright said wearily. He shuffled off the port wing into the pilothouse like an arthritic old man. Fraser walked over to the starboard side of the fire control platform and leaned over the rail. Just inside the pilothouse, he could see the captain slumped in his bridge chair, his feet wedged against the bulkhead. One arm dangled and swayed with the roll of the ship.

They continued to steam south at 25 knots. Dawn found them alone, almost 100 miles south of Java. They were still within range of Japanese aircraft based on Bali or aircraft flying from carriers that might be lurking in the area. Since there was no immediate threat of surface attack, the 4-inch gun crews were broken up and posted as lookouts and as relief crews for the men on the antiaircraft guns. Hours went by and nothing happened, but each hour took them another 25 miles closer to Australia.

Several hours after dawn, Laster and the chief machinist appeared on the bridge to make their reports to the captain. Arkwright motioned Fraser down to join the group.

"What's the status of the engineering plant, Chief?" the captain asked.

"The forward engine room is patched up, Captain. We won't be steaming on either of the boilers in the after fireroom until we get a lot of help from a yard."

"And the men?" Arkwright asked Laster.

"Two dead. Three others with bad burns, including Jack Meredith. We need to get them to a hospital."

"No hope of that for another four or five days," the captain said.

"Can't we go faster?" the doctor asked.

"This is as fast as we can go on two boilers," the captain said. "We'll have to slow down before long. We burned up so much oil at high speed last night, we'll have to economize to reach Perth."

Fraser scanned the sky. He didn't like the idea of slowing down at all. Then he remembered they were down to the forward fireroom. He hoped Simpson had cured the problems there. If he hadn't, they soon might be dead in the water.

After they secured from general quarters late that morning, Fraser barely had time for lunch before he was due on the bridge for the afternoon watch. The four hours dragged by. Fraser shifted his aching feet and looked at his watch; it was almost time for Chuck Steiner to relieve him for the first dog watch. Fraser leaned over the bridge wing and and watched the ship slide through the water. At 15 knots the hull looked like it was coasting. With no fuel to spare for a zig-zag pattern, they were an easy target for any Japanese submarine in their path.

Fraser straightened up and looked in the pilothouse. Arkwright twitched fitfully in his chair with his chin almost on his chest. As the ship rolled in the gentle swell, Arkwright started to slide out of his chair. He awoke with a start, but his eyes seemed unfocused. The captain shook his head painfully.

Fraser joined Chief Jablonski at Arkwright's side. "Captain, you don't look so good," Jablonski said.

"I'll be okay. Just tired." A chill shook the captain's body, rattling his teeth.

"We'd better get you down to Doc Laster," Fraser said.

"No! Let me alone!" Arkwright said with a fierce look that sent Fraser and Jablonski to the chart table where they exchanged worried glances.

When Fraser returned to the bridge that evening after having the short dog watches off, he found Arkwright still in his bridge chair, barely awake. Fraser spent most of his time leaning on the bridge wing watching their slow progress over the moonlit sea and checking the captain. Fraser was bone-weary, but he had managed to go below for an occasional catnap during the previous four days. Arkwright had not even visited the pipe rail bunk in the charthouse for three days and nights. Fraser had only seen the captain manage a few nodding moments of semiconsciousness in his bridge chair, but the unyielding back was fixed in an upright position and not built for comfort.

Arkwright began to slide out of the chair. Chief Jablonski reached the captain first and gently grabbed his shoulders and pulled him upright. Arkwright opened his eyes, stared vacantly, and mumbled, "Must've gone to sleep."

Fraser leaned over him. "Captain, you've got to turn in. You can't take much more of this. It's dark now. If we run into Japs on the surface, I'll have time to call you."

"Can't. Gotta get us to Australia."

Fraser reluctantly went back to his position on the wing and watched Arkwright with growing concern. In a few minutes, the captain slid all the way to the deck, where he floundered like a helpless fish.

"That's enough," Fraser said as they lifted the captain back into his chair. "Messenger, get Doctor Laster and have him bring his black bag."

Minutes later, Laster appeared, his face lined with fatigue. "What's wrong? I've got some sick people below."

Fraser nodded at the captain, who was beginning to slide down in his chair again.

"He needs a seat belt," Laster said.

"Try to tell him that," Fraser said. "I'm worried. He looks completely exhausted. He had shaking chills earlier. See if you can get him to lie down in the charthouse and sleep. He refuses to leave the bridge."

Arkwright caught himself with a start and regarded Laster. "What're you doing here, Doc?" he slurred.

"Here on business, I'm afraid. You need some rest."

"Go 'way. Lem'me be. I have a job t'do."

Laster shook his head. "I think you've already done it. You won't be able to do anything with a case of the dengue fever. I know one when I see one."

"Hell, you say," mumbled Arkwright.

"I say you can't even get out of that chair by yourself," Laster said.

"Watch this." The captain swung his feet down and tried to stand, but he slid to the deck, like a khaki-colored lump of jello.

Laster kneeled down and checked him rapidly in the moonlight. "Looks like dengue all right. Exhaustion to boot. Must be a hell of a strain on his system. We should get him down to his cabin."

"Better put him in his bunk in the charthouse, or he'll raise hell," Fraser said.

"All right. As long as he'll sleep."

They carried Arkwright back to the charthouse and lifted him to the pipe-rail bunk. Arkwright lay on his back and began to take deep shuddering breaths.

Fraser led Laster out to the bridge wing. "Maybe we'd better talk this over, Doc. How long will he be down?"

"Depends. You had a pretty easy case when you had it. Plus you were younger and not on the brink of total exhaustion. He should be really sick for a couple of days. Then he may feel better for a day or so until the usual relapse."

Fraser shook his head. "Jesus!"

His thoughts were interrupted by a muffled thump from the charthouse. "Messenger," Arkwright's voice rasped, "help me out to the bridge!"

Laster and Fraser ran back to the charthouse and picked the captain up and forced him back up to the bunk. "You're going to have to knock him out, Doc. He just won't quit."

"Ummm. He is the captain. Is that legal?" Laster asked.

"We'll worry about that later. Is it the right thing to do—medically?"

"Definitely. Might kill himself if he keeps this up."

"Give him a shot then. Let Jack know he's in charge when you go below. He can figure out what to do."

"Sorry . . . Jack has some nasty burns. He's in no condition to do anything but lie in his bunk."

"Oh, Lord."

"That means you're temporarily in command," Laster said.

Fraser thought for a minute, praying Arkwright would jump up and reassert command.

A chill shook the captain.

"Okay," Fraser said. "Let's give him that shot and hope he's better by morning. If he decides to court-martial me, that's too bad."

Arkwright never moved as Laster raised his sleeve and slipped a needle into his upper arm. In a few minutes, the shuddering breathing eased, and he slept peacefully. "I didn't give him much. But that should keep him asleep for a while."

"But he's definitely out of it now?"

Laster looked up at Fraser. "For about eight hours. When this wears off—who knows? With dengue and exhaustion, he might be down for days, or he might be able to function. Anyway, I agree we have to sedate him. A tough decision."

"I hope you'll remember that on the witness stand."

"What do we do now now?" Laster asked.

"Good question. Officially, I'm supposed to report his incapacity to the division commander and others up the chain of command. I'd rather not break radio silence. The Japs might use the transmission to find us."

"Hmmm," Laster said. "We're the only two who know he's sedated. The rest of the world can think he's sleeping."

Fraser went forward to the bridge and wedged himself into his favorite spot at the forward corner of the port wing. He watched the empty sea ahead as the gentle swells rolled in from the south. He looked up at the full moon, which was almost directly overhead. Memories of the last three full moons and Ilsa flooded his mind. December—their last night in Manila when her cool exterior had suddenly melted. January—the party at the Surabaya Hotel when she had trembled in his arms on the dark terrace. February—their wedding night. Now the March full moon was overhead and he didn't even know whether she was still in Java or heading for Australia.

Chuck Steiner was at his elbow ready to relieve him. After Fraser had briefed him, Steiner nodded. "Where will you be if I have a problem?"

Fraser suddenly realized his new responsibility was a 24-hour burden. Before, he had carried the mantle of officer of the deck for four hours and had then been free to go below. On the bridge he had been able to call the captain if the situation became difficult. With the captain unconscious, there was no one to turn to. Fraser realized he was entrusted with the safety of the *O'Leary* and the lives of her crew. He would just have to do his best and hope it was good enough.

Fraser knew his bunk was too far away in case there was an emergency. But he had to lie down; his feet felt like lumps of lead, and his throbbing calves were ready to cramp. His body was screaming for sleep. There was no way he could stay awake all night. "Chuck, I'm going up to the fire control platform and lie down. Any problems, call me. Pass the word on to Woody when he relieves you."

Fraser pulled himself up the ladder and stretched out on the wooden grating with his head pillowed on a life jacket. It wasn't comfortable, but he didn't care. He closed his eyes and slept.

"Mr. Fraser."

"Unnph." Fraser rolled over and saw the messenger.

"Mr. Korchak says it's time for morning G.Q. in another ten minutes, sir."

Reality flooded back in his foggy brain. He was in charge. "Okay. Tell him I'll be right down."

When the alarm sounded, the men took their positions as they had hundreds of times before. Fraser had Chief Hanlon take over the director platform. The predawn light revealed no sign of friend or enemy. As the sun rose over the horizon, Korchak looked at Fraser expectantly.

Fraser looked around for the captain to give the order to set the Condition III watch. Then he realized that was why Korchak was looking at him. "Secure from G. Q.," Fraser said. "Set up each watch section like yesterday. We want the 3-inch and the fifties manned and ready. If we get jumped, it's going to be from the air."

Fraser searched the horizon and then hustled below for a quick meal at the almost empty wardroom table.

"Doc, how's the captain this morning?" Fraser asked.

"He's still almost delirious. The sedative has about worn off, but he's too sick to care about much."

Fraser remembered how the dengue had incapacitated him. "Keep me informed, Doc. I'll be on the bridge with the watch."

After Fraser relieved Korchak, the hours crawled on. Fraser prowled the wings. "Keep checking the sun sector," he told the drooping lookouts.

By 1100, the high clouds were more numerous, and Fraser began to worry. He felt a nagging apprehension; the clouds would provide good cover for attacking aircraft. Fraser scanned the sky. As the sun approached its zenith, Fraser felt even more vulnerable. He stationed himself on the port wing of the bridge and confined his search to the area around the sun.

Suddenly, two specks broke out of a high cloud. Fraser whipped up his binoculars. Single engines, fixed landing gear with spat-like fairings—they were carrier dive bombers. The two planes confirmed his identification by rolling over into a steep dive out of the sun. Fraser shouted, "Right full rudder! All ahead full! Sound the general alarm!"

The *O'Leary* trembled as the throttlemen poured more steam to the turbines. The blower whine increased in pitch, and the ship's stern began to swing out to port. Fraser looked up to the fire control platform where Chief Hanlon was wearing the headset connected to the guns. "Two dive bombers coming out of the sun!" Fraser shouted. "Commence firing just before they're in range!"

"Air action port! Coming out of the sun!" barked Hanlon into his phone set.

Chief Jablonski stood by Fraser as the enemy continued their long descent. "Sir, shouldn't you go to emergency flank speed?"

Fraser shook his head as he continued to watch the diving aircraft through his binoculars. "Not yet," Fraser said. "Rudder amidships!"

Seconds later, the 3-inch gun on the fantail began its periodic bark. One .50-caliber machine gun stuttered even though the attackers were still far out of range. A thin curtain of 3-inch bursts began to blossom, and defiant streaks of .50-caliber tracers arced skyward, still well below the diving Japanese.

Fraser bit his lip as he watched the bombers react to his initial turn by reducing the angle of their dive. Fraser turned toward the pilothouse. "Left full rudder! All ahead emergency flank!"

The helmsman spun his wheel until the spokes became a silver blur. The man at the engine-order telegraph mashed the levers forward three times, the signal for the throttlemen below to open their throttles fast and wide. Seconds later the *O'Leary* surged again, and the foaming wake boiled up almost level with her fantail. The rudder bit into the water, and the stern began to bound in ragged jumps as it fought its way across the bow wave and the small swells.

The two attackers screamed down through the 3-inch barrage and neared the arcing .50-caliber tracers. The enemy aircraft, which had been black specks when they started their dives, were now close enough for Fraser to see the lead dive bomber in chilling detail. A bomb nestled against the bottom of its fuselage between the faired landing gear. The nose was black; the top surfaces, a dark green. The graceful sweep of the wings was broken by extended flaps and dive brakes.

Undaunted by the *O'Leary*'s meager antiaircraft fire, the dive bombers tried to steepen their dive angles to compensate for Fraser's second maneuver, but the first enemy pilot was too late with his correction; the black speck that separated from the belly of the bomber passed over the *O'Leary* and exploded 40 yards to starboard.

The second aircraft had a few extra seconds in which to adjust; the last bomb seemed to be dropping right toward the *O'Leary*. But the destroyer's propellers were still accelerating the ship from 20 to 25 knots. To Fraser, it appeared as if the bomb were being deflected by an invisible hand; instant by instant, the bomb began to drift aft and to starboard. It slammed into the sea 20 yards off the starboard quarter where it blasted a huge column of white water skyward. The concussion shook the ship and squeezed the air from Fraser's chest.

There were scattered cheers from the after gun crews. Fraser and Jablonski had moved aft near the starboard signal flag storage to watch the bomb hit the ocean. Jablonski gripped a nearby rail with whitened knuckles. Fraser tried to look calm, although his knees were watery and his leg muscles trembled. He cleared his throat and broke the silence. "Let's keep an alert lookout! There may be more where those came from."

But there were no other attackers. As Fraser crossed the signal bridge to go over to the other wing there was a weak croak from the charthouse doorway. Fraser spun around. The captain was hanging on the door. "Nice job."

Fraser felt a surge of guilt. "Sorry, Captain, I should have called you, but there wasn't time. Besides, Doc wants you to stay in your bunk."

"You did fine without me. I saw the whole thing. Maybe somebody'd better help . . . me." Arkwright slowly slid to the deck. Fraser and Jablonski rushed over and picked him up. Fraser gave the conn to Korchak and helped Jablonski carry the captain into the charthouse, where they hoisted him back to his bunk.

Arkwright lifted his head. "Ross, one . . . last test before you're . . . qualified for command. You have to learn . . . to sleep in that damned captain's chair . . . without falling out. Start practicing." The captain's head fell back on his pillow.

Fraser nodded. "I'll give it a try."

When he returned to the pilot house, Fraser regarded the

captain's chair. It wasn't much. Just an uncomfortable wooden chair mounted on the forward bulkhead of the bridge. But it symbolized the authority and responsibilty that went with command of a ship. The night before, he had wanted to be rid of the responsibility for the *O'Leary* as soon as possible. Now he wondered. Maybe I can handle it, he thought. Maybe I might like it someday.

Fraser went out on the starboard wing and searched the sky, particularly around the sun. There was a good possibility more Japanese carrier aircraft would arrive soon. Fraser called Chief Jablonski out to confer.

"Have we got any fuel to spare?" Fraser asked.

"A little, if we slow even more for the last few days to Perth."

"Okay, let's stay at 25 knots as long as we can and get away from here."

"Good idea," Jablonski said. "Might make us tougher to find. We'll have to slow down again by dark, and we won't have any reserve left."

"Worth the risk," Fraser said.

There was no sign of the enemy as the afternoon dragged on. Fraser lowered his binoculars and turned to Chief Jablonski. "No Japs. Hope our luck holds."

Jablonski shrugged. "Could be the two that attacked us were out at the limit of their range."

By late afternoon, they had burned their cushion of fuel, so Fraser slowed to 12 knots. He found himself thinking that maybe command wasn't as difficult as he'd feared. Footsteps rocked the wooden grating behind him. It was one of the radiomen.

"Something for us?" Fraser asked.

"Not exactly, Mr. Fraser. It's a distress signal."

Jablonski plotted the position on the chart. It was 300 miles to the northwest. "Must be a ship that left Tjilatjap," Jablonski said.

Tjilatjap! The name exploded in Fraser's mind. Ilsa could be on that ship, he told himself.

By the time Fraser settled his thoughts, the radioman returned with another distress signal. Chief Jablonski took the slip of paper and plotted the position. Fraser shuddered as he realized the crosses looked like grave markers.

"Even farther back," Jablonski said.

"The Japs are busy." Sweat poured down Fraser's body. "Check your calculations on fuel again, Chief."

Jablonski looked up through his glasses. "Aye, aye, sir." His stubby pencil hovered over the scratch pad while Fraser prayed Jablonski had made a mistake earlier.

"Same results, Mr. Fraser. We're going to have to stay at 12 knots just to have enough fuel for a straight shot to Perth. Those two ships back there are out of the question."

Fraser felt his fingernails digging into his palms. "Jesus, those people are dying back there." And one of them might be Ilsa, he told himself.

Jablonski's eyes were sympathetic. "Nothing you can do for those folks, sir. It'd be suicide to go back."

Fraser trudged out of the pilothouse, leaned on the bridge wing, and stared at the horizon. He wanted desperately to turn the *O'Leary* around and respond to each distress call to guarantee that Ilsa wouldn't be left adrift in the Indian Ocean. He thought of her dying of thirst under the brutal sun, the seagulls pecking her flesh.

But even if he had the fuel, should he turn back? The distress calls were ample evidence of the Japanese presence. If he went back for all the distress calls that came in, he would be throwing the *O'Leary* away—no great loss as far as the ship was concerned—but what about the men? The Navy would desperately need professional sailors to man new ships coming off the building ways. But apart from the Navy's needs, how could he sacrifice men like Hanlon, Landry, Egan, Jablonski, Meredith, Steiner, Eckersly?

Fraser looked up at the fire control platform where Chief Hanlon was searching the sky with his binoculars. Fraser wondered how Hanlon's former wife and in-laws could have given him anything less than their total respect. Fraser remembered Ilsa wasn't the only loved one who had been left behind. Hanlon had left Maria behind in the Philippines. Landry had returned to the *O'Leary* rather than deserting to stay with his girl. Morales and the other Filipino stewards had left entire families in the Philippines.

Fraser knew the men aboard the *O'Leary* were incredibly lucky to have made it this far. They had escaped all the Japanese could throw at them for the first three months of the war. The Navy had given them obsolete and ineffective weapons and no reinforcements. Any chance of defending the Philippines had been squandered by the disaster at Clark Field.

After all the *O'Leary* had survived, Fraser desperately wanted to take this ship and her crew back into peril. He felt himself being pulled back north. Memories of his wedding night flooded his mind. Ilsa. Oh, God! Ilsa!

Fraser looked into the pilothouse where the radioman was handing Chief Jablonski another message. Jablonski bent over the chart. The radioman looked out and caught his eye. Fraser saw weariness, doubt, and even a little fear in the man's eyes.

Good God, thought Fraser, he's thinking I'm going to kill us all. That's probably just the way I used to look at the captain. The captain . . . Somehow Arkwright did it. He got us out of there. He didn't charge at the Japs again . . . Christ, he could have done that two or three times. Fraser turned and gripped the edge of the wing. He realized the captain had managed to surmount his personal demons. Arkwright had made the right moves to save his ship and crew. The captain had denied himself the fulfillment of an honorable death and had carried out his responsibility to his crew. Arkwright had won a great victory. Fraser knew he was ready to throw it all away by turning back.

Fraser suddenly realized he was about to do exactly what he had feared the captain would do. If he turned the ship around, he would sacrifice the crew for the sake of his personal interest.

Fraser looked down where his hands were turning white as he gripped the bulwark. He relaxed his painful grip and plodded into the pilot house where Jablonski and the radioman waited.

The radioman licked his lips. "One of our old gunboats that left Tjilatjap is sinking—she reports being hit by carrier aircraft."

Jablonski looked up from the chart where he had penciled

another cross even farther to the north. Jablonski's face was twisted. "Goddamn it all. Those are our people up there."

There was a long silence. "I know all about that," Fraser said softly. "My wife might be on one of those merchant ships."

Jablonski straightened up. "Oh, no. I'm sorry, sir."

Fraser stared at the chart. The gunboat had been hit by carrier aircraft. The air south of Java must be thick with them.

Jablonski slid his parallel rulers aimlessly across the chart. "Maybe if we went back, we could find somebody with fuel oil between there and Australia."

"Even if the Japs don't get us, give me odds on finding fuel," Fraser said.

Jablonski lowered his gaze to the deck. "Poor—at best. Most of the merchant ships still burn coal."

Fraser closed his eyes. Ilsa . . . Ilsa . . . Ilsa. How could he not turn back? She was everything to him. The rest of life stretched ahead. It seemed empty—meaningless without her. Fraser had long since realized he was no hero, but he was ready to risk his life for the chance of saving Ilsa. But there would be more at stake than his own life—the lives of the men he was now responsible for.

I don't have the right to throw them away, he thought. No one does.

"Damn! Damn!" he said softly. "We have to keep going south."

Jablonski adjusted his wire-rimmed glasses. "Aye, aye, sir. We're already on the right course."

Fraser felt incredibly drained. He looked over at the captain's chair. He shuffled across the pilothouse and hoisted himself up. The captain was right. It was a hard seat.

CHAPTER TWENTY-SEVEN

The next three days crawled by for Fraser. Alone, the *O'Leary* slid through the Indian Ocean at 12 knots to conserve fuel. On the third morning, Fraser went below for coffee in the wardroom, where he found Laster.

"You look discouraged, Doc. How's Jack?"

"He should be all right after a few weeks in the hospital. Two of the others may not make it." Laster gazed at Fraser appraisingly. "You don't look so good yourself. Are you sick—or just worried about Ilsa?"

"I'm beat. It's hell not knowing whether my wife is still alive."

"There's nothing you can do, except get us to Australia."

"Damn, I want to be in control of my destiny."

Laster took off his glasses and polished them. "Some things we can't control. Sometimes life is a rollercoaster. You just hang on. Only choice is whether to scream or not."

Fraser lifted his chipped cup and sipped steaming black coffee. "Doc, this war isn't what I expected. At the academy, military history seemed so clear-cut. The reality—it's a mess, especially on the losing end. Now, to top it off, my wife may have been killed."

Laster stared at his tea. "Warfare's been with us for thousands of years. Ought to stop glorifying war and expose it as the killing and maiming bastard it is."

"I can't get over how many good men have already been killed."

Laster grunted. "They won't be the last. Amazing . . . murder is the worst of crimes. Do it in a war and you're a hero."

"Some of the heroes are killing women and children," Fraser said, thinking of Ilsa.

"That's the worst of all."

Fraser realized he'd better get back to the bridge. "Thanks, Doc. We really haven't solved any problems, but I feel better for getting them off my chest. Gets pretty lonely inside this head sometimes."

"I know the feeling well," Laster said.

The bridge messenger poked his head in the wardroom door. "Mr. Fraser, the crow's nest has spotted land."

"I'll be right up."

"Wait for me," Laster said. "I need to go up to the charthouse and check the captain. He was starting to come out of it this morning."

Fraser hoped so. It had been a lonely three days with the responsibility for the *O'Leary*. At least it had kept him too busy to dwell on Ilsa. As they climbed the ladders, he was tormented by the thought she might have been caught by the Japanese. In the charthouse, Fraser stood by as Laster examined the captain.

"Sir, we'll be entering port soon," Fraser said.

"How much fuel do we have left?" Arkwright asked.

"A few thousand gallons. We just made it."

Arkwright swung his feet over the edge of his bunk. "Help me out to the bridge chair."

Laster put down his stethoscope. "You still don't look too good, Captain."

"I'm not going to a beauty contest."

"You're the captain," Laster said.

As they steamed toward the Australian coast, Arkwright looked through the message board. "A lot of ships not answering up to their radio calls."

Fraser filled the captain in on what he knew. The other four destroyers that had escaped through Bali Strait were safe.

Many other ships were unaccounted for. *Houston* and *Perth*, the cruisers that had headed for Sunda Strait, were silent. *Exeter*, *Encounter*, and the four-stacker *Pope*, which had left Surabaya bound for Sunda Strait were unheard from. Four-stackers *Whipple* and *Parrot* had escaped from waters south of Java, but they had been lucky. Destroyers *Edsall* and *Pillsbury*, as well as the tanker *Pecos* and the gunboat *Asheville* were missing.

"Counting the *Peary* and *Stewart*, the Japs got five of our four-pipers," Arkwright said.

"Would have been almost all of us if our group hadn't made it through Bali Strait," Fraser said.

Arkwright lowered the message board to his lap. "The Allied force we fought with in the Java Sea last week—our destroyers seem to be the only survivors."

Fraser thought for a minute. Every other Allied ship had been sunk during the battle or had failed to escape. Fraser shuddered as he realized how lucky they were.

Arkwright's pale eyes mirrored the emptiness of the Indian Ocean astern. "The ships caught trying to escape—those men gave their lives and we don't even know what happened to them. It's going to be hell on their families not knowing something definite."

Fraser realized that thousands of families would have to share the agony of uncertainty he now felt about Ilsa. I don't even know if she ever left Tjilatjap, he thought. She must have. His fingernails dug into his palms as he wondered what had happened to her.

The *O'Leary* steamed past Rottnest Island and toward the mouth of the Swan River and the port of Fremantle, which served the city of Perth 11 miles farther upstream. When the *O'Leary* completed mooring alongside a pier on the Fremantle waterfront, Fraser got permission to go ashore. He spent the better part of that day and the next making inquiries about ships that had arrived from Java. The Dutch consulate had no information about Ilsa.

Discouraged after his second fruitless day, Fraser returned to the *O'Leary* and wandered about the decks. The cooling afternoon breeze the locals called "The Doctor" cut through his shirt. When Fraser lifted his eyes from the deck, he was reminded they were no longer in the tropics. Gone was the lush vegetation of the Philippines and Java. The low hills in the distance were dusty and brown.

"Different world," Fraser said softly.

He could tell the crew had already begun to snap back from their ordeal. The lined, gaunt faces were returning to normal. But many of the men still had a haunted look around their eyes; they evidently knew how lucky they had been to escape the fate which had overtaken almost half the Asiatic Fleet.

Unlike his shipmates, Fraser found it impossible to unwind. For him, the ordeal continued. He slept poorly and had nightmares about leaving Ilsa behind to die. The third day in port, he sat at the wardroom table with a cup of coffee, his head down. He heard footsteps and felt a hand on his shoulder.

"Captain."

"Yes. I'm up again. Doc says I'm over the second stage. I'll just have to take it slow for a while."

"That should be easy," Fraser said. "It's going to take a few weeks to repair the after fireroom."

"You don't look so hot yourself."

"Still no news about Ilsa."

"Ross, I want you to go over to the Dutch Consulate several times each day until you hear something."

Fraser raised his head. "Thank you. At least that lets me feel like I'm doing something."

Their morose silence was broken when Woody Korchak slammed the wardroom door open. "Mail Call!" Korchak tossed the bags on the table, opened them, and began sorting as the other officers filtered in.

Arkwright sat at the head of the table with only a few official envelopes. Fraser felt almost guilty as he sorted through a stack of letters from his parents. There was a muffled groan from the head of the table.

A silence settled over the wardroom as, one by one, the officers looked up from their mail. "What is it, Captain?" Fraser asked.

Arkwright's expression was unreadable. "This letter's from a friend of mine on the destroyer staff in Pearl Harbor. He says the *O'Leary* will be ordered to return to the East Coast for conversion to a convoy escort."

"Is that all, Captain?" Durham asked.

"No. My friend says I can expect orders to command a new destroyer when we get back."

There were congratulations for the captain who accepted them with a pensive look. Fraser realized that their own Navy would soon break up a group of men who had survived all the Japanese had thrown at them.

Korchak handed Fraser an official envelope. It contained orders for him to be detached and report as the assistant gunnery officer of a new cruiser under construction in San Pedro, California. Fraser knew that this was exactly what he had wanted for months, but now that he was faced with leaving the *O'Leary* and people he had come to regard as family, his emotions were mixed.

Fifteen minutes later, they found out who would relieve Fraser. It was Chief Hanlon, who had been selected for promotion to ensign.

Durham laughed. "Just think, Mortland may be next. He'd make an interesting addition to the wardroom."

Arkwright cleared his throat. "I'm not sure the Navy is ready for that. Let's eat."

After lunch, Fraser found Hanlon on the after deckhouse, supervising work on the number four gun.

"Afternoon, Mr. Fraser. I think we'll have this fixed by tonight," Hanlon said. "But the fire control equipment on number one is out again. Lord knows when we'll track that problem down. Hell of a note, wasting good men on these old ships."

"We'll be getting new ships and planes before long."

Hanlon shrugged. "Most of the men riding them will be fresh-caught civilians instead of the professionals getting killed out here. Could have saved the civilians a lot of dying if they'd given us something decent to fight with."

"Chief, some of those civilians are going to have a fine officer. As soon as we swear you in, you'll be commissioned as an ensign."

"Did I get orders too?"

"You're taking over my job. I've been ordered back to the states to a new cruiser."

"Congratulations, Mr. Fraser." Hanlon was silent for a few moments as he stared over the rail.

"Problems, Chief?"

"Just trying to adjust to the news. Always been an enlisted man. You officers seemed in a different world."

"Chief, you'll adapt. You're as intelligent as most officers I've known."

"Never been one to worry about fancy manners. Ever since I enlisted, seems like folks have looked down at me."

"That's their problem, not yours. A person should be judged on merit. Chief, you care about people and take care not to embarrass them. That's what a real gentleman does."

Hanlon nodded, but then looked sad.

"Something else bothering you?"

"I wish Maria could be here for this."

"I know how you feel, Chief. I don't even know where my wife is."

"All we can do is keep going and hope things get better."

An hour later, the officers and Chief Hanlon assembled in the wardroom. The stocky Hanlon wore an immaculate uniform and stood in front of the captain.

Arkwright cleared his throat. "Chief, repeat the oath after me."

Hanlon, in his firm voice, followed the captain's recitation of the oath, phrase by phrase:

> I, Byron Hanlon, solemnly swear to support and defend the Constitution of the United States against all enemies, foreign and do-

> mestic; to take this obligation freely and without any mental reservation or purpose of evasion; and to well and faithfully discharge the duties of the office on which I am about to enter.

As the chief recited the oath, Fraser watched pensively. With each phrase Fraser felt a fresh resolve to continue the long struggle that lay ahead of them.

When Hanlon finished, the captain shook his hand. "Congratulations, Ensign Hanlon. Welcome to the wardroom. Your promotion is well deserved."

"Thank you, sir." The newly commissioned officer turned to accept the congratulations of the other officers.

Fraser spent the rest of the afternoon turning over his responsibilities to Hanlon. The formal relief process required several inventories of equipment. When they finished signing the official records, Hanlon said, "I relieve you, sir."

Fraser shook Hanlon's hand. "I stand relieved. It'll be a few days before I can pack and arrange transportation out of here, so I'll say goodbye later. But you know how I feel about you and the rest of the men. Take care of them."

"You can count on that, sir."

Fraser felt suddenly free of all responibility. Then he thought of Ilsa. He headed ashore to the Dutch Consulate's office, but there was no information about her. He found two merchant ships that had left Tjilatjap, but none of the officers knew anything about medical evacuees.

Fraser trudged back to the *O'Leary* and went down to his stateroom. He lowered the desk top, looking for a new pencil. Tucked in a cubbyhole was the box Ilsa had given him in Manila. He opened it and lifted the bagpipe chanter from the tissue paper. He felt an urge to play it, but he wasn't ready to listen to any complaints, so he went ashore and found an empty pier nearby.

Fraser sat on a mooring bollard in the twilight and played "Flower of the Forest," the song he had played for Ilsa on their wedding night. It sounded better than he had ever played it, but near the end he stopped in mid-note and lowered the chanter, feeling an urge to hurl it in the water. He looked down at it; aside from his wedding ring, the chanter was all he had left of his wife. He didn't have a letter or even a picture of her. Nothing—only the slender piece of wood and ivory. Fraser knew he would never play it again, but he held it tightly and watched the last light leave the western sky.

Landry squatted on the forecastle, chipping loose paint around a patch of rust.

"Don't take all morning, Landry!" Chief Mortland said. "I've got a new job for you."

"It's time for a break, Chief."

"Break, hell! You're gonna think the last three months were a holiday. This ship looks like a tired old whore. If we chip and paint her, we'll feel like we're riding the *Queen Mary.*"

"Not even if you close your eyes real tight," Landry muttered.

Mortland rubbed his thick hands together. "Landry, you're gonna be our new side cleaner and painter."

As Mortland walked away, another deck hand shook his head. "You're in for it now. Ain't no Chinese or Filipinos around to do all the work for you."

Landry clenched his fists. "Dammit! Painting sides ain't gonna get us back to Manila."

Late that afternoon, Landry swung precariously on a long board supported by two lines secured to the life lines above. He slopped a rag in the bucket of soapy water suspended beside him and rubbed it against the seemingly endless expanse of the *O'Leary*'s side. The bell on the quarterdeck sounded eight times.

Landry tossed his rag in the bucket. "God! I can't stand this!" He pulled himself up one of the lines and swung a leg over the top life line.

Chief Mortland was waiting for him. "Enjoy your evening ashore. It's going to take a few weeks to whip the sides into shape."

"Nope. I'm gonna transfer to another division."

"The hell you say."

"I'm putting in a chit."

"I'll talk Mr. Durham into tearing it up."

"I'll bet Mr. Fraser can change his mind."

Mortland smiled slyly like a poker player uncovering an ace. "Maybe, if you work hard enough, I'll give you the new whaleboat when it comes. That change your mind?"

"No."

Mortland's jaw muscles bulged. "Okay . . . you win. I'll take you off the sides tomorrow. The new whaleboat's yours."

"No. That's not enough, anymore." Landry turned and walked away.

Five days after their arrival, Fraser tried the Dutch consulate again with no success. He walked the narrow streets of Fremantle. Headed in the direction of the waterfront, he lost his way in the winding streets, which were packed with small stores and two-story Victorian houses. His despair deepened as he thought how Ilsa would have enjoyed the walk. She would have admired the wrought-iron decorations on the limestone houses.

Fraser wondered if the pain he felt would ever diminish. He thought over his decision not to turn back. Maybe, just maybe, I could have found Ilsa, he thought. But there were so many distress calls. I couldn't have stopped with just her ship. We all would have died.

Fraser knew all he would have done was sacrifice the *O'Leary*'s crew. There was some comfort in that he hadn't done that. Fraser realized he now knew some of the pain his captain had lived with. At least he didn't have to bear Arkwright's burden of guilt. Lord, Fraser thought, if it's any worse than this, he must be in hell itself.

At the end of the winding street, Fraser spotted a flash of blue water. He decided to canvass the waterfront again to see if he could find out something. When he emerged from the shadowy street, he found one of the piers dotted with uniformed men and ambulances. A battered merchant ship steaming up the Swan River was down by the bow and scarred by machine gun fire. Her upper decks were crowded with refugees who leaned over the rails and waved. Fraser scanned the distant rows of faces for his wife but couldn't find her. A flash of light brown hair behind a row of refugees caught his eye. The flow of the hair in the wind, the tilt of a shoulder gave him momentary hope.

"Ilsa!"

But the woman ducked into the bridge structure without pausing to look at the pier or waterfront. Fraser's spirits sank. Another dead end, he thought. Ilsa would be at the rail looking for the *O'Leary*.

Still, he refused to abandon hope. Fraser waited impatiently as a tug pushed the ship alongside the pier. He bounded up the brow as soon as it was in place and threaded his way through the mass of unwashed humanity, working his way forward toward the bridge. As he passed a doorway, a voice halted him. "Maybe I could help you, Lieutenant."

"Ilsa! Thank God!" They were in each other's arms. Ilsa was crying and laughing at the same time, and Fraser found words impossible. The woman in his arms was alive, warm, real.

Finally, she pulled away. "I have to get some patients ready for unloading. Then I can leave with you."

Fraser helped carry the stretchers down to the pier. He was stunned by what the war had done to some of the men. Arms legs, eyes—the war had shown no respect for the human body. He shuddered when he passed a row of bullet holes in a lifeboat and realized how close Ilsa had come to death.

Later, Fraser and Ilsa stood on the pier and watched the last ambulance roll away. "Let's go find a hotel room," Fraser said. "We have some catching up to do."

"If you'll go aboard and help me with my things."

"Of course. I'll bet you brought several steamer trunks."

"No, I'm traveling light. At least I was," she said sadly. She led him aboard and into the dining room, where a nurse sat beside a cardboard box. "Thank you," Ilsa told the woman. "I'm ready to take over now." She took Fraser by the hand and led him over to the box. "I'd like you to meet Dirk Jansen, Junior."

Fraser looked at the infant, who was sleeping peacefully. "Good-looking kid—a real sack artist. Where's Marta?" He dreaded the task of telling Marta about her husband.

Ilsa told him of Marta's death and the baby's birth. "I promised the doctor I'd be responsible for the baby."

Fraser was stunned by Marta's death. He led Ilsa to a nearby chair. "Dirk is dead. I talked to some of the survivors who told me he went down with his ship."

"Oh, God," Ilsa said softly. "And my father?"

"I don't know. The *De Ruyter* was sunk at night with few survivors. I just don't know." He sat next to her and put his arms around her while she sobbed on his shoulder. Fraser rocked her gently. "Come on, we don't want to wake up the baby. It looks like he's ours for a while."

Ilsa wiped her eyes. "I think it may be permanent. Dirk was an only child and both his parents are dead. Marta's family is in Holland. I know she lost her brother when the Germans invaded. I'm not sure if her parents are still alive. There's no way to find out with the war in Europe." She sighed. "Was I wrong to take this responsibility? I know we wanted time to enjoy each other before having children."

Fraser hadn't even considered parenthood yet, but he realized he had no choice in the matter. "Don't worry. You did the right thing. We're both fortunate to be alive. Marta and Dirk weren't so lucky. We owe it to them to raise their son. Let's go find a hotel room for the Fraser family."

"Oh," Ilsa said. "Here's somebody you have to thank first."

Fraser turned and found a weary-looking, grease-covered T. T. Simpson standing behind them.

"Looks like we made it, Mrs. Fraser," Simpson said.

Ilsa rose and gave him a kiss on the cheek. "Yes, we did. Thanks to you."

"What happened?" Fraser asked.

Simpson described the attack by the bomber and how the engine room crew had panicked as soon as they realized the ship was taking on water in one of the forward holds. "The bastards—'scuse me, Ma'am—all jumped in a lifeboat and sailed off. Took a while to find out we weren't going to sink. Two of the wounded were snipes from the *Stewart,* and we showed some of the refugees how to run this old bucket. Wasn't too bad a trip. We had one breakdown—but that made me feel right at home."

Fraser looked at the balding, bespectacled man who had brought his wife to safety. He remembered the night off Olongapo when he had cursed Simpson for jumping over the side. Fraser realized how much Simpson deserved his gratitude and respect; if it hadn't been for Simpson and the other Asiatic Fleet sailors, Ilsa would probably be dead.

But that wasn't all. Simpson had fixed the number two boiler. With the after fireroom hit by the Japanese destroyers, it had been up to the forward fireroom to get them to Australia. Fraser thought over the last three months. There had been so many times the *O'Leary* had faced the Japanese and survived because the crew had done their jobs under the worst of conditions. Fraser knew he owed his life several times over to Simpson and the rest of the destroyer's crew.

"Simpson, I can't thank you enough for what you've done."

Simpson nodded at the sleeping baby. "Just do a good job bringing up that little boy. I don't expect to help another baby come into the world. He's kind of special to me. I'd like to think he's got a good chance of turning out all right."

"We'll do our best," Fraser said.

"Good." Simpson smiled and pushed his glasses back up his greasy nose. "I feel like cleaning up and going ashore. I wonder if these Aussie gals know how to dance?"

"Simpson," Fraser said, "if there's a Ginger Rogers in western Australia, you deserve to find her."

CHAPTER TWENTY-EIGHT

Fraser returned to the *O'Leary* the next morning, weary from fulfilling his marital and parental obligations. He saluted Shifflet, who had the watch on the quarterdeck. "Good Lord, what happened to you?" Fraser asked.

The battered Shifflet shook his head. "Was a bad night. Things went to hell when we took Simpson to a bar called the Waltzin' Matilda."

"Bet he liked that name."

"Yeah, he was pretty well oiled up by that time. Wanted to know where Waltzin' Matilda was. Damn Aussies took him out back. Turned out she was a 'roo."

"A kangaroo?"

"Yup. Simpson tried a few of his dance steps with it, but I guess that animal didn't much like his style because it stomped the hell out of him."

"That doesn't explain why you look so bad."

Shifflet spat over the side through swollen lips. "Those Aussies put money down that the 'roo could lick any of us. That frigging 'roo was more'n I could handle. That animal had some tricks I'd never seen afore."

"I thought you'd seen everything, Shifflet."

"So did I! I wasn't doin' too bad 'til it kicked me in the privates."

"I'm surprised you didn't try that first."

"I did, but it didn't do any good 'cause it was a female."

"Live and learn." Fraser tried not to laugh.

"Yessir, I guess so. Got my butt kicked and lost all the pay I had saved up." Shifflet took a closer look at Fraser. "What happened to your shirt, Mister Fraser? Looks like a baby barfed on your shoulder."

"You're right on target, as usual. I was feeding my new son this morning."

"You just got married last month. I would'a heard if the bride looked that far along."

"She wasn't."

"You mean it's not her kid?"

"Nope. You'll have to excuse me. I'm almost late, and I have to change my shirt." Fraser supressed a chuckle at Shifflet's bewilderment.

Shifflet winked at Fraser. "You're a real devil after all, Mr. Fraser. 'Cept for Mr. Durham, I thought you officers were so damn stuffy. I'd sure like to know how you explained your kid to the new wife."

Fraser returned Shifflet's wink. "It wasn't easy."

On his way to the wardroom, Fraser ran into Simpson, who was sporting a multicolored black eye. "Heard you had some problems last night."

"Got so drunk, everything's a blank. Wasn't 'tubic' this time. I do know that."

"Sure you don't remember anything else?"

"Just an ugly big-nosed broad in a fur coat."

"Is that all?"

"Oh, yeah. She was wearing the damnedest perfume."

Hank Landry stepped out of the galley with a cup of coffee after the noon meal and spotted Lieutenant Fraser crossing the quarterdeck. "Mr. Fraser, just wanted to make sure I got a chance to say goodbye."

Fraser reached out and shook Landry's hand. "I wouldn't even be here if you'd let Simpson drown me off Olongapo."

"We're even, sir. I'd be rotting in the brig somewhere if you hadn't helped me out."

"Anything for the best catcher I ever had. Good luck in your new job."

"Mr. Fraser, thanks for putting in a word with Mr. Durham, or I'd still be taking crap from Mortland. I owe you and Chief Hanlon for putting some good advice in my ear. Some of the things you two said over the last couple of months started making sense."

"We hoped you'd strike for gunner's mate. But we're not disappointed. Good luck—Mabuhay."

"Mabuhay," Landry said.

Landry turned and opened the hatch down to the forward fireroom. When he reached the grating on the lower level, he picked up a wrench and eyed the pump he was supposed to take apart. The number two boiler roared softly as it burned fuel oil to provide steam for auxiliary services. Landry could almost feel the power harnessed in the pipes around him. He was no longer afraid of the boilers. He had felt death brush by in the dark water off Bali. He had faced death and lost his fear of it; death would come when it was ready.

Steam hissed from a leaking valve overhead and triggered a vague memory buried in the back of his mind. Landry closed his eyes, and he was a boy again standing in the cab of a huge Union Pacific steam locomotive. His father had his hand on Landry's shoulder as steam hissed from another valve. "Steam is power, son," his father's deep voice said proudly. "I feed in the coal and this engine will pull a whole train right up a mountain. But you have to know how to control power. It can burn a man too. You just have to do your best and take your chances."

Landry opened his eyes. He could almost feel the hand still on his shoulder. He realized he hadn't completely understood why he had transferred to the engineers until that moment. He looked over at the boiler and felt a life force flowing from it. Somehow, he knew his father was there with him—and always would be. The bitterness and anger that he had carried for so long seemed to drain into the bilges.

Hours later footsteps rattled the ladder down to the lower level. "How did you like your first day as a snipe?" Simpson asked.

Landry looked around the forward fireroom where he had been working all day. "Ain't so bad down here now that we're not in the tropics."

"Can be damn nice down here when there's a blizzard outside," Simpson said.

"Won't see any weather like that until this old bucket goes to the North Atlantic. Then she'll roll her guts out."

Simpson shook his head. "Some people are never happy."

"Hey, I'm not complaining," Landry said. "Rebuilding that pump today—I feel like I did something worthwhile. And I didn't have to listen to Mortland."

"By the way," Simpson said, "we have an initiation ceremony for you."

"Oh," Landry said warily.

"Yeah, something special since you're an ex-deck hand. We don't get many of you guys shifting down here."

Landry decided to get his medicine over with. "Let's get on with your ceremony."

Simpson led Landry up the ladder from the lower level and along the grating between the boilers. Simpson called the other men in the fireroom around them. "We want to welcome a new man down here today."

"He's gonna lose that nice suntan before long," one man said.

Landry felt his neck redden. Then he realized he was among men who would accept him for how hard he would work. "I won't lose all of it. My grandmother was an Arapaho Indian." He felt a new sense of pride and remembered how his father had never seemed ashamed of his heritage.

Simpson looked at him for a few seconds, smiled, and patted his bald head. "For once I'm glad I don't have any hair. You boys better not rile Landry or he'll scalp you so you'll all look like me."

"Take a whole tribe to do that much damage," one engineer said.

"Nothing to worry about," Simpson said. "I'll vouch for Landry. He's a good worker and that's what we want down here. Snipes work harder that anybody in this Navy—and proud of it too. If our boilers and engines don't work, the ship won't move and can't fight!"

"Damn right!" one man said while the others clanked wrenches and tools against the railing in approval.

The door from the airlock opened and one of the greasy engineers emerged. "Just like usual. Mortland's on the foc'sle for a smoke before his afternoon inspection."

"Wind still from astern?" Simpson asked.

"Almost perfect."

Simpson turned to Landry and gestured to the metal chain hanging down from the top of the number two boiler. "Have at it, Landry. Blow tubes all over that big bastard."

Landry reached up and grabbed the chain. He hesitated a few seconds to savor the moment and then yanked it down. The forward fireroom was filled with the roar of steam rushing though the fire box of the boiler, carrying soot from the boiler tubes up the stack and into the breeze. When Simpson nodded, Landry released the chain, and greasy men clapped him on the back. Landry suddenly realized he didn't miss his whaleboat anymore. It had only been a boat—a thing. These men were offering him something more—friendship. Landry shook their hands, one by one.

Suddenly, the fireroom reverberated with a furious knocking.

"Sounds like Mortland's beating on our hatch with a swab handle again," Simpson said.

Landry cocked his head and listened. "You know, that sounds kind of like . . . music."

Simpson shoved his glasses back up his nose. "Damned if it don't."

Ilsa wrapped her arms around Fraser's neck. "I think we have a while until the next feeding. Let's not waste it."

An hour later Ilsa nestled against him. "Ummmm. The second time was even better than the first."

Fraser stared up at the hotel ceiling where a network of cracks fanned out and intersected like a drugged spider's web.

"You seem a long way off," Ilsa said.

"Just some things on my mind."

"Not another woman, I hope."

"Of course not. It's my orders."

"What's the matter with them."

"Not sure . . . they're just what I spent months hoping for."

"Maybe you've changed your mind about some things."

Fraser thought for a minute. "You're right. I don't want to leave. When I walked down the brow tonight, I felt like I was leaving my family behind. When I thought of a cruiser, it seemed too big. I don't want to hide on a big ship anymore."

"Maybe the captain can help you."

"The orders I have mean I can help you get back to the States. We'll have some time together before I go back to sea." Fraser watched her consider the implications.

Her eyes misted. "You should do what's right for you."

Fraser thought of what she had already been through—losing a mother, losing a fiancé, and now the uncertainty about her father.

She took his hand. "Many people spend their lives doing jobs they hate. If you've found something you can care about, you should do it."

Fraser kissed her and held her tightly hoping he wasn't asking her to carry a heavier load than she could bear. He pulled away. "I have to go back to the ship—right now."

"Can't it wait until tomorrow?"

"There's something else that's bothering me—the captain. He looked terrible at lunch today. Sadder than I've ever seen him look. Tomorrow may be too late."

Thirty minutes later, Fraser paused at the captain's doorway before knocking. There was no sound from the room.

"Come in," Arkwright said.

Fraser pushed aside the curtain.

The captain was sitting at his desk. The black .45-caliber pistol lay in front of him. There was an awkward silence.

"What can I do for you?"

Fraser stared at the pistol. "Ah . . . it's my orders, sir."

"I thought a cruiser was what you wanted."

"I did, too, but I don't want to leave. Can you have my orders cancelled? I feel bad about leaving the people here."

Arkwright frowned. "There's nothing I can do about that, Ross. Besides, most of the crew will be ordered to new ships as soon as we return to the States. With your experience, you're too valuable to leave aboard this old ship."

"A cruiser's just too big."

Arkwright smiled slightly. "I agree. There's something special about a destroyer, isn't there?"

"Yes, sir. There is."

"I think I can help you there. I can write a few letters that will get your orders changed. You'd like a newer one?"

Fraser thought for a few seconds. "Yes . . . if I can't stay here."

"Fine, I'll do the letters before . . . before I . . . sleep. Arkwright's pale eyes were on his pistol. "Is that all?"

Fraser felt his mouth go dry, and he rose to leave. "Ahh . . . yes. Thank you, Captain."

"There's something I want you to have. I've already wrapped it for you." Arkwright handed Fraser a box with his name on it. "It's my model of the *O'Leary*. If my son were still alive I'd give it to him. You were actually in command for three days so it's fitting . . ."

"Captain, I can't take this. It should be yours."

"I want you to have it. You'll see it's not quite done. It needs a touch here and there. Add a few details of your own. Fix some of the things that aren't quite right. That way it will be as much yours as it is mine."

Arkwright stood and extended his hand. "Good . . . night."

Fraser took the stubby hand and grasped it firmly. Something welled up inside him. The man in front of him was the captain—a man he had held in awe, almost like a god. But over the months, he had glimpsed something of the man behind the facade, a man in terrible pain. Fraser had shared a part of that pain until Ilsa arrived in Fremantle. Fraser knew what Arkwright was about to do.

He summoned the courage to confront the captain. Fraser pointed at the pistol on the desk. "That pistol is going over the side before I leave tonight. You're ready to use it, aren't you?"

There was a long silence. "I've been ready to use it for a long time." The captain stared at the picture of his dead family.

"My God, can't you forgive yourself, Captain?"

"You're the only person aboard I've told my story to." Arkwright looked down at the linoleum-covered deck. "Can't you just leave me alone? I did my job and got us out. When I leave this ship, I'll lose the only family I have."

"Then people on your new ship can become your new family. Captain, I can't just walk away. I'd never forgive myself. Beyond my feelings—your next ship will need you as much as this one did. If you blow your brains out, they'll probably give your ship to some jackass like Beringer."

"God forbid," Arkwright said bleakly.

Fraser picked up the picture of Arkwright's family. The smiling woman and children looked out across the years—images caught and frozen—a woman never to know the gentle joys of old age, children never to grow into adulthood. Fraser felt some measure of the ache in Arkwright's soul. He gazed at the woman's eyes and found a message in them.

"Your wife's smile is beautiful . . . Did she love life?"

"Yes . . ."

"Don't you think your wife . . . and your children would want you to keep going—to find some meaning in your life? Suppose your wife had been behind the wheel and you had died. What would you tell her if you could?"

Arkwright put his head in his hands. After a minute, he looked up. "I suppose I'd want her to make the most of her life . . . to enjoy whatever it had to offer."

"Exactly. The fact that you came to care about this crew shows that you can do it. It . . . it proves that you can keep finding something to live for—no matter how great your loss. You . . . just have to find the courage to keep going."

"And if that's not enough to get me through the night?"

"Then think what your suicide will do to the men of this ship.

Every man aboard would feel diminished if you took your life—as if he had failed you somehow."

Arkwright thought for a long time. "I can understand what you're saying. It's not easy. Christ, I hurt. Emotionally . . . I wonder if I can get through tonight . . . tomorrow night.

Fraser saw the pain in Arkwright's eyes and wondered if he had the right to ask the captain to endure any more. Fraser decided that a painful life was better than no life. "Let's make it easier for you to get through tonight."

"How?"

"Sign this," Fraser said.

"What is it?"

"A survey form reporting the loss of that pistol."

"But it's not lost."

"We'll lose it tonight."

Five minutes later, the two men stood on the port wing of the bridge, looking at the dark water below. Ventilators whined, and the deck vibrated underfoot. "Almost like she's alive," Arkwright said.

"She is, in a way, as long as there's a crew aboard to give her life."

Arkwright held out his hand. "Ross, this is something I have to do myself. Would you please wait on the other wing?"

Arkwright's expression was unreadable in the dim light. Fraser hesitated, hefting the weight of the cool weapon. He handed it to the captain. Fraser reluctantly crossed the bridge to the other wing, where he leaned against the bulwark and hoped he'd done the right thing. Agonizing minutes passed while Fraser gritted his teeth and waited.

Suddenly, there was the sound of the slide of the .45-caliber pistol running back and forth as a round was chambered. Fraser felt his knees turn to jelly. Before he could move, the night was shattered by the roar of the large pistol. Fraser rushed across the pilothouse and recoiled from the sight. The bridge bulwark was splashed with blood and pieces of hair and flesh. A leg twitched uncontrollably. Fraser looked into Arkwright's staring eyes. Fraser prodded the body with the toe of his shoe.

"Damned rats!" the captain said, gazing distainfully at the furry remains. "I wish I could kill them all."

Fraser let out his breath. "Captain, you scared the hell out of me!"

"Sorry."

Feet pounded up the ladder to the bridge. Eckersly's solemn face appeared at the top of the ladder.

"It's all right," Fraser said. "Just a little Aussie-style rat hunting. You can use your expertise to conduct a rat funeral in a half-hour."

Eckersly looked at the rat for several seconds as if measuring it for a casket. "Aye, aye, sir. I'll let you have a few last moments alone with the departed."

After Eckersly retreated down the ladder, Arkwright shuffled over to the wing of the bridge, paused, and tossed the pistol over the side. Fraser walked over and watched the faint trail of bubbles rising from the harbor bottom. Ripples spread but gradually diminished, and then they were gone as though they never had been there at all.

"That wasn't easy," Arkwright said.

It took Fraser two days to get reservations for a flight out of Perth to take him and his family across Australia to Sydney, where they would board a ship for the States. He was grateful for the delay because it gave him an opportunity to spend time with Ilsa at the hotel.

Fraser took a turn giving the infant a bottle. "It's not everyone who gets to spend his honeymoon feeding his new son."

"Just wait until you're finished with him. I'll make it worth your while, Lieutenant."

She did, too.

Several hours before their departure from Perth, Fraser and Ilsa took a taxi to the *O'Leary*, where Ilsa sat in the wardroom with the baby and visited with the officers while Fraser packed. When Fraser left his room for the last time, a cockroach skittered across the deck. "We may beat the Japs, but we'll never beat the roaches."

After lunch, he walked around the ship and said goodbye to the crew. Fraser hated to leave the officers and men who had become as close to him as his family. He was comforted by the fact that he might run across some of them in the future.

As Fraser was getting ready to say his final goodbyes in the wardroom, Arkwright walked in. A new uniform fitted him well, but Fraser could still see a haunted look around the eyes. Arkwright had survived the last two nights. That and the new uniform were a start.

The captain cleared his throat. "I thought you might like to hear some official news before Ross leaves. When Jack Meredith comes back from the hospital, he'll take over the exec's job. After the overhaul, Jack will probably get command. If anyone deserves the promotion, he does."

Bull Durham chuckled wickedly. "Jeeze, I feel sorry for the poor guy who's ordered in to be the engineering officer. He'll never have any time to get ashore."

"Ahhh . . ." the captain said. "Our new engineering officer . . ." Arkwright's head swiveled, and his gaze rested on Durham. A smile flickered around the captain's mouth, spread ever so slowly, and finally warmed his bleak eyes. His faint chuckle grew into a guffaw and ignited the rest of the officers into laughter.

Durham slid down in his chair until his chin was almost on the table. "Oh, no! Not that! I'll never have any time for the ladies."

"I'll be happy to come down and transcribe the details of your former activities," Laster said.

"You'll never get my secrets," Durham said.

"Cheer up, Bull," Laster said. "Think how all those neglected women will improve the morale of the rest of our fighting men."

"What about my morale?"

Arkwright said, "Bull, you can go ashore as long as all the engineering plant's problems are solved."

"In that case, I'd better get to work." Durham pushed back his chair and limped out.

Laster said, "The irresistible force is about to meet the immovable object."

When it was time to leave Fraser walked Ilsa down the brow

and helped her and the baby into the waiting taxi. The officers and men who were on deck laughed and waved. Fraser and Ilsa waved back as the cab bumped down the pier. Soon, the *O'Leary* was almost hidden by the other ships moored nearby. The last they saw of her were the tops of her four stacks. From the second one, a small feather of steam began to rise.

Fraser cleared his throat and blinked rapidly. "That number two safety valve looks like it's leaking again. Simpson will be on his way down to the forward fireroom."

"Simpson, all of them—they're fine people," Ilsa said.

"They deserve to go home. They did their best with what they had—which wasn't much. Fraser thought over the last three months with a trace of bitterness. "Most Americans will never appreciate the Asiatic Fleet or the men trapped in the Philippines."

Ilsa squeezed his hand. "At least a few ships escaped."

"We were the lucky survivors. When we get some new ships, the Japs may not find it so easy."

Ilsa was silent for over a minute as the cab bounced over some potholes. "I suppose you'll be back out here before long."

"I don't have any choice. I . . . I'd just as soon this war had never started. Three months ago I didn't think much of the Far East, but you . . . Mohammed . . . Chief Hanlon . . . all of you made me see it in a different light. Yes, I'll be back."

Ilsa put her head on his shoulder. "I can't have you to myself for long, so we'd better enjoy the time we have."

"We seem to have made a good start on that."

When the cab left the outskirts of Fremantle, Ilsa looked back toward the waterfront. "Look, there's the *O'Leary*."

Fraser searched the piers and saw a black plume drift from the number two stack as the engineers blew tubes. "There's some life left in her yet. She may be old, but she was too tough for the Japs to sink."

As cab turned, the old destroyer disappeared, but Fraser knew that the *O'Leary* and her crew, like the woman and child beside him, would remain a part of him forever.